LANDS AND PEOPLES

LANDS AND PEOPLES
EUROPE

Volume 3

GROLIER
EDUCATIONAL

DANBURY, CONNECTICUT 06816

CONTENTS
EUROPE
Volume 3

FLAGS OF EUROPE

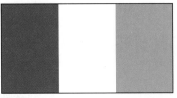

IRELAND

UNITED KINGDOM

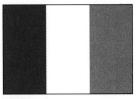

FRANCE

MONACO

LUXEMBOURG

BELGIUM

NETHERLANDS

GERMANY

SWITZERLAND

LIECHTENSTEIN

AUSTRIA

This lovely resort on Lake Como, nestled in the Italian Alps, typifies the regal splendor of European scenery.

EUROPE: AN INTRODUCTION

The waning of the Cold War, the collapse of the European Communist regimes, and the introduction of a common currency called the euro in 11 West European countries close the dramatic and eventful 20th century. When the Communist regimes were collapsing like dominoes, there was an air of excitement and hopefulness because the whole world seemed to be changing for the better. A much more cautious mood has set in since then.

The ethnic wars in Croatia and then in Bosnia and Herzegovina reminded Europeans of World War II. Thanks to the United States, the fighting stopped in 1995 after agreements were signed by the warring parties in Dayton, Ohio. Soon, however, another armed conflict erupted, this time in the Yugoslav province of Kosovo, a sacred region for Orthodox Serbs but inhabited mostly by Muslim Albanians. Farther east, the dissolution of the Soviet Union and the disintegration of the once-iron rule by Moscow first let loose ethnic clashes in Moldova in 1992–93 and, shortly thereafter, a full-scale war in the Russian republic of Chechnya.

Meanwhile, Western Europe has steadfastly pursued the building of a "common European house." The last decade of the century began with the signing of the Treaty of Maastricht in December 1991 and ended with the introduction of a common European currency—the euro—on January 1, 1999. The Maastricht Treaty, establishing a common market of goods, labor, and capital among the 12 countries of the European Union (EU), was followed by the admission of three new members: Sweden, Finland, and Austria. During that same time, most former European Communist countries signed association agreements with the EU and began to prepare for their eventual entry into this organization.

The countries of Europe now fall into several groups. Fifteen Western states—Germany, France, the United Kingdom, Ireland, the Netherlands, Belgium, Luxembourg, Denmark, Sweden, Finland, Austria, Spain, Portugal, Italy, and Greece—are members of the EU. Eleven of them (not counting the United Kingdom, Sweden, Denmark, and Greece) will become members of the European Monetary Union (EMU) on January 1, 1999. Two small island countries—Malta and Cyprus—are expected to join the EU during its next enlargement. Iceland, Norway, Liechtenstein, and Switzerland belong to a smaller organization, the European Free Trade Association.

Three Central European countries—Poland, the Czech Republic, and Hungary—have been in the forefront of post-Communist transformation, and are expected to join the European Union shortly after 2000. Two other small nations—Estonia in the Baltics and Slovenia, formerly the northernmost republic of Yugoslavia—will be in the same group.

The next category includes Slovakia, Romania, Bulgaria, Croatia, Macedonia, and Albania. The post-Communist developments in these countries have been much more difficult. In Slovakia, an increasingly authoritarian prime minister and his government have tried to curb civil rights. In Romania and Bulgaria, economic transformation lagged for several years and gathered speed only in the late 1990s. Croatia has had to repair the damage caused by the war of 1991–92, and the other former Yugoslav republic, Macedonia, was involved in protracted disputes with Greece concerning its name and national symbols. Albania experienced repeated economic crises and, in 1998, was overwhelmed by waves of Albanian refugees from the Yugoslav province of Kosovo.

Bosnia and Herzegovina is emerging from years of war, and NATO troops are overseeing postwar reconstruction. Unfortunately, the region has seen new violence: in 1998, fighting between Albanians and Serbs broke out in the Yugoslav province of Kosovo.

Compared to the successful Estonia, its two Baltic neighbors, Latvia and Lithuania, are much behind in economic transformation, but in other ways they have drifted far from their Communist past. Of the other former European Soviet republics, Moldova is managing relatively well.

Ukraine, slightly larger than France, seemed on the verge of economic collapse in 1993, but then rebounded. The country was united with Russia for centuries, and many people still prefer to speak Russian rather than Ukrainian. The forging of a separate national identity proceeds, however, and the Ukrainian government cultivates contacts with the West to counterbalance its continuing dependence on Moscow. Belarus, on the other hand, is interested in forging closer ties with Moscow. In 1997, a cooperation treaty between Belarus and Russia was signed.

Stretching from the Baltic Sea across the whole of North Asia to the Pacific, Russia is in a category of its own. As the heir of a nuclear superpower, the country aspires to a special international status, but its economic performance has deteriorated steadily. The country faces tremendous internal problems: corruption has reached unprecedented levels, and organized crime is powerful. Although relations with the West are generally positive, the future of the Russian giant continues to be unpredictable, and the country is enduring much turmoil.

The collapse of Communism is receding into the past, and young people in the former Communist countries have quickly become accustomed to the new freedoms and now cannot imagine a return to the past —despite all the problems and difficulties. Yet not much more than a decade ago, the Communist empire seemed solid as a rock. Underneath, however, it was rotting. The growing internationalization of the world economy—with its computer links, telephones, and satellite communications—made it possible for citizens of the Communist countries to be in touch with the free world. The need for external trade and foreign exchange made opening to the West more and more important, which in turn led to an increasing awareness of the multiple failings of the Communist system. Economic and political pressure within the Soviet Union, combined with Western military steadfastness, finally resulted in an irresistible demand for profound change.

The tasks now facing the European nations are, in the first place, to overcome the Cold War division and to clear up old historic enmities, and also to provide new jobs, reform the social-welfare systems, and curb racial violence. All this will require a great deal of work, but it will be worth it.

Unification of Europe

The union of the nations of Europe is an ancient dream. In 1961, Swiss writer Denis de Rougemont published a book with the evocative title *Vingt-Huit Siècles d'Europe* ("Twenty-eight Centuries of Europe"). In it he quoted hundreds of authors who, in one form or another, raised and defended the idea of a union of European countries. Through the centuries, philosophers, poets, and reformers have urged the nations of Europe to unite and thus end the innumerable wars that set one nation against another. Now, after two world wars and a long Cold War, most European countries finally seem prepared to work together.

As early as the end of World War I, Aristide Briand, then French minister of foreign affairs, presented the idea of a European federation to the League of Nations. The proposal was vague, and the political climate of the time was not propitious. Communism, fascism, and Nazism were opening ever-deepening ideological chasms in Europe, and Briand's attempt had no success.

At the end of World War II in 1945, the dominant idea in the policy-making circles of Western nations was the maintenance of the alliance made with the Soviet Union. The United Nations was created to settle the problems posed by peace. In 1946, however, Winston Churchill declared in two historic speeches that the Soviet Union presented a danger to the free world, and he insisted that the countries of Western Europe unite for their defense and economic recovery.

In 1948, a congress that was to have historic importance met at The Hague. All the movements whose goal was the propagation of a united Europe were represented there. It was no longer a question of noble but vague discussions of a great idea, but rather a question of considering a boldly practical way to realize that idea. In 1949, the Council of Europe and its consultative parliamentary assembly were created. Three years later, in 1952, the Coal and Steel Community was born as the first supranational authority in Europe.

In 1955, at the Messina Conference in Sicily, the idea of a united Europe was sensationally reborn. The six governments whose countries belonged to the Coal and Steel Community—Belgium, France, West Germany, Italy, Luxembourg, and the Netherlands—decided to create among themselves an economic community that would encompass agriculture, industry, transportation, finance, currency, and politics. After years of often passionate and dramatic debate, the treaty concerning this economic revolution was signed in Rome in 1957, and the European Economic Community (EEC)—known as the European Community (EC) from 1967 on—was formed. Three new countries—the United Kingdom, Ireland, and Denmark—formally joined the original six in 1973. Greece became a full member in 1981, and Spain and Portugal joined in 1986.

In the late 1980s, the EC began to prepare for a common market of goods, labor, and capital among the 12 member countries, which took effect on January 1, 1993. A milestone declaration was signed in December 1991 in Maastricht, the Netherlands, changing the name of the community to the European Union (EU) and pledging to create a single European currency by 1999.

By January 1995, three new members had joined the EU—Austria, Sweden, and Finland. Norway also had been admitted to the EU, but Norwegian voters rejected the membership in a November 1994 referendum.

Meanwhile, most post-Communist countries signed association agreements with the EU and began discussions about full membership. In early 1996, the Intergovernmental Conference began its sessions to prepare for the admission of new members. It is expected that the first to join, shortly after the year 2000, will be Poland, the Czech Republic, Hungary, Slovenia, and Estonia.

During the time of the Maastricht Treaty signing, Western Europe seemed excited about the approaching unity, but in the following years the enthusiasm declined somewhat. "Euroskeptics" in various countries could be heard more loudly. The European Union, with its seat in Brussels, is indeed an easy target for criticism. Its maze of regulations and red tape can seem stifling. When the "club" consisted of only a few countries, it was relatively easy to devise rules; but with 15 current members and more to join soon, rule-making has become much more difficult.

Consider the question of languages. Since the EU is an organization of equal partners, there are currently 11 official languages, and all important meetings must be simultaneously interpreted into these languages. In the mid-1990s, the EU employed more than 2,000 interpreters, who had to service more than 10,000 sessions. The written documents—more than 1 million pages annually just for the European Commission, one of the key bodies of the EU—must then be translated. All this is cumbersome and expensive. Yet many believe it is worth the cost because a unified Europe is the best safeguard of peace.

In the mid-1990s, many doubted that the proposed Economic and Monetary Union would be introduced as planned, but the deadline was kept. On January 1, 1999, the national currencies of 11 EU members are scheduled to be replaced by a new currency called the euro. The national currencies will coexist with the euro until June 2002, and then will be abolished. During the transition period, all companies, government agencies, and other organizations must convert their accounting systems. This costly change will be pervasive (for instance, about 3.5 million vending machines must be adapted), but it is expected to save money in the long run. The advocates of the EMU hope that the euro will eventually become as strong an international currency as the U.S. dollar.

Interlaken, Switzerland, is one of Europe's scenic resorts.

EUROPE

Is Europe a continent? The answer to the question is both yes and no. The textbook definition of a continent is "one of the great divisions of land on the earth," and most continents can be easily identified on a world map or globe. Europe, however, looks like a western extension of the huge Asiatic landmass. It is, in fact, a peninsula that stretches westward from the main body of Eurasia, as the entire landmass is called. Because of Europe's enormous importance in world history, however, it has been considered a separate continent for a very long time.

The people of the ancient Middle East divided the world they knew into three parts. One division was the area in which they lived. They called the land to the east of them Asu—"land of the rising sun." The land to the west was called Ereb—"land of the setting sun." It may be that our names for Europe and Asia come from these ancient words.

Most of Europe's boundaries are clearly marked by the seas and oceans that lap its shores. And the separation from Africa and Asia, except for the Russian part, is a sharp one: the Mediterranean and its open connection with the Black Sea by way of the Dardanelles and the Bosporus.

Hammerfest
• Vardo

B a r e n t s
S e a

Ivalo •
Murmansk •

White
Sea

Kemi •
• Archangel

FINLAND

• Kuopio
Lake
Onega

• Syktyvkar

Tampere •
Lahti •

Lake
Ladoga

• Kotlas

★ Helsinki
of Finland

• Perm

★ Tallinn

St. Petersburg •

ESTONIA

R U S S I A

• Sokol

• Izhevsk

• Kirov

★ Riga
Novgorod •

Volga R.

• Kazan

• Ufa

LATVIA

Nizhni Novgorod •

LITHUANIA

Tver •

★ Moscow
Ryazan •

• Kuibyshev

Vilnius ★

• Roslavl

• Tula

★ Minsk

• Saratov

• Uralsk

KAZAKHSTAN

BELARUS

• Kursk

• Voronezh

Ural R.

• Lutsk
Dnieper R.

Kiev ★

• Kharkov

Don R.

• Guryev

Aral
Sea

Lviv •

Poltava •

Volgograd •

UKRAINE

Donets R. Voroshilovgrad •

UZBEKISTAN

Dniester R.
Dnepropetrovsk •

Garlovka •
• Zavetnoye

• Astrakhan

Botosani •

Krivoi Rog •
Makeyevka •

MOLDOVA
Zaporozhe •
Donetsk •

Jassy •
Chisinau •

• Rostov

ROMANIA

• Nikolayev

Sea of
Azov

• Stavropol

C a s p i a n   S e a

TURKMENISTAN

Brasov •

Odessa •

Europe C a u c a s u s

Ploesti •
Galati •

• Yalta

Asia

• Grozny

★ Bucharest

GEORGIA

Constanta •

B l a c k   S e a

40°E

★ Baku

Danube R.

• Varna

AZERBAIJAN

BULGARIA

ARMENIA

50°E

• Plovdiv
• Bourgas

Bosporus

Istanbul •

Europe

Kavalla •

Asia

Dardanelles

T U R K E Y

I R A N

Aegean Sea

30°E

I R A Q

Crete

CYPRUS

SYRIA

NORTH AMERICA

GREENLAND

North Pole

Arctic
Ocean

• Novaya
Zemlya

Atlantic
Ocean

EUROPE

ASIA

AFRICA

Equator

Ural Mts.

Europe Asia

Fishnets dry in the sun on Mykonos, a Greek island popular with tourists.

Geographers have long debated the location of Europe's eastern boundary, but most now draw the line along the Ural Mountains, the Ural River, and through the Caspian Depression to the Caspian Sea. Russia is thus divided into two parts—European Russia and Asian Russia.

A large number of islands are also part of Europe. They include Spitsbergen and Novaya Zemlya in the north, and Great Britain, Ireland, the Hebrides, Orkney Islands, Shetland Islands, Channel Islands, Isle of Man, Faeroe Islands, and Iceland in the northwest. There are many islands in the Baltic Sea. The Balearic Islands, Corsica, Sardinia, Sicily, Malta, and the Greek islands are in the Mediterranean Sea.

Including the adjacent islands and European Russia, the continent covers roughly 4,200,000 sq. mi. (10,878,000 sq. km.), the second-smallest continent after Australia. Europe's smallness is in dramatic contrast to the gigantic size of Russia, which alone covers 6,591,104 sq. mi. (17,070,959 sq. km.) and stretches from the Baltic Sea to the Bering Strait across almost 180 degrees of longitude, or about half the globe. Peninsulas, bays, islands, and fjords give Europe very irregular coastlines. As a result, the coast is quite long for the total area, about 50,000 mi. (80,500 km.).

The Nations of Europe

Today 44 nations occupy the continent of Europe, a large number for such a small area. The most northerly countries, which are called the Scandinavian nations, are Sweden, Denmark, and Norway. Finland and Iceland are sometimes included in this group, too.

Belgium, the Netherlands, and Luxembourg, which are often grouped as the Benelux nations or the lowland countries, are on the northern edge of Western Europe. France, Ireland, and the United Kingdom are also in Western Europe.

The walled city of San Marino is one of Europe's countless historic landmarks.

Italy occupies its own peninsula in Southern Europe; Spain and Portugal share the Iberian Peninsula in the southwest; and Malta occupies an island in the Mediterranean. Greece, European Turkey, Bulgaria, Albania, and most of Romania are on the Balkan Peninsula in the southeast. This peninsula is also the home of the former Federal Republic of Yugoslavia, which split into five new countries in 1991 and 1992: Slovenia, Croatia, Yugoslavia (consisting of Serbia and Montenegro), Bosnia and Herzegovina, and Macedonia. The nations of Central Europe include Switzerland, Austria, and Germany. Poland, the Czech Republic, Slovakia, and Hungary are emerging from decades of Soviet domination. Seven new republics arose in late 1991 in the European part of the former Soviet Union: the three Baltic states—Estonia, Latvia, and Lithuania—and Ukraine, Belarus, Moldova, and Russia itself. Europe also contains five tiny nations renowned for charming settings and fascinating histories. Vatican City and San Marino are located in Italy; Monaco is on the southern coast of France; Liechtenstein is tucked between Switzerland and Austria; and Andorra is set high in the Pyrenees.

EUROPE AND THE WORLD

Europe's nearness to Asia and Africa and the open sea-lanes to the Americas have made it possible for Europeans to spread ideas that have shaped and influenced the modern world. The voyages of discovery and exploration, religious missionary efforts, and colonization helped disseminate European beliefs, traditions, and languages around the globe. Three other continents—North and South America in the Western hemisphere and Australia—are inhabited largely by descendants of Europeans who speak European languages. Europeans have also greatly influenced the other two continents—Asia and Africa.

INDEX TO EUROPE MAP

FACTS AND FIGURES

LOCATION: North central and northeastern hemispheres: **Latitude**—71° 08′ N to 36° N. **Longitude**—66° E to 9° 30′ W.

AREA: Approximately 4,200,000 sq. mi. (10,900,000 sq. km.) with adjacent islands.

POPULATION: 728,000,000 (1998; includes entire population of Russia).

PHYSICAL FEATURES: Highest point—Mount Elbrus (18,481 ft.; 5,633 m.). **Lowest point**—Caspian Sea (depression) (92 ft.; 28 m. below sea level). **Chief rivers**—Volga, Danube, Dnieper, Don, Pechora, Dniester, Rhine, Elbe, Vistula, Loire, Tagus, Neman, Ebro, Oder, Rhone, Neisse, Po, Thames, Seine, Arno, Tiber, Severn.

For several centuries, Europe ruled vast portions of the globe, but its importance was due not only to its military power and technological innovation. Europeans speaking Latin, Greek, French, German, Spanish, Italian, Portuguese, and English carried ideas about life and death, government and religion, art and music, and literature to the rest of the world. Their influence was so great that, to this day, in order to understand almost anything—from such large problems as the turmoil in Asia to smaller and pleasanter ones like the literature of South America—one must first know something of Europe.

Among Europe's most enduring legacies are ideas about how to govern. Ancient Greece gave the world the concept of democracy and of the democratic state. Rome added the idea of just laws stressing obedience to government. England contributed the whole body of English law, based on the theory that the individual's life, liberty, and property must be protected by the government. And from Europe, too, came the patterns for constitutional, or limited, monarchies; representative government; and the notion that government must attend to human rights and hopes. Social legislation and the use of the power of the state to support the individual in his or her drive for economic security came from Europe. Socialism and Communism also were born in Europe.

COUNTRIES OF EUROPE

COUNTRY	AREA (sq. mi.)	(sq. km.)	POPULATION (latest estimate)	CAPITAL
Albania	11,100	28,750	3,293,252	Tirana
Andorra	174	450	74,839	Andorra la Vella
Austria	32,375	83,850	8,054,078	Vienna
Belarus	80,151	207,590	10,439,916	Minsk
Belgium	11,780	30,510	10,203,683	Brussels
Bosnia and Herzegovina	19,781	51,233	2,607,734	Sarajevo
Bulgaria	42,822	110,910	8,652,745	Sofia
Croatia	21,829	56,537	5,026,995	Zagreb
Czech Republic	30,387	78,703	10,318,958	Prague
Denmark	16,639	43,094	5,268,775	Copenhagen
Estonia	17,462	45,226	1,444,721	Tallinn
Finland	130,127	337,030	5,109,148	Helsinki
France	211,208	547,030	58,211,454	Paris
Germany	137,803	356,910	84,068,216	Berlin
Greece	50,942	131,940	10,583,126	Athens
Hungary	35,919	93,030	9,935,774	Budapest
Iceland	39,768	103,000	272,550	Reykjavík
Ireland	27,135	70,280	3,555,500	Dublin
Italy	116,305	301,230	57,534,088	Rome
Latvia	24,749	64,100	2,437,649	Riga
Liechtenstein	62	160	31,461	Vaduz
Lithuania	25,174	65,200	3,635,932	Vilnius
Luxembourg	998	2,585	422,444	Luxembourg
Macedonia	9,781	25,333	2,113,866	Skopje
Malta	124	320	379,365	Valletta
Moldova	13,012	33,700	4,475,232	Kishinev
Monaco	.77	2	31,892	Monaco-Ville
Netherlands	14,413	37,330	15,653,091	Amsterdam
Norway	125,181	324,219	4,404,456	Oslo
Poland	120,726	312,680	38,700,291	Warsaw
Portugal	35,672	92,391	9,867,654	Lisbon
Romania	91,699	237,500	21,399,114	Bucharest
Russia	6,592,772	17,075,200	147,987,101	Moscow
San Marino	23	60	24,714	San Marino
Slovakia	18,859	48,845	5,393,016	Bratislava
Slovenia	7,821	20,256	1,945,998	Ljubljana
Spain	194,884	504,750	39,244,195	Madrid
Sweden	173,730	449,960	8,946,193	Stockholm
Switzerland	15,942	41,290	7,248,984	Bern
Ukraine	233,089	603,700	50,684,635	Kiev
United Kingdom	94,525	244,820	58,610,182	London
Vatican City	.17	.44	850	Vatican City
Yugoslavia	39,517	102,350	10,655,317	Belgrade

Although none of the world's major religions were born in Europe, it was in Europe that Christianity grew and flourished. The Roman Catholic Church inspired Europeans after the decline and fall of imperial Rome. Later, after the Protestant Reformation, other Christian denominations arose in Europe. Disagreements about doctrine led to bitter wars, but they also led dissenters to establish the colonies that ultimately became the United States.

Europe's educational institutions, which were at first mainly religious, grew secular over the centuries. The emphasis on the idea of the dignity and equality of individuals led finally to the concept of universal education. Such ancient universities as Padua, Bologna, Florence, Paris, Oxford, Cambridge, Uppsala, Prague, and Heidelberg sent their scholars and their ideas to every corner of the globe.

Europe's beaches, such as this one in the Netherlands, draw big summer crowds.

In the arts, as in government, religion, and education, the influence of Europe has been far greater than the continent's small size would lead one to guess. In painting, sculpture, architecture, music, and literature, Europeans blazed trails that are still being explored. Painters everywhere study the work of Europeans who discovered new ways of painting perspective and of showing light and shadow. Techniques for depicting religious scenes, satirical scenes, or simply portraying a human face on wood, stone, and canvas were developed and perfected in Europe. From the most elaborately decorated Gothic cathedral to the most starkly modern office building, European architects developed new ways of using stone and wood, steel and glass to shelter and inspire people.

Such musical forms as the symphony, concerto, sonata, opera, operetta, and ballet originated in Europe. And every educated person is aware that Europe gave the world of literature the essay, the ode, the lyric, and the sonnet. No matter where a person lives, his or her life is enriched by the works of such European giants as Homer, Virgil, Dante, Chaucer, Shakespeare, Milton, Voltaire, Goethe, Tolstoi, and many others.

In such fundamental matters as how to live better with the resources of the continent, Europeans also developed techniques that made life easier. It was probably northern Europeans who first discovered that the soil could be used longer if crops were rotated. This made it possible to settle in one place and establish permanent homes. With permanent communities came the growth of the villages, towns, and cities that became centers of commerce and culture.

The Greeks are usually credited with being the first to inquire scientifically into human life and the environment, seeking rational explanations of such natural phenomena as the seasons of the year and the tides of the sea. The speculations of the ancient Greeks about the nature of the universe led to the beginnings of astronomy, medicine, physics, and psychology. As the centuries passed, more and more Europeans added to our knowledge of this world. It was a European who discovered that the Sun rather than the Earth is the center of our universe. Other European scientists provided the basic knowledge of gravitation, thermodynamics, and the laws governing motion, sound, and light. The list of European contributions is endless, ranging from medical discoveries that lengthen human lives to the discovery of radio waves, which are able to bring people together no matter how far apart they may live. The extraordinary number of contributions made by Europeans to scientific knowledge and the way in which we live can be measured by imagining what the world might be like if the philosophers Aristotle and

A pastry shop tempts a young Frenchman.

Plato, the physicians Hippocrates and Galen, the astronomers Copernicus and Galileo, the scientists Newton, Pasteur, and Einstein, the psychoanalyst Freud, and countless others of their stature had not lived.

A disposition for scientific inquiry and an abundance of natural resources such as coal and iron led to the Industrial Revolution, which began in Europe in the mid-18th century. Machines powered by steam and coal replaced tedious hours of human labor. Industries grew that altered the face of the world completely. Factories were built, and railroads spread their iron tracks across the land. And as the new industries flourished, people had increasingly more leisure time for entertainment and enjoyment of the arts.

Today travelers by the millions visit Europe, seeking the beauty and inspiration of the continent that has in many ways been the cradle of modern civilization. They go to Athens, birthplace of democracy; to Rome, which for so long was the capital of much of Europe and now contains the seat of the Roman Catholic Church; to Paris, a wellspring of history and art; to Vienna, a pivotal city in European events; to Moscow, the capital of Russia; and to London, the still-splendid capital of the vanished Empire and of the living Commonwealth. In smaller cities, there are memories of the past as well. In Prague, one is reminded of the forerunners of the Protestant Reformation, and in Seville, one finds the meeting of two great cultures—the Muslim and the Christian. The distant past of the first Europeans can be evoked at Altamira in northern Spain, where the cave walls are covered with paintings made in prehistoric times, or at Stonehenge in England, where a great circle of stones may represent a primitive astronomical calendar. Closer in time are the medieval walled cities such as Carcassonne in central France, the majesty of Westminster Abbey in London, and the hill towns of Italy.

Visitors crowd the museums—the Louvre in Paris, the Hermitage in St. Petersburg, the Rijksmuseum in Amsterdam, the National Gallery in London, the Prado in Madrid, the Uffizi in Florence—to see masterpieces of world art painted by geniuses of the past. In Denmark, Norway, and Sweden, there are museums recalling the triumphs and conquests of the seafaring Vikings. In Munich's Deutsches Museum, the adventures of science are explored. Hundreds of towns have smaller museums, featuring exhibitions of all kinds, from armor to glassware, cuckoo clocks, butterflies, and 19th-century safety matches.

Just as the human past has been preserved in museums, monuments, and historic buildings, Europeans strive to keep from destroying the natural beauty of the continent. Despite the environmental dangers posed by the steady growth of population and industry, the majestic Alps, the fjords of Norway, the golden beaches of the Black Sea coast, the vast plains of the Ukraine, and the jewel-like lakes of northern Italy

Few Russians can afford to shop at the smart boutiques that have opened in Moscow in recent years.

Most of Europe receives enough precipitation to support agriculture without the need for irrigation. In England (above), the cool, moist climate helps the landscape maintain a lush green color.

still offer their special charms and their recollection of Europe before nations grew crowded for space and fought for preeminence.

The continent has for centuries been the site of numerous conflicts, and indeed, scarcely a corner of Europe has not been witness to bloodshed. The fierce nationalism and religious feuds so prominent in European history still survive, as has been demonstrated in Ireland and in the former Yugoslavia. Mostly, however, the old historic animosities have virtually disappeared. One can now hardly imagine Britain and France, or France and Germany, at war with one another.

THE PEOPLE

Europe, including the European part of Russia, accounts for more than 14 percent of the world's population crowded into about 7 percent of Earth's land area. In addition, the people of Europe are divided into many ethnic groups, which differ in language, culture, and customs. A detailed map of Europe's ethnic groups looks like a crazy quilt. A boundary change often means not only a change in language but in religion as well. Where the Europeans came from and how they diversified into so many nations is a long story that begins in prehistoric times.

Present-day Europe reflects the result of many movements of population. The various groups blended and consolidated finally into national groups and states. Influenced by existing civilizations—Greek, Roman, Byzantine, and later Latin Christian—they became a part of Europe, regionally different, but nevertheless European.

In the story of human development, Asia served as a kind of reservoir from which peoples moved in all directions. What caused those migrations is not yet clear. Perhaps climatic changes, such as long dry periods, caused people to wander. The approach over the Russian plain was wide open, but the complex landforms of Europe then broke the advance into smaller units. Existing populations were destroyed or assimilated. Some of the earlier inhabitants, however, retreated into less hospitable environments. The Basques settled in the northern Pyrenees; the Celtic peoples in Wales, Scotland, and Ireland; and the Britons in the Britanny region of France. In isolated corners, these peoples have preserved their languages and customs.

From the Middle East came the Jews in a steady stream, beginning more than 2,000 years ago. There were never great numbers of them, but they played a significant role in European history. Out of Central Asia arrived waves of migrant raiders, beginning with the Huns in the 4th century A.D., and ending with the Mongols (Tatars) in the 13th. Most of them were stopped militarily or ran out of steam and returned to Asia. The Magyars, who settled on the Danubian Plain in what is present-day Hungary, and the Bulgars, after whom Bulgaria is named, remained to form European nations. In the 14th century came the Ottoman Turks, who twice advanced to the walls of Vienna and controlled the Balkans until the 19th century. Also from Asia, but by way of North Africa, came the Arabs, who overran the Iberian Peninsula in the 8th century A.D. and ruled it until the end of the 15th.

Germanic Migrations.   One great migration merits special attention because it has influenced the history of Europe up to the present. This was the westward movement of Germanic tribes of east-central Europe into the weakening Roman Empire in the early centuries after Christ. The Rhine and Danube rivers had been the boundaries of the Roman state. East of that line lived certain Germanic tribes whose independence had been protected by the dense forests of central Europe. When Rome began to weaken in the late 2nd century A.D., those tribes invaded Roman territory. One group, the Lombards, occupied Italy and settled in the north—in present-day Lombardy. Another Germanic tribe, the Goths, occupied Spain; still another Germanic tribe, the Vandals, even moved into Africa; and the Franks took over France, which is named after them. Other tribes such as the Jutes and the Danes crossed over into the British Isles. They were relatively few in number, and in due time were assimilated into the existing population. The Elbe became the eastern boundary of the Germanic people; beyond the river a kind of vacuum was left that was occupied by Slavic peoples.

In the 11th and 12th centuries, when conditions in Western Europe had stabilized, the Germanic peoples reversed their interest and looked east across the Elbe, intending to reclaim that land. They moved into what was then Slavic territory and occupied wide areas—a process that continued up to the last century. Large regions, particularly in present-day Poland and the Czech Republic, were entirely Germanized; in others the rural population was left alone, while the Germans controlled the towns.

Poland was the first important state to obstruct this eastern march, but by the end of the 18th century, Poland was defeated and divided up completely among Prussia (a German state), Austria, and Russia. The Russians were the last obstacle, and some observers regard the German conquest of western and southern Russia in both world wars as part of that historic Germanic drive. But in both wars the Germans were defeated and lost most of the territories they had taken from the Slavs. After World War I, Poland was reborn; after World War II, the Soviet Union was enlarged to the west, and Poland was ceded large tracts of German territory. This resulted in tremendous displacement of ethnic Germans.

The Slavs. The original homeland of the Slavs lay between the Volga and Oder rivers. In the 6th century, Slavic tribes began to migrate, probably in conjunction with the movement of Turkic Avars, and by the end of the 1st millennium, there were three distinct groups of Slavic peoples. The West Slavs, ancestors of modern Czechs, Poles, and Slovaks, settled in north-central Europe. South Slavs, ancestors of Bulgarians, Serbians, Croatians, Macedonians, and Slovenians, became established in the Balkan Peninsula. The largest Slavic group, the East Slavs—the future Russians, Ukrainians, and Belorussians—advanced to the sparsely populated east.

Beginning in the 16th century, the Russians began to try to expand westward into Europe proper. This movement was blocked by a line of countries that were to fall only gradually under Russian control. Before World War I, Russia included Finland, the Baltic states (Estonia, Latvia, Lithuania), the eastern part of Poland, and part of Romania. All this territory was lost at the end of the war. Poland was re-created, as were the Baltic states and Finland, while Romania reclaimed its lost territory. In 1939, however, thanks to an agreement with Nazi Germany, the Soviet Union regained most of these areas, except Finland, which remained a free state. After World War II, Poland acquired part of eastern Germany, while the Soviet Union absorbed part of eastern Poland, formerly held by imperial Russia. The introduction of non-Slavic peoples into the Soviet empire produced strong ethnic and political tensions. This became evident once Soviet central control weakened after 1989, leading to independence movements in the Baltic states and elsewhere.

Language and Religion

The existence of a state is based on the desire of a group of people to be politically independent. That desire is generally influenced by a common background, common customs, and a common language. It seems logical that an ideal state is one in which those principles are realized: one country, one language, and perhaps also one religion. In most of Europe, religion has ceased to be a deciding element, and religious minorities are regarded as equal. There are exceptions, particularly in Ireland and the former Yugoslavia. Northwestern Europe, except for the Irish Republic, is chiefly Protestant; parts of eastern and southeastern Europe are Eastern Orthodox; and the rest of Europe is largely Roman Catholic. Interspersed are areas in the Netherlands, Germany, and Switzerland where Catholics and Protestants are about equally represented. Growing immigrant populations have created Muslim concentrations in many urban areas, straining traditional religious tolerance in some countries.

Language remains one of the chief unifying factors for a state, and a linguistic map of Europe reflects the political units. There are three major language groups—namely, the Germanic, the Romance, and the Slavic, all of them belonging to the large family of Indo-European languages. In addition to these, there are numerous small linguistic groups, such as Basque, which is a separate non–Indo-European language that may be distantly related to the family of Caucasian languages; the three Ural-Altaic languages, Finnish, Estonian, and Hungarian; and the remnants of the Baltic branch of the Indo-European family, Latvian and Lithuanian. Until World War II, many Jewish communities in Central and Eastern Europe spoke Yiddish, predominantly a Germanic language, but with strong elements of Hebrew and Slavic languages.

The Language Structure of Europe

Iceland and the Scandinavian nations—Norway, Sweden, and Denmark—have Germanic languages, related but somewhat different. Finland has its own language (Finnish), but on the coast, Swedish is spoken, and the two languages are both recognized as national. The people of each of the Baltic states—Latvia, Lithuania, and Estonia—speak their own languages. The British speak a Germanic tongue with some Latin influence due to the impact of the Norman invasion of William the Conqueror in the 11th century. However, in northwest Scotland, Gaelic is still spoken, as is Welsh (Cymric) in Wales. Most of the people in Ireland speak English, but both Irish Gaelic and English are accepted as national languages. Germany and the Netherlands speak their own Germanic language. Belgium is bilingual; in the north the Flemings speak Dutch, and in the south the Walloons speak French. Luxembourgers speak a Germanic dialect, but French is the official language. France is a Latin country, but there are some linguistic minorities.

Switzerland is quite special. It has three major language groups as well as a remnant language, Rhaeto-Romanic (Romansh), spoken in the eastern mountains by about 1 percent of the population. About 70 percent of the Swiss people speak a German dialect (German Swiss); 19 percent speak French; and 10 percent speak Italian.

Spain and Portugal speak a Latin language. Basque, a relic of the past, is spoken on both sides of the northern Pyrenees, in Spain as well as in France. The people of Italy speak Italian, a Latin, or Romance, language. Austrians speak German, and the Poles speak Polish, a Slavic language. Czechs and Slovaks speak related Slavic languages, but culturally and historically, they are different, as the Czechs were long under Austrian domination, and the Slovaks under Hungarian. Hungarians speak their own Magyar language brought by invaders from Asia in the late 9th century A.D. Albanian is an Indo-European language, but it stands on its own.

The peoples of the former Yugoslavia speak related South Slavic languages: Slovenian, Croatian, Serbian, and Macedonian. The Greeks speak a modern version of ancient Greek. Bulgarians speak a Slavic language. Romanians speak a greatly changed Latin language that, in spite of many invasions, has been preserved since Roman times.

Russian is spoken not only by Russians but also in most former Soviet republics. Ukrainian and Belorussian are other East Slavic languages. Most people in Moldova speak Romanian.

Gothic cathedrals are soaring monuments to the central role of religion in the lives of medieval Europeans.

WAY OF LIFE

Obviously the vast numbers of people who live in the many countries of Europe lead lives that vary a good deal. What is surprising is that Europeans as different from one another as the English, Poles, Austrians, Greeks, or Italians have so much in common. While living under different types of government, influenced by manifold climatic conditions and landscapes, and speaking various languages, the European is a member of a cultural family that has been influenced by common social and intellectual currents and by much common history.

The day-to-day life of the average man and woman and of schoolchildren in Moscow, London, Budapest, or Stockholm does not differ as much as their lives differ from the day-to-day lives of their own countrymen who live in rural areas. City people lead quite different lives from country people in most countries of the world. City people share many of the same pleasures and same concerns all over Europe.

Folk customs vary widely across Europe. In the Black Forest region of Germany, certain holy days are commemorated by religious processions with marchers wearing traditional costumes.

Most Europeans work or go to school five days a week, but many ambitious young professionals also work on weekends and evenings. Thousands of employees in services, particularly those related to tourism, also work on weekends. In large cities, Europeans suffer the miseries of traffic jams or crowded public transportation during their commutes.

For centuries, European fathers came home for their midday meal. Offices and shops were closed, and that was the time when the family assembled for the main meal. Today that is less and less true, except where the climate, such as in southern Italy, Greece, and Spain, is conducive to a siesta after the noon meal. In the extreme south of Europe, when it is possible, businesses close for two to four hours, and then reopen in the midafternoon and stay open until early evening. In most European countries, however, the workday schedule is like that in North America.

Everywhere in Europe, cities are growing and becoming more crowded as people move—as they are doing all over the world—to the metropolitan centers. Most come, especially the young, because they are bored on the farm or because modern technology has reduced the need for human agricultural labor. They also seek the education, job opportunities, and stimulation offered in the cities. Housing is in short supply in many European cities, especially in eastern Europe.

Most of the cities of Europe are a fascinating combination of old and new. In Lisbon or in Rome, it is still possible for someone living in the shadow of a modern office building to go to a fountain in the square to obtain water. Narrow, cobblestoned streets run between rows of old houses, some of which have been occupied for hundreds of years. Centuries-old churches occupy places of prominence in these old quarters. But European cities are beginning to be filled with modern concrete-and-glass structures, office buildings, and apartments. European cities share with large cities all over the world the plagues of air and water pollution caused by wastes from cars, homes, and industry.

Even in the newest areas of European cities, an old custom has been preserved. Nearly always there is a pleasant café where one may stop and enjoy a drink or snack. You may sit outdoors on the sidewalk surrounding a square, as in Rome or Athens, or you may be inside the café, cozy and snug while it rains outside, as it often does in Dublin, London, or

Europeans are renowned for their fine handicrafts.

Brussels. What you eat or drink may differ. It can be beer or tea in a London pub or tearoom, or a glass of local wine in any of the cities of Europe. And often today, in almost any country, it might be Coca-Cola or Pepsi-Cola, even as far east as Moscow. But whatever the drink, the time spent is time for chatting and discussing literature, movies, or politics, especially among the older generations. The young are more likely to be found in discos or at rock concerts.

Europeans share an avid interest in theater and opera. Long ago, strolling players sang, danced, recited poetry, and performed plays. Traveling Punch-and-Judy shows entertained young and old, and so did itinerant trainers and their performing bears or dogs. In many European countries today, opera, symphony, drama, folk dance, and ballet companies are subsidized by the state and are a subject of great national pride. Knowing and responsive audiences greet the Royal Ballet of Denmark, the St. Petersburg and Moscow ballets, the La Scala Opera Company of Milan, the British National Theatre Company, the Swedish Royal Opera, the Vienna Philharmonic, and other renowned ensembles. American movies are popular, especially among young people, but many European countries have flourishing film industries. Italian, French, Swedish, British, Polish, and Czech movies continue to attract large audiences.

Europeans are great sports enthusiasts. In Spain and Portugal, they pack the bullrings to see the bullfights. In Switzerland, skiing is a national pastime. In Russia, thousands of people watch the gymnastic and figure-skating exhibitions. The Dutch in Holland take their skates out to the frozen canals in the winter. The Danes, Swedes, and Norwegians sail in their northern waters. Sometimes there are special national variations of well-known games, such as boccie (Italian bowling) or pelota (Spanish handball). All over Europe, there is intense interest in soccer, whether it is played by schoolchildren or by professional teams. Tennis is also played everywhere. For years, Czechoslovakia had a veritable "tennis factory" that turned out a stream of world champions. Where geography and climate permit, people flock to the beaches—on the Black Sea of Romania, Bulgaria, Ukraine, and Russia; on the Adriatic coasts of Italy and Croatia; and on the Mediterranean of France, Italy, and Spain. In the summer, many central and northern Europeans travel to the warmer beaches of southern Europe, to the islands of the Mediterranean, to Turkey, to the North African coast, or to the Azores in the Atlantic.

Europeans enjoy bicycling and hiking. They often take vacations by hiking through the many lovely forestlands of Europe and camping beside sparkling streams. It may be in tiny Luxembourg, in the Swiss or Austrian Alps, in the French or English countryside, or in almost any country of Europe. In dozens of countries, there are attractive campsites and inexpensive hostels to accommodate these hikers.

Each spring, summer, and autumn, thousands of Europeans go to spas, a tradition that dates from Roman times. Hotels, rest homes, and sanatoriums cater to the people who come to these resorts to bathe in and drink the waters from underground springs, whose mineral properties are supposed to aid in the treatment of some ailments.

In recent years, Europeans have become even greater travelers than in the past. It is not a long trip for anyone, except a resident of the central area of Russia, to get to a foreign land in Europe. In most countries, it is less than an hour by plane. In most areas, frontiers are barely noticed, and people can go quite freely from one country to another. The removal of barriers between Eastern and Western Europe, and the 1992 economic union among Western countries, has made travel even easier. In August, the almost universal European vacation month, it often seems as if all Europeans are on the go—by foot, bicycle, motorbike, train, car, boat, or plane. With their high standards of living and their strong national currencies, Europeans also make up a large percentage of tourists throughout the world.

The 1992 economic union has also accelerated the movement of workers between countries. Citizens of any European Union member state now have the right to work in any other member state, a system that has produced migration from countries with high unemployment to those with labor shortages.

These workers, who often remain for a few years and then return home, demonstrate that there are great variations in the prosperity of the different countries of Europe. Switzerland has the highest standard of living (per-capita income) in all of Europe, and one of the highest in the world. Albania has the lowest per-capita income in Europe. In between are countries in many stages of industrial development and opportunity for employment. The highly industrialized countries of Northern Europe not only provide jobs, but also a great variety of social benefits for their citizens, and their high social-welfare benefits have attracted immigrants from many countries, such as Turkey and former African colonies.

The economies of the former Communist countries are being transformed at an unequal rate. Outwardly, many parts of Moscow, Budapest, Warsaw, Prague, and other Central and Eastern European capitals look completely Westernized—with flashy cars, McDonald's restaurants, and luxury stores—but behind this front there linger many remnants of the totalitarian past. The Central European trio—Poland, the Czech Republic, and Hungary—have been in the forefront of changes, and by the late 1990s two other small nations—Estonia and Slovenia—had caught up with them. These five countries are negotiating their admission to the European Union, which is currently envisioned for sometime shortly after the year 2000.

By the late 1990s, the economic situation had also begun to improve in Bulgaria and Romania, where privatization had picked up speed, and in Bosnia and Herzegovina, which was rebuilding its war-shattered economy. Farther east, on the contrary, economic transformation had stalled, particularly in Russia.

All across Europe, the differences between rural and city life persist to this day, even though the vast growth in communications—especially the spread of television—is lessening this difference. In rural areas, people still live more confined lives that are often centered around their homes and churches. Even remote villages have their cafés or pubs, but in many countries (particularly in southern Europe) these are frequented only by men. Young people, in search of opportunity and excitement, often leave the farms for cities, and the rural population dwindles. Yet thanks to greater efficiency, a shrinking number of farmworkers can feed the growing urban population.

The role of women in society differs greatly from country to country in Europe. In Sweden, women hold many public offices, and there are day-care centers to take care of children while mothers work. In some countries—particularly Spain, Greece, and Portugal—women are still ordinarily found at home. Some European women had to wait a long time for the right to vote: for instance, in France women could not vote until 1945, and in Switzerland, not until 1990.

In the former Communist countries, women were constitutionally recognized as equal and were strongly represented in many professions (for instance, most Soviet doctors were women), but actually very few women had leading positions anywhere. The main reason why most women were employed was economic necessity: one salary was generally not enough to provide for essential expenses. In most post-Communist countries, there are very few women in political and public life.

There are some differences in what are regarded as essential rights of citizens in the countries of Europe. In London's famous Hyde Park, any man or woman can bring his or her own box or platform, mount it, and proceed to say whatever he or she pleases about any subject. In Denmark, there is no restriction on the publication of any material, even what Americans might consider outright pornography. However, most citizens must carry national identity cards, and police at times are given greater latitude than might be permitted in the United States.

A great expansion of civic freedoms has occurred in the former Communist countries. Several are now fully comparable to Western democracies, but in most of them some vestiges of totalitarian practices continue. This is not surprising, particularly because such countries as Russia, Romania, and Bulgaria lack strong democratic traditions. The inhabitants of these nations thus have yet to develop an understanding of the personal responsibility that comes with political freedom.

All the countries of Europe have been greatly influenced by the American way of life. Today blue jeans are seen much more often than the embroidered peasant costumes of the past. Radio, films, television, and travel have brought many Americanisms to the most remote parts of Europe. American "fast-food" outlets provide hamburgers, pizza, and fried chicken to their fans in many parts of Europe.

Many intellectuals and also groups of young anarchists and ecologists have criticized the Americanization of Europe, but the United States continues to attract people from all parts of the continent, and American products are popular with the European public. In the 1990s, hundreds of American investors set up firms in Central and Eastern Europe. At the same time, European automobiles, foodstuffs, and many other products found markets in the United States.

The American influence and the rapid industrialization of much of Europe have brought many changes. Education for the technological society, involving vast public-education systems ranging from elementary schools to universities and requiring higher levels of basic education for all citizens, has broken down class barriers. Competition for top jobs in management is intense, and positions more often go to the ablest than in former days, when they might have been inherited or gone to political-party functionaries. The rush to the cities has brought a breakdown in the old family structures and also in the authority of the church. The industrial society has enabled people to live better and work fewer hours, but it has also brought the inevitable problems of overcrowding, pollution, and a concentration on material values.

THE LAND

A relief map of Europe shows a confusing mass of mountains, plateaus, and lowlands. However, it is possible to bring some order out of the confusion and recognize four major physical regions—the Northwestern Uplands, the Central Lowlands, the Central Uplands, and the alpine mountains.

The Northwestern Uplands

Uplands—rugged mountains, high plateaus, and deep valleys—stretch from Brittany in western France through the British Isles and Scandinavia all the way to the Arctic Ocean. The uplands vary greatly in height from rather low in Brittany to high in Scotland and Norway. These areas have been only thinly settled because the land is generally too rocky and mountainous for farming. The climate can be summed up in one word—"wet." In the northern uplands, moors and bogs are typical. In the far north, snow covers are permanent, and glaciers inch down toward the coast. In fact, during the Ice Age, most of this region was covered by ice. Today the landscape has many glacial features such as U-shaped valleys, lakes, and fjords—arms of the sea that often stretch far inland and are bordered by steep mountains.

Where the uplands are broken up or have a low elevation, living conditions are better. Good examples are central Ireland, which is a saucer-shaped lowland basin with an upland frame; the central valley of Scotland; and the area around Oslo in Norway. But people in the Northwestern Uplands live mainly along the coasts, where the fish-rich oceans offer a better living than does farming the rocky land itself. The land's importance comes from the minerals that are mined there and from the forests, which are an important source of timber.

The Central Lowlands

The Central Lowlands are the most densely settled part of Europe. They extend from the Garonne Valley in southwest France to the Ural Mountains. The lowlands are rather narrow in the west, and then widen to embrace all the space between the Arctic Ocean and the Black Sea. They include northern France, most of Belgium and the Netherlands, southeastern Britain, northern Germany, Denmark, Poland, the Baltic states, Belarus, Ukraine, and practically all of European Russia. The Central Lowlands are perfectly flat in the Netherlands, but elsewhere they are hilly with isolated elevations or long ridges. These ridges are called downs in Britain and *côtes* in France. Around the Baltic Sea, Ice Age glaciers have left their mark with terminal moraines—mounds built up of rock debris carried down by the glacier to the point at which it stopped. After the ice receded, most of the great lowland area became densely forested, but it was cleared by early settlers to make room for growing crops. However, the wetter western part of the Central Lowlands was probably always covered by grass and used for grazing.

Today the Central Lowland region is the home of most Europeans. The largest cities, the densest networks of transportation, and the heaviest concentration of industry are there in Europe's core area. Only a few parts of the region are still uncrowded, perhaps because the soil is poor or the climate too extreme, as in the north, with its short growing season, or the southern part of European Russia, where the climate is very dry.

The Central Uplands

A band of uplands lies between the Central Lowlands and the alpine mountains, and stretches from the Atlantic coast of Spain through France and Germany to Poland. Among the most important of these uplands are the Meseta in Spain, the Massif Central of France, the Ardennes of Belgium, the Vosges of France, the Black Forest of Germany, and the mountain rim around the Bohemian Basin in the Czech Republic. It is a somewhat more hospitable region than the Northwestern Uplands, but many parts are only sparsely inhabited.

The Alpine Mountains

The most dramatic physical features of Southern Europe are the alpine mountains, which stretch from Spain to the Caucasus. These mountains are young as geologists measure time, and there is still some mountain building going on, as demonstrated by the eruption of such active volcanoes as Vesuvius, near Naples, Italy; and Etna, on the Italian island of Sicily; and by disastrous quakes that shake the earth in a band extending eastward from Portugal.

Moving from west to east, the alpine mountains include the Sierra Nevada in Spain; the Pyrenees between Spain and France; the Apennines, which run like a spine down the Italian Peninsula; and such mountainous Mediterranean islands as Corsica, Sardinia, Sicily, and the Balearics. North of the Po River are Europe's most famous mountains, the Alps, which curve in a great arc before dividing into two branches. The Carpathian and Balkan mountains form the northern branch; the Dinaric Alps form the southern branch.

The Caucasus Mountains, between the Black and Caspian seas, are a nearly impenetrable wall separating Europe from the Middle East. Unlike the Caucasus, the low, forested Ural Mountains, which form Europe's eastern border, are easily crossed, so that there is no natural wall separating Europe and Asia.

Over thousands of years, glaciers like this one shaped the European continent.

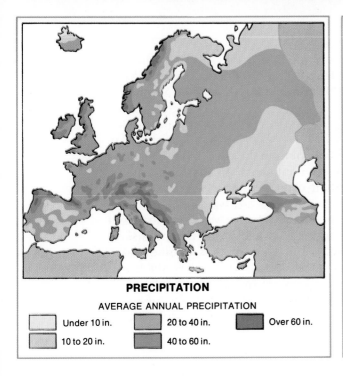

PRECIPITATION

AVERAGE ANNUAL PRECIPITATION

Under 10 in.	20 to 40 in.	Over 60 in.	
10 to 20 in.	40 to 60 in.		

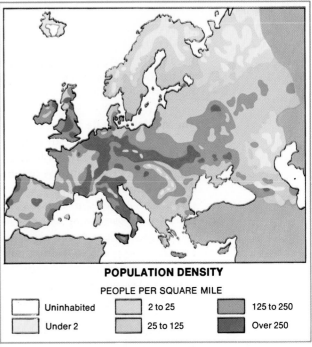

POPULATION DENSITY

PEOPLE PER SQUARE MILE

Uninhabited	2 to 25	125 to 250	
Under 2	25 to 125	Over 250	

The alpine mountain region is quite thinly populated except for some of the larger valleys. The outstanding example is Italy's Po Valley, which is really not a valley at all, but a depression between the Alps and the Apennines, and is one of Europe's most-crowded areas. Other rather densely settled parts of this region are the Swiss Plateau and the Danubian Plain. The narrow coastal plain of the Mediterranean Sea has been densely settled since early in history.

THE CLIMATE OF EUROPE

Climate is the most important factor in the physical environment of humans. It influences their life, their work, and their products. Some geographers believe, for example, that Western civilization was born in the Mediterranean region because the climate was neither extremely hot nor extremely cold, neither too rainy nor too dry. This, they say, made it possible for humans to work efficiently the year round without having to devise special clothing to protect themselves, or special buildings to protect the harvest of grain, which they could grow easily in the mild climate. Humans slowly grew more adept at building and heating their houses and at using tools. They found ways to grow crops in more-extreme climates and then to keep the crops from rotting. All of these developments made it possible for them to settle parts of the continent where the climate was not quite as gentle as in the south. It has been suggested that northwestern Europe's climate, with its cool (but not usually cold) winters and warm (but rarely hot) summers and abundance of precipitation, may be the ideal climate for people to live and work in.

Because Europe is located on a much higher latitude than the United States, Europe's southernmost point has approximately the same latitude as Cape Hatteras, North Carolina, and most of Europe is at the latitude of southern Labrador. The North Atlantic Drift of the Gulf Stream, which washes the coasts of northwestern Europe, causes mild sea air to warm up the winter temperatures.

Europe's three major climatic regions are the Atlantic, which is greatly influenced by the ocean currents; the Continental, which is typical for Central Europe and most of Belarus and Russia; and the Mediterranean in the south.

The Winter Climate

In winter, Atlantic air masses move in from the west, but are blocked in their eastern course by permanent continental air masses. There is, therefore, a great contrast between the climate of the west coast and that of the interior. Relatively warm temperatures are typical for the west coast. The Atlantic air masses also penetrate into the Mediterranean, but the winter storms are less severe, and, about half of the time, the skies are clear. Temperatures around 50° F. (10° C.) make the Mediterranean an attractive place to live and alluring to tourists.

The eastern part of Europe is influenced by the continental high-pressure system. Moscow has a January average of 15° F. (−9° C.). Farther east, toward the Ural Mountains, it grows even colder. Precipitation in the continental-climate zone is rather low, but the snow that does fall does not melt, and the wind piles the snow in drifts.

There is no distinct break between the Atlantic climate and the Continental one. The battle between the two climatic regions shifts constantly. Freezing cold weather at times comes quite close to the west coast. Warm air masses occasionally invade Russia. Even the mild Mediterranean region is at times invaded by cold continental air masses, and snow may fall over Rome and cover the Apennine Mountains in Italy. The Netherlands in northern Europe also experiences climatic variations of the usual pattern. The usual winter weather is cloudy, windy, and rainy, with temperatures close to 40° F. (5° C.) But at times, generally for a short period, the eastern air masses move in; temperatures drop below freezing, ice covers the canals, and the Dutch have wonderful ice festivals and enjoy great skating. There may be snow and a great deal of fog. As a rule, as one goes farther east in Europe, these cold periods become more frequent and last longer.

The Summer Climate

In summer, conditions change. The Atlantic has a cooling influence on the warmer land. The westerly winds are still there, but cyclonic storms are less severe, and the winds are less strong. July averages are still relatively low, in the 60s° F. (10s° C.); even Paris has a July average of only 65° F. (18° C.). The continental high in the east is replaced by a low-pressure area, and Atlantic air masses move into Siberia without obstruction. Temperatures are warmer than in the west—in the low 70s° F. (20s° C.). This is the rainy season for eastern and also central Europe, with storms caused by convection of air that has been heated over land, although the amounts of precipitation are not high. The mountains capture more rain, and have a large range of climatic conditions depending upon their height and orientation in relation to the prevailing winds. During the summer in Switzerland, for instance, it is often cool and wet. In fact, a snowfall in July at an altitude as low as 4,000 ft. (1,220 m.) has been recorded.

Summer climatic conditions in southern Europe are quite different because the subtropical high-pressure zone has moved in. The sky is

The city of Béziers in southern France dates back to Roman times.

generally clear, rain is scarce, and the temperatures are well up in the 70s° F. (20s° C.) and 80s° F. (30s° C.). In the summer, there is a zone of transition between the Mediterranean and the rest of Europe. Northern Italy, for instance, is still warm, but there is also precipitation. Generally, even the warmest European regions seldom experience the high humidity typical of much of the American East Coast.

Each of the three major climatic regions has its good and bad points, but people are able to live and to adjust their lives and economy to them. However, two additional climates are represented in Europe, and both are unfavorable for humans because they are either too dry or too cold. In the dry climates, lack of water prevents the growing of crops except when irrigation is available. This is true of part of the Spanish Meseta, which has a basin shape with a mountain rim that keeps out the moisture-bearing winds. Southeastern European Russia, behind the Carpathian Mountains, is also dry. The other unfavorable climate is one where freezing temperatures are permanent or the growing season too short. These cold climates are found in the high mountains and along the shores of the Arctic Ocean in the so-called tundra belt.

VEGETATION

Tundra and Taiga. The tundra belt, which covers northern Russia and Lapland, takes its name from a Finnish word meaning "barren hill." During most of the year, the soil of the tundra is permanently frozen, and strong winds make it impossible for trees to grow. It is only during the very short Arctic summer that the temperatures rise enough to melt the top layer of the soil.

South of the Arctic tundra belt, there is a zone where evergreens predominate. "Taiga" is the name of this wide belt, which starts in Norway and continues through Sweden, Finland, and Russia all the way to the Pacific. Part of this tremendous forest is still untouched, but the pines and spruces of this zone are Europe's foremost source of lumber.

Mixed Forests and Grasslands. Where the growing season is longer, mixed forest of beeches, oaks, and pines replaces the taiga. Over the years, a great deal of this mixed forest has been cleared to make room for crops and grassland, but large stands still exist, and the Central Lowlands are far from treeless. Trees line the roads, surround the farmhouses, and often form the border between properties. The English park landscape is famous for its large individual trees set on grassland. Along the Atlantic coast, with its wetness, strong winds, and lack of sunshine, grass replaces the forest. Ireland is known as the Emerald Isle because of its grassy green landscapes, and the Netherlands is known for its beautiful green meadows. On the high Alps, above the line where trees can grow, are the alpine meadows, where beautiful wildflowers are found and cattle graze in summer.

Mediterranean. This zone has special vegetation—plants and trees that are able to withstand the long, warm, and dry summers because

This field in southern Spain has typical Mediterranean vegetation.

of their deep roots, thick bark, thorns, or tough leaves. Evergreen oaks, cypresses, cedars, olive trees, and eucalypti are common in the Mediterranean. Where humans have felled the trees in large quantities, the trees have been replaced by a dense mixture of scrub plants called maquis. Maquis flower in spring, but grow brown and lifeless in the summer.

Steppe Vegetation. On the steppes—the level, treeless plains of the lower Danube and southern European Russia—where the climate is dry, grasses thrive. Most grassland is plowed under to provide cropland. In drier areas, such as around the Caspian Sea, saltbushes grow.

ANIMAL LIFE

Wild animals such as the musk ox, ibex, bison, and chamois, which used to be found in large numbers in Europe, must now be protected from hunters and the encroachment of modern life by special laws, game preserves, and even cages in zoos. To see the now-rare European bison, one must travel to the Bialowieza Forest, the national park in eastern Poland. Ibex and chamois—swift-footed alpine animals—can be found in Italy's Gran Paradiso National Park; chamois, lynx, and brown bear are found in a preserve in the High Tatra Mountains.

Some animals still live free, such as the polar bears of Spitsbergen and the wolves and wild boars in eastern Europe. Mouflon, wild sheep with curling horns, roam the hills and mountains of Corsica and Sardinia, off Italy's west coast. Saigas, Europe's only native antelope, live in the dry steppe region between the Volga River and the Ural Mountains.

Rabbit, hare, deer, and fox are still hunted in Europe; but important fur-bearing animals such as mink, ermine, and sable, for which Russia is especially famous, are now carefully raised on fur farms because they were nearly exterminated by trappers.

The birds of Europe have survived better than the mammals, except when they have tempted people by being delicious to eat, as is the case with grouse, wild ducks, larks, and partridges. Other familiar birds such as the cuckoo, skylark, and nightingale are still seen and heard.

Fish such as trout, carp, and the sturgeon of the Caspian Sea—which is caught for its roe (caviar)—are also still plentiful. The pollution in many rivers has eliminated some fish species, but ecological measures have started to reverse some of this damage.

ECONOMY

The Roman historian Tacitus wrote that Central Europe "either bristles with woods or festers with swamps." If he were to revisit the continent today, he would see vast changes in the landscape. Over the centuries, people have slowly cleared the land of the great forests, filled in many of the swamps, and reclaimed land from the sea to make farmland. Bustling industrial cities have replaced most of the forests and swamps.

Food Supply

European farmers have learned to make the most of their not-always-fertile land. The simple tools of the earliest European farmer have been replaced nearly everywhere by modern farm machines and modern farming methods. As early as Roman times, farmers knew the value of enriching the soil with manure, of rotating the land on which crops were

Vines like these in France are the source of Europe's well-known wines.

grown, and of irrigating the dry land. The Romans grew olive and other fruit trees, cultivated grapevines, and carried their agricultural arts to the most distant parts of their empire. Some of the vines growing on the terraced slopes of the Rhine were probably planted by Roman soldiers.

As time passed, villages and towns grew into cities. Once, most of the population lived on the land and grew their own food. Then a slowly increasing number of people began to live in the cities and needed to buy food. As the first large trading cities grew up in northern Italy, southern Germany, and in Flanders (now part of Belgium), and then in England and France, the farms that provided their food had to be changed to meet the new demand. Fields and pastures that had once been shared were enclosed and individually owned. Crop rotation replaced the method of letting a field lie fallow between plantings. Cattle were more carefully selected for breeding, with the result that larger and more-profitable animals were raised. New plants were introduced.

But there were other factors that were beyond the skill or control of Europe's farmers. Uncertain weather could ruin a crop—as is periodically the case with the wheat crop in Ukraine and Russia. A blight of unknown origin could destroy the staple food of a nation, as happened with the potato crop in Ireland in the 19th century. Famine, disease, and desolation were terrible threats that could and did alter the face of Europe. Beginning in the 17th century, another factor had an important effect on Europe's agriculture. The size of the population, which had remained nearly the same since A.D. 1000, slowly began to increase. Between 1750 and 1850, the population of Europe grew from about 140 million to 260 million. By the beginning of World War I in 1914, the population of Europe numbered 400 million. In the British Isles alone, the population grew from about 8 million in the early 18th century to some 21 million a century later. These figures are the beginning of an explanation for the enormous waves of emigration from Europe. The small continent, even with its relatively advanced farming methods, could not support its population. As many as 40 million Europeans settled in the Americas, Australia, New Zealand, and other parts of the world.

Today about 30 percent of the total area of Europe is devoted to agriculture, 20 percent to pasture, and a little less than 30 percent to forests. These percentages are quite high compared to other continents, but they tell only a part of the story because they say nothing about yields per acre and total production. In general, yields are high in Europe, but there are great differences between nations. A Dutch farmer produces four times as much per acre as a farmer in Portugal because of differences in climate and methods of farming.

Except for Britain, Europe is self-sufficient in food production, although some tropical products and fodder for livestock are imported. Part of this self-sufficiency is based on higher yields. Europeans have also seen great changes in their diets. There has been a shift from cereals to meat, fruit, and dairy products. Prosperity has made that shift possible: the Italians eat less spaghetti, and the French, less bread. Europe generally eats well. Ireland is estimated to have the world's highest calorie intake per person.

In some former Communist countries, particularly in Russia, Ukraine, and Belarus, agriculture is much less developed and agricultural machinery is scarce; in remote villages, farming has changed little since the 19th century. So far, however, most people have managed to scrape together the basic necessities. Even in Bosnia and Herzegovina, which has been convulsed by war, food has been always available, often thanks to humanitarian aid from the West.

The type of food produced is to a large extent based on climate: dairy products come from the wet northwest; cereals (rye and wheat) and sugar beets are grown in the Central Lowlands. Corn is cultivated in the transition zone between the Mediterranean climate and that of central Europe. In the Mediterranean lands, wheat, fruits, and vegetables are raised, partly with the help of irrigation. Other important factors operate despite, rather than because of, climatic conditions. These are the demands of the market and the concentrated production of perishable foods near the areas of greatest population.

In the industrialized countries of central and northwestern Europe, the farming population continues to leave the land for factories and big cities. This is less true for the south. In Greece, for instance, the farming population is about 30 percent of the total, compared to the average of about 7.6 percent for all of the members of the European Union.

It is not only the land that gives Europe its food; there is also the ocean. The coastal waters of Western Europe abound in fish: herring and cod in the north, sardines and tuna farther south. The former Soviet Union had one of the largest fishing industries in the world, and its annual fish catch was the second largest in the world, after that of Japan. Iceland's economy is based on fishing; its production is one-quarter that of the United States, which has 1,000 times as many people.

Strangely enough, the Mediterranean, which teems with fish, has never become an important fishing ground, primarily due to its warm water. In cold water, fish species appear in schools, and the catch is generally of one or two kinds. In warm water, however, fish do not congregate; the catch is a colorful display of all kinds of fish—interesting, but commercially of little value. Furthermore, the growing pollution of the Mediterranean poses a serious threat to its fish population.

Modern methods of canning, freezing, and preserving have made it possible to enjoy European foods thousands of miles from the continent. English sole, Belgian endive, and wild strawberries from France are welcomed on American tables, while stores have shelves loaded with wines from France, Italy, Germany, Greece, Spain, Portugal, and Hungary. Long white asparagus from France, hams from Poland and Denmark, canned fish from Scandinavia and Portugal, and cheeses from the Netherlands, Switzerland, and Italy are only a sampling of the fine foods that Europe exports to the world.

Industries, Products, and Services

Power Resources. From the time of the waterwheel and the windmill through the Coal Age and the beginning of the use of hydroelectricity, Europe had all the power it needed. When oil became a major source of power, Europe west of Russia was in trouble. Oil is found in many parts of Europe, but generally in small amounts. These amounts were sufficient in preindustrial Europe for such novel experiments as the lighting of some streetlamps in Prague with oil in 1815, but they are insufficient for power industries and vehicles. The Ploesti oil fields in Romania, which were the largest in Europe outside the former U.S.S.R., are no longer as important as they once were. Petroleum from the North Sea, discovered in the 1970s, is providing an important supply of this valuable resource for the nations of Western Europe. And an enormous natural-gas field was discovered in the northern Netherlands. But the need to import oil and natural gas continues in much of Europe, and their rising cost has threatened economic growth.

The former Soviet Union had about 58 percent of the world's proven petroleum reserves and about one-third of the world's proven reserves of natural gas. In 1974 it passed the United States as the world's leading petroleum producer, but the recent political upheavals led to a significant decline in oil production. The once-great Caucasus oil fields around Baku, in Azerbaijan, are now less important than those in Central Asia, particularly Kazakhstan. Pipelines extending from these newer fields into Europe could regain their importance when Central Asian oil production begins to profit from cooperation with Western oil companies.

Tankers transport oil from the Middle East and North Africa to the other nations of Europe. Rotterdam, at the outlet of the Rhine River, is the world's greatest oil port. In its huge refineries, crude oil is transformed into its final products. Pipelines carry the oil to the nearby German industrial region. North African oil goes chiefly to Europe's Mediterranean ports, especially Genoa, Italy, and Marseilles, France. Pipelines also cross the Alps to Switzerland and Germany. A 3,700-mi. (5,950-km.) pipeline to carry natural gas to Western Europe was completed in 1983.

Historically, the coal-producing areas in countries such as the former Soviet Union, the United Kingdom, Belgium, France, Germany, and Poland were the first centers of manufacturing. Coal is not as important a power source as it was in the past, but it is still used in large quantities, and Europe has enough to meet its needs. Russia is Europe's largest coal producer.

The availability of hydroelectricity depends on plenty of running water—if possible, throughout the year—and a difference in elevation because the water must drop rapidly, as over a waterfall, to supply power. This is why power plants are usually built on mountains that have plenty of precipitation, such as those of Scandinavia, the Alps, and the Pyrenees. Norway and Sweden are major producers of hydroelectric power, and could produce more if there were an outlet to less-fortunate countries. However, transferring hydroelectric power over long distances is still a problem.

France, Italy, Switzerland, Austria, and Spain also have a great deal of waterpower. This is especially important in Italy and Switzerland, as both have practically no coal resources. Alpine valleys, especially those in Italy, are carefully utilized; one dam (with a dammed lake) and power plant follows the next one downstream because, in contrast to coal, water can be used over and over again. Hydroelectric power in Russia is based on its rivers, where huge amounts of water compensate for small differences in elevation. Two of the largest hydroelectric dams in the world are on the Volga River in European Russia. More recently, a huge new hydroelectric system has been constructed jointly by Romania and Yugoslavia at the historic Iron Gate gorge on the Danube River, and both countries draw power from it.

Iceland, the volcanic island off Europe's northwest coast, has a unique power source—hot springs. The Icelandic Government plans to use these hot springs to produce electricity at low cost to users. The hot springs, once only columns of steam roaring up from mud pits to the amazement of visitors, have already been tapped to pipe heat to nearby farmhouses, greenhouses, and nearly all the homes of Reykjavík.

Some people consider the power resource of the future to be nuclear energy, which could replace the waning reserves of traditional sources such as coal and oil. A number of European nations have used nuclear energy for peaceful purposes such as generating electricity. But the expansion of the use of nuclear power as a source of energy has slowed as some people have become concerned about the safety of nuclear-power plants and the disposal of radioactive wastes. A major accident in 1986 at the nuclear-power plant at Chernobyl, in the former Soviet republic of Ukraine, with its loss of many lives and widespread radioactive fallout, reinforced such fears.

Mineral Resources. Europe west of Russia is not blessed with many minerals. The important exception is iron ore. The combination of coal and iron ore was to a large extent responsible for the Industrial Revolution. Britain, for example, was extremely fortunate in having its coal and iron-ore deposits close to each other. While iron ore is mined in many parts of Europe, there are two areas of outstanding production. Lorraine, an area in eastern France (extending into Luxembourg), is located close to the coal of the Saar Basin in Germany. The other important iron-ore mines are in northern Sweden, from which the ore is brought by ship to the industrial regions of Europe.

Otherwise, Europe is not an important producer of the major metallic minerals. Copper is mined in some quantities by Finland, Norway, Sweden, Yugoslavia, and Spain. Germany, Spain, and Sweden produce small quantities of lead ore. Zinc production is slight, and the tin mines in Cornwall, England, which once attracted traders from as far off as the eastern Mediterranean, are now empty. The picture is brighter in alloy metals such as tungsten, which is found in Portugal and Spain, and chromium, mined in what was Yugoslavia. Europe is also quite well supplied with some of the minor minerals: mercury from Spain and Italy, and sulfur from Italy. Bauxite, for aluminum, is also found in adequate quantities. In fact, its name comes from the small town of Les Baux in southern France, where it was first discovered.

Inside Russia the mineral-resource picture changes dramatically. This vast country has large quantities of nearly every metallic mineral, but much of it is in its Asian part. In the Ukraine, the nation's production

High-quality European automobiles and farm equipment have found worldwide markets.

European aircraft manufacturers have made steady inroads into what once was a U.S.-dominated industry.

of iron ore, the most important mineral, surpasses that of the United States. The chief source is the Krivoi Rog area west of the bend in the Dnieper River. It is also supplied with bauxite, copper, lead, nickel, molybdenum, and manganese.

Europe's nonmetallic mineral production includes abundant building materials such as stone, clay, sand, gravel, and the world's largest potash deposits. Potash, which is used in fertilizers, exists in such large quantities in eastern Germany that some experts believe it could meet the world's needs for this product for 1,000 years. Salt is mined in some places, extracted from underground brine, and taken from the sea off the Mediterranean coast mainly for use in the chemical industries. Sulfur and magnesite are two other important nonmetallic minerals found in Europe. Even with this seemingly impressive list of mineral resources, Europe must still import minerals to provide for its industries and its agriculture.

Manufacturing.   Generally, early peoples made their own personal tools, weapons, clothing, pottery, and other articles. Gradually, within a group or a city, experts would specialize in certain types of manufacturing (literally, "production by hand"), either for direct consumption or for sale. During the Middle Ages in Europe, experts in the same branch of manufacturing would join in a kind of union known as a guild to protect their industry. These associations often built beautiful guildhalls, such as those that still stand in Brussels.

The Industrial Revolution, despite its stress on coal and the creation of many new, generally ugly, towns of factories and row houses, did not entirely destroy the former craft specialties. Glasswork in Venice, steel blades in Toledo, watches in Switzerland, blue chinaware in Delft in the

Netherlands, lacework in Flanders, and linen in Ireland are examples of such specialties that are still produced. But the main emphasis of the Industrial Revolution was on heavy industries and mass production, using power-driven machinery.

In the 19th century, Europe, with its coal resources and its good transportation, became the world's greatest manufacturing area. Heavy industries developed near the coalfields in Britain, northern France, Belgium, Germany, and Poland. Later, when hydroelectric power was introduced, the already-existing industries of central Sweden and of northern Italy expanded. Large cities attracted factories. Harbors became prime locations for manufacturing industries where imported raw materials were most cheaply available. One of the largest European steel plants is located on the shore of the North Sea at Ijmuiden, the outlet of the Amsterdam shipping canal.

The post–World War II development in Europe would not have been possible without American help, principally the Marshall Plan of 1948. Moreover, the United States has invested many billions of dollars of private capital in Europe. American know-how and efficiency have also contributed much to Europe's industrial development. But, finally, it was the Europeans themselves who performed the economic miracle (as it is sometimes called) with their own hard labor, thrift, and intelligence.

Manufacturing in the Former Communist Countries. After the Bolshevik revolution in 1917, transforming the Soviet state into a top industrial-manufacturing power was a constant preoccupation of the Communist regime. Similar emphasis on heavy industries, especially those connected with the military, characterized the development of Soviet satellites in Eastern Europe following World War II. Meanwhile, stores were few and far between and often sparsely stocked.

The political and economic upheavals of recent years laid bare the inherent problems of Communist-managed industrial development. These flaws included complicated red tape that had always discouraged personal initiative, wasted energy, and technological backwardness. In the Czech Republic, for instance, many workers still use machines from the 19th century.

The modernization of huge former Soviet industrial centers—particularly those around Moscow, in the middle Urals, or in the Donets Basin in Ukraine—is an overwhelming task. Many factories will soon close. In Central Europe, heavy industry is being scaled down and services are expanding.

Tourism. It is impossible to talk about the economy of Europe without mentioning tourism. Most of the traveling is done by Europeans themselves, although Americans, Japanese, and other affluent non-Europeans provide a good percentage. Tourism as it is now is quite different from what it used to be. Until the end of World War II, relatively few people traveled abroad. It was a pastime of the rich living separately in luxury hotels. Now everybody travels, by private automobile as well as by the large buses utilized by travel clubs—those organizations offering their members a selection of various trips for a small monthly payment. The mass of cars leaving Paris on the first of August, the traditional beginning date of French vacations, is almost unbelievable. Many stay in France, generally on the coasts, but more and more visit other nations, including increasing numbers who visit the United States. The warm

Mediterranean is a special attraction in summer, and along the Alpine crossings, cars drive or stand bumper to bumper.

Of course, tourism means welcome income for a nation. Spain, for example, can be called a tourist miracle. Until relatively recently, Spain was a forgotten country as far as most tourists were concerned. Roads, except for a few major ones, were bad; and hotels, except in the big cities, were few in number. Then Spain was "discovered," and people poured in across the Pyrenees. Roads were improved; new hotels arose everywhere. The main attraction is the Mediterranean coast: the Costa Brava—"wild coast"—between the Pyrenees and Barcelona, and more recently the Costa del Sol—"coast of the sun"—west of Málaga.

Tourism to and between the former Communist nations is also increasing. The removal of travel restrictions in many countries and the relative bargain prices have attracted visitors to the rich historical and natural treasures of the region. After decades of limited access, tourists are bringing much-needed foreign exchange to the economies that are struggling to shed the Communist ways of doing business. Indeed, travel to the countries that had been separated by the "Iron Curtain" had become the "in" thing for Americans by the early 1990s.

Transportation

Roads. The impulse for the construction of better roads in Europe came initially from the military. Ancient Rome was the first to build roads for the swift movement of its troops. Napoleon constructed the French road system for similar reasons, and Hitler was responsible for the network of superhighways called *autobahns* in Germany. In later years the development of mass automobile production in Western Europe and the desire to attract tourists became the impetus for building first-class roads. Car tunnels such as the 7.5-mi. (12-km.)-long Mont Blanc Tunnel connecting France and Italy greatly shorten travel time. In Central Europe, the highways are generally narrower, but in relatively good condition. Farther east, the quality of roads declines and there are fewer of them.

The number of cars on the roads has increased rapidly since the end of World War II. Sweden has more than one car for every three inhabitants. In Northern Europe, bicycles are still popular, especially in the Netherlands and Denmark, and bicycle paths are often found on either side of the road. Since the fall of the Iron Curtain, the number of cars in the former Communist countries has mushroomed. In Prague, for instance, there are now twice as many cars as there were in 1989.

Railroads. Railroads started in Europe. In 1804, the world's first steam locomotive pulled a train of cars loaded with coal from a mine in Wales. In 1825, the Stockton and Darlington in England became the first railroad to be opened to the public. Gradually, the European rail network grew into the densest system in the world. In contrast to those in the United States in recent years, European passenger trains have increased in number and speed, and passenger traffic is heavy. Trains are generally comfortable, and many of them are excellent. With airports usually far from town, and traveling distances relatively small, trains continue to compete with planes. A network of EURO-CITY and INTER-CITY trains now reaches into former Communist countries. The Chunnel, a train tunnel under the English Channel, was opened in 1994 after seven years of construction.

Airlines. Europe was the home of the world's first commercial airline, Royal Dutch Airlines (KLM), established in 1919, and aviation has been important since the beginning of the century. Today practically every European country of any size has its own airline. Air France is the world's largest airline in terms of route mileage served. Some European countries, such as Denmark, Norway, and Sweden, have pooled their resources to operate a joint airline (Scandinavian Airlines). England and France together built and operate one of the world's two supersonic airliners, the Concorde. (The other is the Tupolev TU-144, an aircraft developed by the former Soviet Union.) Airlines connect all cities of any importance and, of course, connect Europe with all parts of the world. Such European "gateway" airports as Heathrow in London, Orly in Paris, and Schiphol in Amsterdam handle vast amounts of traffic annually. The ongoing modernization of Prague's airport will soon make it a Central European traffic hub.

Waterways. Since ancient times, rivers have been major arteries of transportation. The main international rivers of Europe, the Rhine and the Danube, have played a part throughout history. The Rhine was used by the Romans, who also controlled its outlet. The Normans sailed up the rivers to plunder the commercial cities along their courses. In modern times, both the Rhine and the Danube are under international supervision. Of the two, the Danube is longer and connects more countries, but the Rhine is the more important economically. The Danube flows away from the main European markets and empties into the somewhat isolated Black Sea. The Rhine, however, serves Europe's most industrialized area; the port at its mouth at Rotterdam handles more freight than any other in the world. Rhine barges, under their own power or pulled by tugboats, go all the way to Basel, Switzerland. A narrow old canal connecting the Rhine with the Danube (and thus the North and the Black seas) has been replaced by a new shipping canal that opened in 1992.

Most rivers in the Central Lowlands, such as the Elbe and Oder in Germany and the Seine and Loire in France, are connected by a maze of canals, which had their period of glory before the railroads came. England also had its canals, now somewhat forgotten. It is still possible, however, to cross most of Europe by small boat, going from the North Sea to the Mediterranean Sea, ending in Marseilles by way of a mountain boat tunnel.

Large shipping canals have been constructed in modern times. The New Waterway, the artificial outlet of the Rhine, looks more like a river than a canal and is lined for 16 mi. (26 km.) by harbor basins, which are part of the Rotterdam harbor complex, called Europoort by the Dutch. The Germans constructed the Kiel Canal as part of the trade route between the North Sea and the Baltic. Manchester, England, has its shipping canal to the Irish Sea. Antwerp, Belgium, has a canal joining it to the Rhine so that it can share in the Rhine trade. Romania recently completed a new shipping canal connecting the Danube, near its mouth, with the Black Sea.

Being primarily lowlands, Russia is a country of large rivers. Except for those toward the Arctic, whose outlets are blocked by ice most of the year, these have long been major routes of transportation. The Volga, the longest river in Europe, is for Russia what the Rhine is for Germany, a river of folklore and historic significance as well as great economic

Its setting, history, and art make Venice a popular goal for tourists.

The Grenadier Guards at Windsor Castle represent the pageantry in English life.

importance. Other large rivers are the Dnieper and the Donets.

The largest waterway is, of course, the ocean, and harbors are the contacts between continent and ocean. Europe has a great variety of coasts, some favorable, some unfavorable for shipping. In old times a port was adequate if it could serve ships of up to a few hundred tons; now there are supertankers of 300,000 tons. Some of the most important European ports are London and Liverpool in Britain, Rotterdam in the Netherlands, Antwerp in Belgium, Hamburg and Bremen in Germany, Le Havre and Marseilles in France, Genoa and Naples in Italy, Gdańsk and Szczecin in Poland, and Odessa in Ukraine.

Megalopolis

Since the Industrial Revolution, people have flocked into towns, where jobs are readily available. In capital cities, the government is usually the largest employer. Most Europeans are thus town or city dwellers. In Britain, for instance, 80 percent of the population lives in urban districts. More than 30 European cities have passed the 1 million mark, and many others are quite close to that number. The European successor states of the former Soviet Union have eight cities with more than a million inhabitants, led by Moscow. These statistics are often given for urban agglomerates, which mean the cities proper plus their suburbs. Generally, the old city core loses part of its population to the suburbs, where life is more pleasant.

For still-larger urban concentrations, the word "megalopolis" has been coined. On the whole, "megalopolis" signifies a gigantic urbanized area, but it does not have to be continuous, and open spaces (greenbelts) may occur. In the United States, the word describes the coastal zone from Portland, Maine, to Washington, D.C. In Europe, a megalopolis is developing comprising northern France, central Belgium, the western Netherlands, and the lower Rhine region of Germany; its population may exceed 40 million.

Europe's Economic Future

With the economic integration of 1992 and the planned admission of former Communist countries into the European Union, Europe is turning into an economic giant. Yet it is not smooth sailing. In the early 1990s, the wealthy West European countries suffered from increased unemployment and have increasingly had to grapple with the overburdened social-security system. Indeed, it seems that the much-admired Western European system, in which citizens pay high taxes but receive extensive benefits, will have to be significantly revamped.

Another problem is red tape: as Europe unites economically, the maze of rules and regulations (concerning even such matters as the allowable curvature of a banana) sometimes becomes stifling.

Europe's economic future will also depend on the pace of economic transformation in the former Communist countries, and on political and economic developments in Russia.

HISTORY

The Europe of the earliest settlers was an uninviting place. Vast glaciers still covered much of the land. The climate was unpleasant—cold and damp. The vegetation was probably of the tundra type that is still found in the most northerly parts of the continent. The inhabitants of Europe during the Paleolithic period (Old Stone Age) did little to change the appearance of the land. These first Europeans lived as nomads—hunting animals, catching fish, and gathering food. Their skills were extremely limited, and the tools they made of bone, stone, and flint were rough and unpolished.

As the glaciers retreated, the climate gradually became more moderate, and the vegetation of Europe began to resemble that of the continent today. Waves of invaders, mainly from the east, brought new ideas and techniques that slowly altered the way of life of the first Europeans. The culture of Southwest Asia is believed to have entered Europe by way of three routes—the Aegean Sea, the Morava-Vardar River gap to the plains of the Danube, or the Bosporus to the lower Danube. Among the most enduring contributions of these invaders were language, tools, and the knowledge of how to live as settled farmers. Indo-European—the ancestor of all the modern European languages except Estonian, Finnish, Hungarian, and Basque—may have come with the invaders.

The knowledge of farming that developed in India, Mesopotamia, and Egypt spread slowly into Europe. It led to the establishment of permanent communities that shared their tools for farming and pooled their resources for mutual defense. A gradually increasing knowledge of the continent's resources—ranging from the tin of Cornwall to the copper of Austria—made it possible to make better tools for farming and defense. Animals, including horses, were domesticated. Wheeled carts and ships were built. Routes for trade in such commodities as amber, which was highly prized for jewelry, began to spread across the continent—the forerunners of today's network of rails and highways.

THE CLASSICAL CIVILIZATIONS

The combination of a rather mild climate and the nearness of the more highly developed cultures of the East acted as a stimulus to the first great European civilizations, which grew up on the northeastern edge of the Mediterranean Sea. From about 1600 to 1400 B.C., the Minoan civilization of the island of Crete dominated the Aegean. The Minoans, whose name may have come from Minos, a legendary priest-king who ruled over them, were a community of farmers, seafarers, traders, and artisans. Their culture is known for its emphasis on good taste and elegance. The houses of the wealthier citizens often were five stories tall and had terraces and individual wells.

The Civilization of Ancient Greece

The Minoans' development was first paralleled and then surpassed by the Mycenaeans, whose life centered around the city of Mycenae on the mainland of Greece from about 1600 to 1200 B.C. An elaborate government ruled over a community whose organization and variety are indicated in its preserved tax records and occupation census, where jobs are listed ranging from longshoreman to bath attendant. Although plentiful gold ornaments suggest that the Mycenaeans were as luxury-loving as the Minoans, they had a disposition to wage war. Their most famous conflict, under the leadership of their king, Agamemnon, was the 10-year-long Trojan War. This, the first recorded war in European history, is known to us through the first great European literary work, Homer's

Delos, one of the Cyclades Islands, offers evidence of the glories that were Greece.

epic the *Iliad,* which was composed several centuries after the Trojan War ended.

In the years between 1200 and 750 B.C., the older cultures of Crete and Mycenae disappeared, and successive waves of Dorian invaders from the north took over the Greek Peninsula and the nearby islands. Refugees from the Dorian invaders found a home in Athens, where the ancient cultures were preserved. In the upheaval caused by the invaders, only the smallest political units survived—the city-states, whose governments (whether they were tyrannies, aristocracies, or later, democracies) exerted a profound influence on all European political development. Despite the division into hundreds of political units, the Greeks were united by their language, their alphabet, and the beginnings of a political philosophy. Each adult male was responsible to his city, and the city in its turn was responsible for protecting the citizen by law and by arms.

Wine, olives, and wool were the chief products and the basis of Greek trade. But constant wars and a shortage of land plagued the Greeks, who did not know how to rotate crops, and thus often had large tracts of land lying fallow. As the population became too large for the land to support, Greek colonists settled in Ionia (the coast of Asia Minor) and in regions as distant as the Black Sea coast, Sicily, Massilia (Marseilles), and Tarraco (Tarragona, Spain). The seeds of modern European ideas based on Greek thought swept into Europe with the Greek traders who followed the Rhone River north to trade in Gaul (most of modern France and western Germany) and perhaps even in Cornwall and Ireland.

During the 5th century B.C., the Athenians and the Spartans turned back the Persians who threatened to occupy their lands. The defeat of the Persians in 480 B.C. marks the beginning of the most glorious, if brief, moments in human history—the Golden Age of Greece, when art, literature, and government reached heights that have scarcely been equaled since. Then the rivalry between the cities of Sparta and Athens led to the Peloponnesian Wars, which marked the close of the Golden Age and the defeat of Athens as a great power. But during the century that followed, some of the greatest Greek thinkers of all time lived. They included Socrates, his student Plato, and Plato's student Aristotle.

Aristotle, whose ideas were to dominate science for centuries, was himself the teacher of Alexander the Great, a man of action rather than reflection. Yet it is through him that so much Greek thought spread around the world and has come down to us. In 336 B.C., Alexander began a program of conquest that swept over Greece and across the Middle East to India and included all the lands along the eastern Mediterranean. In the city of Alexandria, which Alexander founded in Egypt, Greek ideas continued to be studied long after Alexander's vast empire had been divided.

The Rise and Fall of Rome

After Alexander's death in 323 B.C., the center of political power moved slowly westward to the Italian Peninsula, especially the city of Rome. Rome began as a city that was a sort of transition point between the culture of the Greek cities of the south and the Etruscan domains of the north. Rome gradually dominated the entire peninsula. It eliminated the threat of a rival imperial power, Carthage, in the course of the long Punic Wars (264–164 B.C.), and thus added the Carthaginian territories of Sicily, Spain, and parts of North Africa to its own growing empire. Threats from Macedonia and Greece were met by armed intervention, and soon Rome held outposts along the eastern coast of the Adriatic Sea. By A.D. 14 the Roman Empire had grown to include all the lands to the north as far as the Rhine and Danube rivers. In this way the civilization of the Mediterranean world become a part of the fabric of European life.

The ruins of the Roman Forum bear testimony to the grandeur of Europe's ancient civilizations.

Medieval castles were built of stone and surrounded by water-filled moats, to ward off attackers.

A highly centralized government, Rome was administered first as a monarchy, then as a republic, a military government, and finally, beginning in 27 B.C., as an empire. For some two centuries, from 30 B.C. to A.D. 193, Rome ruled its widespread empire in relative peace. Greco-Roman ideals, the Latin language, and an effective network of roads combined with a large standing army to unite people as different from each other as the Belgians, Iberians, and Britons. Art, literature, and philosophy flourished. Sciences grew more accurate. For the bureaucrats and landholders, life was fairly easy and comfortable. For the dispossessed—peasants, slaves, and the unemployed—life was often harsh and difficult.

The most important religion that developed in the late Roman Empire was Christianity, which gradually replaced the cults of pagan gods. Groups of Christians grew larger in spite of persecution, and in A.D. 380, Christianity was proclaimed the state religion. Increasing numbers of Roman government officials became Christian bishops.

The First Barbarian Invasions

Barbarians had been pressing in on Rome's territory since the 3rd century A.D. To fend off invasions, Emperor Diocletian (A.D. 284–305) decided to divide the empire into an eastern and a western half so that it could be administered and defended more easily, and he shared power with a co-emperor. Although in A.D. 324, Constantine became sole emperor and the two halves were united, the empire was split again when Emperor Theodosius died in 395.

The richer Eastern Empire, Greek in culture, ultimately developed its own form of Christianity that came to be known as Eastern Orthodoxy. The poor western division, initially less cultivated because of continued fighting with barbarians, followed a different form of worship under Roman bishops, using Latin. Thus the faith branched out on two separate paths, although the final split between the East and western Roman Catholicism did not take place until 1054.

Pressing in on this divided state from the west and the south were Germanic tribesmen. Some joined the Roman army, others were enslaved, and still others became farmers. But they were never fully absorbed into Roman life, and as the need for land grew, they turned to conquest. In 410, the Goths attacked, looted, and burned the city of Rome. The city that for eight centuries had represented order and civilization worldwide had fallen.

By the end of the 5th century A.D., the Roman Empire in the west was ended, although the eastern half, centered at Constantinople (now Istanbul), continued to exist until the mid-15th century. The dream of reviving the huge, united Roman Empire lingered on for a long time in European civilization, and the title of "Roman Emperor" was also revived, in various forms, at later dates.

THE EARLY MIDDLE AGES

Historians writing in the 18th century viewed the history of Europe as the steady progress of humanity to the high point marked by the cultivated society of their own time. The period of the barbarian invasions, with its restless movement of populations, chronic warfare, and neglect of classical learning, seemed to the 18th-century mind to be the "Dark Ages." The six centuries following the Dark Ages are often called the Middle Ages. Generally the Middle Ages covers the era of European history from approximately the 8th to the 14th centuries. These years witnessed the last of the barbarian invasions, the triumph of Christianity as a unifying force, the clearing and settlement of forest and fringe lands, and the establishment of nearly all the towns and cities of Europe.

The peopling of Europe was almost completed by the beginning of the Middle Ages. The Bulgars settled in the state that bears their name. Hungary dates its founding to the establishment of the Magyar Empire in 896. During the previous century, Arabs had conquered Spain and threatened to overrun southwestern France.

The *Völkerwanderung*—as the movement of the Germanic tribes is called—left a lasting mark on Europe. They destroyed the Roman Empire in the west. In its place came the scattered kingdoms of the Ostrogoths in the lower Danube, northern Italy, and southern Gaul; the Franks' occupation of France, parts of Germany, Belgium, and the Netherlands; and the occupation of the lowlands of Britain by the Angles, Saxons, and Jutes.

Church and State

In a remarkably short period, the Christian faith spread across Europe. The political unity that Rome had provided was replaced by the Church, whose faith and whose language—Latin—shaped a new spiritual unity. The Church gave Europe a standard of values, a system of governing, and a link with the achievements of the classical past. The

Vatican City, an independent state surrounded by Rome, is the headquarters of the Roman Catholic Church.

kings of the new political units and the bishops of the Roman Church often worked together—the kings gaining power as they spread the gospel in the name of the Church to the remaining areas of paganism. In the monasteries, to which devout men retreated to worship and to study, a new band of teachers was born.

From the Irish monasteries, monks went to preach the faith to the Franks. In 597 Pope Gregory sent an Italian missionary, who later became St. Augustine of Canterbury, to England to convert the king and his subjects. In 716 a Benedictine monk named Boniface set out from England to ally the eastern Frankish Church with the popes. His success was capped by the elevation of Pepin as king of the Franks "by the grace of God" by the pope in 751. Not only had the kingship been made sacred and hereditary, but the indebted king could now be called upon to defend the Papal States that had grown up in central Italy. The king, for his part, could call upon the Church for support. The first powerful alliance between the temporal and spiritual world had been made. Such alliances were to be important for centuries to come.

By the time Pepin's son Charlemagne came to the Frankish throne in 768, everyday life in Western Europe was regaining the stability it had lost in invasions and wars. New lands were opened for cultivation, and improved farming methods were developed. Industry and trade also grew. Charlemagne added another element to this changing scene—a revival of the ideal of a politically united Europe. In the course of many campaigns, Charlemagne's Frankish armies drove the Avars out of Hungary, the Lombards out of the Papal States, set up the east march (or border) that formed the basis of the Austrian state, took Barcelona from the Muslims, and unified western Germany.

In A.D. 800, Charlemagne was named Roman emperor by the pope. Charlemagne established a strictly organized government, revived education, and sponsored the arts. After the death of Charlemagne in 814, his empire was divided and subdivided much as Alexander the Great's had been. The enfeebled successor states became easy prey to the seafaring warriors of Scandinavia—the Vikings.

The Vikings

"From the wrath of the Norsemen, O Lord, deliver us!" was perhaps the most common prayer heard in the 9th century. It reflected the terror of the population of Western Europe at the repeated attacks of Viking seamen from Scandinavia. They attacked towns as distant from their homeland as Cádiz in Spain and Pisa in Italy.

No one is quite sure what caused the sudden explosion of these seafarers from their coastal homes in Scandinavia. It may have been over-population or a hunger for wealth and power that drove them out of their homeland in their superbly built, oar-driven longships. The ancestors of the modern Danes, Norwegians, and Swedes followed different courses of plunder and trade. Danish Vikings took their ships to the nearby coasts of continental Europe and to the British Isles. By the middle of the 9th century, they had settled forces along the mouth of the Thames, the Loire, and the Seine. From these bases, they were able to send out fleets to besiege London, Paris, and other prosperous cities. Gradually, however, the invaders settled down. The name of Normandy in France, for example, reflects its settlement by the Norse.

Norwegian and Swedish Vikings ambitiously sailed farther from their bases in Scandinavia. The Norwegians occupied Ireland for about two centuries, and also succeeded in colonizing the Faeroes, Hebrides, and Orkney Islands, Iceland, and Greenland; in about the year 1000, they reached North America. The adventurous Swedish Vikings followed still another course of conquest and trade. They penetrated northern Russia, and then sailed south along the Volga and the Dnieper rivers. From their trading settlements at Nizhny Novgorod and Kiev, they took furs, amber, and slaves to trade with the inhabitants of the then-remote and wealthy cities of the Middle East. The unusual goods—such as silver, spices, and brocades—that they brought back provided the Swedish Vikings with the basis of a flourishing trade with the merchants of England, France, and Germany.

The years of the Viking conquests, which lasted from about A.D. 800 to 1000, had significant results for Europe. One of the most important results was that these fearless sailors traveled the seas of northern Europe. They opened up new routes of trade that rivaled and then eclipsed the local trade of the Mediterranean Basin. The Swedish Vikings, by becoming the rulers of their territories, helped establish the first Russian state. Russia may even have taken its name (Rus') from *ruotsi* (rowers), the Finnish word for the Viking invaders. Finally, the threat posed by the Viking raiders to the scattered and disunited governments of the continent led to the formation of institutions that were better equipped to deal with the realities of war and peace.

Feudalism

Europe at the time of the Viking raids was broken up into hundreds of poorly fortified communities. The basic political units were villages clustered around the castle of the local lord or the abbey of the monks.

Both the abbey and the castle served as fortresses when necessary. "Men of prayer, men of war, and men of work," as the 9th-century King Alfred the Great of England called them, made up the three large divisions of early medieval society.

The disasters caused by repeated invasions led to the growth of the feudal system. The system was based generally on an exchange of land for protection in time of need. Feudalism was based on the overlord's granting land—a fief—to a vassal. In exchange for his fief, the vassal would swear homage to his overlord. This meant that a vassal could be called upon to provide a certain number of knights to serve in the lord's army. The size of a man's landholding and the number of knights that he commanded determined his rank. Unfree peasants, called serfs, who actually farmed the land made up the broad base of the social structure. Over them, in order up to the overlord, were the squires, knights, and the nobles. The trained warriors provided by this system; improvements in weapons, armor, and the use of cavalry; and the growth of heavily fortified towns and cities helped bring some stability to the continent.

The feudal system prevailed in most of Europe until the 14th century, by which time the greatest and most powerful overlords had transformed themselves into hereditary monarchs. By the end of the 16th century, serfdom, too, had disappeared from Western Europe, although in central and Eastern Europe, it was not abolished until the 19th century. Traces of the feudal structure also remained in some areas such as parts of Italy, Germany, and Russia into the 19th century. In other parts of Europe, hereditary kings and standing armies provided a more effective response to the threat of war and served to protect the rapidly growing commerce of the cities.

THE LATE MIDDLE AGES

The end of the invasions and the organization of Europe into stable units of government, beginning in the 11th century, were heralds of

Cardiff Castle in Wales is a typical medieval fortress.

modern times. From England to Russia and from Norway to Italy, the forerunners of modern nations were evolving. The Church, under the guidance of outstanding popes, embarked on a series of reforms to strengthen and purify itself. In the arts the growing prosperity of the times was reflected in the building of magnificent and richly decorated churches. Education in schools and newly founded universities was extended to the laity as well as the clergy.

The increased productivity of the farms, which was based in part on crop rotation and technological improvements such as heavier plows pulled by draft animals, began to provide a surplus of food that freed some farmworkers to join the tradesmen in nearby villages. As the economy grew, villages became towns, and towns expanded into cities. Paris, Rouen, Hamburg, Cologne, Prague, Venice, Genoa, Florence, and Pisa became centers of trade.

The woolen textiles of Flanders, the metals of Bohemia, the wines of France, the swords of Toledo, and the leather of Córdoba were traded at markets and fairs all over Europe. The increasing wealth of the city merchants gave them enough political power to form a new middle class that had the independence to accept or reject the rule of an overlord. A new ideal of freedom and dignity for every man was striking at the foundations of the rigid feudal system.

Outside Influences on Europe

The many factors that shaped the relative peace and prosperity of Europe from the 11th to the 13th century freed Europeans to look beyond their own territories. The once-powerful empire formed by the Muslims was losing its unity, and the centuries-long reconquest of Spain by Christian warriors was under way. In the east was the Byzantine, or Eastern Roman, Empire. Constantinople, the capital, was the seat of a powerful, cultured Christian empire separated from the west because it was Greek in its traditions and because its church leaders refused to acknowledge the supremacy of the Roman Catholic pope. Beginning in about the year 1000, however, the Byzantine Empire started its decline. It was threatened by the Muslim Turks in the east and by the rising power of such city-states as Venice.

When the Roman Catholic popes rallied Western Europeans to recapture the Holy Land from the Muslims, Crusaders easily cut across Byzantine territory (1097–99, 1147–48), and in 1204 they turned on Christian Constantinople itself, capturing and sacking it. The Byzantine court returned to Constantinople in 1261, but the territory it ruled until it was finally overthrown by the Turks in 1453 was a collection of virtually independent states rather than a united empire.

One branch of the Orthodox Christian community survived far to the north of Constantinople in the disunited and troubled Russian principalities. But the life of these scattered Russian ministates was repeatedly threatened by nomadic invaders from the east. In the early 13th century, Mongols from Asia reduced almost all of Russia to the status of a tribute-paying state. The collection of the tribute to the Mongols' Golden Horde was the job of the grand dukes of Moscow, who thus slowly grew in power and prestige. By the end of the 15th century, Ivan III of Moscow was powerful enough to stop sending the tribute, an important step in shaping Russia's future as a major nation.

The Crusades

In the west the power of the popes continued to grow—a fact that was reflected in their successful control of the Holy Roman emperors and of the dramatic response from all Europe to the call to free the Holy Land from the "infidel" Muslims. Thousands sought that end in nine separate Crusades between the 11th and 14th centuries. Although the Crusaders succeeded in freeing Jerusalem for only about 100 years, these warrior pilgrimages had important repercussions in Europe. Since most of the Crusaders took the land route to the Holy Land, they passed through Constantinople, which was still the most cultured and important city in Europe. The influence of Byzantine culture on the relatively unlettered Crusaders was profound. The contact with the Muslims had the important effect of renewing the bonds between Europeans and the civilization of their Greek ancestors, whose learning had been preserved by Mohammed's followers.

The Crusades had other significant consequences for Europe. The money needed to outfit and transport the Crusaders was circulated in coins made of precious metals. Where money was not immediately available, forms of credit were devised—the forerunners of modern banking. The taste of new, exotic goods that was stimulated by the Crusaders' discoveries in the Middle East helped to stimulate trade and growth of the merchant class.

The mixture of nationalities represented in each Crusade reflected both a united Christendom and the birth of national awareness. Men from hundreds of isolated localities in Europe, unified only by their religion, met and fought side by side in the Crusades. Unavoidably, a sense of national differences arose and provided a powerful impetus to the development and support of centralized monarchies.

In England, a strongly centralized government was formed in the 11th century by William the Conqueror. When the barons forced King John to grant the Magna Carta—Great Charter—in 1215, an important step had been taken in the evolution of England's unique form of constitutional monarchy. France was united under the reign of Saint Louis (1226–70), and solidified its position on the continent in the Hundred Years' War (1337–1461), which ended England's claim to the French throne. In Scandinavia, Russia, Austria, and Hungary, monarchies were also well established by the end of the Middle Ages. By 1492, the Spanish had succeeded in driving the Muslims out of their land and forming a central government. Elsewhere in Europe, less centralization was still the rule. Germany and Italy remained divided into a number of small separate states until the 19th century.

Renaissance and Exploration

Two important movements mark the close of the Middle Ages in Europe and the beginning of modern times. They were the Renaissance (as the rebirth of interest in classical civilizations is called) and the great explorations of European seamen.

The Renaissance, which started in the prosperous commercial cities of northern Italy in the 14th century, had spread across Europe by the 16th century. The Renaissance is set apart from the Middle Ages because people actually changed their way of looking at the world. Such outside influences as the Crusades combined with the growth of the European

Wealth from trade and exploration helped to develop the Netherlands.

economy to make people more curious about themselves, their lives in this world, and the universe as a whole. The period was marked by an effort to revive classical ideals and forms. There was a widespread revival of interest in the writings of ancient philosophers and poets, as the Italian poet Dante's *Divine Comedy* demonstrates. There were also remarkable developments in art. Purely religious art, which had flourished throughout the Middle Ages, was replaced by realistic portrayals of everyday events and people. The development of linear perspective, which makes a two-dimensional picture seem to have three dimensions, is considered one of the major contributions of Renaissance artists. Such creative giants as Leonardo da Vinci, Michelangelo, Machiavelli, Shakespeare, Rabelais, Montaigne, and Erasmus provided new perspectives on every phase of human life. Through the variety of their achievements, these men earned fame as "universal men"—the ideal of all Renaissance people because it represented the highest achievement possible on this Earth.

Just as the Renaissance opened up new perspectives in art and thought, so the great voyages of exploration revolutionized knowledge of Earth. Sailing under the flags of the major merchant kingdoms of the continent, such explorers as Christopher Columbus (1451–1506), Vasco da Gama (1469?–1524), and Ferdinand Magellan (1480?–1521) opened up the world's sea-lanes and revealed the existence of the Americas as well as new routes to Africa and Asia. The wealth of Africa, Asia, and the Americas first poured into Portugal and Spain. When the English, Dutch, and French expanded their influence overseas, they built up even larger and more durable empires. The development of powerful navies that could control the sea-lanes provided the basis of power for the great colonizing nations until the 20th century.

THE BIRTH OF MODERN EUROPE

The growing prosperity and spiritual unity of Europe was shattered at the beginning of the 16th century. In 1517 a German priest, Martin Luther, launched a protest movement against what he felt were abuses by the Roman Catholic Church. Neither the pope nor the Holy Roman emperor was able to contain the Protestant movement. Emperor Charles V, who also ruled as the king of Spain, was preoccupied protecting his own far-flung possessions. The Church itself was at first too entangled in local politics to concern itself with Luther's heresy. By the time the pope and the emperor were free to act, Luther's Protestant followers numbered in the thousands. The Counter Reformation launched by the papacy and supported by the Habsburg Holy Roman emperor reformed and reorganized the Church and succeeded in retaining most of its followers in southern and central Europe.

Yet national ambitions and religious beliefs continued to fan the flames of war. Throughout the closing years of the 16th century, civil wars raged in France, ending only when Henry of Navarre abandoned his Protestantism to become King Henry IV. However, he gave a wide degree of freedom to the Protestants in his kingdom. Spain's provinces in the Netherlands gained what amounted to independence in the early 17th century and divided along religious lines—a fact that is reflected today in the existence of predominantly Catholic Belgium and the largely Protestant Netherlands. The civil war that raged in England between 1642 and 1648 involved Protestant sects, but was caused by questions about Parliament's power as well. By 1689 the issue was resolved in favor of the Anglican Church and the supremacy of Parliament.

The most terrible religious wars of the 17th century were caused by the Habsburg emperors' efforts to suppress Protestantism in Bohemia (now part of the Czech Republic) and Germany, and ultimately involved Sweden, Denmark, and France. The Thirty Years' War (1618–48), as it is known, resulted in the worst devastation Germany was to experience until World War II. The German states remained divided between the Roman Catholic and Protestant faiths. Politically, a union of the German states was delayed by the religious issues. The powerful, united monarchy of France became the leading European state.

By the middle of the 17th century, the religious quarrels were largely settled, and the interests awakened by the Renaissance could be pursued again. The work of such scientists and philosophers as Sir Isaac Newton, René Descartes, Baruch Spinoza, and John Locke seemed to show that humans and their universe were subject to natural laws that could be observed, measured, and predicted. If, indeed, the world was based on these orderly, clockwork principles, it meant that people and their institutions could be improved by using reason. History itself was seen as a staircase on which humankind was rising to higher levels.

Throughout the 18th century in Europe and America, educated people explored the philosophic, scientific, economic, political, and religious consequences of these theories. The result was an intellectual revolution. Humans, whom religion had portrayed as helpless victims of uncontrollable forces, were transformed into rational creatures capable of guiding and improving their own destinies. Such ideas fitted the views of the prosperous, self-made middle class perfectly, but threatened the very existence of organized religion and absolute monarchy. The political theorists of the 18th century first thought that the most appropriate form of government would be "enlightened despotism"; that is, government based on the rule of an intelligent monarch who could impose and enforce reforms. Such monarchs as Catherine II of Russia, Joseph II of Austria, and Friedrich (Frederick) II of Prussia seemed to embody the virtues of the enlightened despot. In France, with its absolute monarch, and in the American colonies, ruled by a distant king, the ideas of the Enlightenment were the seeds of revolution.

Two Revolutions

From the end of the religious wars in the mid 17th-century until 1789, France was a flourishing but troubled nation. The middle class increasingly disliked the absolute rule of its kings, who claimed to rule by "divine right." Prosperous merchants hoping for a voice in government were unhappy to hear the legendary remark of King Louis XIV, "*L'état c'est moi* [I am the state]." The revolution that began in France in 1789 was based on the "enlightened" hope that the government could be reorganized to serve all French citizens equally. The results were less clear-cut than the philosophers had hoped, and various groups came into conflict over what was the best route for France to follow.

Politically, one of the obvious achievements of the revolution was the overthrow of the monarchy and an end of the feudal tradition in France. The middle class achieved a central role in national life, as it would all over Europe in the course of the next century. The triumph of "Liberty, Equality, and Fraternity" was not reflected, however, in the realm of government, which was taken over by General Napoleon Bonaparte in 1799 after years of chaos. Through internal reforms and brilliantly executed military maneuvers, Bonaparte made France the leading power

Versailles, a French palace, symbolized royal power and prestige.

The National Museum of Natural History, in Paris.

in Europe. Napoleon's decision to invade Russia, however, proved disastrous. Napoleon's final downfall came at the Battle of Waterloo in 1815. Yet France's dramatic rise to immense power under Napoleon left its mark on the subsequent history of Europe.

An entirely different kind of revolution stemming from the Enlightenment began in the middle years of the 18th century. The Industrial Revolution, as it is called, replaced manpower with the power of machines. Harnessing the resources of the earth began the period of change that would literally alter the face of the globe and the life of people everywhere. Where wind- and waterpower had once been the chief substitutes for individual labor, there emerged a host of machines using coal as a power source. The revolution began in England, where James Watt's steam engine (invented in 1769) was followed by such devices as the flying shuttle, spinning jenny, and power loom for use in large-scale textile production. The work of thousands of skilled individuals was replaced in a matter of years by the work of machines. A similar change followed in the mining of coal, the manufacture of machinery, and the processing of metals. Green landscapes were replaced by clusters of factories and houses for industrial workers. Canals, roads, and later railways and steam-driven ships provided new links between mines and factories, factories and consumers, and finally between nations.

In the course of the 19th and 20th centuries, the Industrial Revolution created more far-reaching changes in Europe than any other event in its history. The leaders of the Enlightenment surely would have considered the Industrial Revolution a sign of progress. Thousands and thousands of people were made more nearly equal by the provision of standard goods for all who could afford them. A surplus of food became available. Advances in medicine helped eliminate diseases that had destroyed entire generations, and advances in housing and education provided obvious benefits.

Yet some observers soon began to point out that industrialization was a mixed blessing. The beauties of the countryside were blotted out by factories and squalid houses. The long hours of routine factory work proved to be dull and dispiriting, and craftsmanship and a worker's pride in a job well done were lost. The relationship between a factory worker and his or her employer was often less stable than the one that had existed between a farmer and his lord. If business was bad, workers were laid off and left to survive as best they could. And so, along with liberalism—the political, social, and economic philosophy of the capitalist middle class—there developed the theory of socialism, which attracted many members of the working classes. The most important proponent of economic equality and justice was the German philosopher Karl Marx (1818–83), who developed a vision of "classless society," or Communism.

Meanwhile, the extension of European power outside the continent, which had begun 1,000 years earlier with the Vikings, reached its height in the last years of the 19th century. At that time, several nations of Europe constituted what amounted to a world superpower, directly controlling dozens of countries around the globe.

Many European cities have sidewalk cafés or coffee shops where pedestrians can relax and enjoy refreshments.

Paris' Arc de Triomphe, the world's largest triumphal arch, was built as a memorial to Napoleon's victories.

The 20th Century

In 1900, European leaders were still for the most part hereditary kings and emperors. France alone among the major European nations was a republic. When the German states were finally united in 1871, the new nation was organized as an empire, and it surged to a leading position on the continent, threatened only by its powerful rivals, England and France. German fears of encirclement by its enemies, and its enemies' fears of German preeminence, led to World War I (1914–18), which was much more brutal than all previous European military conflicts. For the first time, the new destructive instruments of airpower, tanks, submarines, and chemical weapons were used. Germany and Austria-Hungary were eventually defeated by the Allies—France, England, and the United States—but at a tremendous cost: 10 million people killed and 20 million wounded. It seemed impossible that people would ever seek war as a solution again. Indeed, contemporaries called the conflagration "the war to end all wars." The subsequent establishment of the League of Nations and the Versailles peace treaties seemed to ensure a peaceful future for both the old and the newly established European states.

In place of the vast Austro-Hungarian Empire, which had ruled much of Central Europe, there now appeared Poland, Czechoslovakia, Hungary, Yugoslavia, and the small Austrian Republic. Russia, which had been convulsed by revolution in the closing years of the war, emerged as the Communist Union of Soviet Socialist Republics—a massive counterbalance to the nations of Western and Central Europe. Germany itself became a republic and was forbidden by treaties to manufacture weapons; in addition, it was required to pay enormous reparations to the Allies.

The rebuilding of a new Europe out of the rubble of the war, however, was soon undermined by inflation in the 1920s and by the worldwide Depression of the 1930s. Millions of people became unemployed and impoverished. Labor unrest then led to the rise of fascism in Italy, under Benito Mussolini, and to Nazism in Germany, under Adolf Hitler. The stage was set for World War II.

This conflict, which started in 1939 and soon involved countries from three other continents, seemed to herald the final destruction of European civilization. It is estimated that there were almost 15 million military deaths and probably an equal number among civilians. Millions of Jews, as well as members of other ethnic groups targeted by the Nazis and their allies, were exterminated in Hitler's concentration camps. These dreadful events added a new horror to warfare—genocide, the murder of an entire people. But the tide turned against Hitler when, like Napoleon before him, he attacked the Soviet Union. A war fought on two fronts—one in the west against the growing underground resistance aided by Allied bombings, the other in a long battle against the Soviets in the east—finally overwhelmed the Nazi war machine in 1945.

This time, Europe's economic recovery was remarkably swift, particularly in the western half, which allied itself with the United States. But even in Eastern Europe, increasingly dominated by the Soviet Union, the scars of war soon disappeared. Most of the remaining European colonies in Asia, Africa, and Central America gained their independence after World War II.

The United States and the Soviet Union were both founding members of the United Nations in 1945. But soon after the war ended, the

The Palais des Nations in Geneva, Switzerland, is the European headquarters of the United Nations.

The Berlin Wall long symbolized the opposing philosophies of the Communist East and the democratic West.

Soviets' determination to extend their political and economic control throughout Eastern Europe fractured the wartime alliance and launched the Cold War. Its symbol, the "Iron Curtain," was a heavily fortified barrier constructed by Communist regimes, not only to exclude Western people, goods, and ideas, but also to keep their own populations from fleeing. Where it passed through the divided city of Berlin, the barrier was actually a solid wall of masonry. Two different political, religious, social, and cultural systems developed on the opposing sides of the Iron Curtain. Free-market capitalism and liberal democracy flourished on the Western side of the boundary, while Marxist-Communist regimes in the East attempted to exercise central control over all aspects of the lives of their people. The tension and hostility between the two parts of Europe produced two military alliances: the North Atlantic Treaty Organization (NATO), established in 1949 and including the United States, and the Warsaw Pact, established in 1955 and headed by the Soviet Union.

And so in the late 1940s, Europe became a continent divided and remained so for the next four decades. The center of world power shifted outside Europe to the two nuclear superpowers, the United States and the Soviet Union.

In 1949, the Council of Europe was founded in Strasbourg, France, as part of a cooperative effort at reconstruction. Other cooperative organizations followed, and the large Western European nations thus became closely intertwined. In 1957, six countries formed the European Economic Community (or Common Market), the precursor of the future European Union.

The United States played a crucial role in Western European development: it provided massive economic aid in the form of the Marshall Plan, which helped Germany and other nations to rebuild their bombed cities, repair damaged roads and bridges, and revitalize industry. The United States also protected Western Europe by maintaining its military bases there, mainly in Germany, but in other countries as well. As the leading member of NATO and the Organization for Economic Cooperation and Development (OECD), the United States became much more involved in European affairs than ever before. Western Europeans occasionally resented certain American policies or actions, but a generally positive attitude prevailed, and the peoples of the two Atlantic outposts of democracy became great friends.

On the other side of the Iron Curtain, the Euro-Asian Soviet Union ruled with an iron hand. In contrast to Western Europe, the "satellite" Eastern European countries were kept under Soviet domination by force. Whenever citizens in those countries showed the slightest disobedience to Moscow, they were severely punished. In 1953, Soviet troops suppressed a workers' demonstration in East Germany. In 1956, the Soviet army brutally crushed a Hungarian uprising, killing thousands. And in 1968, half a million Warsaw Pact soldiers invaded Czechoslovakia to put an end to the liberalization policies known as the Prague Spring. Ironically, this was the only military operation of the Soviet-dominated Warsaw Pact.

The Soviet Union also bound its satellites in an economic alliance known as COMECON (Council for Mutual Economic Assistance), set up in 1949. In contrast to Western European economic organizations, which supported regional cooperation, COMECON's primary purpose was to serve the interests of the Soviet Union. Many Eastern European countries felt that they were being exploited by their "Big Brother." The only advantage of COMECON for them was the supply of inexpensive Soviet oil.

Contemporary architecture in Europe has assumed a distinctly abstract form.

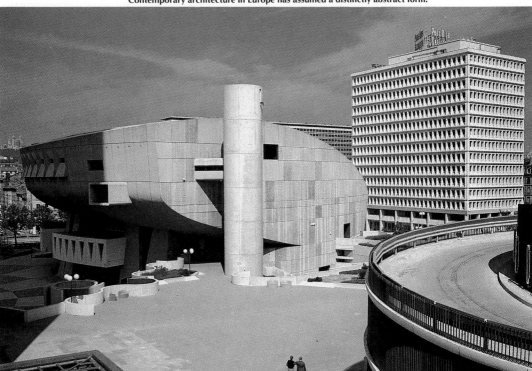

CONTEMPORARY EUROPE

In March 1985, the last of the old guard of Soviet Communist leaders died; he was replaced by a representative of the new generation, Mikhail Gorbachev. Intelligent and forceful, Gorbachev tried to reform the Soviet system, but it was like trying to square a circle. Only his "new thinking" in foreign policy proved to be a success, because it led to the end of the Cold War.

The dramatic events of 1989 and the following few years changed the face of Europe and made the whole world a different place. In 1989, Communist leaders in Poland, Hungary, East Germany, Bulgaria, and Czechoslovakia stepped down with astonishing restraint. Only in Romania was the change bloody. In 1990, East Germany and West Germany were united, and early the following year, Albania held its first-ever free elections. The violent breakup of Yugoslavia also began. And then in August 1991, the unsuccessful coup of Soviet hard-liners initiated the collapse of the Soviet Union. On December 25, 1991, an era came to an end, as the red Soviet flag with hammer and sickle was lowered to signify the dissolution of the Communist superpower.

The earthquake that completely rearranged the former Communist world came at the same time that Western Europe was under the spell of the "spirit of Maastricht." The name of this small Dutch town came to embody the Western European unification effort. In December 1991, 12 member countries of the European Community signed a treaty at Maastricht, renaming their organization the European Union and pledging to coordinate their economic, social, and foreign policies, and to create a single European currency before the end of the century.

In the years following these historic events, new challenges have appeared. Before the year 1990, many imagined that once the Communist regime was toppled, a rosy capitalist and democratic future would lie ahead. In reality, the transformation has been much more arduous. Even though Communism as a system is gone, the former "nomenclature" (party members of high standing) continues to hold power, particularly in the economy. In many countries, corruption has increased dramatically.

The worst developments occurred in the former Yugoslavia and in the Russian republic of Chechnya. In both these places, tens of thousands of people lost their lives and saw their homes destroyed. Many also became refugees.

Meanwhile, Western Europe has been concentrating on the Economic Monetary Union, to be put in place on January 1, 1999. The enthusiasm for unity, however, has waned, and many "Euroskeptics" fear the loss of their national identities. Most wealthy West European governments are also devising ways to curb their extensive social-welfare systems, but they are repeatedly challenged by unions and the population at large.

Contemporary Europe thus faces many uncertainties and dangers. Sometimes, in contrast to the vigorous United States, Europe seems rather old—a stodgy, bickering continent. Nevertheless, thanks to its diversity, sophistication, and maturity, Europe remains a place of great potential. If no serious crisis erupts in Russia, if the monetary union works well, and if the admission of former Communist countries to the European Union proceeds as planned, the continent could enter the third millennium stronger than ever.

JOSEPH F. ZACEK, State University of New York at Albany

Ireland is truly an "emerald isle."

IRELAND

The island of Ireland, a land of great natural beauty, forms the western boundary of the Eurasian landmass. Its most remarkable natural feature is its greenness, which has given it the title of the Emerald Isle.

Ireland has had a long and often tragic history. For over 700 years the people fought for the right to rule themselves. They struggled against oppression, famine, and disease. And yet the Irish have managed to enrich the world. They have produced an extraordinary wealth of great literature. And so many Irish men and women have emigrated to other countries that this small, isolated land has had a far-reaching impact. Since the 1950's Ireland has started catching up with the industrialization of the Western world and has begun to provide a better life for its people.

THE LAND

Ireland resembles a saucer, with a fertile central plain and a rim of hills and low mountains. The most famous of the mountain ranges are the Macgillycuddy's Reeks, where Ireland's highest peak, Carrantuohill,

Peat being cut in County Donegal for use as fuel.

rises 3,400 feet (1,040 meters) above sea level. Everywhere the Irish coast is broken by indentations. The west coast is a place of wild grandeur, with sheer cliffs broken by mysterious coves and inlets.

Central Ireland is a region of meadows, bogs, lakes, and many twisting, turning rivers. Peat covers much of the surface of the island. These peat bogs are a mixture of mosses, heather, and other materials that, because of special soil and climatic conditions, have become compressed and carbonized over the centuries. The peat is cut and dried to be used as fuel in homes and in industry. As the bogs are cleared, the land is being made usable for planting. About one fourth of Ireland is cultivated and one fourth is occupied by peat bogs, marshes, mountains, and lakes. The rest is meadowland, where the world-famous Irish horses and cattle graze.

Rivers and Lakes. Running through the island is the great Shannon River, the longest river in the British Isles. For over 200 miles (320 km.), the Shannon serenely winds its way through the beautiful Irish countryside, widening out at places to form spectacular lakes, such as Lough Allen, Lough Ree, and Lough Derg.

Climate. Ireland is so far north that one would expect severe winters. In fact, the weather is relatively mild all year long. The North Atlantic Drift brings the warm waters of the Gulf Stream to the coast of Northern

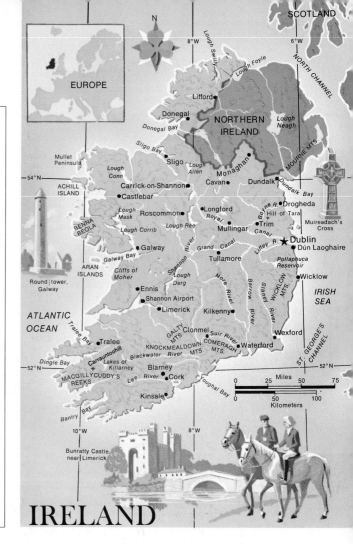

FACTS AND FIGURES

OFFICIAL NAME: Ireland.

NATIONALITY: Irish.

CAPITAL: Dublin.

LOCATION: Island in eastern North Atlantic Ocean. **Boundaries**—Northern Ireland, Irish Sea, Atlantic Ocean.

AREA: 27,135 sq. mi. (70,280 sq. km.).

PHYSICAL FEATURES: Highest point—Carrauntoohill (3,415 ft.; 1,041 m.). **Lowest point**—sea level. **Chief rivers**—Shannon, Boyne, Blackwater, Lee, Suir, Nore, Barrow, Liffey, Slaney. **Major lakes**—Lough Neagh, Lough Allen, Lough Corrib, Lough Mask, Lough Conn.

POPULATION: 3,555,500 (1997; annual growth –0.42%).

MAJOR LANGUAGES: Irish, English.

MAJOR RELIGIONS: Roman Catholicism, Anglicanism.

GOVERNMENT: Republic. **Head of state**—president. **Head of government**—prime minister. **Legislature**—bicameral Parliament.

CHIEF CITIES: Dublin, Cork, Limerick, Waterford, Galway, Dundalk, Kilkenny.

ECONOMY: Chief minerals—zinc, lead, natural gas, petroleum, barite, copper, gypsum, limestone, dolomite, peat, silver. **Chief agricultural products**—livestock and dairy products, turnips, barley, potatoes, sugar beets, wheat. **Industries and products**—food processing, brewing, textiles and clothing, chemicals and pharmaceuticals, machinery, transportation equipment, glass and crystal. **Chief exports**—dairy and meat products, data-processing equipment, livestock, machinery, chemicals. **Chief imports**—food, animal feed, data-processing equipment, petroleum and petroleum products, machinery, textiles.

MONETARY UNIT: 1 Irish pound = 100 pence.

NATIONAL HOLIDAY: March 17 (Saint Patrick's Day).

IRELAND

Europe. At the same time, because of the westerly Atlantic winds, it brings the rainfall that with the mild weather makes Ireland so intensely green. In the west as much as 80 in. (200 cm.) of rain falls in a year, while in the east it may be only 30 in. (80 cm.).

THE PEOPLE

The Irish are a people of predominantly Celtic stock, who were for many centuries under English rule. In 1922, 26 largely Catholic counties became independent of Britain, while the mainly Protestant northeastern counties secured a parliament of their own, subject to the Parliament of the United Kingdom of Great Britain and Northern Ireland.

John Millington Synge (1871–1909), an Irish playwright, said, "It's in a lonesome place, you do have to be talking with someone. . . ." And the Irish do indeed love to talk—at any time, to anyone, anywhere. Words flow melodiously, rivers of words full of wit and color. But Irish wit, humor, and warmth are mixed with a sense of fatalism and a deep reverence for religion. The Irish constitution separates church and state, but recognizes the "special position" of the Roman Catholic Church. A sign of the pervasive strength of traditional religious feelings was the overwhelming defeat of a 1986 referendum to legalize divorce. The defeat contributed to the fall of the ruling party, Fine Gael.

A pub—public house—is a popular meeting place in Ireland.

As in many countries where the Industrial Revolution came late, there is a great difference in the way families in rural Ireland and those in the industrial centers live. However, everywhere in Ireland family life is close, and there is great devotion to parents. In rural Ireland particularly, the pub is the man's social club, where he may have his glass of black stout, the famous Irish beer, and enjoy the company of his neighbors. Wives in small villages do not usually go with their husbands to the local pubs, but there are occasions for family outings. Sunday Mass is a social gathering for the whole family.

The Irish are passionate sportsmen. Traditionally they have always hunted and fished. They love horses, and horse racing is a great national sport. The Irish Derby is one of the world's most famous races, and betting on the National Sweepstakes, run for the benefit of the Irish hospitals, is virtually a national industry.

Among the most popular sports is the ancient game of hurling. It is a type of field hockey played with a curved ash stick and a small leather ball by two teams of 15 players, who need great strength, skill, and timing. Gaelic football (a combination of soccer and rugby), soccer, rugby, golf, bowling, and sailing are all very popular.

Céad míle fáilte ("a hundred thousand welcomes") is the traditional Irish greeting, and the Irish are renowned for their hospitality. A visitor will be urged to come for a drink or a meal.

Dublin University (Trinity College), a world-famous institution.

Language and Learning

Irish, one of the oldest languages in Europe, was the speech of the Celts in Ireland. Its use began to decline early in the 1800's. When the Irish Government was set up in 1922 strenuous efforts were made to revive Irish. The teaching of Irish was made compulsory in all schools, and it became the language of instruction in the teachers colleges. In the Irish Constitution of 1937, Irish was declared the "first official language" of Ireland, English the second. The drive to revive Irish has not been entirely successful. The difficult language is commonly spoken only in a few remote areas. English is the language of most of the people, but schoolchildren learn Irish. Public signs are in Irish, but the ancient language will probably not take the place of English in Ireland.

Education is free and compulsory for all children between the ages of 6 and 14. Secondary education is free as well. Schools are generally run either by the Catholic or Protestant churches, but are supported by state funds. There are two universities in Ireland—Dublin University (which is also called Trinity College) and the National University, with colleges in Dublin, Cork, and Galway. Dublin has two fine schools of technology, where architects and engineers are trained. And in Dublin and Cork there are well-known schools of music and art. The National Museum of Ireland is located in Dublin as is the National Gallery of Ireland. The James Joyce Museum has relics of the world-famous author.

Irish Literature

Long before any school existed in Ireland, there was a great native oral tradition. The earliest known literature of Ireland dates from the 8th and 9th centuries when the poet-singers, or bards, recited the romances, or sagas, of their heroes. The Ulster Cycle relates the story of the great hero Cuchulain. The collection of tales known as the Fenian Cycle deals with the exploits of Finn Mac Cool and his band of warriors, the Fianna. Poets enjoyed the patronage of kings in the old Gaelic society. Many of their works were court poems in honor of the kings and their chiefs. But they also recorded history and dealt with law, medicine, and religious subjects. During the troubled years of wars and conquest, the songs of Ireland became sad songs. The poets, forbidden to sing openly of their love for Ireland, addressed instead a mythical queen, Cathleen Ní Houlihan, one of the poetic names for Ireland.

Some poetry is still written in Irish in the new Ireland, but it is writing in English that has made Irish literature famous throughout the world. Jonathan Swift, Dean of St. Patrick's Cathedral during the first half of the 18th century, was the first of a long line of what have been called Anglo-Irish writers. *Gulliver's Travels* is read today as a delightful fantasy, but it was written, as were many of Swift's works, as a bitter satire on English rule in Ireland, as well as on humanity in general. Other great Irish literary figures of the 18th century wrote and lived in England. They included Oliver Goldsmith, the poet, novelist, and playwright; Edmund Burke, the political philosopher; Richard Brinsley Sheridan, the dramatist; and Richard Steele, the essayist. Possibly the best-known 19th-century Irish writer was the poet, novelist, and playwright Oscar Wilde.

The 20th century has come to be known as the period of the Irish literary renaissance. The fight for independence aroused interest in the Irish past, and ancient sagas were revived. Ireland's greatest modern poet, William Butler Yeats, was inspired by the old tales and stirred by the heroism of the struggle for independence. Together with Lady Augusta Gregory, Yeats in 1897 helped found the Irish National Theatre in Dublin. It is famous throughout the world as the Abbey Theatre, the home of the Abbey Players. Yeats influenced John Synge to return from abroad to write in his native Ireland. Synge's ability to record the poetry of peasant speech and to write about the poor honestly, compassionately, and beautifully is best illustrated by his play *The Playboy of the Western World*. Another famous Irish playwright, Sean O'Casey, also wrote for the Abbey Theatre.

Ireland's best-known dramatist, George Bernard Shaw, lived and wrote in England. *Candida, Arms and the Man, Caesar and Cleopatra, Man and Superman, Major Barbara, Pygmalion,* and other plays are about contemporary social problems and sparkle with Irish wit and satire.

The writer who is often called the greatest literary figure of this century, James Joyce, also lived and wrote abroad, but his work was about his native Ireland. *Ulysses,* his most famous novel, is about a day in Dublin, June 16, 1904. Joyce vividly records everything that his three main characters did, thought, and felt during that day and night.

Wherever books are read, Irish writers of this century are well-known. Liam O'Flaherty, Sean O'Faolain, Frank O'Connor, Samuel Beckett, Oliver St. John Gogarty, and Brendan Behan are just some of the writers that Ireland has given to the world.

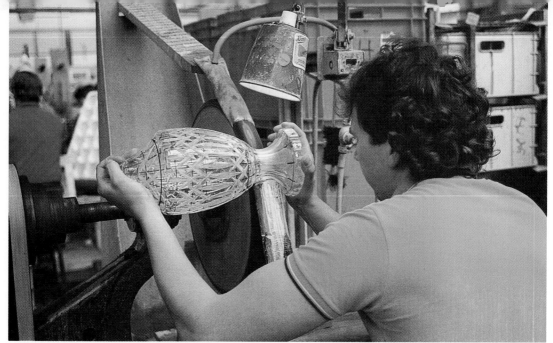
Finely crafted Waterford crystal is one of Ireland's best-known exports.

ECONOMY

There have been many changes in modern Ireland, with industry displacing agriculture as the most important source of income. Although some two fifths of the population is rural, less than one fifth of the labor force works in agriculture. The high rainfall and the moderate temperature make Ireland one of the finest grass-growing countries in the world. As a result most of the land is devoted to pasture.

Livestock is the mainstay of the economy. Cattle and milk account for about 85 percent of all agricultural production. Sheep, pigs, and the famous Irish horses are also very important. The principal field crops are barley, oats, potatoes, wheat, and sugar beets.

The government is doing much to promote progressive farming, to develop better strains of livestock, and to increase the average size of farms by programs of land reform. There are large stud farms, cattle ranches, and dairy farms, but most Irish farms are still too small to raise beef cattle profitably. And as in other countries, thousands of young men leave the farms annually to seek industrial jobs in cities, both in Ireland and abroad.

For many years Ireland's greatest preoccupation has been with industrial development in an attempt to raise the standard of living, to give employment to the young people from the farms, and to stem the flow of emigration. Ireland possesses few natural resources. Peat bogs provide an almost unlimited amount of turf for fuel, but coal and oil must be imported. There are only a few minerals.

A large portion of Ireland's industry is related to processing agricultural products into food, drink, and leather. Recently many new industries based on imported raw materials have come into being. Workers now find employment in oil refining, shipbuilding, and in the manufacture of clothing, textiles, chemicals, and machinery. Nearly all the new industrial plants have been built by investors from abroad.

Many Irish exports are well-known. Waterford crystal has been admired for years. Irish whiskey, stout, oatmeal, and hams are sold in many countries, as are clothing and other products. The bulk of trade is with the United Kingdom, and it is largely from the United Kingdom that Ireland obtains coal, machinery, and vehicles. Ireland's banking and monetary system is closely allied to the British system. British currency circulates freely in Ireland, although the Irish pound is the monetary unit of the country. In 1973 Ireland, together with Great Britain and Denmark, joined the European Economic Community, an organization which is probably better known as the Common Market.

Ireland's largest new industry is tourism. Today an ever-growing number of tourists come to Ireland from the highly industrialized Western countries to enjoy the unspoiled beauty, the leisurely way of life, and the great sporting opportunities.

DUBLIN, IRELAND'S CAPITAL CITY

Dublin, the heart of Ireland, is set on a wide, sandy bay on the Irish Sea. In the distance you can see the heather-covered slopes of the hills of Wicklow. An old city, Dublin was first mentioned by the Alexandrian geographer Ptolemy in A.D. 140. It is a city where much of Ireland's history has taken place, and many of its buildings bear the scars of battle. Some of the finest buildings, such as the Customs House and the Four Courts Buildings, were destroyed in the fighting of the 1920's but have been restored.

The museums are filled with treasures of the past. In Trinity College is the great Book of Kells, the 340-page hand-illuminated Celtic manuscript of four books of the New Testament. Beautifully painted and inscribed by 9th-century monks, it is considered by many to be the most beautiful manuscript in existence. The old parliament house (now the Bank of Ireland), the Abbey Theatre, famous churches, elegant Georgian town houses, and great parks and gardens grace the city. Phoenix Park, with its racecourse and famous zoo, is one of the largest and finest enclosed public parks in the world. Dublin was a city of great elegance in

O'Connell Street, Dublin's main thoroughfare, is named for a 19th-century Irish patriot.

The colorful horse show is an annual event in Dublin.

the 18th century and at one time was considered to be second only to London. After the Act of Union in 1800, when the old Dublin parliament ceased to exist, the city gradually fell into decay. Many of the magnificent Georgian houses became tenements, and the glow and glamour of life began to fade away. Since Dublin became a seat of government again in 1922, it has indeed expanded in a new way. It has now become a thriving industrial complex, with all that this involves in factories, supermarkets, and office blocks. However, a shadow of the old elegance still haunts such streets and squares as Harcourt Street, Merrion Square, and St. Stephen's Green.

Other Cities of Ireland

In the south is **Cork**, the Republic of Ireland's second city. It has less than one-fourth the people of Dublin, but it, too, played a large role in the fighting of the 1920's. The oldest part of the city is ringed by the two channels of the Lee River. The loveliness of Cork is heightened by the palms, azaleas, and bamboo that flourish there and by the hills that form the backdrop for the old streets. Near Cork is the legendary Blarney Castle, where the visitor must bend over backwards to reach the fabled Blarney Stone and thus acquire the power of eloquence.

Westward from Cork is **Killarney**, known for hundreds of years as one of the grandest areas of natural beauty to be found anywhere. Killarney, where "the long light shakes across the lakes and the wild cataract leaps in glory," is only one of the magnificent stops in the Ring of Kerry, a 110-mile (175 km.) circle that encompasses lakes with mysterious islands, mountains with crashing cataracts, silent forests, sleepy valleys, and mountain passes—as well as historic abbeys and castles.

A quay on the Lee River in Cork, Ireland's second largest city.

Near Shannon, in the southwest of Ireland, is **Limerick**, once noted for its lacemaking. It is also another center of great natural beauty. Nearby are barren hills with strange Arctic and Mediterranean flowers existing side by side. And on the coast are the spectacular Cliffs of Moher, rising 700 feet (210 m.) and extending along the pounding Atlantic Ocean.

Galway, in Ireland's west, is another ancient town with winding streets, old houses, and broad quays. Near Galway are interesting archeological remains and many strange subterranean streams under the grassy limestone plain.

In the southeast is **Waterford**, an old port, famous for its glassware, and **Wexford**, where the Opera Festival brings visitors each autumn to hear rarely performed works.

HISTORY

Earliest Inhabitants. Hunters and fishermen, whose name and race we do not know, came to Ireland about 6000 B.C., but they left little trace of their existence. After 3000 B.C., during the late Stone Age, farming was introduced, and the people of this era left behind tombs constructed with stones so huge that legend says they were built by giants.

The Irish-speaking Celts may have appeared in Ireland about the middle of the 4th century B.C. They came from the continent, conquered the primitive tribes on the island, and established a complex civilization. There were seven small tribal kingdoms, where each king ruled surrounded by lawmakers, soldiers, poets, and musicians. The high king, the Ard Rí, whose seat was at Tara in the kingdom of County Meath, ruled over all the kings. Every third year he presided over the Feis of Tara, a great assembly for law, music, games, and literary contests. This

The formal gardens at Powerscourt, an old estate in County Wicklow.

highly developed society continued uninterrupted for 1,000 years, because Ireland, on the edge of Europe, escaped Roman invasion.

The Golden Age.   Christianity came to Ireland in A.D. 432, with the coming of Saint Patrick. Patrick was a slave in Ireland who escaped, may have studied for the priesthood on the continent, and returned to Ireland as a bishop. The people were rapidly converted to Christianity, and Ireland became renowned for its great monastic schools. Students came from all over Europe to the monasteries, such as Clonard and Clonmacnoise. During a time when civilized Europe was falling to invaders from north and east, Ireland became the haven for ecclesiastical learning. This time has become known as the golden age in Ireland. After the decline of Rome, the Irish were among the first European peoples to produce a literature in their native language, Irish.

These days ended when the Vikings, sailors from northern Europe, raided the undefended monasteries during the 9th and 10th centuries. They established settlements on the Irish coast and at Dublin, Cork, Waterford, Limerick, and other places, and remained in control for many years. Their power was finally broken in A.D. 1014, at the battle of Clontarf, near Dublin. The High King Brian Boru defeated the Danes in this battle, but was slain at the moment of victory. No high king of similar strength succeeded him. The divided country was no match for the Norman knights who came to Ireland in 1170. The Normans then submitted to the English king, Henry II.

English Rule.   For 750 years Gaelic chieftains attempted to carry on their struggle against the English, but gradually the English rulers tightened their grip. In 1366 the repressive Statutes of Kilkenny were passed to keep the English and Irish apart. It became illegal for the English to intermarry with the Irish or for anyone to speak Irish, to use Irish dress or customs, or to employ Irish musicians or storytellers.

Henry VIII (1491–1547) was the first English monarch to add "King of Ireland" to his title. He began the policy of trying to impose the Protestant Reformation upon the Irish. Succeeding English rulers continued to deprive the Irish of their lands. Queen Mary "planted" two midland counties with English settlers. Queen Elizabeth I took land in southwest Ireland and gave it to Sir Walter Raleigh (1552?–1618), who brought the potato to Ireland.

The Irish resisted strongly, and there were many bloody encounters, but their fate was determined for hundreds of years by their defeat at the battle of Kinsale in 1601. Oliver Cromwell (1599–1658), the Puritan leader of England, cruelly crushed all remnants of Irish resistance. His army laid waste much of the country and massacred thousands of people. Many soldiers were exiled to France and Spain, and many men and women to the West Indies and Virginia. Cromwell filled the country with English settlers. In 11 years the Irish population was reduced to less than half the number it had been when Cromwell came to Ireland. Three quarters of all Irish land passed to Protestant landlords, many of them living abroad. But the only English plantation that was ultimately successful was the plantation of Ulster, established after the battle of Kinsale.

At the end of the 17th century Ireland was the scene of the struggle between William III (William of Orange), a Protestant, and James II, a Catholic, for the British Crown. William was the victor at the battle of the Boyne in 1690. Because the Irish Catholics had opposed William, the English Parliament passed the Penal Laws of 1695, which assumed that every Catholic was an enemy of England. Irish Catholics were forbidden to vote, to hold office, or to retain military, civil, legal, or teaching positions. Catholic schools were abolished. More land was confiscated, and no Irish Catholic was allowed to own a horse of any value. The Penal Laws, which reduced the Irish to terrible poverty, were finally repealed in 1829, but even greater hardship was in store for Ireland.

The Famine.   The most terrible times in these long, unhappy years for Ireland started in 1845. A famine, which lasted 4 years, was caused by a fungus that attacked the potato crop and thus wiped out the basic food supply. It would be hard to exaggerate the suffering of the Irish during these years. Even before the famine, people often went hungry between the end of the old potato crop and the time when the new plants were ready. Most of the farmers were tenants who farmed tiny plots owned by absentee landlords. The famine made it difficult and even impossible for farmers to pay their rent, so the crop failure caused people to lose not only their source of food but also their homes. Landlords evicted tenants and often burned their homes to clear the land for pasture, since they found it more profitable to use the land for grazing cattle grown for export. Thousands of men, women, and children, dressed in rags, roamed the muddy roads during the chill, rainy weather looking for food and shelter. Often they lived in ditches. An epidemic added to the horror. At least 1,000,000 Irish died of starvation and disease. Another 1,000,000 emigrated to North America. These emigrants traveled in poor cargo ships, which have become known as coffin ships because so many people died en route.

Home Rule. The spirit of independence in Ireland had been aroused by the French and American revolutions. A rebellion in 1798 was put down, and in 1800, Ireland and Britain were united by the Act of Union. In the 19th century, Daniel O'Connell and Charles Stewart Parnell became leaders of the Home Rule movement. Through O'Connell's efforts, the Penal Laws were repealed and Catholics were admitted to Parliament. Both leaders, however, failed to gain home rule for Ireland.

During World War I, many Irish joined the British army to fight against Germany, but others joined the Irish Volunteers. This group was the military arm of a political party, Sinn Fein ("ourselves alone"), which was formed in 1904. The Volunteers and the Citizen Army attempted to capture Dublin on Easter Monday, 1916. They called themselves the Irish Republican Army (IRA) and raised their green, white, and orange flag over the Dublin Post Office. After about a week, they had to surrender to the British. Many of their leaders were executed.

Until 1921, a bitter guerrilla war raged in Ireland. The IRA fought no pitched battles, but they were very successful in quick raids and harassment. The British acts of reprisal were harsh. King George V intervened, and a settlement was worked out whereby 26 of the 32 counties of Ireland became a self-governing free state in the British Commonwealth. Six counties of the northern province of Ulster remained a part of the United Kingdom. Even though the treaty was accepted by Dáil Éireann, the Irish parliament, no immediate peace followed. Eamon de Valera led the forces opposed to the treaty, and a civil war started. In 1923, peace was restored with the defeat of those opposing the treaty.

In 1926, De Valera founded a new party, the Fianna Fáil (Warriors of Destiny). When the Fianna Fáil and De Valera came to power in 1932, they abolished the oath of allegiance to the British Crown and other restrictive clauses of the peace treaty. In 1937, a new constitution was adopted. It declared Ireland to be a sovereign, independent, democratic state. The following year, Britain gave up its naval bases in Ireland. During World War II, Ireland remained neutral. In 1948, the Irish government announced that "the description of the State shall be the Republic of Ireland," and the British government said this placed Ireland outside the Commonwealth. A completely separate state had finally been achieved after generations of striving and bloodshed.

GOVERNMENT

The head of state is the president, elected for a term of seven years by all citizens over 18. He or she may serve two terms. In December 1990, Ireland's first woman president, Mary Robinson, took office. She was succeeded in 1997 by Mary McAleese, Ireland's first president from Northern Ireland. The Oireachtas (parliament) consists of two houses. Dáil Éireann (House of Representatives) has 166 members elected by proportional representation, which guarantees representation of every substantial minority. Seanad Éireann (Senate) has 60 members. The actual head of the government is the *taoiseach* (prime minister), who is nominated by Dáil Éireann and appointed by the president. For most of modern Ireland's history, the Fianna Fáil (the Republican Party) has been in power. In December 1994, however, a three-party coalition that excluded the Fianna Fáil took control of the government; it was led by a new prime minister, John Bruton of Fine Gael, the nation's leading opposition party.

Dublin is Ireland's chief port, handling more than half of the nation's seaborne trade.

Modern Ireland

A new political generation came to power in the early 1960s. It faced the future with new self-confidence and new demands for industrial and social reforms. Changes within the Catholic Church, a freer press, television, and the growth of industries, city life, and tourism helped to create a more progressive attitude and to challenge old beliefs and customs.

The new leaders turned against the old self-imposed isolation of Ireland. They took an important role in the United Nations, playing a major part in the work of the UN Special Committee on Peacekeeping Operations. New industrial goals also led Ireland to look for additional markets and to seek and finally obtain entry into the Common Market (now the European Union, or EU). With industrial growth it was hoped that the tide of emigration would end, just as it was anticipated that modern education, improvements in social and welfare laws, and a freer intellectual climate would help to keep the Irish intellectuals at home. Unfortunately, economic recession led to the resumption of emigration, especially by young people.

The reunification of the northern and southern parts of the island has been controversial for many years. A major step toward resolving this crisis was a peace agreement that was overwhelmingly approved in a popular vote in May 1998. Three interconnected government bodies have been created to handle, respectively, issues within Northern Ireland itself; between Northern Ireland and Ireland; and between Ireland and Britain. The agreement also calls for a referendum on amending the constitution to end the country's claim to Northern Ireland. Unfortunately, terrorism remains a problem: several factions oppose the peace plan, and some of them are still using violence in an attempt to derail the process.

THOMAS FITZGERALD, Department of Education, Dublin, Ireland

UNITED KINGDOM: AN INTRODUCTION

by C. P. SNOW
Author, Strangers and Brothers

What does England mean to an Englishman? Not the island that one has to call Britain—though that is a political, not a conversational, term —but just *England,* the stretch of land from the Channel to the Scottish border. It is a very small stretch of land by the standard of modern nations. I don't think Englishmen feel for it the passionate, emotional, almost sensual attachment that Frenchmen feel for the *pays sacré de la France*—"sacred land of France"—or Russians for the earth of Mother Russia. On arriving home from abroad one looks at the English countryside with a kind of domestic pleasure: it is pretty rather than picturesque. Although England is, of course, still one of the four or five great industrial powers, there is a surprising amount of the gentle, well-kept, grassgreen landscape. Even the outskirts of the big industrial towns, including London, are leafy. The English dedication to gardening, and the soft climate, take away a lot of harshness; the whole country looks as if it had been cared for affectionately, and for a very long time. That happens to be true. Most of the English landscape was being man-made 1,400 years before the Allegheny frontier ceased being virgin forest. The Saxons, technologically better farmers than the Romans, were blazing down the trees and using their heavy plows on the clay soil not long after A.D. 400. There is very little of the English countryside that hasn't been shaped, altered, tended by man. So one feels for it nothing extravagant, but a kind of indulgent possessive affection.

And Englishmen don't feel for the language that desperate without-it-we-are-lost yearning that a good many other nationalities do. That is perhaps because, more than any language before it, it has become world currency, so that other people, who use it in their own fashion, have as much right to it as the aboriginal English. The forms of American English are slightly different from the forms of English English (not British English, which has no meaning whatsoever), but just as legitimate. And so on with Australian English and the rest. The chief peculiarity of English English is that its users, after 20 or 30 generations of playing with the language, have adapted themselves, quite unconsciously, to a more complicated syntax than anyone else. Compare the elaborate English conditionals. "I suppose you wouldn't happen to have a match?" would sound bizarre in New York; yet you can hear it any night in an English pub.

So neither the land nor the language have the first claim on an Englishman. Nor, in any direct sense, has the history. The vast majority of Englishmen live as industrial workers in the great towns. Their knowledge of their own history is pretty perfunctory compared with their knowledge of the local football teams.

So far as they know about their great men, they have never hero-worshiped them (except that they have come to attach a special charisma to the royal family). The hagiology of Winston Churchill is American, not English. The natives of Stratford-on-Avon, when they turn their attention to Shakespeare at all, domesticate him much as we have managed to domesticate the English landscape.

And yet, after all, something has percolated through to most of us. If I have to put it in one word, it would be "comfort." Yet England is having its strains along with the rest of the advanced world—crime, juvenile delinquency, protest, purposelessness. It remains, though, of all advanced countries among the most comfortable to live in. Partly, perhaps, because it has been lived in such a long time, and the inhabitants have become, within the limits of quarrelsome humanity, more easygoing than most. But partly, I believe, there is another reason, and a rather curious one.

The comfort, the degree of relaxation in English life, wasn't always there. It is relatively new. In some respects, it has increased since the last war. People outside the country have bestowed on us much sympathy because we have "lost" an empire. That sympathy is almost entirely misplaced. A few Englishmen (I have to include myself among them) might prefer the country to exercise maximum responsibility. That wouldn't be the general choice. Having been top nation through the 19th century has left a singular blessing—unrealized, but nevertheless felt—behind it.

There is a sense of how little it matters. The country was a super-power not so long ago, relatively more of a superpower than the United States is now, in fact. What did that mean, in terms of general human satisfaction? Active, fortunate, privileged people enjoyed the scope it gave them. For the rest—that is, 95 percent and more of English citizens —it brought little or nothing. Red on the map. Patriotic songs. Parades and ceremonies (at which the English have always been good). Well, it may have been nice to have. The present has some solider satisfactions.

Whether one is aware of it or not, a long history teaches one something. Stoicism, making oneself as comfortable as may be, getting on with others in the same condition. Things pass; others take their place. There have been so many lives, so many creations, not stopping with ourselves. Life flows. That feeling is part of the common existence in England. It gives a special flavor, and one that—despite our attempts to write off any emotion about our country—we hold dear.

Westminster Abbey, the site of British coronations, also contains the tombs of many distinguished Britons.

UNITED KINGDOM

The United Kingdom of Great Britain and Northern Ireland is a political unit occupying most of the land surface of a cluster of islands off the coast of northwestern Europe. Geographers call them the British Isles. The largest island, Great Britain, is divided among England, Scotland, and Wales. The six counties of Northern Ireland and the republic of Ireland share the second largest. Other islands in the United Kingdom include the Hebrides, Orkney, Shetland, and Scilly islands; Anglesey Island; and the Isle of Wight.

THE PEOPLE

Packing so many people into so little land would be a remarkable feat even if they were all alike in speech, habits, culture, and religion. They are not. There are six types of people who have long lived within the borders of the United Kingdom: English, Welsh, Scottish, Cornish, Protestant Irish, and Catholic Irish. In the past, friction among these people has caused many wars. Today, such friction is still causing trouble in Northern Ireland, also called Ulster. The Catholics are reaching for political and economic equality with the Protestants.

The Scots, the Welsh, and the Cornish have more or less settled their differences with the English, and many of them live in their own parts of the main island, Great Britain (called Great to distinguish it from Brittany in France; in French one is called Bretagne and the other one is called Grand Bretagne).

The Cornish, the Welsh, the Irish, and the Scots are descendants of Celtic and even earlier peoples who lived in the British Isles before the Romans first came in 55 B.C. The Romans were conquerors rather than settlers. They did not displace the natives. After the Romans came other invaders from across the English Channel—Angles, Saxons, Jutes, Danes, and Norsemen. These people wanted land, and they slaughtered or drove off the natives. The survivors were pushed into the western peninsulas, northern mountains, and farther islands, where the ruggedness of the land helped them to hold out.

To this day a line drawn across Great Britain from lower left to upper right will roughly separate peoples as well as the land. To the left are the highlands and mountains. There are the survivors of the Celtic people of Britain. To the right of the line are the lowlands. The stone is soft, mostly limestone and chalk. It has been worn down to a rolling, verdant countryside. There the Anglo-Saxons are dominant.

HOW THE UNITED KINGDOM WAS CREATED

The political consolidation of the peoples living on these islands was often attempted. It was finally completed by the Act of Union of 1707. The phrase United Kingdom dates from that time. So does the official British flag, called the Union Jack. It combined the flag of Saint George, patron saint of England, with the flag of Saint Andrew, patron saint of Scotland. In 1801 the flag of Saint Patrick of Ireland was added.

The English dominate the union symbolized by this flag. Of the total population in the United Kingdom, about 83 percent live in England. Some 9 percent live in Scotland, 5 percent in Wales, and 3 percent in Northern Ireland. Cornwall, Wales, and Ireland were brought into the kingdom by conquest; Scotland by merging the crowns. On the death of Elizabeth I of England in 1603, the English invited James VI of Scotland to become their king as well. In the English line he is called James I. The two countries had separate parliaments until 1707.

GOVERNMENT

The political result of British history is a government that is a constitutional monarchy, presided over by a monarch. The power center is in Parliament. A struggle between sovereign and Parliament was decided, sharply, in 1649. Parliament had King Charles I beheaded. Oliver Cromwell was declared Lord Protector. After 11 years of the "Protectorate" the monarchy was restored. British rulers have been constitutional monarchs ever since, acting largely on their ministers' advice. The monarch's influence can be considerable, but it is usually exercised now in the form of questions put by the sovereign to the prime minister. He calls on the monarch (king or queen) regularly to report on events. A question about a policy or an appointment can lead to a change of decision.

Parliament

The Parliament is descended from early Saxon tribal councils. In medieval times, the king consulted with three groups of leaders: Lords Spiritual (bishops), Lords Temporal (peers), and the Commons—the original "three estates." (The press is called the fourth estate.) Today, Parliament consists of the House of Lords (upper house) and House of Commons (lower house). The Lords is being transformed into an advisory chamber, but it can still delay legislation for 6 to 12 months. The hereditary principle, by which a seat is handed down from father to eldest son, remains, but no new hereditary peerages have been created since 1965. New Lords hold their titles for life only.

The House of Commons is the place in which political power is organized. In theory, the monarch may form a government (select cabinet officers) from any source he or she chooses. In practice (with some exceptions), the cabinet is chosen from the leadership of the majority party in the House of Commons. When the monarch entrusts the leader of the majority party with the responsibility of forming a government, he or she sets out to organize a group that can command a majority in the Commons. If successful, the party leader becomes prime minister.

The prime minister is not the chief executive in the American sense. The official title is First Lord of the Treasury. ("Prime minister" is not a legal title.) In the United Kingdom, political power rests on the "confidence" in the prime minister of a majority of the Commons. The resignation of a prime minister need not cause a dissolution of Parliament. But it may be dissolved on request of the prime minister to the sovereign. The maximum term of Parliament is five years, but elections are often called earlier.

Political control in Britain swings back and forth between the Tories, officially known as the Conservative and Unionist Party, and the Labour Party. The Liberal Party, which was a major political force in the late 19th century, has lost its importance and in 1988 agreed to merge with the Social Democratic Party.

Unity in Spite of Differences

The southern, Catholic part of Ireland broke away from British rule in 1921. There are separatist movements in Scotland and Wales. Northern Ireland had its own parliament from 1921. But in 1972, responding to increasing violence, the British government dismissed Northern Ireland's parliament and began to rule directly from London. The hope has been unfulfilled that direct rule would decrease tensions between Protestants and Catholics struggling for control of Northern Ireland.

One reason for the survival of the British monarchy is that the Crown is an acceptable bond among people who still have much in common, despite their age-old and deeply felt regional and cultural differences. An example of such common interest was provided by the almost 33,000 citizens of the Republic of Ireland (southern Ireland) who volunteered for service in the British army during World War II, although their country was no longer part of the United Kingdom and was officially neutral.

Another example is that while the Republic of Ireland is legally independent of and separate from the United Kingdom, free movement of money, goods, and people between the two countries continues. Economically and culturally, the British Isles are still a single community.

The ceremony of Trooping the Colour marks the Queen's official birthday in June.

SOME FACTS ABOUT THE ROYAL FAMILY

There are no automatic titles for the husband of a queen. They are conferred by the monarch. The wife of a king is called the queen during his lifetime, and the queen mother after his death. A monarch's children are automatically titled royal highnesses (princes and princesses). The first son is heir apparent. By birth he is Duke of Cornwall in English peerage; Duke of Rothesay, Earl of Carrick, and Baron of Renfrew in Scottish peerage; and Lord of the Isles and Prince and Great Steward, or Seneschal, of Scotland. Titles Prince of Wales and Earl of Chester are conferred on him by monarch. Monarch's eldest daughter is usually called the princess royal. She cannot be titled Princess of Wales.

SOME FACTS ABOUT THE PEERAGE

Peerage began with the barons, granted land by the king. Since they were equal in this sense, they were called peers (from Latin *par,* or "equal"). Peerage later came to include dukes, marquesses, earls, viscounts, archbishops of Canterbury and York, and certain bishops. Besides exemption from jury duty, peers have few privileges. (Once they could be tried by peers instead of commoners, and be beheaded rather than hanged if sentenced to death.) Main privilege is membership in House of Lords. There are five categories of peerage—English, created before union of England and Scotland in 1707; Scottish, before 1707; Irish; peerages of Great Britain, after 1707 but before 1800 and union with Ireland; and United Kingdom, after 1800. All peers except dukes are called "Lord" (and their wives "Lady").

Duke—14th century. Comes from *dux,* Latin for "leader." A duke's wife is a duchess.

Marquess—14th century. Comes from Germanic *march,* or "tract of land." A marquess's wife is a marchioness.

Earl—Before 1066. Comes from *jarl,* Old Norse for "chieftain." Earl's wife is a countess, from "count," from Latin *comes,* or "companion."

Viscount—15th century. From Latin *vice* ("deputy") and *comes.* Viscount's wife is a viscountess.

Baron—13th century. Comes from *baro,* Late Latin for "man." A baron's wife is a baroness.

Peerages can be hereditary (title usually inherited by eldest son) or life. A life peerage is a personal honor for the recipient's lifetime. Most new peerages are announced in annual Honours Lists, one published on New Year's Day, and one in June, on monarch's official birthday. Lists also include baronetcies, knighthoods, and other honors.

SOME FACTS ABOUT HONORS AND ORDERS

Baronetcies are not part of the peerage. They date from the 17th century and can be inherited.

Knighthoods, derived from medieval chivalry, are usually bestowed for distinction in a profession or for great national service. Knights are called "Sir," their wives "Lady." Women honored in their own right are made Dames. Principal orders are:

Order of the Garter (K.G.)—Dates from 14th century. Only rank is Knight Companion. Limited to 24 persons besides monarch and Prince of Wales.

Order of the Bath—Established 1725. Military and civilian. Ranks are Knight Grand Cross (G.C.B.), Knight Commander (K.C.B.), Companion (C.B.).

Order of Merit—Founded 1901. Only rank is Member. Limited to 24, plus foreign honorary members. Abbreviation is O.M.

Order of Saint Michael and Saint George—Founded 1818. Ranks are Knight or Dame Grand Cross (G.C.M.G.), Knight or Dame Commander (K.C.M.G.; D.C.M.G.), Companion (C.M.G.).

Royal Victorian Order—Established 1896. Ranks are Knight or Dame Grand Cross (G.C.V.O.), Knight or Dame Commander (K.C.V.O.; D.C.V.O.), Commander (C.V.O.), Member 4th class or 5th class (M.V.O.).

Order of the British Empire—Founded 1917. Military and civilian. Can be conferred on citizens of Allied countries. This is the most widely conferred honor. Ranks are Knight or Dame Grand Cross (G.B.E.), Knight or Dame Commander (K.B.E.; D.B.E.), Commander (C.B.E.), Officer (O.B.E.), Member (M.B.E.).

Order of the Companions of Honour (C.H.)—Founded 1917. Only rank is Companion. Limited to 65.

Eilean Donan Castle

Big Ben

A Village in Devon

UNITED KINGDOM OF GREAT BRITAIN & NORTHERN IRELAND

NORWAY

DENMARK

GERMANY

NETHERLANDS

BELGIUM

FRANCE

NORTH SEA

ATLANTIC OCEAN

IRISH SEA

IRELAND

EUROPE

ENGLISH CHANNEL

SCOTLAND

NORTHERN IRELAND

WALES

ENGLAND

London

FACTS AND FIGURES

OFFICIAL NAME: United Kingdom of Great Britain and Northern Ireland.

NATIONALITY: British.

CAPITAL: London.

LOCATION: Off the western coast of Europe. **Boundaries**—North Atlantic Ocean, North Sea, English Channel, St. George's Channel, Irish Sea, Ireland.

AREA: 94,525 sq. mi. (244,820 sq. km.).

PHYSICAL FEATURES: Highest point—Ben Nevis (4,406 ft.; 1,343 m.), in Scotland. **Lowest point**—sea level. **Chief rivers**—Thames, Severn, Wye, Dee, Clyde, Forth, Bann. **Major lakes**—Lough Neagh, Lough Erne, Loch Lomond, Loch Ness, Windermere, Bala.

POPULATION: 58,610,182 (1997; annual growth 0.19%).

MAJOR LANGUAGES: English, Welsh, Scottish Gaelic.

MAJOR RELIGIONS: Anglicanism, other Protestant denominations, Roman Catholicism, Judaism.

GOVERNMENT: Constitutional monarchy. **Head of state**—king or queen. **Head of government**—prime minister. **Legislature**—bicameral Parliament.

CHIEF CITIES: London, Birmingham, Glasgow, Leeds, Sheffield, Liverpool, Bradford, Manchester, Edinburgh.

ECONOMY: Chief minerals—coal, oil, gas, tin, limestone, iron, salt, clay, chalk, gypsum, lead, silica. **Chief agricultural products**—cereals, oilseed, potatoes, vegetables, cattle, sheep, poultry, fish. **Industries and products**—machinery and transportation equipment, metals, food processing, paper and paper products, textiles, chemicals, clothing, electronics and communications equipment. **Chief exports**—manufactured goods, machinery, fuels, chemicals, transportation equipment, semifinished goods. **Chief imports**—manufactured goods, machinery, foodstuffs, consumer goods.

MONETARY UNIT: 1 British pound = 100 pence.

NATIONAL HOLIDAY: Second Saturday in June (Celebration of the Queen's Birthday).

THE UNITED KINGDOM—FROM EMPIRE TO COMMONWEALTH

The British have played a remarkable role in world affairs, often brilliant and decisive. One measure of the importance of this role is that the empire of which the British divested themselves from 1931 onward was the largest (in population) in world history. At its height, it included almost one fourth of the world's land and one fifth of its people. It is another measure that this was their third, not their first, empire.

Three Empires

The first British empire came about when the Norman, William the Conqueror, added England to his holdings in what is now France. From the Norman Conquest (1066) to the end of the Hundred Years War (1453) the sovereigns of England claimed, and most of the time held, a varying portion of the old feudal lands of the dukes of Normandy in France. At times they even held Paris. They clung to the French port of Calais down to 1558. The Channel Islands survive from that first empire.

A second empire consisted mostly of territories in North America, including the island of Bermuda and some islands in the Caribbean. Only Bermuda and a few Caribbean islands remain from this empire.

The third empire was put together out of coaling stations and trading posts picked up around the world during and shortly after the Napoleonic Wars. It was formalized officially in 1876, when Queen Victoria was proclaimed Empress of India. It ended in 1948, when King George VI gave up the title of Emperor and settled back into being just King of Great Britain and Northern Ireland.

In 1875 Prime Minister Benjamin Disraeli (later Lord Beaconsfield) pulled one of the great coups of statecraft by purchasing the Suez Canal. Through an intermediary, he bought the controlling block of shares in the Suez Canal Company. Because it connected the Mediterranean and the Red seas and thus greatly shortened the distance between Europe and Asia, the canal was a vastly important channel for world trade and commerce. When Britain gained control of the canal, it also became the military line of communications between Britain and India.

In 1871, after a Prussian victory over the French, Germany had been united as an empire. Queen Victoria's German relatives suddenly became Imperial Highnesses. Her children and grandchildren in Britain were still only Royal Highnesses. They were outranked and upstaged by scores of other Imperial Highnesses—Austrian, Russian, Turkish, Japanese, Ethiopian—and now German! She begged Disraeli to correct this socially distressing situation, and in 1876 Victoria was declared Empress of India.

Thus was born the most famous British Empire, upon which, it was said, "the sun never sets." It lasted precisely 72 years. The second empire had lasted 163 years. The original empire had a life span of 387 years. The Victorian empire was spectacular, but it was not long-lived.

THE COMMONWEALTH OF NATIONS AND THE UNITED KINGDOM TODAY

The empire was followed by a political device called the Commonwealth—a voluntary association of the United Kingdom and independent nations that were once part of the British Empire. The Commonwealth was formed to ease the liquidation of the empire and make it palatable to "empire loyalists" in Britain.

But the important thing about the United Kingdom today is not its departed imperial glory, but its surviving industrial energy and its social pioneering. The British islanders started the Industrial Revolution and have been in its front rank ever since. Hovercraft and short take-off and landing planes (STOL) are merely the latest in the long line of modern devices that were invented or pioneered by the British. The list of British firsts includes the steam engine, penicillin, the jet engine, radar, much of the original work in both radio and television, and the decisively important early work in nuclear energy.

After the Empire—Changes at Home

The political energy that once went into the empire has been transferred since World War II to Britain's internal social problems and the creation of the "welfare state." The British system of national insurance protects the old, sick, handicapped, deprived, unfortunate, and unemployed from acute distress or destitution. Compulsory contributions paid by all who have an income are paid out to all who would be unable to stay alive in modest comfort without help. The National Health Service, which is only one part of the system, provides medical and hospital service for all. It is no longer free, as it was when it was introduced in 1948, except to children and the aged. The payments required are small.

Among the big industrial countries Britain is in the front line in wiping out slums, poverty, human misery, and economic inequality. The worst of London's once notorious East End slums have largely disappeared—after being hard-hit by Hitler's bombs in World War II. The infamous Gorbals—the Glasgow slums—have come down.

This concentration on social progress at home has been accompanied by a remarkable flowering of the arts. Though Britain was always known for its theaters, museums, and great literature, before World War II no one thought of it as a wellspring of music, ballet, films, and fine food. It is now.

Economic and social historians will want to study the causes of this third flowering of the arts in Britain. The first came in the reign of Elizabeth I (1558–1603); the second with the restoration of the Stuart dynasty under Charles II in 1600. The third began in 1954, immediately after the lifting of most, though not all, of the controls and rationing left over from World War II. A great sense of freedom and relaxation was felt in Britain for the first time in over 20 years. The rise in the level of achievement in all art forms took place almost immediately, and it carried the British islanders in a few years from the grim austerity of World War II to the gaiety of what has been called a second Restoration. Small wonder that to many British islanders this aftermath of empire has been tastier than its glory and its power. There has been little looking back with regret.

The 1970's, however, were a bad decade, marked by open warfare in Northern Ireland, terrorist attacks in England, high inflation, and increasingly sharp industrial strife. The decade culminated in the "winter of discontent" of 1978–79, when a wave of strikes paralyzed the economy. Economic dissatisfaction led to the defeat of the Labour Party in 1979 and the election of the nation's first woman prime minister, Conservative leader Margaret Thatcher. Her government embarked on a sweeping reorganization of the economy, which included lower income taxes, "privatization" of a number of state-owned enterprises, and a promotion

Stonehenge, on Salisbury Plain, is a relic of prehistoric Britain.

of "popular capitalism," that is, increased home ownership and a much greater number of stockholders. These changes brought about widespread unemployment, but, despite that, Margaret Thatcher won a landslide victory in 1983. In 1987, Thatcher won a third term, making her the longest-tenured British prime minister in the 20th century. Her popularity fell over tax policies, and in November 1990, she resigned. John Major was elected to succeed Thatcher; he won reelection in 1992, but was soundly defeated in May 1997 by Labour Party leader Tony Blair.

After the Empire—Changes in World Status

An incidental victim of the shift from world power to social progress at home was British influence in Europe. At the end of World War II, the leadership of Europe was Great Britain's for the taking. It passed up the chance. The saddest misjudgment in postwar history was the British decision to step out of the negotiations for the European Common Market.

The European Economic Community (EEC)—the Common Market—was established in 1958, but the British did not apply for membership until 1963. Negotiations began, but France suddenly vetoed the British application. The British persisted, however, and in 1973, Great Britain entered the Common Market.

Today, Britain is preparing for the closer integration of the European Union (EU). It approved a treaty of political and economic union negotiated in Maastricht, the Netherlands, in 1991. Britain's future lies in this cooperation with its European neighbors. In 1994, the "Chunnel," a tunnel running under the English Channel, was completed, connecting Britain to France and the rest of Europe for the first time since the Ice Age. Great Britain's dedication to European integration was severely tested in 1996, when the EU banned the export of British beef due to fears of so-called mad-cow disease, and again by growing doubts about the adoption of the Euro, the single European currency favored by the EU.

JOSEPH C. HARSCH, C.B.E. (Hon.), Chief editorial writer, *Christian Science Monitor*

Queen Elizabeth II and Prince Philip lead a procession from Windsor Castle to St. George's Chapel.

ENGLAND

For many American travelers approaching England by air, the first surprise is that "it really is green!" Below them is the land they have read about in hundreds of books—Shakespeare's "demi-paradise" and "blessed plot" and poet William Blake's "green and pleasant land"—and it looks so much as they expected that it is a surprise. England has always been an exciting combination of expectations fulfilled and undreamed-of surprises.

It has also been a land of contradictions. Divided from the continent by a body of water some 21 miles (34 kilometers) wide at its narrowest, England is of Europe but not in Europe. Its history parallels that of Europe and yet shows striking differences. But if water divides, it also protects and can be dominated. England has not been successfully invaded for more than nine centuries. And from the security and fastness of their island, Shakespeare's "water-walled bulwark," the English built and ruled for hundreds of years over an empire so far-flung that later its citizens could confidently say "the Sun never set" on it.

THE LAND

England occupies the southern half of the island of Great Britain. Scotland occupies the north; and Wales, an outlying section of the west. Both Scotland and Wales are mountainous, but England is generally low-lying, as if a colossus had forced the southeast corner of the island down until the water lapped over its edge. Except in the north, where the rugged Cheviot Hills form the border with Scotland, and the west, at the Welsh border, England is surrounded on all sides by water. No place in England is more than 100 miles (160 km.) from the sea.

The neat green fields of England.

Southern England, bounded on the north by the Thames and Severn river valleys and on the west by the Exe River, is an area of rolling, wooded hills and winding streams and rivers. It is farm country, with fields bordered by dark green hedgerows. It is the land of the fabled white cliffs of Dover (though they appear truly white only when their chalk surfaces gleam in the sun), backed by grassy ridges called downs. And it is the land of London, England's capital and one of the largest cities in the world. (An article on LONDON follows.)

The long tail of England—including Devon and Cornwall—which lies on the other side of the Exe and trails off into the Atlantic, is called the West Country. Here the landscape is fairly rugged, with deep valleys, rocky plateaus, and vast, windswept moors. Here, too, there are apple orchards and dairy farms, tiny fishing villages and the great port of Plymouth. The granite spur called Land's End, which points westward past the tiny Scilly Islands, across the pounding Atlantic surf to Newfoundland, also belongs to the West Country.

The English Midlands are that part of the country up to the Trent River, including the southern ranges of the Pennines, the long chain of mountains often called the spine of England. Starting in the late 18th century, thanks to deep veins of coal and abundant water, the Midlands became England's industrial center. There, industry created a new landscape, blackened by the soot of innumerable foundries and dominated by factory smokestacks. It is not surprising that some Englishmen still refer to the Midlands as "the black country," though the area is no longer truly black.

Beyond the Midlands lies the North Country, a long upland strip that runs to the Scottish border. Coal and other minerals also changed the look of the land here. In the great industrial cities of the north, one can still see the "dark, Satanic mills" Blake described in the 19th century.

But the North Country also has the most varied landscape in England. Not far inland from the Irish Sea and the Isle of Man are the Cumbrian Mountains, the northwestern extension of the Pennines. The Cumbrians include Scafell Pike, at 3,210 feet (978 meters) the highest point in England.

Set among the mountains are 15 mirrorlike lakes, including Derwentwater, Windermere, and Buttermere. Sparkling waterfalls add to the unexpected wilderness of this part of England. Now a national park, the Lake District was not really appreciated until the early 1800's. Then such Romantic poets as William Wordsworth and Samuel Taylor Coleridge extolled the region's beauties—and became known as the Lake Poets.

Still farther north is the Scottish border country—almost grim and yet beautiful, with yellow trefoil and purple heather on the slopes and green valleys where brooks tumble and waterfalls splash. To the southeast, beyond the foothills of the craggy Pennines, are the Yorkshire moors. They are used for sheep grazing, as they have been for centuries. But the modern world has reached even remotest Yorkshire. In winter, when some of the higher passes may be snow-blocked, helicopters are used to drop hay to the animals.

Climate

Snow in Yorkshire is one surprising facet of the English climate; palm trees in Devon and Cornwall are another. Though the country lies as far north as part of Labrador, winds from the North Atlantic Current of the Gulf Stream bring warmth and moisture to the land. Winters are generally mild and summers fairly warm; blizzards and heat waves are equally rare.

Westerly winds are also responsible for the variability of the climate. In the 1st century A.D. the Roman historian Tacitus wrote, "Britain's sky is overcast, with continual rain and cloud." Today, many Englishmen claim that their country has no climate, only weather. At all seasons, rain, clouds, and sunlight chase each other across England's skies. A bright, clear morning is no sure sign of a bright, clear day. Shakespeare wrote of the "uncertain glory of an April day"; and in the 20th century T. S. Eliot described April as "the cruellest month." The contemporary Englishman whose umbrella is as necessary as his shoes might agree with both.

AGRICULTURE, INDUSTRIES, AND COMMUNICATIONS

Today few remnants of England's ancient forests, with their massive oaks and yew trees, still stand. Nearly every bit of arable land is under cultivation. Even so, England must import about one third of its food.

In the east, south, and southwest, where the climate is generally mildest, English farmers raise all kinds of vegetables. Here, too, are England's fruit orchards. In Kent, hops are grown for the brewing industry. Wheat is grown in the drier sections of England, as is barley, the leading grain crop. Potatoes do well in the marshy parts of the northwest.

Livestock includes ducks, chickens, pigs, horses, sheep, and cattle. Much of England's meat must be imported, but the dairy herds of Jerseys, Guernseys, and Friesians yield rich milk and cream. Modern farming methods and machines are in use throughout England, and only just over two percent of the population work in agriculture today.

England's great shift from an agricultural to an industrial, urban economy began around 1800. Today, in spite of declining mineral resources, new sources of power, such as North Sea oil and gas, help to maintain the country's position as a leading industrial nation. Tankers bring oil to be processed at vast, modern refineries. Nuclear power plants have been built, and more are planned. The steel industry uses imported iron ore; and imported raw materials go into most of England's industrial output, from automobiles and airplanes to fashions and films.

England has a modern transportation network to take its products to market. There are some 2,500 miles (4,020 km.) of canals and navigable rivers and many excellent highways. Cities are linked, too, by the up-to-date British railway system. At English harbors, merchant ships load and unload goods from all the nations of the world. In addition to its international passenger airlines, British Airways and British Caledonian Airways, England has a large fleet of cargo aircraft.

In the 19th century, a Swiss visitor said that the English "think nothing is as well done elsewhere as in their own country." Today, they take pride in their efficient postal system and in the excellent information services and entertainment provided by the British Broadcasting Corporation (BBC) radio and television, and a commercial television network. England has also made an important contribution to the new field of satellite communications—its tracking station and radio telescope at Jodrell Bank, Cheshire, is one of the largest in the world.

CITIES AND PLACES OF INTEREST

Every Englishman cherishes his own corner of England, and few visitors can resist the spell of this storied land. At every bend in the road, some legend, poem, or novel or some event encountered in a history book seems to come to life.

London's Tower Bridge crosses the Thames.

A NOTE ON THE ENGLISH LANGUAGE

Winston Churchill (who was proud of being half-American) is said to have described England and the United States as two countries separated by a common language. Here are some examples of what he had in mind:

ENGLAND	UNITED STATES
Ground floor	First floor
Biscuits	Cookies
Dustman	Garbage collector
Jumper (women)	Sweater
Lorry	Truck
Flat	Apartment
Lift	Elevator
Queue	Waiting line
Underground	Subway
Subway	Pedestrian underpass
Sweet	Dessert, candy
Bonnet (of a car)	Hood
Boot (of a car)	Trunk
Petrol	Gasoline
Across the road	Across the street
On holiday	On vacation
Chemist	Drugstore
Stalls (theatre)	Orchestra seats (theater)
Interval (theatre)	Intermission (theater)
To stand (politics)	To run (politics)
Fortnight	2 weeks
Caravan	Trailer
Puncture	Flat tire
Jug	Pitcher
Skew-wiff	Cockeyed
Pocketbook	Wallet
Wash up	Do the dishes
Goods waggon	Freight car
Chest of drawers	Bureau
Joint	Roast
Rubber	Eraser
Runner beans	String beans
Scruffy	Messy
Vacuum flask	Thermos bottle
Vest	Undershirt
Waistcoat	Vest
Gods (theatre)	Top balcony (theater)
Dressing gown	Bathrobe
Lounge	Living room
Post	Mail
Pavement	Sidewalk
Kirby grips	Bobby pins
Bowler (hat)	Derby (hat)
To hand	Within reach
Rise (in pay)	Raise (in pay)
Restaurant car	Dining car

ENGLAND

FACTS AND FIGURES

NATIONALITY: English.

CAPITAL: London.

LOCATION: Southern and eastern parts of island of Great Britain. **Boundaries**—Scotland, North Sea, English Channel, Wales, Irish Sea.

AREA: 50,352 sq. mi. (130,412 sq. km.).

PHYSICAL FEATURES: **Highest point**—Scafell Pike (3,209 ft.; 978 m.). **Lowest point**—sea level. **Chief rivers**—Thames, Severn, Mersey, Trent, Yorkshire, Ouse. **Major lakes**—Windermere, Coniston Water, Derwentwater.

POPULATION: 49,089,100 (1996).

MAJOR LANGUAGE: English.

MAJOR RELIGIONS: Anglicanism, other Protestant denominations, Roman Catholicism, Judaism.

CHIEF CITIES: London, Birmingham, Liverpool, Manchester, Sheffield, Leeds, Newcastle, Bristol.

ECONOMY: **Chief minerals**—coal, natural gas, petroleum, clay, chalk. **Chief agricultural products**—barley, cattle, chickens and eggs, fruits, milk, potatoes, sheep, sugar beets, wheat. **Industries and products**—aircraft engines, beverages, chemicals, clothing, electronic equipment, fabricated steel products, wool and other textiles, footwear. **Chief exports**—steel, motor vehicles, machinery, chinaware, textiles. **Chief imports**—fuel oils, food products, chemicals.

Southern England

The port of **Dover** lies nestled in a little valley, interrupting the famous cliffs that rise some 400 ft. (120 m.) from the sea. In 1867, poet Matthew Arnold chose the spot as the setting for his poem *Dover Beach,* which begins, "The sea is calm tonight/The tide is full, the moon lies fair/ upon the straits." On clear days, the French coast can be seen from the commanding location above those straits. In the 1st century A.D. the Romans built a fort and a lighthouse there. Remains of the lighthouse still

The white cliffs of Dover are one of England's best-known landmarks.

stand, and tourists can also visit Dover Castle, built some 1,000 years later by the Normans.

In late Norman times, Dover joined nearby Hastings, Sandwich, Romney, and Hythe to form the Cinque ("five") Ports. They contributed to England's sea defense in return for special privileges. The office of Lord Warden of the Cinque Ports—once held by such men as the Duke of Wellington and Winston Churchill—is a relic of those days.

Twenty miles (32 km.) to the northwest is ancient **Canterbury**, whose archbishop heads the Church of England. The soaring towers of Canterbury's great Gothic cathedral dominate the town. In 1170, after Thomas à Becket, Archbishop of Canterbury, quarreled with King Henry II over the rights of the Church, Becket was murdered. When Becket was made a saint 2 years later, the cathedral became a pilgrims' shrine. The 14th-century poet Geoffrey Chaucer wrote of such pilgrims in his *Canterbury Tales,* and one of the greatest 20th-century poets, T. S. Eliot, described Becket's death in his stark play *Murder in the Cathedral.*

The tiny port of **Hastings** lies in Sussex, on the south coast, past the lovely orchards of Kent and bleak, flat Romney Marsh. Nearby, the Norman William the Conqueror defeated the Saxon King Harold in 1066. Also nearby is Hurstmonceux Castle, which dates from the 15th century and houses the Royal Greenwich Observatory.

Farther west are the **South Downs**, treeless hills that roll back from the coast. In the downs at Wilmington a strange figure—the Long Man—appears on the side of a hill. The Celts are supposed to have gouged it

The "stately pleasure dome" and towers of the Royal Pavilion, in Brighton.

out long ago. Some 230 feet (70 m.) high, with a staff in each hand, it may represent a god of journeys.

Just southeast in **Brighton**—one of England's largest seaside resorts—is an even stranger sight. Brighton became fashionable in the early 19th century—known as the Regency because the Prince of Wales acted as regent for his father, King George III, who was too ill to rule. In 1817, the Prince built himself a fanciful, Oriental pavilion in Brighton. A visit to "Prinny's" pavilion is a trip back to the days when Beau Brummell set men's styles, when England fought Napoleon, and when the "daring" European waltz first shocked the English.

Outside Brighton are the Devil's Dyke (a ravine) and the remains of a camp of the early Britons. From there the whole Weald—enclosed by the Downs—can be seen. (*Weald,* or *wold,* is an Anglo-Saxon word meaning "forest.")

Chichester, about 30 miles (48 km.) west of Brighton, is one of the oldest and most attractive English cathedral towns. Called Regnum by the Romans, it was renamed Cissaceaster by the Saxons. Its cathedral, begun in the 12th century, has a graceful, harmonious combination of architectural styles. Since 1963, the Chichester Festival has combined leading actors and fine plays (from Shakespeare to such contemporaries as Harold Pinter) in productions that delight visitors.

In Hampshire, to the southwest, are the great shipping centers of **Portsmouth** and **Southampton**. Admirably sheltered by the Isle of Wight, the two harbors also have double tides, which prolong high water.

Southampton is England's biggest passenger port, and many great transatlantic liners and cargo ships dock there. In the Royal Dockyards at Portsmouth, England's biggest naval base, is the *Victory*—Admiral Horatio Nelson's flagship in the battle of Trafalgar (1805), which turned the tide against Napoleon. From the *Victory* it is a short walk to the tiny house where Charles Dickens was born in 1812. A museum today, it contains first editions of such novels as *David Copperfield* and *Oliver Twist* —often considered the most vivid pictures of life in 19th-century England.

To the west, past Bournemouth, is **Dorset**. In the 1870's Thomas Hardy called the county where he was born Wessex and made it the setting for such brooding novels as *The Return of the Native*.

Southwest of Dorset are the **Channel Islands**—the largest are Jersey, Guernsey, Alderney, and Sark—known around the world for the cattle bred there. The islands, once part of the medieval Duchy of Normandy, have been united with England since 1066. Their laws are based partly on medieval Norman laws, and the islanders still use some old Norman words (as well as English and French). Actually closer to France than to England, the islands were occupied by German troops in World War II.

The West Country

In the valleys of Devon, to the west, there are unspoiled villages, dreamlike in the spring when the fruit orchards around them are in bloom. On the coast there are tiny fishing villages, some with streets so steep they threaten to pitch everything on them on a headlong slide into the sea. **Exeter** and the port of Plymouth are the only large cities in Devon. Located on the Exe River, Exeter has been inhabited since Roman times, and its ancient walls can still be seen. Its Guildhall has a sword given by King Edward IV during the War of the Roses—the 15th-century struggle between the houses of York and Lancaster for the English throne. Exeter's cathedral was heavily bombed during World War II, but it has been restored.

According to legend, these ruins in Cornwall may have been King Arthur's castle.

Southwest of Exeter is **Dartmoor**, a vast plateau, where masses of granite form outcrops called tors. Clear streams race through the moor, pausing now and then in quiet pools where wily trout lurk.

In coastal resorts such as Paignton and Torquay palm trees flourish in the mild climate. **Plymouth**, in the southwest, is another major port. It was the starting point for many of the expeditions that made England a world power in the time of Elizabeth I. Sea captains like Sir John Hawkins and Martin Frobisher brought England its first empire, and Sir Francis Drake led English ships in the destruction of the Spanish Armada in 1588. Three decades later the *Mayflower* set sail from Plymouth on its great venture to the New World.

Cornwall once had busy ports, too, but today they are all peaceful fishing villages or resorts. The only industry is the mining of kaolin clay around St. Austell, where the great white heaps of waste make a moon-like landscape. Cornwall is rich in ancient remains and folklore. At Helston a winding trail of people still dance up and down the steep streets and in and out of the houses in the annual Furry Dance (or Floral Dance), a relic of pagan times. On the north coast is Padstow, famous for its own pagan rite, when flower-decked young people follow the prancing Hobby Horse through the town on May 1.

On the breezy downs of the peninsula called the Lizard the heather blooms, and among its cliffs are secluded coves that once made excellent pirate hideouts. In 1879, William Gilbert and Arthur Sullivan immortalized the area in *The Pirates of Penzance,* one of their operettas popular to this day. On the high moors inland stand the giant dish aerials of the satellite-tracking station Goonhilly Downs, and only 50 miles (80 km.) away is the ruined castle at Tintagel, thought to have been King Arthur's. Many Arthurian legends are associated with Cornwall and were handed down in Cornish, a Celtic language now long extinct.

About 120 miles (192 km.) to the northeast is the port of **Bristol**. In 1497 one of John Cabot's voyages of discovery started there; and in 1838 the *Great Western,* an early transatlantic steamship, was launched at its docks. Today Bristol is a shipbuilding center, and its other industries include candy making, aircraft manufacture, and flour milling. It has a university and is the home of the Bristol Old Vic, a fine theater group.

From the South to the Midlands

Bath lies some 10 miles (16 km.) southeast. The town takes its name from the baths built in the 1st century A.D., when the Romans discovered its mineral springs. One of England's best preserved examples of Roman architecture, the baths draw many visitors. But many also come to see 18th- and 19th-century Bath—the graceful Royal Crescent or small, shop-lined Pulteney Bridge. In the Grand Pump Room and Assembly Rooms, it is easy to imagine the characters of Jane Austen's novels, such as *Pride and Prejudice* or *Persuasion,* alive again. Jane Austen was only one of the well-known people who lived and worked in Bath. In the 18th century, statesmen Edmund Burke and William Pitt lived there. So did Samuel Johnson—author of one of the best-known English dictionaries—and his biographer James Boswell; and Thomas Gainsborough, one of England's greatest portrait painters. Some years later Lord Byron, a leading Romantic poet, shocked the Assembly ladies with his unconventional behavior.

Limestone cottages are typical of many villages in the Cotswold Hills.

On Salisbury Plain in Wiltshire, southeast of Bath, stands **Stonehenge**. This great ring of towering stones is thought to have been a place of worship or an astronomical clock for the ancient Britons who built it. But whatever Stonehenge's purpose, scholars still do not know how the giant stones—some as high as 21 feet (6 m.)—were brought there, thousands of years ago. The city of **Salisbury** itself includes one of England's loveliest cathedrals—a perfect example of English Gothic architecture, with the tallest spire in the country.

Near **Reading**, in Berkshire some 50 miles (80 km.) to the northeast, John Galsworthy set part of his *Forsyte Saga,* a multi-volume story of a late 19th- and early 20th-century English family. The Forsytes became so real to their readers that a leading English newspaper reported the death of a principal character in its headlines.

Galsworthy was an Oxford graduate, as were many other English writers and statesmen. **Oxford** is located on the edge of the Cotswold Hills, the most truly inland part of England. A visit to Magdalen (pronounced "maudlin") or All Souls colleges, or to the Bodleian Library, is like stepping into a special world "through the looking-glass." (In 1872 Charles L. Dodgson, an Oxford mathematics teacher who used the pen name Lewis Carroll, coined that phrase in his *Alice's Adventures in Wonderland.*)

Although both of England's great universities date from the 12th century, **Cambridge** is slightly younger. In a lovely setting on the Cam River in east central England, Cambridge, too, is a group of colleges. The most famous are King's College, with its beautiful chapel; and Trinity, known now as the college attended by Prince Charles—one of the first members of the British royal family to have a regular university education. John Milton, one of England's greatest poets and author of *Paradise Lost,* studied in the 17th century at Christ's College. Cambridge takes pride in its Cavendish Laboratory of Experimental Physics, where scientists like J. J. Thom-

Punts move lazily down the Cam—part of university life at Cambridge.

son and Ernest Rutherford did much of the early work in atomic theory. A favorite pastime that visitors can share with students is punting on the Cam. Relaxing in a punt (a flat-bottomed boat moved along by a pole) is a peaceful way to spend a summer afternoon.

East of Cambridge, on the North Sea coast, is the tiny fishing village of **Aldeburgh**. The town hosts an annual musical event—the Aldeburgh Festival—founded in 1948 by Benjamin Britten. Britten, whose works include *The Young Person's Guide to the Orchestra,* is England's leading contemporary composer. He represents a tradition that goes back many years, to such 16th- and 17th-century composers as Thomas Tallis, William Byrd, and Henry Purcell, and that also includes such 19th- and 20th-century figures of English music as Edward Elgar and Ralph Vaughan Williams.

North of Aldeburgh are the **Broads**—the flat, shallow lakes of Norfolk. Yachts, cabin cruisers, and other craft ply their waters, as thousands vacation here in summer. Northwest of the Broads, the swampy Fens curve around a wide bay called The Wash. The Romans started to drain the Fens, but not until the 17th century, with Dutch help, was any land successfully reclaimed. Today this rich agricultural region, like the Netherlands it so much resembles, even produces tulip bulbs.

Some 30 miles (48 km.) northwest of the Fens is the town of **Lincoln**. Its cathedral was founded in the 11th century, and much of the town also dates from the Norman period. In the cathedral is one of the four original drafts of Magna Carta.

The North and the Midlands

In spite of the industrial concentration of the North and the Midlands, they too abound with historical and literary associations, as well as surprising areas of natural beauty.

Nottingham, on the Trent River, is an important engineering and textile center, which also manufactures railroad and electrical equipment. The city has a fine university and an excellent art gallery, housed in a castle first built in Norman times.

Nottingham was the military headquarters for two kings who later lost their thrones—Richard III during the War of the Roses and Charles I during the Civil War. But Nottingham is best-known for its legendary outlaw Robin Hood, who escaped to nearby Sherwood Forest with his merry men, outwitting his archenemy the Sheriff of Nottingham.

To the west lies the smaller city of **Derby**. Its industries include textiles, leather goods, and the delicate Crown Derby chinaware. It is also the home of the nationalized Rolls Royce Company, which manufactures not only cars that are a worldwide symbol of elegance and fine engineering, but also jet aircraft engines. In the 19th century, George Eliot (Marian Evans), author of the popular novels *Silas Marner* and *The Mill on the Floss,* lived in Derby; and in the 20th, D. H. Lawrence, whose best-known novel is *Sons and Lovers,* decried what industrialization had done to the land and to the men of the area.

North of Derby is **Sheffield**, a steel-making center since the 14th century. Today, most of its population works in Sheffield's countless foundries, mills, and machine shops. Sheffield products, from needles and scissors to rails and girders, are well-known and are found all over the world.

Leeds lies some 30 miles (48 kilometers) to the north, in central Yorkshire. Its industries include woolen milling and the production of clothing and heavy machinery. Leeds is near the tiny village of Haworth, where, in the early 19th century, Charlotte and Emily Brontë wrote their romantic novels *Jane Eyre* and *Wuthering Heights.*

On the Ouse River to the northwest is **York**, a smaller manufacturing city. The Romans, who occupied the city for some 300 years, called it Eboracum and made it a military center. From the city walls, there is a fine view of the Guildhall, the many churches, and the narrow, winding streets of medieval times. Its great cathedral, or York Minster, was begun in the 11th century and is second only to Canterbury in importance. York Castle was the home of the dukes of York, including Richard III before he took the throne.

The port that serves most of the industrial northeast—taking in vital iron ore and other raw materials and shipping out steel, textiles, and machinery—is **Hull**, near the mouth of the Humber. Even farther north is **Newcastle-upon-Tyne**, a shipbuilding and manufacturing center. But it is principally known as a coal-shipping port, and the expression "carrying coals to Newcastle"—which means doing something useless—has been part of the English language since the 16th century.

In the Scottish border country to the west are the high fells that mark the northern end of the Pennines. There, too, is all that remains of **Hadrian's Wall**, planned by the Roman emperor in the 2nd century A.D. to keep out northern barbarian tribes. The wall cut clear across England, some 75 miles (121 kilometers) from the estuary of the Tyne on the east to the Solway Firth on the west.

Down the coast from the Solway, past Blackpool, a popular resort, is **Liverpool**, on the Mersey River. England's second largest port has ultra-modern facilities to handle the goods that move through its docks—

Hadrian's Wall once marked the northern frontier of Roman Britain.

The beach at Blackpool is a favorite vacation spot in northern England.

textiles and heavy machinery from the northwest and the Midlands, as well as flour and other products made in Liverpool itself. It is also England's cotton-importing center. In the 1960's this city, whose inhabitants are called Liverpudlians, gained new fame—as the home of the internationally acclaimed rock group, the Beatles.

Inland is **Manchester**, which has been the center of the textile industry since the late 18th century, when James Hargreaves invented the spinning jenny, and Richard Arkwright used water to power the new machines. Manchester's mills now produce artificial silks and other synthetics and cotton and wool. The *Guardian*, widely considered one of England's finest newspapers, was founded there, and Manchester also takes pride in two of England's top football teams.

Some 35 miles (56 kilometers) south is the city of **Stoke-on-Trent**, comprising the "Five Towns" sometimes called the Potteries. In 1769 a master potter named Josiah Wedgwood built a factory nearby, and this was the foundation of Stoke's fame and industry. Wedgwood is only one of the well-known companies based in the city today, all turning out fine china prized around the world.

Birmingham, England's second largest city, lies to the southeast. In its 80-square-mile (207-square-kilometer) area this hub of heavy industry produces metals, machinery, cars, chemicals, soap, and hundreds of other goods. Birmingham has a leading repertory company, an important art gallery, and a fine municipal orchestra.

Coventry, near Birmingham, has been the center of the English bicycle and automobile industries since the 1870's. During World War II, its cathedral—one of the most beautiful in England—was largely destroyed in German air raids. A new cathedral, completed in 1962, draws many visitors today. One of the best-known English legends is associated with Coventry. It is said that an 11th-century countess named Godiva rode through the marketplace clad only in her long hair. Her husband had agreed to lower Coventry's taxes if no one looked at Godiva. When one citizen was unable to resist, he became the original "peeping Tom."

To the west, in the windswept hills and meadows of Shropshire, now renamed **Salop**, the gale still "plies the saplings double" as it did in the bittersweet poetry of A. E. Housman. And to the southwest, on the Avon River, is the small town of **Stratford**—birthplace of the writer whose works are England's principal gift to world literature. Three of William Shakespeare's greatest plays, *Hamlet, King Lear,* and *The Tempest,* were probably written in London. But scholars believe that the life he knew in 16th-century Stratford colors all Shakespeare's plays, giving them the essential humanity that appeals to people of all times and nationalities.

Visitors to Stratford can tour the houses where Shakespeare was supposedly born and died, the church where he is buried, and the cottage associated with his wife. They can also attend performances of Shakespeare's plays in a memorial theater. The theater was opened in 1932, over three centuries after those plays first delighted the English people.

WAY OF LIFE

England is one of the most densely populated regions in the world. England is crowded, too, with millions of cars and all the paraphernalia of modern industry—power stations, pylons, and pipelines.

This cottage in Stratford was the birthplace of William Shakespeare.

Yet, even in this hectic world of automation, the English have managed to preserve many traditions born in more graceful times long past. Some observers believe that so long as they cling to their traditions "there'll always be an England."

Education

One of the most important factors in shaping a society is education. Under the education acts of 1902, 1918, 1921, and 1944, England has a free, compulsory school system. Every child must attend school from the age of 5 to 16. The dreaded "11-plus"—an examination taken at the age of 11 to determine whether a child goes to an academic "grammar school" (leading to a university) or to an ordinary secondary school—is disappearing with the introduction of the "comprehensive" secondary school in which children of all levels are educated together.

The Public Schools. But in education, too, England has its special traditions, summed up in the great old schools—Eton, Harrow, Winchester, and Rugby—and scores of others less well-known but cast in the same mold. If the school system is compared to a triangle, these are its apex, and to have a son become an Old Etonian or Wykehamist (Winchester alumnus) is a cherished goal for many English families.

Though private and expensive, they are still called "public schools," a reminder of the days when they were founded centuries ago (often by royal charter) to provide free education for boys from nearby towns. Many of their traditions seem to belong to those times as well. Perhaps

An Eton tradition—boys still wear these distinctive morning coats to classes.

the best-known description is in *Tom Brown's Schooldays* (1857). At 19th-century Rugby, there was "fagging," by which younger boys did chores and errands for older ones, and there were canings and often brutal beatings for infractions of the rules. (Of course, there were also cricket and football—one variation of which is named for Rugby.) With modifications, some of these practices continue today, and it is easy to see why many Englishmen describe their school days with a sort of horrified nostalgia. George Orwell, author of *1984* and *Animal Farm* wrote, "Indeed, I doubt whether classical education ever has been or can be successfully carried on without corporal punishment." Whether it can or not, it is a system that still produces many of the students at English universities.

The Universities. Until 1836 there were only two universities in England. Today there are more than 40, most of them offering higher education as good as or better than that available at Oxford and Cambridge. Nevertheless, many English students still hope to go to the two ancient schools, known familiarly as Oxbridge. (Some of the other universities are called Redbrick, for their once prevalent architecture.)

University admission is by examination, and scholarships are widely available. Most 3- or 4-year courses lead to a bachelor's degree, either general or honors (specialized). Students attend lectures, seminars, and, especially at Oxford and Cambridge, tutorials. These are private meetings with dons or supervisors to discuss the student's work. The universities are co-educational, but not until 1920 and 1948 did women become full members of Oxford and Cambridge.

Together with the public schools, Oxford and Cambridge are often accused of maintaining a rigid class structure in England, one divided into those at the top—the Establishment—and the rest. It is true that members of the government as well as leaders in business and the arts still tend to be graduates of these schools. But as educational opportunities are extended, class lines are being blurred.

Sports

As an old man, the Duke of Wellington—the victor of Waterloo—is supposed to have said that the great battle in which Napoleon was finally defeated "was won on the playing fields of Eton." Whether the story is true or not, it is symbolic, for it underlines the meaning of sports in English life.

Not only in the public schools, where "being good at games" is still important, but everywhere in England, sports matter. Cricket is England's national game, and many of the little boys who practice daily in the parks dream of growing up to play in county cricket or in the Test Matches, the "world series" of cricket. Football (rugby or soccer) also involves thousands, from local teams to great professionals who are idolized heroes to those who attend the games or follow them on radio and television.

Polo, which came to England from India, has many fans, and Prince Philip, the Duke of Edinburgh, is only one of a growing number of players. Horse racing (with legalized off-track betting) is a leading spectator sport. Many Englishmen ride, and in spite of the increasing outcry against fox hunting, many still ride to hounds. (The sport was scornfully described by Oscar Wilde in 1893 as "the unspeakable in full pursuit of the uneatable.") Regular hunting, known in England as "shooting," is popular, too, and England's rivers and streams are a paradise for fishermen.

Pubs. For the active sportsman who has worked up a thirst, or for the less energetic who prefer a leisurely game of darts, the pub is still the most traditional form of relaxation. The word itself is a shortened

Cricketers play the game known around the world as England's national sport.

version of "public house," and country or city, elegant or plain, every Englishman has his favorite. It is usually a local place where he knows everyone and everyone knows him. Englishmen regard their pubs as unofficial clubs, and they often end the day there talking with friends over a drink. Pubs also offer the pleasant break called a pub lunch—including such dishes as crusty steak-and-kidney pie.

English Food

For many years, almost the only English dishes known beyond English shores were roast beef with Yorkshire pudding and fish and chips. Especially after World War II, when rationing continued, English food was often contemptuously dismissed—even by Englishmen—as consisting of overcooked vegetables, warm beer, and cold toast. Today, however, more and more visitors are discovering the huge variety of tempting fare English kitchens can produce.

Among these dishes, many named for the areas where they originated, are the Cornish pasty, flaky pastry with a meat filling; and Lancashire hot pot, a delicious lamb, oyster, and vegetable stew. English cheeses are as varied as English dialects—blue-veined Stilton, tangy Cheshire, and sharp Cheddar are only a few. English biscuits, marmalades, and fine beers and ales are prized everywhere.

The rich harvest of the seas graces English tables, too, from Dover sole, kippers and bloaters (smoked salted herring), and plaice (flounder) to shrimp, prawns, oysters, and lobsters. And game of all kinds is still a favorite ingredient in English cooking, especially grouse, pheasant, and partridge.

Cakes and desserts include Bath buns, bursting with candied fruit; trifle and fool, rich concoctions of cake, custard, fruit, and jam; and Devonshire's thick "clotted cream," especially good with ripe Devonshire or Kentish strawberries. But the most famous "sweet" (dessert) is still plum pudding, the crowning glory of Christmas dinner. After the meal, the pudding is brought in, described by Dickens as "blazing in . . . ignited brandy, . . . Christmas holly stuck into the top." The visitor who shares this treat with an English family might sigh, with Dickens, "Oh, a wonderful pudding!"

And, of course, there is tea—tea with breakfast; a morning tea break called elevenses; and afternoon tea (cake, cookies, bread, butter, and sometimes cold meats and salads). But, more than a drink or a meal, tea is a tradition. The idea of the Englishman, no matter what the crisis in which he finds himself, making time for his cup of tea, has amused and puzzled many a foreigner. It is a tradition even Englishmen no longer attempt to explain—it simply is.

Crown and People, Pomp and Circumstance

Though tradition is associated with all of England's institutions, it often seems odd that today this nation—among the most modern in Europe—still maintains its monarchy. But the visitor has only to attend a ceremony like Trooping the Colour to understand at once the emotional ties of the English for their royal family. The Queen is more than a figurehead (a position that could be filled by a president), she is a personal symbol of continuity with the past.

The pageantry, the peerage, and the strict rules of procedure are the forms, not the substance, of an older world. They conceal the flexibility of the English system of government—based on a few documents and on many unwritten laws that change with the times—that has developed over the centuries.

HISTORY

The story of man's occupation of England is a long one. Flint tools and weapons used by those who lived before the dawn of history have been found in many parts of the country.

When—after conquering most of Gaul (parts of present-day France, Germany, Belgium, the Netherlands, and Switzerland)—Julius Caesar's Roman legions invaded Britain in 54 B.C., the country was inhabited by Celtic tribes. The Celts practiced agriculture, worked bronze and iron, and traded—especially in Cornish tin—with places as far away as Greece. According to Caesar's *Gallic War,* in battle they stained themselves blue with woad dye to frighten their enemies. But Caesar soon had to turn his attention back to Gaul, and the legions were withdrawn.

In A.D. 43, under the Emperor Claudius, the Romans began the conquest of Britain in earnest. They took most of the island, even parts of Scotland. Unable to hold all of this territory, however, early in the 3rd century they retreated behind the wall built by the Emperor Hadrian some 85 years before.

The Roman way of life began to take root. The lowlands were soon dotted with luxurious villas, resorts such as Aquae Sulis (Bath), and fortified towns such as Regnum (Chichester) and Londinium (London). Most important, the Romans laid a network of roads that for centuries was the basis of the English road system.

The Germanic Invasions

But later Roman emperors had to recall troops, and by the 5th century, barbarians, especially three Germanic tribes—the Angles, the Saxons, and the Jutes—were swarming in. Settling at first in the southeast, the Anglo-Saxons used the rivers and Roman roads to penetrate ever deeper west and north. These invaders, too, overcame the Britons. But this time, those who were not killed or enslaved were pushed to outlying parts of the island—to the valleys of Cornwall and the mountains of Wales—where their ancient languages survived for many centuries, away from the mainstream of civilization.

Instead of seafarers, the Anglo-Saxons became farmers. They set up a social system based on a powerful chieftain, or king, under whom were lesser lords, down to peasants at the bottom of the scale. Over the years, seven kingdoms were established—Northumbria, Mercia, East Anglia, Kent, Sussex, Essex, and Wessex. By 596, when Augustine was sent from Rome to convert the Anglo-Saxons, the country was called Engla land—"land of the Angles"—the source of its modern name.

In spite of rivalries between kingdoms, 9th-century England united to meet an outside threat. Danish Vikings had been raiding coastal settlements for some years, and in 865 they invaded in force. King Alfred of Wessex led the resistance, but not until 878 were his armies able to push the Danes out of Wessex. In 886 Alfred and the Danish king, Guthrum, signed a treaty defining the limits of their power. Guthrum ruled the northeast (the Danelaw), and Alfred the southwest.

In an age when Latin was the language of learning and few besides priests and monks could read, Alfred had books translated into Anglo-Saxon and schools set up to teach reading. He had the laws codified. Also, through his efforts, many Danes accepted Christianity.

The kings who succeeded Alfred the Great won back the Danelaw, and the country prospered. But in the 11th century, after new Danish invasions, England became part of the Danish kingdom. The last Danish king of England died in 1042; and when his successor, Edward the Confessor (Alfred's descendant), died in 1066, the English throne came into dispute. Harold, a leading earl, was crowned king, but William, duke of Normandy in France—and Edward's distant relative—claimed he was the rightful heir. Shortly after William's army invaded England, the succession was decided at the battle of Hastings. Harold was killed, and William became king.

Norman and Medieval England

The Normans brought some new laws, customs, and most important, a new language to England. At first, French was spoken only at the royal court. Anglo-Saxon (Old English) was the language of the ignorant—and the conquered. But slowly, French came into more general usage, starting with words for important aspects of life such as law, food, war, and religion. Gradually, Anglo-Saxon and Norman French combined to produce the basis of modern English.

Most Saxon lands were given to Norman nobles; the people were heavily taxed. (The *Domesday Book*—England's first census—was drawn up to facilitate tax collection.) Norman control also included part of Ireland. Over the years William and his successors strengthened the monarchy.

But in the 12th and 13th centuries, royal power came into conflict, first with the Church and then with the nobles. The first struggle culminated in 1170 in the murder of Thomas à Becket, Archbishop of Canterbury. The second resulted in the document that became the foundation of the English Constitution.

Magna Carta. King Richard I, the Lion-Hearted, died in 1199. His brother King John tried to extend royal power and frequently placed himself above the law. A group of barons—supported by the Archbishop of Canterbury and powerful London merchants—drew up a charter of their rights as free Englishmen. The most important points laid the basis for trial by a jury of equals and stated that taxes could be levied only by "the Common Council" (consent) of the kingdom. The barons forced John to sign the Great Charter (Magna Carta, in Latin) at Runnymede, near London, in 1215. In succeeding centuries the principles of the Magna Carta gradually came to apply to all Englishmen.

By the mid-14th century, when Edward III involved England in the Hundred Years War, the Common Council had developed into a two-chamber parliament. (The word comes from the French *parler*, "to speak.") The barons were the upper house (not called the House of Lords until the 16th century) and the representatives of the people, or the Commons, the lower.

At this time England was undergoing great change. Trade with continental Europe expanded, particularly in wool. Cities grew rapidly, and merchants became wealthy. Powerful craft guilds, called ministries or "mysteries," regulated many aspects of members' lives. Though farm villages remained fairly isolated, England was becoming one nation.

The principal development in this process was the spread of English, specifically that spoken in London—the seat of wealth and power. English became official in courts, was used in schools, and, after Chaucer (a Londoner), in literature. William Caxton introduced printing into England in 1476, and by the 16th century, London English had become the language of the kingdom.

The War of the Roses and the Tudors

During the Hundred Years War, Richard II was forced to abdicate by his cousin Henry Bolingbroke. Bolingbroke—King Henry IV—and his son Henry V established the House of Lancaster as the royal family. But in the second half of the 15th century, the Duke of York also claimed the throne. The resulting civil war—called the War of the Roses because the Yorkist emblem was a white rose and the Lancastrian, a red one—was not settled until 1485. In that year Henry Tudor, a descendant of Edward III, killed King Richard III at Bosworth Field. He became Henry VII.

Under Henry VII, Parliament passed the Navigation Acts protecting English trade, and new shipping routes opened new markets for English goods. When Henry VIII became king in 1509, Tudor England was flourishing and the monarchy was strong. But Henry and his queen had no sons; and after the Pope refused Henry a divorce so he could remarry and perhaps have a male heir, the King used his power to break with the Church of Rome. Henry had Parliament pass acts abolishing papal power in England. Church property was confiscated. The King became the head of the Church of England, or the Anglican Church.

Although he married six times, Henry only had one son. After the boy-king Edward VI (the prince in Mark Twain's *The Prince and the Pauper*) died, Henry's daughter Mary—a Catholic—came to the throne. Under Mary and her husband, Philip II of Spain, Protestants were so harshly persecuted that the Queen was called "Bloody Mary." Opposition increased when she involved England in Spain's war with France. When Mary died in 1558, England had lost Calais, its only remaining continental possession; and at home, the people were ready for revolution.

The Elizabethan Age. Mary's half-sister Elizabeth, daughter of Henry's second wife Anne Boleyn, ruled England for 45 years. Under "Good Queen Bess" England returned to Protestantism, and, after defeating the Spanish Armada in 1588, entered a period of unparalleled prosperity. Men like Drake and Frobisher sailed on voyages of discovery. Trade increased, chartered companies were founded, and England began to acquire distant colonies. Wealth and security brought a flowering of the arts. This was the age of Shakespeare and his contemporaries Christopher Marlowe and Ben Jonson, of poet-adventurer Sir Walter Raleigh, and an age when men like Edmund Spenser, author of the *Faerie Queene*, could think of nothing more fitting than to dedicate their works to Elizabeth I.

The Stuarts and Civil War

In 1603 Elizabeth was succeeded by James VI of Scotland, who became James I of England. A scholarly king, he authorized a new translation of the Bible, the King James Version (1611), which had a lasting influence on English literary style. But the son of Elizabeth's rival, Mary Stuart, failed to understand his new kingdom. He ignored the Navy and shipping and spent extravagantly. Conflict arose between the King and Commons—by then an established part of government—over his constant requests for money.

And once again, there was religious strife. The Puritans—who believed in simple ritual—felt the people had too little say in controlling the Church. The King wanted to continue his influence by appointing bishops. Matters came to a head in the reign of James's son. For 11 years after 1629, Charles I called no parliament, obtaining money by other

"Mrs. Grace Dalrymple Elliott" (1778?) an oil painting by Thomas Gainsborough. Metropolitan Museum of Art, New York City.

means. Through his Archbishop of Canterbury, William Laud, he tried to suppress the Puritans.

Laud's harsh measures led to a Scottish rebellion in 1640, and the King had to call Parliament. Though he dissolved it after several weeks, he was soon forced to call it again. The Long Parliament (not dissolved until 1660) had tired of the King's sidestepping of the law. In 1642 Charles's supporters, including many Catholics, fought the first battle of the Civil War with Parliamentary forces led by Oliver Cromwell. Four years later Cromwell's Roundheads (they had short haircuts) defeated Charles's Cavaliers. In 1649 the King was executed by Parliamentary order, and traditional government was at an end. Cromwell ruled England as Lord Protector from 1653 until 1658. But dissatisfaction spread anew, and in 1660 a parliamentary proclamation called Charles's son to the throne, restoring the monarchy.

Charles II died in 1685, and his brother James—a Catholic—became king. When James tried to reconvert England to Catholicism, Parliament raised an army against him, with the help of William III of the Netherlands—a Protestant. In 1688 James was deposed and fled the country. William and his queen (James's Protestant daughter Mary) ruled England jointly until 1702.

In 1689 Parliament passed the Bill of Rights, which completed the process begun by Magna Carta. The bill defined royal power and made Parliament the real ruler of England. Also, by another act, religious toleration was extended to Protestants outside the Anglican Church.

18th-Century England

Many English political institutions—especially the party system, with the leader of the Parliamentary majority as prime minister—first developed in the 18th century. Then, too, English trade doubled and redoubled, and England went to war with France to protect its interests. Led by the great general John Churchill, Duke of Marlborough, England defeated France and gained new outposts—especially in the Mediterranean and North America. (Queen Anne authorized the building of Blenheim Palace, near Oxford, as a mark of the nation's gratitude to the Duke.) The chartered companies extended English holdings in India and Africa. And the Act of Union (1707), joining England and Scotland politically, created the United Kingdom of Great Britain.

Queen Anne died in 1714. None of her children survived her, so the German House of Hanover (descendants of James I) became the royal family. At the end of the century, though it had lost the American colonies, England was one of the strongest nations in Europe—and, thanks to its empire, one of the richest. But the monarchy feared the ideas of the French Revolution and the military might of Napoleon. In 1793 the two nations went to war.

Although the great admiral Horatio Nelson died in the battle of Trafalgar, off southern Spain (1805), the Navy did maintain its mastery of the seas. And the Army, led by the Duke of Wellington, was instrumental in Napoleon's final defeat at Waterloo, Belgium, in 1815.

The 19th Century—The Industrial Revolution and Imperialism

The French threat had been ended, but another revolution was sweeping England. Out of a series of 18th-century inventions—including

The High Street in Oxford, one of Europe's oldest university towns.

the steam engine, the spinning jenny, and the use of coal to smelt iron—a pattern was taking shape. Cheap power meant faster, cheaper production and the rise of the factory system. Communications improved. Roads and canals were modernized; then a railroad network spread across the land. Cities grew—especially in the North and Midlands.

There were other changes, too. The rate of enclosures—a system of fencing off former communal farmlands—was increasing, and small farmers could no longer compete. And many farm workers were displaced by machines that did 10 times the work in one tenth the time. Those who left the land crowded the cities. As the cities grew, so did slums and disease. Factory workers—including women and children—put in long hours, often in indescribably unhealthy conditions. For the jobless, there were the poorhouses and debtors' prisons—the dark side of Dickens' novels.

The Industrial Revolution drew a line between the old England and the new. Mine and factory owners formed the core of a middle class—one with money but little voice in government. Members of Parliament often stood for "rotten boroughs"—with few and occasionally no people—while thousands went unrepresented. And demands increased for legislation to help the workers. In 1832 the government passed the first Reform Bill, extending the vote and reforming the rotten boroughs. Inspection acts and other measures slowly improved social conditions. (By 1884, after two more Reform Acts, most Englishmen had the vote.)

After 1837, the 19th century was also the age of Queen Victoria and of her two great prime ministers Benjamin Disraeli and William Ewart Gladstone. Today the word "Victorian" often means an exaggerated sense of propriety and a stuffy, rigid morality. Many Victorians—especially members of the middle class—did exhibit these characteristics. But this was also a period of experimentation in many areas. It was the time of Joseph M. W. Turner, whose paintings captured the effects of light and air; and of Charles Darwin, whose book *On the Origin of Species by*

Means of Natural Selection (1859) revolutionized man's view of the natural world.

And it was the age of imperialism. With thriving industries and trade, attention turned as never before to empire building. England consolidated power in its old possessions and—in competition with continental nations—gained new ones. Instead of the East India Company, the British Government ruled India. Australia and New Zealand, colonized in the 18th century, flourished in the South Pacific. Colonies and areas of British influence were developed in the Middle East, Asia, and Africa. This era of general prosperity and peace was marred twice—in the Crimean War (1854), after Russian attempts to gain control of the Dardanelles outlet to the Mediterranean; and in the Boer War (1899), after conflict with the original Dutch settlers of South Africa. In 1875 England acquired the controlling shares in the Suez Canal, which became the lifeline of the empire because it shortened the route to India and the East.

Some Victorians regarded imperialism as a duty and a glorious crusade—ideals best expressed in the patriotic poetry of Rudyard Kipling. Although they carried the "white man's burden" of civilization around the world, the English colonialists adopted very little from their surroundings, and have been described as living "inside invisible stockades."

The 20th Century—Two World Wars and a Changing World

By 1910, when Edward VII was succeeded by George V, industrial and imperial expansion had reached a zenith. But problems remained—social inequality, the power of the House of Lords, and the Irish question.

A series of welfare acts during the period provided old-age pensions, unemployment compensation, and better wages and working conditions. Unions became a powerful political voice for the workers, and in 1900 the Labour Party was formed. The Education Act of 1902 gave England its first national educational system.

The Parliamentary problem was settled in 1911, by an act stating that money bills no longer required the Lords' consent, and that severely curbed their powers in other areas. But after a troubled 700-year association, marked by repression and bloody strife between predominantly Catholic Ireland and Protestant England, the Irish question was less easily resolved. In the 1850's, Irish agitation for independence reached a point at which it could no longer be ignored. Although it later gained the support of Prime Minister Gladstone, the Irish Home Rule Bill was not passed until 1914. In that year, however, all normal life in England was suspended, not to be resumed for almost 5 years.

World War I—"The Lamps are Going Out." In the early 20th century, military competition between the nations of Europe—especially between England and Germany—had grown intense. England was also part of the tangled skein of European alliances. In 1914, after the assassination of the Austrian archduke by Serbian nationalists, all of Europe went to war. But nothing in the proud military past had been preparation for years of trench warfare or for the efficient use of new weapons such as tanks and machine guns. England and its allies won the war, but when the 1918 armistice was signed, nearly 1,000,000 English and British Empire troops had been killed, and the economy was at a standstill.

Postwar recovery was slow and marked by labor troubles, including the General Strike of 1926, and by the worldwide Depression of the

1930s. After 1933 Germany, led by Adolf Hitler, again presented a threat to world peace.

World War II—"Blood, Toil, Tears, and Sweat." By 1939 it was clear that Britain's policy of appeasement—conceding to Hitler's demands in order to maintain peace—was a failure. Germany's invasion of Poland resulted in England and France going to war with Germany once more.

The fall of France in 1940 left England the lone European holdout against Nazi Germany's might. Hitler's Luftwaffe (air force) subjected English cities—especially London—to merciless bombing. But two factors, combined with English courage, enabled the country to survive the Battle of Britain. One was the Royal Air Force (RAF), which first regained mastery of the English skies and then went on to rain destruction on Germany. The other was one man, Prime Minister Winston Churchill, who seemed to sum up in himself everything essentially English—the tenacity, the national pride, even the sense of history.

England Today and Tomorrow

Of all the postwar changes, the greatest were in relation to the Empire and to England's position as a world power. A 1931 act of Parliament had established the Commonwealth of Nations—"united by a common allegiance to the Crown. . . ." Today many of England's former colonies are members of the Commonwealth.

The British accepted that they no longer dominated the map of the world. Their prime concern after the war was rebuilding at home. This was one reason for remaining outside the European Economic Community (EEC, or Common Market), established in 1958. (Later, however, England reversed this position and eventually received Common Market membership.) At home the first postwar election had given the Labour Party a majority. The Labour government nationalized the railroads, coal mines, gas, and electricity. A National Health Service, assuring medical care for all who need it, went into effect in 1948.

From the 1950s to the 1990s, the pace of change accelerated in the British Isles. For the first time in centuries, the British people began to question the role of royalty in society. The royal family, for the most part treated with respect in the early part of the 20th century, became the subject of persistent media fanfare. Bowing to growing public furor, Queen Elizabeth II agreed to pay taxes for the first time in the monarchy's history. The failed marriages of three of her children, Prince Charles (the heir apparent), Prince Andrew, and Princess Anne, were accompanied by sensational tabloid reports. The popularity of the royal family hit a modern low following the news that its most popular member, Diana, the Princess of Wales, had been killed in a Paris car accident on August 31, 1997. Many loyal British subjects began to view the monarchy as a remote and very expensive institution that had outlived its usefulness. Still, the majority support the royal family, seeing it as a thread that holds together the traditions that define the British character.

Author C. P. Snow wrote that the English have an "indulgent . . . affection" for their country. Another English writer once said of England that there is "something in it that persists," for it is "a family . . . [with] its private language and its common memories. . . ." It is that heritage of "memories" that will shape the country's future.

Reviewed by DAVID DE BOINVILLE, British Embassy, Washington, D.C.

London

London's landmarks are familiar to anyone who ever heard a nursery rhyme, sang songs, played games, read books, attended the movies or theater, or only watched television. Just recall in your mind's eye the Tower of London with its Beefeaters and ravens, Tower Bridge, St. Paul's Cathedral, Westminster Abbey, Piccadilly Circus, 10 Downing Street, the British Museum, Trafalgar Square, the Houses of Parliament and Big Ben, and Buckingham Palace. Conjure up the image of a London bobby or a double-decker London bus. And of course everyone has heard of Scotland Yard.

The capital of the United Kingdom and political hub of the Commonwealth, London is a focal point for much of the economic and political life of the Western world. It is also a magnet for many people whose only tie is an emotional one.

In these days when London has been discovered to be "swinging," it is well to recall that for centuries, London was a seat of power. London made the laws for an empire, judged its disputes, coined its money, received its tribute, trained its leaders and some of its followers, set its styles, and wrote and published its books. London was the world's banker and broker. London was the arbiter of fashion, virtue, and justice for much of the world.

In the realm of politics and finance, there can be no doubt that London's fortunes have declined during the 20th century. The British Empire has ceased to be. The Commonwealth ties are unraveling. The power of the pound sterling has been supplanted by that of the dollar, the yen, and the mark. And yet London remains a great and powerful city. It is still a vital influence, due to its political and cultural contributions, as well as its powerful history.

GOVERNMENT

Speaking of "London" can mean either the area called Greater London or the actual City. The City of London is the ancient heart of the capital. "The square mile" has about 4,500 permanent residents, and all the great banking houses are located there. The City's real importance is as the financial and commercial core of Britain and the Commonwealth of Nations. Half a million people work daily in the offices and exchanges located within the City. The western boundary between the City and Greater London is marked by the statue of a griffin, where the Strand and Fleet Street merge outside the Law Courts.

The City has its own lord mayor, selected each year from among the members of the ancient City of London livery companies, the descendants of the medieval guilds. This tradition dates to a charter granted by King John in 1215. The job is purely ceremonial, kicked off by a glittering inaugural parade, the Lord Mayor's Show, each November. Dressed in full regalia, the lord mayor rides in a splendid coach through the streets of his small domain. He also greets the queen whenever she wants to cross the boundary line into "his" City.

Greater London embraces the City and adjacent districts—the 33 metropolitan boroughs plus parts of the neighboring suburban "Home Counties." Greater London covers about 620 sq. mi. (1,600 sq. km.), extending some 12 to 16 mi. (19 to 26 km.) in every direction from Charing Cross, which is the accepted center of London. It has nearly 7 million inhabitants. Until 1986, the elected Greater London Council (GLC) coordinated regional planning and services. Local government details are now handled within the boroughs, each of which has its own mayor, council, and town hall.

London is also considering the idea of creating the post of an elected mayor who would have jurisdiction over the entire city. Unlike the lord mayor of the City, whose duties are only ceremonial, this person would be a powerful political figure with a mandate from the voters. An elected assembly with administrative powers is also being considered. Both questions are being put to the voters in referendum form in the year 2000.

Greater London is protected by the Metropolitan Police, or bobbies. Since 1829, when Prime Minister Robert Peel established the London police, they had remained unarmed. In 1994, however, some of the bobbies were permitted to carry guns in order to help them keep the peace throughout the sprawling city.

Navy-blue-uniformed and helmeted bobbies are a familiar part of the London scene.

THE LONDONERS

Greater Londoners may live in the City of Westminster, the Royal Borough of Kensington and Chelsea, in such famous districts as Hampstead, Holborn, Lambeth, Battersea, Southwark, Paddington, or even the City. But only a few Londoners can claim to be true "cockneys." That title is reserved for those who were born within the sound of Bow bells, the bells of Bow Church (St. Mary-le-Bow), in the City of London. Of course, this can be stretched a bit. It is said that on a clear, still night in summer the sound can carry for 4 miles (6 km.) around.

In the past the speech of the working-class cockney—especially his habit of dropping his *h*'s and adding them elsewhere—was looked down upon. *My Fair Lady,* the musical based on George Bernard Shaw's play *Pygmalion,* tells the story of a professor of linguistics who trained a cockney flower-seller to speak "properly" so she could pass for a lady. When she learned to pronounce "in Hertford, Hereford, and Hampshire, hurricanes hardly happen," she was well on her way. Today, however, to call a man a cockney is not to insult him.

Whether cockney or not, Londoners are a special breed. They

showed their mettle during World War II, sleeping in deep shelters in the Underground (subway), calmly digging friends and families out of bombed buildings. They can be rough and tough, and they have their own special humor and language. "Ta," they will say for "thanks." "Ducks" and "mate" are all-purpose words for addressing strangers or friends. They have infinite patience and line up in tidy queues (lines) for a bus, movie, or tickets to a cricket match.

Until recently, brightly garbed figures in foreign dress were just passing through, obviously visitors. They were students, businessmen, occasional rich sheikhs and rajahs, or honored guests of the government. But a goodly number of Indians, Pakistanis, Burmese, Malayans, Africans, West Indians, and Hong Kong Chinese accepted Britain's offers of British passports and citizenship. They are now Londoners, too.

Now, as always, London has its exquisitely turned-out males. (The words *fop, dandy,* and *beau* first came into widespread use in 18th-century London.) The slim, elegant men in their Savile Row suits still cut a fine figure, with their regimental ties, furled umbrellas, and hats pitched at just the right angle on their heads.

Today, however, these privileged customers of Savile Row tailors are no longer London's fashion trendsetters. Starting in the 1950s, young workingmen discovered fashion, too. They had money to spend, and they wanted something new and trendy to spend it on. Instead of sub-dued tailoring, they wanted bright colors, tight fit, and shock value in their clothing, and they wanted to be able to buy it "off the peg" (ready-made). Their demands for cutting-edge styles were responsible for the many colorful shops that began to crowd the areas around Carnaby Street and Chelsea in the 1960s.

Not to be outdone by the menfolk, London's young women also began to update their look. Lots of them were working, too, away from the watchful eyes of mothers and teachers. In the 1960s they pioneered the miniskirt and the even shorter micromini. More recently they took to raiding grandma's attic for odd bits of Victorian gear they could use.

HISTORY

London was not an important town before the Romans came. But with their usual eye for a communications center, the Romans chose it for a settlement and dubbed it Londinium.

No mention of it turns up in history until A.D. 61, about a century after Julius Caesar's legions first invaded Britain. In that year, according to the Roman historian Tacitus, Queen Boadicea (or Boudicca) of the Iceni, who came from the northeast, rose up against the Romans. She led her followers in sacking Londinium, described by Tacitus as a "busy emporium for trades," and slaughtered its inhabitants.

When the Romans reestablished their authority, they turned to city building. By A.D. 120, in the reign of Emperor Hadrian, London had become a walled city. Portions of that wall can still be seen in the City today.

The Roman legions abandoned London in the 5th century. Celts, Saxons, and Danes fought for it, and the city was partly destroyed. Little is known of London until the late 9th century, when it emerged in the control of the Saxon King Alfred.

After the Norman conquest of England was decided at the Battle of

Hastings (1066), the Saxon leaders of London declared the city's independence. William I, the Norman king and conqueror, had to bargain with the Londoners, and he finally granted them a charter. During William's reign the White Tower, the core of the Tower of London complex, was built.

In the 12th and 13th centuries, London prospered under the Norman and Plantagenet kings. In the last decade of the 12th century, during the reign of Richard I, and in the first part of the 13th century, under King John, London got some of the basic forms of government it still has today.

During the medieval period there was much building: the first St. Paul's Cathedral; Westminster Abbey, future burial place of kings, scientists, and poets; and the four Inns of Court—Lincoln's and Gray's inns, and the Middle and Inner temples—where most of England's lawyers and jurists still learn their profession today.

London thrived in the 16th century, becoming a rich center of trade. Henry VIII, rebelling against the Roman Catholic Church, destroyed or converted many religious buildings. He also took Hampton Court, the great palace of Cardinal Wolsey, who had fallen from power.

London displayed a rich culture and great power under the Tudor Queen Elizabeth I in the 16th century. It was the time of sea-captain Sir Francis Drake and of poet-adventurer Sir Walter Raleigh. It was the time of philosopher Francis Bacon, of poet-playwright Christopher Marlowe, and especially of William Shakespeare and his Globe Theatre on the Thames.

Then in the 17th century came the Stuarts, the beheading of a king, the Puritan Revolution, Oliver Cromwell, civil war, and finally the Restoration in 1660. London survived, prospered, and grew. Then disaster struck. First came the Great Plague of 1665, which took 75,000 lives. In September, 1666, the Great Fire, which lasted some 5 days, leveled most of the City, including St. Paul's.

Soon a new London rose from the ashes. Though his total plan for rebuilding the city was never carried out, the great architect Sir Christopher Wren left his very substantial mark. The spires of 52 Wren churches dotted the London skyline, but his masterpiece, the new baroque St. Paul's Cathedral atop Ludgate Hill, dominated it.

Even now many church spires stand out in London's skyline but postwar high-rise hotels and office buildings really dominate the scene. What is so remarkable about London is that although its skyline changed so little in 250 years, it has completely altered in the last 20.

The German bombers and guided rockets of World War II destroyed or did irreparable damage to scores of landmarks, including a number of Wren's buildings. The fire raids of December, 1940, London's second great fire, were especially disastrous. St. Paul's was a favorite target, but the cathedral was saved by the valiant efforts of its volunteer fire brigades, led by its Dean. The incendiary bombs were immediately removed and extinguished—some by hand—and the cathedral survived almost intact.

When the smoke cleared, St. Paul's stood alone in a sea of rubble. For the first time in years the full splendor of the great building was visible. But St. Paul's splendid isolation was not to last for long, for office buildings soon began to encroach.

THE PANORAMA OF LONDON

To get an idea of London's sprawling immensity an aerial view is best, but the panorama may also be savored at lower altitudes. A boat ride on the Thames through the Port of London offers the excitement of the activity on the riverbanks. Anchored along the route to Greenwich, the spot that is accepted around the world as 0 degrees longitude, are ships flying the flags of all nations. A traveler may also board a London bus and clamber to the top deck for spectacular bird's eye views. However, the most intimate way of all to see London is to walk.

The Houses

From above, London's houses seem remarkably alike, with little backyard gardens and rooftops cluttered with TV antennas and chimney pots—the little pots that jut up from the chimney of nearly every house. (Those coal "fires" helped to produce London's lethal fogs. When the sea fog met the smoke they combined in a horror peculiar to London— the pea-souper. But that is now a thing of the past, thanks to London's massive smoke-abatement program.)

Of course, all London houses are not alike. One can still see lovely squares, terraces, rows, and crescents. Near Regent's Park one can admire the graceful lines of Regency architecture. The eye can delight in the beauty of a few still unspoiled Bloomsbury squares; and even when the houses are not especially beautiful or architecturally pure, they have a certain symmetry, and all seem to fit together.

Many Londoners live in row houses. Nearly 45 percent of all London dwellings are owner occupied.

In London's Trafalgar Square, a statue of British naval hero Horatio Nelson stands atop the tall column.

The Streets

Nowhere in London is there one great, broad unifying avenue as so many large cities have. The city just grew unplanned. There are, of course, some longish thoroughfares; for example, Oxford Street or the beautiful sweep of Regent Street, which dominate their areas.

The wide and splendid Mall, running straight from Admiralty Arch to Buckingham Palace is, in fact, London's one triumphal way. The Queen rides along it on horseback each June on her way to the ceremony of Trooping the Colour, which marks her official birthday. (It is celebrated in June instead of on her actual birthday so that the ceremony and the official garden parties are less apt to be rained on.)

London is a traffic planner's nightmare because of its narrow, winding streets. They often funnel into a central area, and once into the funnel there is no escape. Piccadilly Circus, Trafalgar Square, Hyde Park Corner, and Oxford Circus are such funnels. At the rush hour, traffic creeps along, in and out of the little side streets in routes devised to ease the jams. In the heart of the City, the traffic often stalls for long periods at the Cornhill (site of a corn market centuries ago), as the eight main roads that lead into it disgorge cars, buses, and lorries (trucks).

The Parks

Throughout London there are many green areas—parks, quiet squares, and public and private gardens—the "lungs of London" as the 18th-century English statesman William Pitt, Earl of Chatham, called them.

In the heart of London are the great royal parks. There is St. James's Park with its pelicans, ducklings, and fine views of Buckingham Palace and the government buildings of Whitehall. Then across the Mall is Green Park, extending along Piccadilly to Hyde Park Corner. Together, giant Hyde Park and neighboring Kensington Gardens form a square-mile green space. There Londoners can ride horseback, sun themselves, play cricket, and boat or swim in the artificial lake, the Serpentine.

At the northeast corner of Hyde Park, by the Marble Arch, is the famous Speaker's Corner, where anyone with a flag, a stand, a gripe, or an ideology can get up and make a speech. Heckling from listeners is often fierce, but the watchful bobbies rarely do more than suggest that the crowds "move along."

To the north is yet another large park, Regent's, known for its rose gardens, outdoor Shakespeare theater, and the London Zoo. Not far away is Lord's Cricket Ground, where the crowds reward the players with a faint ripple of applause and a murmured "well played" when the action has been especially spirited.

Still farther north, on one of London's highest hills, is Hampstead Heath. In good weather, it is possible to see all of London stretching off into the distance below. The heath is not a formal park; instead, it has open meadows and gnarled old trees, almost as it did in the 17th and 18th centuries, when it was a favorite hiding place for highwaymen.

The River

A fact that dominates all else in London's story is that it is one of the world's greatest ports. It straddles the Thames some 50 miles (80 km.) upstream from the river's mouth in the North Sea.

The Thames used to be London's highway. Kings and queens were rowed in their barges in stately progress from one palace to another. Heroes returning from battles and triumphs on foreign shores were greeted on it. The famous dead were rowed on it to their lying-in-state. Prime Minister Winston Churchill, who planned his own funeral with his usual superb sense of history, asked to be borne on the Thames as his London farewell after his state funeral at St. Paul's.

At London, the Thames is a tidal river. Seagoing ships come up as far as the Pool, the wide basin between Tower and London bridges. Smaller vessels, barges, and private craft navigate most of its 200-mile (320 km.) length.

The Port of London Authority supervises some 70 miles (110 km.)

The Houses of Parliament, officially known as Westminster Palace, stretch for 950 feet along the Thames.

of the Thames' length. But the true Port of London, through which so much of Britain's trade flows, stretches along the river from Woolwich to London Bridge. The Docklands, formerly a rather run-down but nonetheless fascinating area, is now being renovated into a bustling financial district. The center of this development project, begun in the mid-1980s, is Canary Wharf, a towering complex of offices, shops, and restaurants. A new rail line has also been built.

Fifteen bridges now cross the Thames in London. Westminster, Tower, Waterloo, and Kew bridges have each had their share of history, but first and foremost is London Bridge. Until 1750 it was the only one across the Thames in London. In 1831 a solid, five-arched version was built. In 1968 that edition of the often rebuilt bridge was shipped, stone by stone, to an American corporation that set up the bridge over the Little Thames River in Arizona. A new, third, London Bridge, made of prestressed concrete, had been opened to traffic by 1972.

LONDON LIFE

"Sir, when a man is tired of London, he is tired of life," the 18th-century English writer Samuel Johnson once said to a friend, "for there is in London all that life can afford." It is still true today. There is something in London for everyone.

Sports. Londoners are avid sports fans and troop in the tens of thousands not only to Lord's, but to watch football (soccer) at Wembley, tennis at Wimbledon, horse racing at Epsom (the Derby) and Ascot (the Gold Cup), collegiate rowing on the Thames (Henley), and hundreds of other events at less-hallowed sites.

Arts. The world-renowned Royal Ballet and Royal Opera call the stage of London's Covent Garden home. Seats are booked long in advance, save a few up in the "gods" (the topmost balcony), sold at the last minute. Music lovers have their choice of concerts, from madrigals to "pop," in the cavernous and elderly Albert Hall or the sleek, new Festival Hall with its superb acoustics.

To many minds, it is the theater lover who is best served in London. Performances are exciting, excellent, and most important, accessible. Tickets are reasonably priced and readily available in the West End theater district (roughly in an arc around Piccadilly Circus) for those who still like to see good acting and hear words well-spoken.

Museums and Historic Sites. London has several great museums. The National Gallery, with its classical paintings; the Victoria and Albert Museum with its fascinating miscellany; the Tate Gallery with more recent art; and dozens of other collections—public and private—make London a mecca for art lovers. Even the effigies of famous people and the historic scenes depicted in Madame Tussaud's Wax Museum are art —though of a special sort.

But most fascinating of all of London's museums is the fabulous British Museum. The museum, which includes in its vast treasure trove the Elgin marbles (statues and friezes from the Parthenon in Athens, Greece), the Rosetta stone, and two copies of the Magna Carta, is also the home of one of the world's greatest libraries. Its treasures are priceless and abundant. Beneath the great, domed Reading Room, where entry is limited to true scholars, 5,000,000 books are shelved in a labyrinth of underground passages; the catalogue alone occupies 263 huge volumes. But London's historic sites are museums in themselves—everything about them is aged and worth seeing. Its business establishments often have historic archives and fascinating souvenirs. (Some examples are Lock's and Lobb's, the famous hatters and bootmakers, and Lloyds, the great insurance center in the City.)

The Tower of London, in itself a massive souvenir of the past, also houses the priceless, dazzling crown jewels and a splendid collection of armor. Tourists troop each day where once traitors and enemies of the Crown languished before execution.

Westminster Abbey, England's most sacred shrine, is the very heart of royal London and the place of coronation of England's monarchs. It also houses many of their tombs, as well as those of some of England's great writers, artists, and scientists. The neo-Gothic, 19th-century Houses of Parliament adjoin the remains of the Palace of Westminster, once a home of English kings.

St. Paul's Cathedral, too, is a kind of museum. It contains the tombs of the 17th-century poet John Donne, who was also the cathedral's dean, and of Sir Christopher Wren, who designed it. (On his tomb is the Latin inscription *Lector, si monumentum requiris, circumspice*—"Reader, if you seek his monument, look around you.") Among the other great Englishmen buried in the crypt of St. Paul's are John of Gaunt, the 14th-century head of the House of Lancaster; the 17th-century painter Sir Anthony Van Dyck; and the two great military leaders of England's war against Napoleon—Lord Nelson and the Duke of Wellington.

This then, is a glimpse of London. It may not be quite as Disraeli once described it: "A city of cities, an aggregation of humanity, that probably has never been equaled in any period of the history of the world, ancient or modern," but it has come very close.

JOSEPH C. HARSCH, C.B.E. (Hon.), Chief editorial writer, *Christian Science Monitor*
JUDITH FRIEDBERG, Author and editorial consultant

The tiny village of Maentwrog, in northwest Wales.

WALES

Wales is one of the countries that make up the United Kingdom of Great Britain and Northern Ireland, but it is far different from the others in background and language. The ancient Welsh language, or Cymraeg, is related to the Celtic once spoken in much of northern Europe and throughout the British Isles. By about A.D. 500, two branches of Celtic were spoken in Britain—Gaelic was the language in Scotland, Ireland, and the Isle of Man, while Brythonic was the language spoken in Cornwall and Wales.

The Welsh, thus, are an ancient people—much older than the English—and their national emblems date back to the beginning of recorded history. The flag and crest of Wales both show a red dragon, and its two national mottos are *Ddraig goch ddyry cychwyn* ("The red dragon leads the way") and *Cymru am byth* ("Wales forever"). More than 600 years ago, Edward the Black Prince (because he wore black armor) took three ostrich feathers from the helmet of Bohemia's dying king and made them his emblem, with the motto *Ich dien,* or "I serve." At the investiture of Charles as Prince of Wales in 1969, *Ich dien* and "Wales forever" were combined as "I serve Wales forever." The Welsh people felt this to be a wonderful omen for a future they hoped would find them united and prosperous.

THE LAND

Geographically, Wales is a broad peninsula jutting out of the English Midlands, with an irregular coastline, indented by numerous bays, the largest of which is Cardigan Bay. The Welsh terrain is dominated by mountain ranges severed by swift-flowing rivers. Its backbone is the Cambrian Mountains, rolling uplands with an average elevation of about 1,500 feet (460 meters) that run down the middle of the country in a north-south direction. To the southeast, somewhat higher and more rugged, are the Brecon Beacons. But the highest altitudes are in the northwest, where the land rises in the Snowdon massif, culminating in Mt. Snowdon, the highest point in Wales.

At the northwestern tip, beyond Snowdon, the Lleyn Peninsula points a finger into the Irish Sea. Across the Menai Strait lies Anglesey, a large island often called Mona, Mother of Wales, because there, nearly 2,000 years ago, Druids taught Celtic youth to become priests, judges, and teachers.

Wales enjoys a moderate climate, generally mild and moist. Rainfall varies greatly, depending on the altitude. While the coastal fringes receive 30–35 inches (76–89 centimeters) of precipitation annually, mountain areas may get more than 100 inches (254 centimeters) of rain and snow annually.

Rivers. The principal river is the Dee, which rises in Bala Lake in the north and flows generally northeast and north into the Irish Sea. The river forms part of the English-Welsh boundary. Considerably larger, however, is the Severn, which rises in east-central Wales, but it runs most of its course through England. The "sylvan Wye" separates Wales from England in its lower course.

Resources. Coal is the country's most valuable resource. The richest deposits are located in the southernmost part of the country and slightly less rich ones are in the northeast. Slate and limestone are important quarry minerals. There are also scattered ores containing copper, gold, lead, manganese, uranium, and zinc. Waterpower is a major resource, providing electricity both to Wales and England.

THE PEOPLE

The people who are the present-day Welsh are descendants of the Brythonic invaders of antiquity. But there has been a good deal of admixture from other ethnic groups. Romans, Scots (the so-called Sons of Cunedda), Saxons, Scandinavians, and Normans all added their strains to the original stock. Much later, the Industrial Revolution brought a flood of other people to the coal fields, injecting further diversity. Through all that, however, the Welsh have retained a remarkable degree of their distinctiveness.

Language. Today, about 25 percent of the population can speak Welsh, although most of them speak English as well. Both are official languages. Welsh, a Celtic tongue, is one of the most musical languages in the world, but it is also one of the most complex. It abounds in y's and double l's and d's to the endless confusion of outsiders. Non-Welsh people rarely succeed in spelling or pronouncing the language correctly. A tiny village blessed with the longest place-name in the world always makes an amusing visit for tourists—Llanfairpwllgwyngyllgogerychwyrndrobwllllandysiliogogogoch—meaning "Church of Saint Mary in a hollow of white hazel, near a rapid whirlpool, and Saint Tysilio's Church of the red cave."

Religion. Wales was one of the first countries to be converted to Christianity, beginning about the 2nd century A.D. Near the mouth of the Alun River stands a cathedral dedicated to St. David—Dewi Sant in Welsh—the patron saint of Wales. On St. David's Day (March 1), their national holiday, Welsh men wear the leek and Welsh women the daffodil.

Today most of the Welsh are Protestants, divided mainly between the Calvinistic Methodist church, called the Presbyterian Church of Wales, and the Church in Wales, as the Anglican church has been called since 1920.

Education. The school system of Wales is integrated with that of England, but in predominantly Welsh-speaking areas, the language of instruction is Welsh rather than English. There are also schools with bilingual instruction in those parts that are primarily English-speaking. Higher education is offered in the University of Wales, which has constituent colleges in Aberystwyth, Bangor, Cardiff, Lampeter, and Swansea.

ECONOMY

Ever since the Industrial Revolution, which in Britain began in the late 18th century, Wales has been a country of mining and manufacturing. It is still that way, although mining has much declined and the manufacturing industries have changed with the times.

Conway Castle, in North Wales, dates from the 13th century.

Mining. The best of the coal mines are in the south, in the Rhondda Valley and around Swansea and Carmarthen. Many mines have shut down because of diminished demand, but Wales still produces about one-tenth of all coal taken in Great Britain, and mining remains the single largest source of employment. In former days, considerable iron and copper were also mined, but the ores are now largely depleted.

Manufacturing. Depletion of ores notwithstanding, the processing and refining of metals remains the principal manufacturing activity. The main products are tin plate, aluminum, sheet steel, copper tubing, and other industrial metals made from imported ores. The renewal of the country's industrial base since mid-century has introduced the manufacturing of such modern wares as synthetics, plastics, and electronic equipment. A major oil refinery is located at Milford Haven.

Agriculture. The traditional pastoral activities of the Welsh now occupy less than ten percent of the people, and vast areas of the uplands have been largely depopulated. Most of the farms are in the low coastal lands and in the river valleys, where beef and dairy cattle are the mainstay of farming. The raising of crops—barley, hay, oats, potatoes—is secondary and not nearly enough to feed the population. Sheep are kept in the highlands, yielding quantities of wool.

THE CITIES

Wales is now overwhelmingly urban, and about three quarters of the population is concentrated in and around the industrial centers of the south. But it is a country of small rather than large towns; only three Welsh cities have populations of more than 100,000.

Cardiff, the capital of Wales, was almost completely rebuilt after severe bombing during World War II. Cardiff and **Swansea,** the second largest city in the south, are both coal- and ore-shipping ports. **Newport** has always been a gateway to England on the east, and since 1966 the nearby Severn Bridge (one of the longest suspension bridges in Europe) has provided another link between Wales and England. **Milford Haven,** in the southwest, is one of Britain's largest oil complexes, handling many millions of tons of petroleum products annually.

HISTORY

Records of Welsh history in pre-Roman times are scant. In fact no real history is known until 55 B.C., when the Romans first attempted a landing in southern England. The Roman legions were met by the Britons, who fought from scythe-wheel chariots, backed by pony-mounted cavalry as well as archers and lancemen on foot.

Archeologists have found traces of Stone Age man as well as of the Bronze and Iron ages in Wales. Polished axheads and other artifacts give evidence of a high standard of craftsmanship, suggesting a certain degree of civilization. Rings of hewn stone, which might have been places of worship, point to the importance of religious feeling in pre-Roman Wales. The inner circle and altar slab of Stonehenge, in southern England, were cut from the Prescelly Mountains in western Wales.

When the Romans came again, in A.D. 43, they slowly gained a firm footing despite the continued resistance of the Welsh and other Britons. In A.D. 61 Boadicea, or Boudicca (the name means Victoria), Queen of the Iceni, rebelled against the Roman legate. Her army slaughtered a

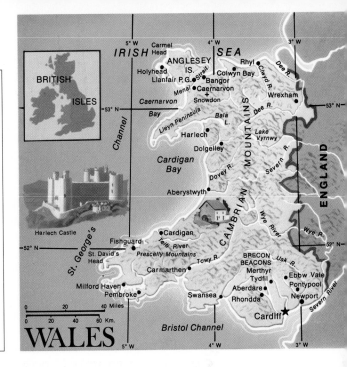

FACTS AND FIGURES

NATIONALITY: Welsh.

CAPITAL: Cardiff.

LOCATION: Southwestern part of the island of Great Britain. **Boundaries**—Irish Sea, England, Bristol Channel, St. George's Channel.

AREA: 8,023 sq. mi. (20,779 sq. km.).

PHYSICAL FEATURES: Highest point—Mt. Snowdon (3,560 ft.; 1,085 m.). **Lowest point**—sea level. **Chief rivers**—Dee, Wye, Severn, Usk.

POPULATION: 2,921,100 (1996 estimate).

MAJOR LANGUAGES: English, Welsh (both official).

MAJOR RELIGIONS: Protestantism, Roman Catholicism.

CHIEF CITIES: Cardiff, Swansea, Newport, Rhondda.

ECONOMY: Chief minerals—coal, slate, limestone. **Chief agricultural products**—barley, cabbage, cauliflower, cattle, hay, oats, potatoes. **Industries and products**—service industries, coal, tinplate, aluminum, sheet steel, oil refining, automobile parts, chemicals, electronic and electrical equipment. **Chief exports**—coal, steel and iron, aluminum. **Chief imports**—fuels, food products, raw materials.

WALES

legion and sacked Roman towns and camps, including London. Finally defeated, Boadicea took poison rather than become a prisoner. The next Roman legate, Agricola, attacked Anglesey as the heart of insurrection because of the colleges. Scholars were put to the sword and the area razed. That destruction of literature and records is the reason that so little is known of early Welsh history.

Post-Roman Wales

When the Romans left Britain in the early 5th century A.D., other peoples invaded the island, and finally the Scandinavian Vikings took most of Britain. The word Welsh dates from this time; it comes from the Saxon *waelisch*, which means "the stranger."

Rhodri (Roderick) the Great, ruler of Wales from 844 to 877, established the houses of Gwynedd in the north and Deheubarth in the south. His sons fought invaders, seaborne corsairs, and Viking raiders throughout their lives. In the 10th century their line produced Hywel Dwa, or Howel the Good, who called himself king of Wales. His legal code, governing social and moral conduct, is known as the Law of Howel. It is believed that in his reign the Eisteddfod—"the great sitting down" where poets, musicians, and choirs compete—became not a local but national event. The Royal National Eisteddfod is still held each August.

Wales and England—Centuries of Conflict

William the Conqueror won England in 1066 by killing the Saxon king, Harold, at Hastings. Under Norman rule, earldoms were set up along England's border, with castles at Chester, Shrewsbury, and Hereford to guard against constant attacks by the Welsh.

In 1267 Llewelyn ap ("son of") Gruffydd was defeated by King Edward I of England. The land was divided into counties. Castles were built as their headquarters. Though they were military fortresses, their names have all the music and poetry of the Welsh language—Caerphilly, Beaumaris, Conway, Harlech, Caernarvon.

But Wales remained disunited. In 1301 Edward offered his newborn son to the Welsh princes as a guarantee of peace—according to tradition —because the infant would be a Prince of Wales who spoke no English!

By the 15th century the Welsh economy was thriving on trade in cattle and textiles. But with the coronation of Henry IV as king of England, Owen Glendower, a Welsh prince, unsuccessfully rebelled against the English. Owen is said to have died in hiding about 1416, but Welsh legend says he will return when his country needs him.

In 1536, during the reign of Henry VIII, an act of Union incorporated Wales into the realm of England, and English common law served both countries. At this time, English became the official language of the Welsh courts. The Welsh language was not to be used in official business.

In 1588, however, a Welsh translation of the Bible by the rebel Bishop William Morgan did a great deal to save Welsh as a language. The heritage of the bards—poet-musicians—and of the *Mabinogion,* a collection of tales including legends of King Arthur, was saved for posterity.

In the 18th century the Welsh Methodist movement printed prayer books and Bibles that helped to raise literacy throughout the nation. In 1811 the Methodists broke away from the Established Church and the dream of worship in Welsh became a reality.

19th Century—the Growth of Industry

At the start of the Industrial Revolution many Welshmen left the farms and went southeast to the Rhondda Valley ironworks and coalfields, where they could earn ten times more in one year than they might

Coal mines still blacken the lovely green valleys of South Wales.

in a lifetime as farmhands. The Rhondda soon held more than half the entire population. Many went into shopkeeping, supply, and transport, and soon young men were sent to college to earn a degree. A new middle class was born within one generation. But many thousands migrated to the United States, Canada, Australia, and New Zealand.

The world's first labor union, formed among the Rhondda miners, was put down by force. But miners are not easily subdued. They soon allied themselves with Scots in London to form a secret labor union that in 1898 became a cornerstone of the labor movement in the United Kingdom.

Many distinguished 20th-century Welshmen were born in or near the Rhondda Valley, notably Aneurin Bevan, the Labour member of Parliament who fought for improved conditions for miners. A little to the west, near Swansea, Dylan Thomas wrote his magnificent poetry, which conveys much of the atmosphere of his homeland. The painter Augustus John came from mid-Wales. David Lloyd George, prime minister of Great Britain through World War I, was raised near Caernarvon.

20th Century—Decline and Renewal

But after World War I oil took the place of coal as a fuel, and hundreds of thousands of men were out of work. The ore fields supplying the ironworks petered out, creating more unemployment. The worldwide Depression of the 1930s enlarged the problems. The Rhondda Valley, once one of the world's largest producers of anthracite coal, became a dead region. Other industries also declined in the 1930s.

World War II brought renewed employment in the mines, but after the war the market for coal diminished once more, and the problem of unemployment recurred. In 1962 Prime Minister Harold MacMillan created the Welsh Office to deal with the effects of an almost ruined economy. Two years later the first Secretary of State for Wales was appointed. An area south of the Rhondda was turned into an industrial center. Today it thrives with new jobs and housing.

But the more things change, the more they stay as they are. Beneath the modernization the Welsh people remain the rebels they always were. In the late 1960s and early 1970s, their rebelliousness took a more serious turn with the formation of Plaid Cymru (the Welsh Nationalist Party) and of a secret "liberation army" that was responsible for acts of sabotage. The British government passed a bill that would grant the Welsh control over their own affairs in 1978. In 1979, Welsh voters went to the polls to vote on the plan, known as devolution.

The majority of Welsh rejected the devolution bill, but the question has come up again and again since then. Finally, in 1997, by an extremely narrow margin, Wales approved the creation of a new assembly, which is scheduled to start meeting in 1999. Apparently Wales still believes in the words of the Welsh prince Cadwallader, who once told Henry II, the 12th-century English king: "This nation, o king, may now, as in former times, be harassed ... but it can never be totally subdued through the wrath of man, unless the wrath of God shall concur. Nor do I think, that any other nation than this of Wales ... shall in the day of severe examination before the Supreme Judge, answer for this corner of the Earth."

RICHARD LLEWELLYN, Author, *How Green Was My Valley* and other books

Urquhart Castle, on the shores of Loch Ness where, over the centuries, thousands of people have reported sighting a large, unknown creature. Whether a "Loch Ness monster" really exists is still actively debated.

SCOTLAND

Scotland occupies the northern third of the island of Great Britain. It is an isolated land made up of rugged terrain, deep coastal inlets, and many islands. This isolation and ruggedness have combined to keep Scotland's population small and its land empty, but they have also helped to make the Scots an independent, proud, and determinedly self-sufficient people.

THE LAND
The country is washed on the north and west by the Atlantic Ocean and on the east by the North Sea. Its breadth varies from 154 miles (248 kilometers) to as little as 26 miles (42 kilometers). The country has 2,300 miles (3,700 kilometers) of coastline, a phenomenal length for the size of the mainland and its surrounding islands.

The Highlands—Their Beauty and Legends
A line drawn from Glasgow to Aberdeen roughly divides the Highlands from the rest of Scotland. In the past it was said that this line also marked the border between civilized Scotland and the region of savage scenery and a reputedly savage people. But what seems to be unfriendliness in the Highlanders is more a sign of independence, probably the result of centuries of life in a harsh, isolated land.

From the top of 4,406-foot (1,343-meter) Ben Nevis, Britain's highest mountain, one can see much of the Highlands. The most striking feature of the view from Ben Nevis is that the Highlands are cut in two by a great hollow, Glen More—the Great Glen—with a chain of lakes that cut across from Moray Firth to the Firth of Lorne. This chain of lakes was linked in 1847 to form the Caledonian Canal. More than 60 miles (96 kilometers) long, it runs from Fort William to Inverness (known as the capital of the Highlands), through 29 locks and through the lochs (that is, lakes) of Lochy, Oich, and Ness. But it never took ships of more than 600 tons and today is hardly used at all. Loch Ness, of course, has been the scene for centuries of a running story—is there a Loch Ness monster?

The huge Highlands region to the north and west of the Great Glen is in effect an island. This land is spectacularly beautiful, with rugged mountains, lovely lochs, and great stone-covered fields—the legacies of the Ice Age—on which nothing can grow. The northernmost reaches of the Highlands are quite desolate—moors and mountains, swept by wind and rain, with few inhabitants and little arable land.

To the east and south of the Great Glen, however, are the Highlands of the tourist brochures, with the Grampian Mountains and the valley of the Trossachs, lochs, rushing streams, and heather-covered fields. There are few towns though, as anyone knows who has crossed the desolate Rannoch Moor or visited Ballachulish and historic Glencoe, where, in 1692, the Campbells turned on their fellow Highlanders, the MacDonalds, in a massacre that has become notorious.

The Southern Uplands

Though somewhat mountainous, the Uplands are tamer than the Highlands. They resemble the parts of northern England with which they form the Border country. This region is one of restfulness, where peace and calm prevail. There are grassy slopes and quiet streams.

Writers have always loved the southwest region. The poet Robert Burns was born and died there, and his works were flavored by it. The historian Thomas Carlyle was also born there. Sir Walter Scott, Robert

Kilts, tartans (plaids), and bagpipes add color to parades during the Highland Games. Many Scottish traditions owe their origin to the ancient clan system.

Louis Stevenson, John Buchan, and Dorothy L. Sayers, the mystery writer, set novels there.

The southeast section of the Uplands is sheep country, the land of the Tweed and the Teviot rivers. Centuries ago, monks who lived in the four great abbeys of the Border—Melrose, Jedburgh, Dryburgh, and Kelso—first saw the value of local wool and established an export trade with the Continent. Today many of the tweed and sweaters that fill world markets are still exported from there.

The Border was known as a lawless region. Sir Walter Scott helped to preserve—and added to—the legends of the Border. His home, Abbotsford, became a place of pilgrimage as his novels became best-sellers.

The Lowlands and Their Cities

The central Lowlands—the broad Middle Valley—hold most of Scotland's people. Commerce and industry are centered in this area. Despite recent attempts to decentralize and move industrialization north and west, most Scots stay in the areas around their biggest cities, Glasgow and Edinburgh.

A glance at the map tells why this is so. The Clyde and Forth rivers penetrate far enough inland to give each city superb facilities for water transport. The depth of that penetration also means that the main north and south roads and rail lines must come together in the area. Scotland's international airport at Prestwick is in the same region.

Abbotsford, home of the novelist Sir Walter Scott.

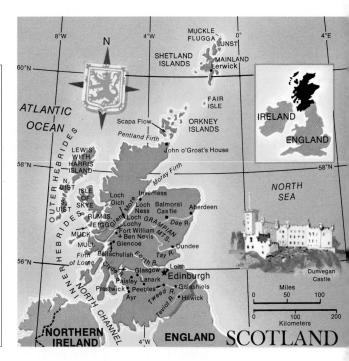

SCOTLAND

Glasgow. A big, sprawling metropolis, Glasgow has been a center of British industry ever since James Watt began to work on the steam engine in the 18th century. The Scots, who harnessed coal, iron ore, and steam together, helped to pioneer the Industrial Revolution and thrived on it. Glasgow's engineers and their products and the ships from its great yards along the Clyde River have reached every part of the earth. Today Glasgow has worldwide competition. The shipyards now produce drilling rigs and platforms, as well as seabed exploration craft, for the North Sea oil industry.

The city of Glasgow has a justly famous art museum and a great 500-year-old university (the 18th-century economist Adam Smith was a graduate and later a professor). But as a city it is gray, solid, and forbidding, though attempts have been made at urban renewal. Its once infamous slums, the Gorbals, are now a wasteland, their people relocated in apartment houses on the city outskirts or in new towns.

Edinburgh—Gracious Capital. Edinburgh has culture and civic pride, and is often called the Athens of the North. Many of its splendid squares display the graceful lines of early 19th-century architecture. Princes Street, the city's main thoroughfare, is bordered on one side by lovely parks and gardens and on the other by the city's most fashionable stores. Visitors are also attracted to the Walter Scott Monument, the Royal Scottish Academy, the National Gallery of Scotland, and the tiny 8th-century West Kirk (St. Cuthbert's Church), which is the oldest religious institution in Edinburgh.

Overlooking all of Edinburgh is the Castle, high on the bluff above the city gardens and Princes Street. The Castle was the citadel of the city and is now its military barracks. During the Edinburgh Festival in the late summer, most visitors attend the superb Military Tattoo on the grounds of the Castle. From the Castle down the Royal Mile, a history-laden thoroughfare, one can see the panorama of Edinburgh—the tall, narrow granite houses; the vast Cathedral of St. Giles, mother church of Scotland and center of Presbyterianism; and the Palace of Holyroodhouse. Built on the site of an abbey, in the late 16th century it was the home of Mary Queen of Scots and her son, James VI of Scotland—who became James I of England.

Though it is the youngest (only 400 years old) of the four old Scottish universities, Edinburgh was for years the most important. Its scholars won worldwide repute in a number of fields, especially medicine. But since the 1960's, other centers, concentrating on the arts and science and engineering, have moved ahead.

Near Edinburgh is its seaport of **Leith,** also the center of Scotch whiskey trade, where much of Scotland's most famous export is blended. Not far away are the great Firth of Forth rail and road bridges, which link Edinburgh with the northeast coast. The coastal city of St. Andrews is renowned for its old university (est. 1410) and as the birthplace of golf. To the north is **Dundee,** known for marmalades and cakes. Up the coast, in an area known for its cattle, is **Aberdeen,** site of a university (est. 1494) and center of the British oil industry.

The Islands of Scotland

The Orkney Islands lie off Caithness, the extreme northeast of Scotland—beyond John o'Groat's House. Treacherous waters surround the islands. Pentland Firth, with its racing tides and skerries (rock reefs), has long been a ships' graveyard.

There is evidence of Stone and Bronze Age settlements in the Orkneys and signs of 9th-century Norse invasions as well. Only about 20 of the 70 Orkneys are inhabited. Though the islands are practically treeless, they are fertile and intensively farmed. The main islands form a sheltered anchorage—Scapa Flow—famous as a war base for the British navy.

Even farther north, past bleak little Fair Isle (known for its traditionally patterned sweaters), are the Shetland Islands. Like the Norsemen from whom they are descended, Shetlanders are seamen and fishermen. Shetland ponies, cattle, dogs, and sheep are special small breeds. The wool from Shetland sheep is especially soft and much sought-after in the world-famous Shetland knits.

The Hebrides, the fabled "Western Isles" off Scotland's western shores, are numerous and well-traveled. Songs and ballads have been written of the Hebrides, such as "I Know Where I'm Going" and "Over the Sea to Skye." Many of the islands have amusing names. There are Rum, Eigg, and Muck, Mull, North Uist, South Uist, and Lewis with Harris of tweed fame. Skye is legendary thanks to Bonnie Prince Charlie, the Scottish pretender who set forth in the 1740's to overthrow the British Crown and re-establish Stuart rule. His dream ended on the battlefield of Culloden in 1746.

THE PEOPLE

Modern-day Scots are the product of an age-old ethnic blend. The original Picts mixed with successive invaders—Celts, Romans, Anglo-Saxons, Scandinavians, Normans—and each group left its mark on the national culture. In later times, many Irish migrated to the industrial areas in the Central Lowlands. Some immigration from eastern and southern Europe also took place.

Scots have long been noted for their frugality, which they have de-

A view of Scotland's capital city from the heights of Edinburgh Castle.

liberately exaggerated and turned into jokes about themselves. But perhaps the best-known feature of Scottish society through the ages is that of the clans—groups of families sharing a common ancestor and the same name. Many Scots still feel strong kinship with their clan, and many Scottish traditions have their origins in that system.

Language. Gaelic, the old Celtic tongue of the Scots, is now spoken by little more than 75,000 people, most of them in the Highlands and the Hebrides. By their acceptance and use of the English translation of the Bible, the Scottish reformers of the 16th century in effect adopted English as the national language. But as any singer of "Auld Lang Syne" knows, the Scots have made the English they speak peculiarly their own. They have retained a high percentage of vocabulary derived from Old Norse and Anglo-Saxon, and they speak with a lilt.

Religion. Scottish Presbyterians have been meeting in "kirk sessions" ever since John Knox thundered his fiery sermons from the pulpit of St. Giles in the 1560's. Today, their denomination is the official, as well as the largest, church in the country. The Church of Scotland, as it is called, claims the adherence of nearly half the population. Roman Catholics, particularly strong in the western Highlands, make up the second-largest group of worshippers.

Education. To the Scots, education is extremely important, and they start sending their children to school at 5 years of age. At 12, Scottish youngsters generally graduate from elementary to secondary schools, where they must continue until they are 16. Most schools in Scotland are supported by public funds. The educational system is administered by a special Scottish Educational Department.

Higher education may be pursued at eight universities and dozens of other specialized institutions. Four of the Scottish universities, those of St. Andrews, Glasgow, Aberdeen, and Edinburgh, are more than 400 years old.

ECONOMY

About three-fourths of the land is used for agriculture—crop culti-vation and animal husbandry. But Scotland is still deficient in food pro-duction and must rely on imports. Manufacturing has long been the mainstay of its economy. With the exploitation of the North Sea natural gas and oil deposits, the extractive industries have entered a new phase and become of major importance.

Manufacturing. Heavy industries, such as steelmaking and ship-building, have been the backbone of the manufacturing sector since the Industrial Revolution. Glasgow is still the principal marine engineering center in the United Kingdom. But foreign competition has forced diver-sification of industries and spurred a movement into high technology and consumer goods. Electronics and computers are among the notable new products from Scottish plants. Scotch tweed and textiles are still in demand, and the nation's world-famous whiskey distilleries continue to flourish.

Mining. Coal used to be Scotland's chief mineral resource, but since the 1970's, coal has been eclipsed by oil. Most of Britain's offshore oil fields are in Scottish waters, and Aberdeen has evolved into head-quarters of the new oil industry. Large refineries have been established at Grangemouth and Dundee.

Agriculture. About half of the country's farmland, especially in the Highlands and Southern Uplands, is used for grazing sheep and cattle. Scotland is famous for its breeds of cattle—Aberdeen-Angus, Galloway, and others—and the peculiar Scottish blackface sheep produce the wool for its tweeds. The major crops raised on the other half of the farmland, the best of which is in the Central Lowlands, are barley, oats, wheat, hay, and potatoes.

Fishing. Depleted stocks and the closing of some traditional fishing grounds in the North Atlantic have created difficulties for many Scottish fishermen. Fishing, however, is still a major industry. Crabs and lobsters are taken in coastal waters, and cod, haddock, and other white fish as far away as Greenland and the White Sea.

HISTORY

Scotland's very remoteness kept it apart from the waves of change that rolled over England from the Continent, whether they were the im-perialism of Rome, the invasions of the Anglo-Saxons, or the institutions of feudalism. The Romans, for example, made occasional forays and built some forts and a wall, but basically they only policed a troublesome border. One enduring exception is Scottish law, which is based on that of the Romans, while English laws are rooted in Saxon codes.

As each movement traveled north it met with increasing resistance from those already in control. Some of these invaders were never strong enough to reach the farthest north of Scotland at all. Thanks to their spirit of nationality Scots were able to hold out against English on-slaughts. Often defeated, the Scots managed to rally time and again and held their own until the Union of the Crowns in 1603. Scotland accepted the fact that its King ascended the English throne, and hence it felt equal to England. The Scots accepted the inevitable Parliamentary Union in 1707, but that feeling of equality did not last long.

Though the English and the Scots share one island and one kingdom, they remain two distinct peoples. By now, the English are used to having many Scots in leading positions in government and industry. Scotland itself used to be viewed as a place to vacation, but not to live. The royal family has a summer home at Balmoral. Great landed families had their estates for hunting and fishing, but few would stay there out of season. Scots made great contributions to knowledge, business, and politics. Since World War II, two British prime ministers have been Scottish —Harold Macmillan and Sir Alec Douglas-Home—and so is the present Queen Mother, Elizabeth, a daughter of the 14th Earl of Strathmore.

In the past, the Scots were often taunted for their accents. Today, a new air of self-confidence has taken root. Scots are expressing their nationalism, but not necessarily as a negative force. Scottish nationalists have been elected to Parliament. In the elections of 1974, the Scottish Nationalist Party (SNP), which advocated self-rule, gained 11 seats. Although it subsequently lost much ground—winning only three seats in the 1992 elections—the SNP is still powerful.

The Search for a Prosperous Future

Many Scots have had enough of conforming to English ways and of accepting London as the center of their world. Although voters in a 1979 referendum showed little enthusiasm for a plan that would have given Scotland home rule, support for independence—or at least for loosened control—increased in the 1990s. When devolution was proposed again to Scottish voters in a 1997 referendum, they approved it by a wide margin. As a result, a parliament with legislative and taxation powers over Scotland will begin serving by the year 2000.

The Scots are trying to reverse a longtime trend—a steady wave of emigration. The oppression of Highlanders for years after the defeat of Prince Charlie's men at Culloden in 1746 helped turn Scots into emigrants. More fateful, though, was the period in the 19th century when lands were needed more for grazing sheep than for people. In that era, the fact that the Highlands were considered economically unimportant led to more emigration. Finally, the Depression of the 1930s made young people think they could do better elsewhere. Highlanders headed first for the cities and then overseas, while Irish immigrants took their places in Scottish industry. These waves of emigration, a huge drain on the nation's labor pool, sent Scots to every part of the world. In the United States, one need only look in the phone books to see Scottish names. Scotland's loss has surely been everyone else's gain. Today's Scots realize that only too well.

Nonetheless, the last quarter of the 20th century marked the opening of an entirely new chapter in Scotland's history. Vast new hydroelectric projects in the Highlands, the development of nuclear energy, and, most important, the discovery of oil under the North Sea off Scotland's eastern and northern coasts have brought Scotland a new measure of prosperity. The nation's manufacturing industries have also undergone great change in recent years. While many shipbuilding and other heavy-manufacturing enterprises have declined or failed, new industries—including businesses that manufacture plastics, electronics, and consumer goods—have risen in their place.

JOSEPH C. HARSCH, C.B.E. (Hon.), Chief editorial writer, *Christian Science Monitor*
JUDITH FRIEDBERG, Author and editorial consultant

The highest elevation in Northern Ireland occurs in the Mourne Mountains of County Down.

NORTHERN IRELAND

Ireland, the small island west of Great Britain, has a divided population and a divided political system. The province of Northern Ireland in the northeast is a part of the United Kingdom of Great Britain and Northern Ireland. The independent Republic of Ireland occupies the rest of the island. The division of the island into two political units is the result of the treaty that ended the Anglo-Irish conflict of 1918–21. From 1800 until 1921 all of Ireland was a part of the United Kingdom. Today the people of the Irish Republic still hope to see the creation of an all-Ireland republic that is separate from Great Britain. The majority of people in Northern Ireland, however, do not want to unite with the Republic, but want to maintain their link with Great Britain. The division of the island into two political units is due mainly, but not entirely, to religious disunity. Most of the people in the 26 counties of the Irish Republic are Roman Catholics. The majority of the people in the six counties of Northern Ireland are Protestant. However, history perhaps as much as religion has played a part in creating strife in the land.

THE LAND

Armagh, Antrim, Down, Londonderry (Derry), Tyrone, and Fermanagh—the six counties of Northern Ireland, or Ulster as it is sometimes called—cover a relatively small but lovely area of hills, glens, plains, and lakes.

Northern Ireland is a land of many rivers, the most important of which are the Lagan, Bann, Blackwater, Mourne, and Foyle. Lough Neagh in the central part of Northern Ireland is the largest lake in the British Isles.

Economy. Although the country has no mineral resources of any importance, there is considerable industry in Northern Ireland. Belfast, the capital, is an important center of shipbuilding and aircraft construction. And all over Northern Ireland there are little towns that thrive on the old industry of linen-processing, or some other local activity. The rest of the countryside is used for farming, usually in small units.

Northern Ireland, like the rest of the island, has an equable climate. The winters are not very cold, and the summers are not particularly hot. This has been favorable to farming and also the principal traditional industry, which was the growing of flax and the production of the famous Irish linen from flax fibers.

Contemporary Belfast contains an unusual mixture of Victorian and modern architecture.

Since the end of World War II, many people have moved away from the farms. Linen manufacturing has declined because human-made fibers have taken the place of the natural product. The government has a policy of building new towns in which factories making many different kinds of goods are being set up. Clothing production is important. There are also many new companies that make chemicals and electronic products. Even so, Northern Ireland continues to be plagued with above-average levels of unemployment.

THE PEOPLE

Perhaps one of the first things that strikes the visitor to Northern Ireland is the way the people speak. Particularly on the east coast, the accent resembles the Scottish dialect. English is spoken by everyone, but there are many words and ways of saying things that come from Scotland. When the country was Gaelic-speaking, the northern part of Ireland was the gateway to Scotland, where the people also spoke Gaelic and had a similar culture. The Scotsmen, who were settled in Northern Ireland in the 17th century by royal decree, were like cousins of the Irish.

Religion. Two major branches of the Christian religion meet in Northern Ireland. About two-thirds of the people are Protestant—mainly Anglican and Presbyterian. The remaining third are Roman Catholic.

Education. Education in Northern Ireland is free and compulsory for children between the ages of 5 and 16. Higher education is available in two universities—Queen's University of Belfast, which was founded in the 19th century, and the recently consolidated University of Ulster at Newtonabbey—as well as in the Belfast College of Technology.

Higher education is available for all students who pass the entrance examinations to the university. No student is kept out of school because of financial reasons. In fact, most students receive some kind of assistance from public or private funds.

GOVERNMENT

The head of state in Northern Ireland is the governor, who is appointed by and represents the British monarch. Until 1972, the legislature consisted of a parliament (known as Stormont) made up of the House of Commons and the Senate. Executive power was in the hands of the prime minister, who was leader of the majority party in the House of Commons. The Northern Ireland parliament had control of education, internal trade, social services, and lower courts of justice. All other matters were handled by the British Parliament (to which Northern Ireland sends 12 members). Because of the crisis in Northern Ireland, Stormont was suspended in 1972, and its functions taken over by the British Parliament under a secretary of state for Northern Ireland. In 1973, a new government was formed, made up of an assembly of 80 members—both Protestants and Catholics. Hostility to this new coalition government, however, led to its suspension, too, in 1974. In the mid-1990s, despite various proposals for constitutional assemblies and elections, London still governed directly.

HISTORY

The seeds of disunion between Northern Ireland and the Republic date from the early years of the 17th century. For centuries, much of the north had been ruled by the great clans of O'Neill and O'Donnell. Dur-

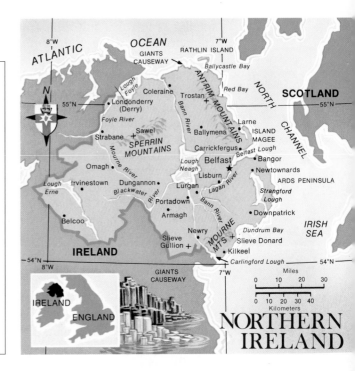

FACTS AND FIGURES

NATIONALITY: Northern Irish.

CAPITAL: Belfast.

LOCATION: Northeastern part of island of Ireland, separated from Great Britain by Irish Sea. **Boundaries**—Atlantic Ocean, North Channel, Republic of Ireland.

AREA: 5,242 sq. mi. (13,576 sq. km.).

PHYSICAL FEATURES: Highest point—Slieve Donard (2,795 ft.; 852 m.). **Lowest point**—sea level. **Chief rivers**—Bann, Lagan, Foyle, Blackwater. **Major lakes**—Lough Neagh, Lough Erne.

POPULATION: 1,663,300 (1996).

MAJOR LANGUAGE: English (official).

MAJOR RELIGIONS: Presbyterianism, Anglicanism, Roman Catholicism, Methodism.

CHIEF CITIES: Belfast, Londonderry, Coleraine.

ECONOMY: Chief minerals—fire clay, limestone. **Chief agricultural products**—cattle, chickens, eggs, hogs, sheep, milk, potatoes. **Industries and products**—linen, textiles, chemicals, aircraft, automobile parts, computer chips, ships. **Chief exports**—linen, machinery, clothing, ships. **Chief imports**—tobacco, metals, motor vehicles.

ing the 16th century, when the rest of the island had been "planted" with Protestant English colonists, the northern clans were able to maintain their independence. However, when O'Neill and O'Donnell marched south to Cork to join with an invading Spanish army, they were defeated in the great battle of Kinsale, in 1601. The battle put an end to the effort of the Irish clans to maintain their ancient Gaelic civilization against the English invaders. O'Neill and O'Donnell were allowed to retain their lands but they no longer reigned as princes. After a few years O'Neill and O'Donnell voluntarily emigrated to Europe with most of their active supporters. The English government then decided to "plant" their lands with Protestant English and Scottish settlers.

In the middle of the 17th century, King Charles I of England was at war with Parliament, a war that ended after the execution of the king in 1649. The Irish Catholics, who distrusted the English Parliament, had given their support to the king. During the civil war in England, English power in Ireland declined. Oliver Cromwell, the lord lieutenant of Ireland, who ruled in place of the king, came to Ireland in 1649. His army crushed the Catholic Irish with the utmost severity. The religious bitterness dates from those unhappy days.

In 1688 William of Orange, Stadtholder of Holland, was invited by the Protestant party to take over the throne of England from the Catholic James II. The resultant war was fought in Ireland, where James had the support of the Catholics. The Battle of the Boyne near Drogheda in 1690 decided the issue in favor of William's forces.

The victory is still celebrated by the Orangemen of Ulster (as the descendants of William's followers are called) on July 12 each year with colorful traditional processions. The men who march on July 12 carry banners painted with historic scenes, and the bands play the familiar old tunes. One of the most popular of these is known as the "Sash," named for the sashes that the Orangemen wear across their chests. The song contains a list of the 17th-century battles that brought King William to victory, and it expresses the sense of historical continuity that the processions are meant to demonstrate. Thus, with the sound of songs, drums, flutes, and marching feet the battle of the Boyne is recalled each year.

King William's victory cast a long shadow over the history of Northern Ireland. During the 18th century laws were enforced in Ireland against people who did not belong to the Anglican Church, which was the state church. The laws weighed most heavily on the Catholics. They were not allowed to take any part in the government of the country. They were not permitted to buy land or to take any but short leases. They were kept from serving in Parliament, in public office, or in most professions. Members of the higher clergy were banished and Catholic religious services were made illegal. Catholics had to pay for the support of the Established Church, as did Presbyterians, who also were excluded from holding public office. As a result thousands of Presbyterians emigrated to the United States. Toward the end of the century a movement arose in which, particularly in the north of Ireland, the Presbyterians joined with some Catholics in rebellion against England. The movement was called the United Irishmen. Its aim was the independence of all of Ireland.

The rebellion of the United Irishmen was unsuccessful, and in 1800 a law was passed by which the kingdoms of Ireland and Great Britain were united. Until then the two countries had shared the same king, but

Dunluce Castle rises dramatically on a rock formation overlooking the east coast. The castle is believed to have been built in about 1300 by the Earl of Ulster.

there was a separate parliament in Ireland that did not have much power. Over the next 30 years, the laws that discriminated against non-Anglicans were removed, and the two main branches of Protestantism agreed to bury their political differences and support the union. Most of the Catholics, however, still hoped that Ireland would become independent.

Just before World War I, a bill was debated in Parliament concerning self-government for the whole of Ireland. Many of the Unionists—people who supported the union with Britain—took arms to resist this step. The crisis was postponed by the outbreak of war in Europe. After the war ended, the Unionists insisted that they should remain under the British Crown. The result was that Ireland was divided. In the north the majority was Protestant, and the substantial Catholic minority was dissatisfied.

Because the Catholics objected to the partition of the island, they were accused of disloyalty to the constitution. There was also a fear that the Catholics would grow to outnumber the Protestants. This made a convenient argument for discriminating against Catholics.

In 1968, a new movement developed to win full civil rights for all people—Catholics and Protestants—in the north. Some leaders believed they could secure full civil rights by peaceful agitation, while the Irish Republican Army (IRA) favored military action to secure a united Irish Republic. The old Nationalist Party in the north hoped for military action from the government of the Republic.

When it appeared as if many hundreds would be killed in clashes between Catholic and Protestant groups, the British government intervened. The British Home Secretary persuaded the government of Northern Ireland to introduce new civil rights. The British army was brought in, and the Northern government rushed through a number of reforms. As a result, Catholics were recruited into the police, and the Special Constabulary (emergency police force), which had been entirely Protestant, was disbanded. An effort was made to provide housing without regard to religious affiliation, and the sectarian local authorities began to lose their powers. But the situation remained grim as Catholics and hard-line Protestants seemed to become even more hostile toward each other. In 1972, the British government took over direct rule of Northern Ireland.

Hopes for peace in the north seemed to grow for awhile under a compromise reached in 1973. It called for participation by both Catholics and Protestants in a new government, and assured that the status of Northern Ireland would not be changed against the will of the majority of its people. But the agreement failed. In 1985, an accord between Britain and the Republic of Ireland was signed, giving Ireland an advisory role in setting policy for Northern Ireland. In 1993, Britain and Ireland declared their goals towards peace in a remarkable peace initiative. Although progress was slow, in 1998 a peace agreement was finally reached, and the Irish enthusiastically approved it in a nationwide vote. Three interconnected government bodies were created to, respectively, mediate issues within Northern Ireland itself; between Northern Ireland and Ireland; and between Ireland and Britain. Also planned is a referendum to amend Ireland's constitution to end its claim to Northern Ireland. Terrorism, however, remains a problem, mainly due to a number of small paramilitary groups that oppose the peace process.

FERGUS PYLE, *The Irish Times*, Belfast
THOMAS FITZGERALD, Department of Education, Dublin

FRANCE: AN INTRODUCTION

by Pierre MENDÈS-FRANCE
Former Premier of France

When I was a child, the map of France filled me with wonder at the image of a perfect creation. The visible evidence of this perfection was the regular hexagon in which France was contained. And because France joined together all climates—because it was at once Nordic and Mediterranean, continental and maritime, mountainous and rich in plains; because it had the highest peak in Western Europe and the biggest sand dunes on the continent; because its rivers spread out in diverging directions to flow into four different seas; because it was ornamented by a glorious array of cities and towns, churches and castles; and finally because Paris was Paris—I cherished its image even more.

Later, I knew other nations; I recognized the complacency and naïveté of my first enthusiasm. Traveling through France, I discovered a very different—and certainly more complex—reality from the one I had imagined. I became convinced that nothing could be more false than being content with a ready-made idea of a country instead of considering its most varied and even its most contradictory aspects. Thus, if all our foreign friends wish to know of France is the monuments of its past, they are misled; as are those who occasionally declare us incapable of adapting to today's world. It is indeed true that Sainte-Chapelle and the Arc de Triomphe are integral parts of us, but it would be wrong to assume from this that in France the clock stopped at the dawn of the machine age. It continued ticking—though often in a highly irregular fashion—and no man of our time can ignore the political, economic, and social realities that are giving today's France a profoundly new character.

Little by little, I became aware of the incredible amount of work invested across the centuries in this country, though some people accuse us of an addiction to laziness. Certainly France's climate is good and its land often fertile, but there is nothing here that was bestowed upon man as a completely free gift of nature. From the polders of our Flanders to the dams on the Loire, there is evidence of a 1,000-year struggle with the waters. From our woodlands in Normandy and Brittany to the terraced farms of Provence and Roussillon, the results of human labor can be seen everywhere. Our ancestors spared neither time nor trouble. To clear the forests that covered our plains took them centuries. It took them centuries to complete the Cathedral of Chartres, centuries to decorate the Lascaux Caves, a whole century to build Versailles.

This heritage was ravaged hundreds of times by those tragedies in which French history is only too rich. Not to underestimate any of these, but only to remember the most recent—the last war brought more destruction and privation, and more ruins, than any of those that went before. In 1944 and 1945 the American soldiers could see the extent of the disaster. Houses had collapsed, factories had been burnt out, machines had been broken, electric power stations had been destroyed, bridges had been blown up, railroads and highways had been torn up. And there was the terrible condition of our fields, our vineyards, and our orchards, deprived for years of fertilizer and of all necessary care. Undoubtedly history offers no comparable precedent of an industrialized nation abruptly paralyzed in all its vital activities. At the time of the Liberation, French production was at about 30 percent of its prewar level. It was relatively easy to put the nation's economy on the road to recovery, but the actual task of rebuilding was slow and laborious and caused much effort, misery, and privation. Since I was among those who continually demanded more order and discipline in this thankless task, I can bear witness to the great work contributed by those men and women who, scarcely past the ordeal of the war, had to sacrifice themselves further to rebuild a country stricken to its very foundations.

But that was not all. The goal of the French was not to regain the mediocre levels of 1939, already depressed by a decade of economic problems of all kinds. They aimed much higher, hoping to put France in the vanguard of modern nations once more. This was only possible if the idea of reconstruction was replaced by those of modernization and expansion. That was the goal of our five 5-year plans, which were soon followed by the sixth.

So one may say that, in the postwar years, France has experienced a genuine economic revolution. Let the traveler, the tourist, look around him; he will see its signs everywhere—the giant silo replacing the traditional barn; vast mechanized farms instead of small ones; huge factories with assembly-line production instead of the old country workshops where the anvil used to ring under the hammer. All this took great effort and sometimes meant painful changes that, the French realize, are not yet ended.

However, the Frenchman has a natural attachment to traditional ways of life and a very human desire to preserve them against the incursions of industrial civilization. These factors, and policies that (it must be said) were too often hesitant, have maintained—in certain sectors and areas—structures that are more or less obsolete. But it cannot be denied that the whole country is on the path toward progress. Industry, agriculture, the universities, intellectual life, the arts—all show the effects of change. There has been the inevitable strife, but also evidence of an irresistible forward movement. The performance of our railroads, the development of our aircraft industry, our huge dams, the transformation of many of our regions, the shining industrial examples of Toulouse, Grenoble, and Rennes, side by side with land improvements in the Camargue and the phenomenon of rapid urbanization—all testify to a renewal worthy of admiration. In the eyes of the visitor or the scholar, the hydroelectric dam at Tignes is no less remarkable than the Pont du Gard.

One after another, the structures least adapted to our century are being transformed. Even if the necessary changes sometimes take place amid confusion, these are all signs of a people becoming young once again. Thus, in France the objective observer can see co-existing a thousand legacies inherited from the distant past, and the vigorous bursting forth of the initiatives and bold promise of a beautiful rebirth.

In the heart of Paris, Notre Dame Cathedral rises above the Île de la Cité, an island in the Seine River.

FRANCE

It has been said that "everyone has two homes—his own and France." For centuries, France has been a wellspring of inspiration in art, music, and literature. For centuries, France has been a fountainhead for many of the world's great ideas. The language of the country is still a second language for many cultivated people everywhere.

In France, taste and elegance are in the air, and simply being there is an exhilarating experience. It is a dynamic country where much of Europe's intellectual and artistic pace is set. As a modern industrial nation with a young population, France is also a country whose people are creating valuable new traditions to add to the glorious old ones.

THE LAND

France, which is the largest nation in Western Europe, has an area of approximately 211,000 sq. mi. (546,490 sq. km.). It borders on Spain in the south, Italy and Switzerland in the east, and Germany, Luxembourg, and Belgium in the northeast. These land frontiers are partially formed by Europe's greatest river, the Rhine, and by several of Europe's

Chamonix, near the foot of Mont Blanc, is one of France's top winter resorts.

great mountain ranges—the Pyrenees, the Alps, and the Jura. In the French Alps in the east there are soaring, snowcapped peaks, including Mont Blanc, at 15,781 feet (4,810 meters). Mont Blanc is the highest in Western Europe.

But about half of France's total border is formed by coastline, with the Mediterranean on the southeast and the Atlantic and the English Channel (La Manche, or "the sleeve," to the French) on the west and northwest.

Climate

Within these boundaries France has a variety of climates. On the shores of the Mediterranean, for example, and in much of southern France, summers are hot and dry. Although winters in the south are extremely mild, cold winds from the Pyrenees and the Alps sweep down across the flatter plains below. One of these winds, the mistral of the Rhone delta, reaches speeds near hurricane force, blowing for 3 or 4 days in a row. Many trees in this region have been permanently bent by the power of the mistral, and the wind is also said to have a psychological effect on the people exposed to it.

In the Alps and the nearby Jura, the mountain peaks are snow-covered all year round. On France's Atlantic coastline, on the other hand,

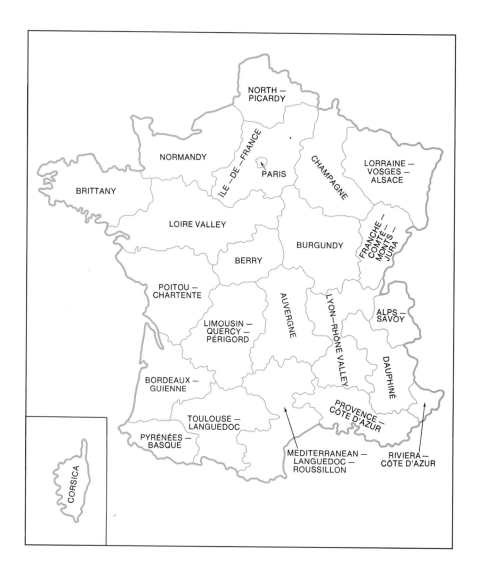

from Hendaye in the south to Dunkirk in the north, winds from the sea carry abundant rainfall to the land. The warm waters of the Gulf Stream also bring generally mild temperatures to this part of France. In the interior, away from both coasts and mountains, the climate is less moderate, but temperatures rarely reach great extremes of hot or cold.

Rivers and Canals

The rivers of France form a vast network that fans out across the land, tying different regions and cities together. The Seine, the country's longest navigable river, flows northwest from eastern France through the great capital city of Paris and empties into the Channel at Le Havre. The Loire—often considered France's most beautiful river—begins farther south, flows northwest to Orléans, and turns west to empty into the Atlantic at Saint-Nazaire. The Garonne, which rises in the Pyrenees, flows northwest past the now industrial city of Toulouse and through the Bordeaux wine country. Where it empties into the Atlantic, the river is called the Gironde.

The Rhone flows southwest from Lake Geneva in Switzerland. South

FRANCE

FACTS AND FIGURES

OFFICIAL NAME: French Republic.

NATIONALITY: French.

CAPITAL: Paris.

LOCATION: Western Europe. **Boundaries**—English Channel, Belgium, Luxembourg, Germany, Switzerland, Italy, Monaco, Mediterranean Sea, Spain, Andorra, Bay of Biscay.

AREA: 211,208 sq. mi. (547,030 sq. km.).

PHYSICAL FEATURES: Highest point—Mont Blanc (15,805 ft.; 4,807 m.). **Lowest point**—sea level. **Chief rivers**—Seine, Loire, Garonne, Rhone, Rhine. **Major lake**—Geneva.

POPULATION: 58,211,454 (1997; annual growth 0.29%).

MAJOR LANGUAGE: French.

MAJOR RELIGIONS: Roman Catholicism, Protestantism, Islam, Judaism.

GOVERNMENT: Republic. **Head of state**—president. **Head of government**—prime minister. **Legislature**—bicameral Parliament.

CHIEF CITIES: Paris, Marseilles, Lyon, Toulouse, Nice, Nantes, Strasbourg.

ECONOMY: Chief minerals—iron ore, coal, bauxite, potash, zinc. **Chief agricultural products**—beef, cereals, sugar beets, potatoes, wine grapes. **Industries and products**—steel, machinery and equipment, textiles and clothing, chemicals, food processing, metallurgy, aircraft, motor vehicles, wine. **Chief exports**—machinery and transportation equipment, foodstuffs, agricultural products, iron and steel products, textiles and clothing, chemicals, wine. **Chief imports**—crude petroleum, machinery and equipment, chemicals, iron and steel products, agricultural products.

MONETARY UNIT: 1 French franc = 100 centimes.

NATIONAL HOLIDAY: July 14 (Bastille Day).

Barge traffic on the Seine—a vital part of France's network of waterways.

of the Burgundy wine-growing region it is joined by its major tributaries, the Saône and the Isère. The Rhone branches out into a wide delta as it nears the Mediterranean. Just before it reaches its delta, the river flows past the town of Avignon. There is a modern bridge over the Rhone at Avignon today, but the ruins of the bridge that gave its name to the song *Sur le Pont d'Avignon* ("On the Bridge at Avignon") can still be seen. Children all over France enjoy singing the ancient song and dancing the circle dance that goes with it.

Some 3,000 miles (4,800 kilometers) of canals link the major French rivers to one another and to the great rivers of Europe. This extensive network carries many of the products of French agriculture and industry. The wheat and grain of the northwest can be taken south to Marseilles for export by river and canal. The iron ore of Lorraine may be exported from the great Channel ports of Le Havre and Cherbourg after a trip on the inland waterways. The steel manufactured in Dunkirk and used in the shipyards of Saint-Nazaire is shipped largely by canal, too.

ECONOMY

In France, since the beginning of the 20th century and especially since World War II, there has been an increasingly rapid shift away from traditional small farms and factories toward larger, more mechanized units. These extensive changes have produced one of the most diversified —and one of the healthiest—economies in Europe.

Sheep graze near a village in the Pyrenees, the mountain range that forms a natural border with Spain.

Agriculture

Since land in France has always been extremely costly, the traditional French farm was small and family-owned. Each farm had its dairy cow, a flock of chickens, and a few pigs. These small farms are gradually disappearing, however, as modern farming methods become more and more prevalent. As a result, French farm output as a whole is increasing.

Today France produces more foodstuffs than any other single Common Market country. One basic crop is wheat, which is grown mainly in the north and northwest. France is one of the few European countries that supplies all of its own wheat and exports the surplus. Barley, oats, sugar beets, and all kinds of vegetables are also raised. French orchards yield an abundance of fruit, from the apples of Normandy and oranges of the Mediterranean area to the cherries, apricots, and tiny, yellow-green mirabelle plums of Lorraine.

Livestock production is increasing steadily. Nearly half of all French livestock is cattle, though sheep, poultry, horses, pigs, and goats are also raised. The dairy herds of Normandy produce the rich milk and cream that are important ingredients in so many delicious French dishes. Much of the dairy yield is also used to make the almost endless variety of French cheeses. French breeders are constantly working to improve their beef cattle. Today France's Limousin and snowy-white Charolais steers, known for their tender meat, have made the country a leader in European beef production.

Cognac, a well-known French product, is aged and blended in wooden casks.

But the best-known product, and one of France's most important agricultural exports, is wine. Wine has been produced in France since Roman times and perhaps earlier. There is hardly a region of France that does not have its vineyards. Ranging in color from pale rose to deep ruby, from golden amber to almost clear white, the wines of France are considered by many to be the finest in the world. There are the rosés of Provence and Anjou, the reds of the Rhone, and the whites of the Loire and Alsace. The sparkling wines of the Champagne region are the only ones in the world legally entitled to use the name. Some of the wines of the Cognac and Armagnac regions are distilled into fine brandies. The great red wines of Bordeaux and Burgundy are justly renowned around the world, though often they may come from holdings only a few acres in size.

Besides the important well-known vineyards, such as Rothschild and Romanée-Conti, there are local wines and everyday wines (*vins ordinaires*), which are rarely exported. Many small farms have their own prized vines, producing just enough for family and friends.

In some parts of France, after picking time, farmers still trudge up the slopes to prune their weathered, gnarled vines with old-fashioned long-handled knives, as they did in the time of Saint Vincent, long ago. According to an old Burgundian legend it was this saint who first taught that severely pruned vines yield more grapes. It takes year-round, unremitting toil to grow the grapes that keep France in the forefront of the world's wine producers.

Industry

France also has the sources of energy for modern industry. At the beginning of the Industrial Revolution in the early 19th century, France was handicapped by not having abundant supplies of coal and iron, which were then the essentials of industry. France's scattered coal deposits never yielded enough to meet the nation's needs. The principal French iron deposits in Lorraine and near the Saar were long regarded as worthless because of their high phosphorus content. France lost these regions to Germany at the end of the Franco-Prussian War in 1871—just when the British were finding out how to make this kind of ore industrially useful.

After World War I, Lorraine was returned to France. Steel production is booming today. French mills turn out steel for agricultural machinery, railroad track, aircraft and aircraft engines, trains, and ships. French steel goes into the finely engineered cars that roll off the assembly lines of Renault, Citroën, Peugeot, and Simca, making France the fourth largest automobile producer in the world. In addition, France is one of the world's leading steel exporters. Since the end of World War II the French Government has made concentrated efforts to modernize mineral production in Lorraine. France today leads Western Europe in the extraction of iron ore, and much of that ore comes from Lorraine. In addition, the per capita daily production of a coal miner in the Lorraine fields is among the highest in Europe.

In today's industrial world, however, other sources of energy supplement or replace coal. France has an abundance of hydroelectricity from damming its many swift-flowing rivers. The rivers have also been responsible for the growth of the French textile industries. Lyons, on the Rhone, was known as early as the 15th century for the fine silks produced there. Today the whole Rhone Valley area is the home of mills that turn out excellent synthetic fabrics, many of them first developed for the *haute couture,* or high fashion, designers of Paris. Rouen, on the Seine, also has a thriving synthetics industry, and cotton and woolen fabrics are made in north and northeast France. Petroleum is still produced in the Parentis field south of Bordeaux, but reserves there are dwindling. France nevertheless has a large-scale oil-refining industry based on imported crude oil from North Africa and the Middle East, and active prospecting continues in the country, both on and off shore. In 1951 large deposits of natural gas were discovered near the town of Lacq in the foothills of the Pyrenees, and the area subsequently became an important center of the French chemical and plastics industry. But these reserves, too, have been almost exhausted, and France now has to import more than half of its needs.

Beyond these energy sources, France has harnessed the seas off Brittany to build the world's first tidal power station on the Rance River near Dinan. The uranium deposits of central France are used to fuel nuclear reactors that run huge generators. At Odeillo, in the Pyrenees, a great experimental solar power station uses the sun's heat to produce energy.

France is also well supplied with the "light metals"—such as aluminum—that are so important in the world's economy today, especially in the transportation industries. Aluminum ore, or bauxite, was named for Les Baux, the town in southern France where it was first discovered and mined in the 19th century.

Although France has all the heavy industries so vital to a modern economy, it is also proud of the many luxury industries for which it has always been known. A label bearing the words "Imported from France" is still a sign of quality and ensures sales in many other countries. French clay is made into the delicate, artistically decorated porcelain of Sèvres and Limoges. Equally famous is the fine hand-cut crystal of Baccarat and St. Louis.

Paris is the traditional center of France's most important luxury industries. There exquisite jewelry, fine handbags, and beautifully made shoes are produced—often by small manufacturers with worldwide reputations. Paris is also—to the delight of women around the world—the home of the *haute couture*. This industry makes an important contribution to the French economy and also to France's fame as a country where styles are set. Today the great names in this field, such as Dior, Chanel, and Givenchy, have been joined by numerous younger designers. There are also style-conscious manufacturers who produce less expensive clothes whose cut and line mean "Paris" in places as far away as Tokyo or Tahiti.

CITIES

All of the cities of France take great pride in their contributions to the nation's past and in their work toward its future. There is hardly a city in France that has not carefully preserved—and often restored—some monuments and relics of French history. The cities are equally proud, however, of their huge power plants and automated factories.

Reminders of the past are kept alive and cherished in modern France.

Marseilles, France's chief port, lies on the Mediterranean.

Because they reflect so much of the country's beauty and diversity, France's cities have been described as the jewels in a crown. Of all the jewels, **Paris** has always been the largest and most dazzling. In the 19th century, the American author Oliver Wendell Holmes wrote, "Good Americans, when they die, go to Paris." For many people, Paris remains their idea of heaven. Other cities are compared to it and are called "the Paris of the North" or "the Paris of the South." There are songs about it in every language, and almost everywhere in the world its name evokes an image of gaiety, elegance, and beauty.

Over the years, the city's atmosphere has made it a magnet for artists and intellectuals from all countries. All of them were drawn to Paris by its freedom, and all of them drew something special from being there. They also helped to give Paris its reputation as *la ville lumière,* the City of Light. (See article on PARIS, which follows.)

Marseilles, on the Mediterranean, is the chief port of France. It is also the country's oldest city and has always been its gateway to the East. Since ancient times, both the goods and culture of Africa, the Middle East, and Asia have entered France at Marseilles' docks.

Almost everything in Marseilles' life has to do with the sea, from the colorful, cheerfully noisy fishmarket to the hilltop church of Notre Dame de la Garde, patron saint of the city's fishing fleet. From the liveliest street, La Canebière, it is only a few steps to the old port. There, dozens of restaurants offer the Marseilles specialty called bouillabaisse—a spicy, delicious fish stew—and a fine view of all the bustle of the busy harbor.

Marseilles is an ideal starting point for trips to the Riviera resorts— Cannes, Juan-les-Pins, Antibes, and Nice—strung out along the Mediterranean shore. Also nearby are the lovely hill towns of Provence and Languedoc, such as Aix-en-Provence, Arles, Avignon, Nîmes, Orange, and Carcassonne. In many of them, ancient theaters and buildings still stand, relics of Roman times.

Some 170 miles (270 km.) north of Marseilles is **Lyons**. Located where the Rhone and Saône rivers meet, it is an important port and

Fresh fish from the Mediterranean tempts shoppers in Nice.

The wide-bodied Airbus aircraft are assembled in Toulouse, the center of the French aerospace industry.

communications center. Lyons is the traditional home of French silk manufacturing, though today many other fine textiles are also produced there. Chemicals, pharmaceuticals, and electrical equipment are some of Lyons' other industries. The city is also known for its annual international trade fair and exhibition. Manufacturers and businessmen from many countries take part in the fair, and treats from all over the world can be sampled, including the many varieties of Lyons *saucisses* and *saucissons* (sausages).

Strasbourg, the capital of Alsace, is France's port on Europe's most important river, the Rhine. Because of the river and its many canals (such as the Rhone-Rhine and Marne-Rhine), the city has long been a cross-roads of commerce and industry. Iron and steel from Lorraine, coal from Germany, and hundreds of other products are shipped through Strasbourg. The city's industries include metalworking, brewing, and food processing. Its best-known food product is the fine goose-liver spread called pâté de foie gras.

Strasbourg was not always French, however. Until 1681, and again between 1871 and 1919, it was a German city, and much of its culture is still German today. In 1949, Strasbourg became truly international when it was made headquarters of the Council of Europe, an organization founded to work toward European unity and progress.

Toulouse, north of the Pyrenees, is the historical capital of the south-

Carcassonne, a medieval stronghold, perches on a hill in southwestern France.

west and a center of the French aircraft industry. There the huge Sud-Aviation plants developed the Caravelle jets widely used in Europe today and worked on the Concorde, the huge supersonic airliner built jointly by France and England. Toulouse has one of the largest airports in France. The city has also made a contribution to French cuisine with its cassoulet —a succulent stew of goose, sausage, pork, and beans.

Other important French cities include Bordeaux, a major industrial city and port as well as a wine center; and Lille, the industrial center of the north.

PLACES OF INTEREST

The French landscape is extremely varied, from the harsh, wind-swept coasts of Brittany, facing the Atlantic, to the palm-lined promenades of Nice and Cannes on the Mediterranean. Each region has some striking features and characteristic beauty to catch the eye. But France is equally rich in the works of man, and Frenchmen and visitors alike can see the whole panorama of history spread out across the land.

In the foothills of the Alps there are towns with steep stair-step streets, such as Briançon. Still crowned with ancient fortifications, Briançon is one of the highest walled cities in Western Europe. Carcassonne, in southwest France near the Pyrenees, is the best preserved. Restoration of the medieval town, with its towers and crenelated walls, was begun in the 19th century under the direction of France's leading architect, Eugène Viollet-le-Duc. The restoration has been so exact that today a visit to Carcassonne makes it seem as if time did not exist—as if the 12th century had come to life again, side by side with the 20th.

About 400 miles (640 km.) to the east are the rolling, vine-clad hills of the Champagne region, near the Marne River valley. This pleasant area, home of the most famous wine of France, also has military cemeteries of both world wars, silent witnesses of past battles. Rheims, the largest city in the Champagne region, has one of the most beautiful cathedrals in France. The cathedral was the site of the coronations of 24 kings of France.

In the south, near the resorts of the Riviera (the Côte d'Azur, or "azure coast," to the French), is dry, windswept Provence. Here gnarled olive trees are silhouetted against bright blue skies, and small houses with characteristic orange tile roofs cluster against the hillsides. It is easy

The spires of Mont-Saint-Michel pierce the sky above France's Channel coast.

A marina at Calais, an ancient city near the narrowest stretch of water separating England and France.

to see why this region has always been such a favorite with artists, both French and foreign.

On the Channel, in the north, there are the dunes of Dunkirk beach and the great ports of Le Havre and Cherbourg. Many of the smaller towns along this stretch of coastline are fishing villages, for France has always used the sea as a source of food as well as a highway of trade. The French fishing fleet was completely modernized after World War II. It still sails from the Channel ports of Boulogne and Dieppe, bringing in huge catches of cod, herring, and sardines from the Atlantic. The icy waters off the rocky coast of Brittany yield lobsters, crabs, and oysters said to be the best in the world. Every year, the tiny Breton village of Locmariaquer celebrates the beginning of the oyster season with a festival in which all the residents—and many visitors—take part.

Down the Channel coast past Cherbourg stands the towering Abbey of Mont-Saint-Michel. Built on a spur of land that becomes an island at high tide, the Abbey has been one of the unique beauties of France for more than 10 centuries. Still farther south along the Atlantic coast, there is more evidence of France's history as a maritime power. Brest is an important Atlantic port, and Saint-Nazaire is the site of the country's largest shipyards, where many of its great transatlantic liners were built.

Pilgrims flock to the grotto at Lourdes where, in 1858, a peasant girl had visions of the Virgin Mary.

In the extreme south, close to the Spanish border, is the town of Biarritz. In the mid-19th century, drawn by the mild climate and the peaceful atmosphere, European royalty began to vacation there. Today Biarritz, with its beautiful beaches, elegant hotels and shops, and busy casinos, is one of the most famous resorts in the world.

Some 80 miles (130 km.) inland to the east lies the small city of Lourdes. There, in 1858, a young girl named Bernadette Soubirous said she had visions of the Virgin Mary. This story and the waters of Lourdes' springs—said to have miraculous healing powers—have made the town the goal of religious pilgrimages ever since. Hundreds of thousands come to Lourdes annually to worship at its basilica and to be cured by its waters.

Amid the wheatfields and flat plains of north central France—the Paris basin—is the town of Chartres. Chartres' massive Gothic cathedral, with its beautiful stained-glass windows, is one of the great achievements of the Middle Ages.

Even closer to Paris are two vast structures built to reflect the power and splendor of the French kings. The palace of Fontainebleau was begun during the reign of Francis I in the 16th century, and every succeeding king added to it. The Forest of Fontainebleau—some 40,000 acres (16,154

The Hall of Mirrors in the palace of Versailles is where the Treaty of Versailles was signed in 1919.

The palace of Fontainebleau is another monument to France's royal past.

hectares) of unspoiled woodland—is under government protection. It is still popular with artists, as it was in the 19th century when painters such as Jean Baptiste Camille Corot and Jean François Millet lived and worked there.

To the northwest of Fontainebleau lies Versailles, the royal palace of King Louis XIV. With its Hall of Mirrors, sweeping staircases, and lovely formal gardens, the palace of Versailles is a reminder of the days when France was the political center of Europe. Every spring and summer *son et lumière* ("sound and light") performances are held at Versailles, with the voices of great French actors evoking the palace's past.

Hundreds of miles to the south, past some of the principal agricultural and industrial areas of France, contrasts still abound. Near Périgueux are the Lascaux Caves, whose walls and ceilings are covered with paintings of animals dating from prehistoric times. The caves have been closed to visitors since 1963, as scientists try to find a way to prevent a fungus from destroying the paintings.

In Avignon, on the banks of the Rhone in southeastern France, there is a 14th-century fortress-palace. The palace—and the walls that surround the town—date from the time when a number of French popes reigned in Avignon instead of Rome.

The island of Corsica, in the Mediterranean Sea off the coast of Italy southwest of Livorno, has been part of France since the 18th century. Once known as a bandit hideout, the mountainous island's chief claim to fame is as the birthplace of Napoleon. The Bonaparte family home may still be seen in Ajaccio, Corsica's capital and an important port. The city has another museum dedicated to Napoleon, and there are streets and squares named for him as well. Visitors can also enjoy the excellent beaches near Ajaccio and elsewhere on the island.

The castle and vineyards in Châteauneuf-du-Pape, near Avignon.

Boats line the harbor at St.-Tropez, a fashionable Mediterranean resort on the French Riviera.

Under the hot Mediterranean sun of the southeast is the town of Grasse. Nearby, fields of roses, violets, and mimosa form a patchwork of color to delight the eye. The flowers' lovely fragrance is captured in essential oils produced in Grasse, "the perfume capital of the world."

To the west, several miles past Marseilles, is the deep-water oil port of Fos. There, mostly in the 1970's, the French erected a gigantic, ambitious complex of modern harbor facilities and industrial plants, producing steel, plastics, and other commodities, in part on filled-in swamplands. This is close to the Rhone delta area known as the Camargue, whose marshes and lagoons have long been a bird and wildlife sanctuary. Herds of small horses still roam the region, while nearby, "cowboys" tend huge *manades,* or droves, of black cattle. Every spring and autumn, the tiny Camargue town of Saintes-Maries de-la-Mer, at the mouth of the Rhone, celebrates a religious festival that dates back many centuries. The ceremonies include the blessing of the cattle, which are driven into the sea to receive a kind of baptism. Side by side with these ancient traditions, however, industries and extensive land reclamation projects have begun to bring the Camargue closer to the 20th century.

Environment Planning

The French people would be deeply upset if industrialization and progress spoiled their land. So government and industry have joined in trying to preserve the natural beauty of the country and the heritage of

Ronchamp chapel, by Le Corbusier (C. E. Jeanneret), France's top modern architect.

the past while promoting the large-scale use of France's resources. Wherever possible, an official policy of *aménagement du territoire* ("environment planning") retains the best features of the countryside as the demands of production are met. The effects of this policy can be seen all over France—in the construction of a modern superhighway system; restoration of a Roman amphitheater or an ancient church; new industrial development; widespread reforestation projects; and the transformation of desolate, mosquito-infested wastelands, such as along the extreme western shore of the Mediterranean, into up-to-date resorts.

THE PEOPLE

Concern with making money, and then more money, in order to buy the conveniences and luxuries of modern life, has brought great change to the lives of most Frenchmen. More people are working than ever before in France. In the cities the traditional leisurely midday meal is disappearing. Offices, shops, and factories are discovering the greater efficiency of a short lunch hour in company lunchrooms. In almost all lines of work emphasis now falls on ever-increasing output. Thus the "typical" Frenchman produces more, earns more, and buys more consumer goods than his counterpart of only a generation ago. He gains in creature comforts and ease of life. What he loses to some extent is his sense of personal uniqueness, or individuality.

Some say that France has been Americanized. This is because the

United States is a world symbol of the technological society and its consumer products. The so-called Americanization of France has its critics. There is also widespread criticism in France of industrialization and modernization. The critics fear that "assembly-line life" will erase the pleasures of the more graceful and leisurely (but less productive) old French style. What will happen, such critics ask, to taste, elegance, and the cultivation of the good things in life—to joy in the smell of a freshly picked apple, a peaceful stroll by the river, or just happy hours of conversation in a local café?

Since the late 1950s, life in France has indeed taken on qualities of rush, tension, and the pursuit of material gain. Some of the strongest critics of the new way of life are the young, especially university students. They are concerned with the future, and they fear that France is threatened by the triumph of this competitive, goods-oriented culture. Occasionally they have reacted against the trend with considerable violence. In 1968 and again in 1994, student dissatisfaction spread from Paris across the nation. Unrest swept the country when industrial workers staged a series of crippling strikes. France's public workforce also held a number of labor strikes between 1994 and 1996.

In spite of the critics, however, countless French citizens are committed to keeping France in the forefront of the modern economic world. They find that the present life brings more rewards, conveniences, and pleasures than that of the past. They believe that a modern, industrial France is preferable to the old.

Changing Population

Since the 1940s and the wartime German occupation, the French population has been growing at a rapid rate. The total number of inhabitants now exceeds 58 million. Approximately 27 percent—more than 15 million people—are under the age of 20.

Such a large youthful population means an urgent demand for better schools to train young people in the skills needed in today's world. It necessitates creating new jobs to bring millions of young men and women into productive careers. It results in a great deal of purchasing power in the hands of teenagers and young adults. These are buyers who want to enjoy what they can get now, who are confident of tomorrow, and whose tastes show a willingness to experiment, to sample the new, and to use up and replace goods. This is a startling contrast to the traditional French attitude of making what one has last as long as possible.

The people of France, the country's greatest resource, have always been a mélange (mixture). The reasons for this are not hard to find. First, France has no really formidable natural frontiers—even the Pyrenees and the Alps have passes through them—so it was always accessible by land. The extensive coasts, washed by the Channel, the Atlantic, and the Mediterranean, and marked by the mouths of navigable rivers such as the Seine, the Loire, the Gironde, and the Rhône, have made the land accessible by water, too.

First there were cave dwellers, and then explorers and traders—notably Phoenicians and Greeks from the eastern Mediterranean—some of whom stayed and settled. Over the years came Celts, Romans, Teutons (such as the Germanic Franks), Norsemen, Saracen North Africans, and Jews. All of these contributed significantly to the French of today. More recently the many elements in the modern French nation have come to include descendants of the Senegalese, Congolese, Indo-Chinese, and other African and Asian peoples, as well as Germans, Russians, Poles, Italians, Spaniards, and others.

The French are tolerant of differences of all kinds. This is not to say that the French are wholly without prejudice, but in general they do not systematically exclude whole groups. There has always been fairly continuous assimilation of newcomers. Thus, to be French is not so much to claim any certain ancestry as it is to "feel" French.

Education

One of the strongest influences in the making of the French is education. Today the French schools are playing a vital role in the transformation of France into a modern society. In the past the cultural heritage was transmitted only to a small elite of each generation. Now, all French children have the chance to discover and develop their abilities and aptitudes. As the result of a series of reforms, two major changes have taken place in education. First, there is a variety of courses, allowing all students a wide choice of the professional and technical careers necessary in today's world. Then, parents and schools work together so that a program may be chosen that best suits the unique needs and abilities of each child.

School is compulsory for children between the ages of 6 and 16. There are both government-run and private *écoles maternelles,* or nursery schools, some taking children as young as 2. In the eighth grade if pupils want to prepare for the traditional "classic" higher education, they begin to study Latin and sometimes Greek. There are also other programs, including those with the study of two modern foreign languages. Or they may go into general education combined with vocational training.

Those students who do go to the 3-year academic high school, or lycée, have a variety of majors to choose from—literature, social sciences, mathematics, pure and applied science, and an important recent addition, industrial technology, reflecting the new needs of the economy. At the end of the three years, the students take stiff examinations for their baccalaureat (or "bac") degree.

At the university level, too, important changes have taken place. In the wake of the student protests of 1968, most of the larger universities were subdivided into smaller units to make them more responsive to the students' needs. Students and teaching staff were given a role in their administration, and instead of central control of budgets and curricula by the ministry of education, the reorganized multidisciplinary universities were made into autonomous institutions. Again, more science and technology courses have been added. Although such curricula are fairly new in French education, the students who choose them are nevertheless following an old and honorable French tradition. Many important advances in science and medicine were made by French people or others who had made France their home.

Recreation

Young people in France today take their education as seriously as their parents take their jobs and professions. But the French are nevertheless aware that "all work and no play makes Jacques a dull boy." Popular pleasures and pastimes abound, and there is something for every taste.

In many households, television fills a large amount of leisure time. There are several commercial networks, and American programs are common. This wave of American culture has provoked a good deal of opposition from those who feel French culture is being submerged. In a further infiltration of American entertainment, in 1992 a huge Euro Disneyland complex was opened near Paris. Popular music, from folk to hard rock, is popular, often with the characteristically French themes of love and its joys and sadness.

A singer has really arrived when he or she performs at the Olympia, long Paris's best-known music hall. There, *chanteurs* and *chanteuses* set records for coming back year after year to sing to their adoring fans. In-person appearances in the provinces, too, are now a regular part of the French entertainment scene. With state subsidies for the arts, theaters have multiplied so that almost every French city has a thriving popular theater, even down to tiny houses seating 50 people at most. But wherever the theater and whatever the play, prices are low and theaters are

This meat market offers the raw materials for a delicious French dinner.

packed. This, too, is in keeping with the old French tradition of universal interest in the arts.

French Food

Another universal French interest is food, for good eating has always been one of the favorite pastimes of the French people. In caves near the hill town of Roquefort in south-central France, a tangy, blue-veined cheese is cured. Roquefort, made of sheep's milk, is a gourmet treat around the world, as are Brie, Camembert, Port Salut, and Coulommiers. Over 400 different cheeses are produced in France, and they are only one indication of the French love of fine food.

Le bon goût ("good taste") is as important when it comes to food as it is in every aspect of life in France. It is not unusual to see a butcher or grocer arranging his wares with all the care an artist might devote to a still life painting, and French housewives take pride in preparing even the simplest meal well. From the smallest bistro to the most elegant restaurant, dining is a pleasure in France. Every meal offers foods with a distinctly French flavor. For breakfast, there are flaky croissants, brioches, crisp *petits pains,* and other rolls to enjoy with jams and a piping hot cup of café au lait. Other meals present such delights as *soupe à l'oignon* (onion soup), served bubbling hot with cheese on top; *escargots bourguinonne* (snails prepared with garlic and herbs); or *pot-au-feu,* a savory stew; all of them accompanied by enough long, crusty loaves of bread to enjoy the last of the sauce or gravy. Countless varieties of fluffy omelets are consumed daily in France, and *bifteck et pommes' frites* (steak and french fried potatoes) are ever popular. For dessert, there are literally hundreds of different patisseries to choose from. Or the lucky visitor might select a *mousse au chocolat,* a *crème caramel,* or simply end his meal with a *glace* (ice cream).

In the *grand luxe* restaurants of France, especially those of Paris, sparkling crystal, dazzling white linens, and silverware placed "just so" form a backdrop for the best of *gastronomie* (fine eating). There a chateaubriand or a soufflé is prepared to order and served with elegant precision and even drama. One seemingly simple dish may take the combined efforts of six chefs to produce. French food is a joy the visitor can share with the French, and it is also an art form that is admired and imitated everywhere.

Sports

With the growing youthfulness of the population, active sports are becoming increasingly popular. Physical education is now compulsory in the schools and universities. An expanding government program is making sports facilities—swimming pools, stadiums, and gyms—available to everyone. This new emphasis has made the French "physical-fitness conscious" as never before, and has brought new ideas of fun into their lives. The top team sports are soccer and basketball. Among individual sports, skiing leads the field. Geography and climate have blessed France with snowy slopes, especially in the Alps and nearby Jura Mountains. Clustered in valleys or nestled at the foot of snowy peaks such as Mont Blanc are dozens of winter resorts, including Mégève, Chamonix, and Albertville—site of the 1992 Winter Olympics. Many smaller ski towns such as Courchevel, Font-Romeu near Prades, and Barcelonnette are

Skiers enjoy the slopes at Montgenèvre, near the Italian border.

Saint-Malo is one of the most popular Channel resorts in France.

The Vingt-Quatres Heures of Le Mans thrills Frenchmen and foreigners alike.

rapidly gaining popularity. Almost any Frenchman can learn to ski today, for there are frequent excursions to low-cost resorts. In winter whole school classes move to ski areas, and skiing is added to regular studies during these *classes de neige* ("snow classes").

Other popular sports are judo, sailing, and water-skiing. *La chasse* ("hunting") is a passion for many Frenchmen, reflecting their love for *gibier* ("game")—from partridge to wild boar—on the table. The rivers and streams of France provide excellent fishing—another well-loved recreation.

In every season there is something for everyone in France, but August is still when most Frenchmen enjoy their *vacances* ("vacation"). The average Frenchman has little taste for wandering to exotic corners of the world. Even in this age of great mobility, he is likely to find true contentment in a return from the city in which he lives to the small corner of France where he feels his roots are. Many Frenchmen still show this love of the land by taking camping trips or annual family excursions simply to "breathe the country air." Nevertheless, more and more young people are traveling today. Many low-cost vacation groups have been set up—some with their own resorts—not only in France but all over Europe and North Africa.

Another great French love is automobiles. This fascination with cars is evident in the excitement generated by the great annual race, the grueling Vingt-Quatres Heures ("24 hours") of Le Mans in western France. Each spring sees hundreds of thousands of Frenchmen crowding the route of the classic in western France and cheering wildly for their favorite drivers. International bicycle races, such as the 3,000-mile (4,800 km.) Tour de France, are equally popular with Frenchmen, and their mud-splattered winners become heroes all over Europe.

But in spite of the increasing interest in sports and popular entertainment, the serious culture of France still plays a real part in the lives of its people. To many people, both Frenchmen and foreigners, the very essence of France is its richness in the arts of the past and present.

Medieval illuminated manuscript from "Le Livre de la Chasse" ("Book of the Hunt") by Gaston Phoebus. The Cloisters, Metropolitan Museum of Art, New York City.

The Fine Arts

Playwright Jean Giraudoux's statement *Sans style rien ne vit et rien ne survit: tout est dans le style* ("Nothing can live or survive without style: style is everything") is particularly true of the fine arts in France—a country that has always cherished and promoted great artistic works. One of the oldest surviving examples of the artistic spirit among remote, primitive ancestors of the French is found on the walls and ceilings of the Lascaux Caves, in southwestern France. These graceful paintings of animals were discovered during World War II, and scientists estimate that they are over 20,000 years old.

The art of medieval France, from tapestries, illuminated manuscripts, and stained glass to altarpieces and sculpture, was largely done for the Church. But the most important art works were actually the churches themselves. In the 12th century, French builders began to develop the Gothic style. With its graceful pointed arches and slender spires pointing toward heaven, Gothic architecture spread all over Europe in the next 4 centuries.

In the 16th and 17th centuries, French Renaissance architects were influenced by styles from Italy. One of them, Francois Mansart (the mansard roof is named for him), used Italian ideas to form his own style. He built many palaces, châteaux, and public buildings during the reigns of kings Louis XIII and Louis XIV.

French Renaissance painters were also strongly influenced by Italian works. Seventeenth-century artists were often inspired by the classics and painted subjects from the Bible and Greek and Roman mythology.

By 1700 France had become the most powerful nation in Europe, and the court of King Louis XIV, who died in 1715, had become the artistic as well as the political center of the world. As the 18th century went on, French styles in painting and architecture became more ornate and decorative. They were imitated all over Europe. The major artistic figures of the period painted graceful scenes of garden parties and actors, dancers, and jugglers, or they depicted the simpler life of the times.

At the end of the 18th century, along with the political revolution, a kind of revolution took place in French art. Painters became increasingly experimental and adventuresome. The Romantic painters of the mid-19th century took an interest in the vivid colors and swirling action of such exotic lands as North Africa.

In the mid-1800's, Jean Baptiste Camille Corot was the leading nature painter. His sun-drenched landscapes and lakes surrounded by silvery birches show his great love for the French countryside. Edouard Manet was another artist of the time who believed in painting from life.

The leading French artists of the late 19th and early 20th centuries are known as the impressionists. They painted from life, but not with photographic realism; instead they tried to capture on canvas the subtle effects of changing light.

One great French influence on 20th-century art was Paul Cézanne, the leading post-impressionist. Cézanne's interest in shape and structure was the beginning of a great change in world art. By the 1920's Georges Braque and the Spaniard Pablo Picasso (a resident of France) helped to develop cubism, in which various planes of an object or person are shown at once. Things are reduced—or abstracted—to their essential shapes.

"Girl with Green Eyes" (1909), oil painting by Henri Matisse. San Francisco Museum of Art, Sarah and Michael Stein Collection.

"A Sunday Afternoon at the Grande Jatte" (1855), an oil painting by Georges Seurat. Metropolitan Museum of Art, New York City.

"Mont Sainte-Victoire" (1885?), oil painting by Paul Cézanne. Metropolitan Museum of Art, New York City. H. O. Havemeyer Collection.

"Dancers Practicing at the Bar" (1877), oil painting by Edgar Degas. Metropolitan Museum of Art, New York City. H. O. Havemeyer Collection.

Centuries of Great Literature

From the days of the medieval singers who traveled from town to town or knightly court to knightly court, France has made major contributions to world literature. Many of the significant trends in Western poetry and prose originated or developed in France. During the Middle Ages, poetry expressed the ideals of the time—chivalry, honor, and courtly love.

The literature of 16th-century France includes the fullest expression of the Renaissance (the word itself, meaning "rebirth," is French). All of the spirit of discovery and the joy in human abilities characteristic of the period were reflected in the works of French writers such as François Rabelais and Michel de Montaigne. But less than 100 years later, partially as a reaction to the exuberant Renaissance style, French literature changed again. The 17th-century playwrights, especially Pierre Corneille and Jean Racine, emphasized a return to older traditions. Using stories from classical mythology and ancient history, they imposed rigid limits of subject, time, and place on their work. They described the struggle of human emotions against reason and order. Their contemporary Molière (Jean Baptiste Poquelin) made fun of everyday life. Many of their plays are still performed by the world-famous Comédie-Française, the oldest of the French national theaters.

In *A Discourse on Method* (1637) René Descartes, mathematician, scientist, and philosopher, expressed the feeling of the age that man was fundamentally a thinking—and questioning—creature.

Belief in man as a reasoning being was central to the classicism of the age, which sought order, form, and style in every human expression. It was natural, therefore, that the French language should come under scrutiny. Based on Latin and enriched over the centuries by borrowings and additions from other languages and dialects, French was becoming unmanageable. In 1635 the Académie Francaise was established. Under the patronage of Cardinal Richelieu (King Louis XIII's chief minister), the academy's task was to guide the development of the language and to insure its purity. It still serves largely the same purpose today.

By the early 18th century, French writers had turned to observation of the quality of human life—especially in the areas of politics and social criticism. They began to question the nature of government and the proper relationship of kings to those they ruled. Their writings began to reflect the discontent developing in France. As a group they were known as *les philosophes,* or "the philosophers," and they expressed the principles of *liberté, egalité, fraternité* ("liberty, equality, fraternity") that culminated in the French Revolution in 1789.

A kind of revolution swept through French literature, too, and by the 1830's, feeling and imagination had become the key themes in French writing. The novels and poems of 19th-century France are vivid examples of this new Romantic spirit.

In the mid-19th century Charles Baudelaire, in his poems *The Flowers of Evil,* used the French language to create word pictures or image music. The symbolist poets who followed Baudelaire also used words to suggest intense feelings and ideas, rather than to make simple statements.

Marcel Proust's *Remembrance of Things Past,* a multi-volume portrait of an era, began to appear in 1913. It exerted a great influence on later 20th-century writers in France and all over the world.

Plays, novels, poems, and philosophical essays continue to flow from the pens of French authors in the second half of the 20th century. Book publishing is still a major industry in France today, and the French public reads avidly. The annual announcements of winners of the important literary competitions (such as the Prix Goncourt and the Prix Femina) are awaited by some as eagerly as soccer fans await the results of a major match.

Music

French contributions in the realm of music—from the songs of the medieval troubadours, to the precise, courtly measures of Jean-Baptiste Lully, to the sometimes dissonant scores of today's composers—have long been well known.

Much of the music of medieval France was church music, often based on the Gregorian chant. Also, biblical stories were set to music and performed. An important composer of secular music during this period was Josquin des Prez, whose melodies became known all over Europe in the late Middle Ages.

As secular music developed, 15th- and 16th-century French composers wrote battle songs and music based on sounds of nature. In the 16th and 17th centuries, as royal power grew, the courts at Paris and Versailles became musical centers. Composers of the period wrote music for court theatricals and ballets, as well as individual pieces. Music was supported —and even produced—by the kings; King Louis XIII himself was a composer.

But possibly most often played are the rich, rolling works of the 19th century, especially the symphonies of Hector Berlioz and the Belgian César Franck, and the piano compositions of the Pole Frédéric Chopin. Equally popular are the colorful, romantic French operas; perhaps the best known are Charles Gounod's *Faust* and *Roméo et Juliette* and Georges Bizet's *Carmen*.

In the late 19th century, at about the same time that painters were developing Impressionism, music, too, took a new turn. After Claude Debussy and Maurice Ravel, the first musical "impressionists," came the musical "cubists" Erik Satie and Francis Poulenc. Their compositions were often as startling to their audiences as a Picasso or Braque painting was to its viewers.

France today is as much a musical center as ever, and its influence continues to be felt all over the world.

French Films

In today's world, new media have enlarged the scope of art. No view of French life and culture would be complete without noting French achievements on the screen. From the very beginning of this art, French contributions have been among the most significant. As films became more sophisticated, French directors were always among the leaders of the new art form. In the 1950s the young directors of the "New Wave" made film even more an art for its own sake. France also produces many screen actors, such as Gérard Départieu and Catherine Deneuve, who are well known to film lovers everywhere.

HISTORY

By 51 B.C., Roman legions under Julius Caesar had conquered much of the land called Gaul—an area that includes all of present-day France as well as Belgium and Switzerland. Though Greek and Phoenician traders had settled on the Mediterranean coast centuries before, Caesar's victory marked the beginning of more than 5 centuries of outside rule.

Under the Romans, cities (including Lyons, Nîmes, and Arles) were built, and a communications network—roads, bridges, and aqueducts—was set up to serve them. Some of the bridges, such as the Pont du Gard in Languedoc, are still used today. In many parts of France modern highways lie above the ancient Roman roads. Roman civilization came with conquest, and in culture and language Gaul gradually became a Latin country.

In the 3rd century A.D., Gaul experienced the first invasions across its eastern boundaries by wandering Germanic tribes. Over the next 2 centuries more and more of these invaders—notably Franks, Burgundians, and Visigoths—swept into Gaul. Rome no longer had the strength to push them back. So in some cases the invaders settled down and set up their own areas of control side by side with lands that remained under nominal Roman rule. Toward the end of the 5th century, the Franks decisively defeated the last remnants of Roman power and gained control of most of Gaul. By 500 a Frankish kingdom under King Clovis had accepted Christianity. The kings who followed Clovis had to fight off new invaders. In 732 the Franks defeated a Muslim army that had

The Pont du Gard, near Nîmes, was used to carry water for more than 1,000 years.

crossed the Pyrenees from Spain. By 800, when Charlemagne was crowned Holy Roman Emperor by the Pope, the Franks had extended the borders of their kingdom to include parts of present-day Austria, Germany, Italy, and Yugoslavia. Under Charlemagne (Charles the Great), the Holy Roman Empire grew even larger. Charlemagne set up schools, gave France a code of laws, and strengthened the emperor's authority.

After Charlemagne's death, however, central power declined, and his kingdom was divided among his grandsons. The western part became Francia, the nucleus of today's France. The king's authority grew very weak in the second half of the 9th century, and disastrous raids by Vikings weakened it even more.

The Middle Ages

In 987 Hugh Capet was elected king of France by the nobles. Slowly, with the support of merchants and the growing middle class in the cities, the Capetians strengthened the monarchy. By the 13th century the king of France had become the most powerful ruler in Europe. French agriculture flourished. Guilds in the towns and cities turned out quality products. Foreign trade increased. French universities attracted scholars from all over Europe. In every way France became a European center of styles and ideas.

During the later Middle Ages serious conflict arose between the king of France, Philip IV, and the Church. In 1305 a Frenchman was elected Pope Clement V. He had the papal palace moved to Avignon, in south-

The Château of Chenonceaux is one of the loveliest in the Loire Valley.

ern France; and, for some 70 years, the popes were almost puppets of the French Crown. In 1378, the papacy returned to Rome. (Even today, a wine grown in the Avignon area is called Châteauneuf-du-Pape, or "the Pope's new chateau.")

The Hundred Years War

In 1066 William, the Duke of Normandy—a large region in northern France—became king of England. From that time on, English kings held sizable lands in France. Almost 300 years after William conquered England, Edward III even laid claim to the French throne. In 1337 Edward invaded France. Although hostilities actually lasted longer than a century, the conflict came to be known as the Hundred Years War. The English won many victories—notably Crécy, Poitiers, and Agincourt—but they were never able to seize and hold the throne of France. In the 1420's Joan of Arc, a young farm girl, appeared at the French court. She said

Orléans. In 1429, Joan of Arc led in lifting the English siege of the city.

God had commanded her to lead the French armies and to have the Dauphin—the rightful heir to the throne—crowned at Rheims. Joan's leadership helped to turn the tide. Although she was betrayed and burned at the stake, her courage so inspired the French that they were finally able to drive the invaders out. In 1429 the Dauphin was crowned King Charles VII, and by 1450 the French had recaptured most of their land. When the war ended, the French Crown was far stronger and the land of France more unified than before.

Religious Strife

In the 16th century the Reformation, based on the ideas of Martin Luther, swept France. Many noblemen and even some members of the royal family became Huguenots, as the French Protestants were called. There were violent clashes as King and Church tried to wipe out the Huguenots. France was divided into factions, and civil war broke out. In 1572, by royal order, thousands of Huguenots were massacred in Paris and other French cities.

Henry IV

Stability returned in 1598, when King Henry IV, who had been converted from Protestantism to Catholicism, issued the Edict of Nantes. This allowed the Huguenots some religious freedom.

Under Henry agriculture was encouraged, and the French economy was reformed. As France regained its prosperity, there was an increase in trade. French ships ranged far from home in search of new sources of wealth. In this way France began to acquire colonies in the New World.

But 12 years after the Edict of Nantes, Henri IV was assassinated. His queen, Marie de Médicis, became regent for their young son, Louis XIII. There was division and dissent among the nobility, and, once more, there was conflict between Huguenots and Catholics. Royal power was weakened.

Richelieu and the Sun King

Cardinal Richelieu began his rise to power under Marie de Médicis in 1614. He eventually became Louis XIII's chief minister, with nearly absolute control over all aspects of French government. For almost 20 years he worked not only to restore royal power but to make France the strongest state in Europe.

Richelieu crushed all opposition inside France, including the Huguenots and the nobility. He levied high taxes, especially on peasants and city merchants. He encouraged foreign trade and expanded the French Empire in North America, the Caribbean, and elsewhere.

In foreign policy Richelieu opposed the powerful Habsburg monarchies of Austria and Spain. The Cardinal allied France with the Habsburgs' enemies in the Thirty Years War. His work set the stage for the absolute monarchy of Louis XIV.

Louis came to the throne as a child, in 1643. For the first 18 years of his 72-year reign, his chief minister, Cardinal Mazarin, continued Richelieu's policies. Opposition within France, which had flared into the open under a child-king, was again suppressed and France's position abroad was consolidated. When Louis XIV began to rule for himself, he was the strongest king in Europe. In 1685 he revoked the Edict of Nantes, and the Huguenots either fled or suffered gross indignities and even death if they refused to convert. Louis involved France in costly wars with Spain, the Netherlands, and England but actually gained little for his country. He summed up his theory that he was God's representative on earth (and responsible to no one) with the words, *"l'état c'est moi* [I am the state]."* Everything Louis did was a reflection of the centralized power of *le roi soleil,* "the sun king."

In the early 18th century, Louis XV succeeded his great-grandfather as king. Royal power seemed as strong as ever, but below the surface trouble was developing. France was defeated by England in the Seven Years War and lost much of its territory in North America. By 1774, when Louis XVI became king, dissatisfaction with social, political, and economic conditions, along with the growth of an able, educated middle class, had created an inflammable situation. Protests, riots, and dissent grew into a revolution that swept away the old regime. Crown, Church, and privilege were destroyed.

The French Revolution

French aid to the American colonies in their revolt against England strained finances past the breaking point. To raise money, the King in 1789 called a meeting of the Estates-General (representatives of the clergy, the nobility, and the middle class) for the first time in over 175 years. After an unauthorized meeting in the Jeu de Paume—or royal indoor tennis court—some representatives, mostly middle-class deputies, banded together in a national assembly and vowed to write a constitution for France. Shortly after, on July 14, 1789, a Parisian mob stormed the Bastille, an ancient prison that symbolized all the oppressions of the old regime. Next, in August, the assembly issued the Declaration of the Rights of Man. The revolution had begun.

The revolution rapidly grew increasingly violent. France was declared a republic in September, 1792; and Louis XVI and his queen, Marie Antoinette, were beheaded a few months later. Radical leaders, such as Maximilien Robespierre, took over. A reign of terror swept the country as these men tried to exterminate all enemies of the Revolution.

Meanwhile France was also engaged in foreign war. Fear of the revolutionary events in France had spread all over Europe. Every crowned monarch felt gravely threatened by what had happened to Louis XVI. Thus France, from 1793 onward, found itself at war with five major powers, including England.

The war continued even after 1795, when the Reign of Terror ended and the Revolution became more moderate. For the next 4 years France was governed by the Directory, a five-man executive board. But internal dissent continued, and the government became increasingly dependent on army support.

Napoleon Bonaparte

In 1799 Napoleon Bonaparte, a young Corsican general who had won brilliant victories for France, took control. He eliminated all opposition and set up the Consulate, a committee of three. As First Consul, Napoleon made all the decisions. France began to enjoy stability, although freedom had been lost.

Napoleon believed that he was the repository of the people's will. He had a legal code drawn up for France. (The Code Napoléon, as it came to be known, is still the foundation of French law and of the laws in many areas that were once under French influence.) In 1801 he signed the Concordat, making peace with the Pope and gaining Church support. He reformed the educational system and set up a professional civil service for which people were chosen on the basis of ability. Napoleon's armies continued their victories in Europe, carrying French ideas far beyond French borders. In 1804, Napoleon crowned himself emperor of France. Gradually extending his empire, Napoleon defeated most of France's enemies—Austria, Prussia, Russia, and Italy. Finally only England remained free of French control, thanks to its sea power. The armies of the French Empire had redrawn the map of Europe.

In 1812 Napoleon decided to crush what remained of Russia's strength. He led the Grande Armée—over 600,000 men—in the invasion. After several great victories, the French occupied Moscow, which had been abandoned and set on fire. The Russians retreated constantly, destroying all supplies as they went. Finally Napoleon ordered the long march back to France. But the snows and bitter cold of the Russian winter soon set in, and Russian soldiers harassed the retreating French. Only about one sixth of the glorious army survived to return home. The empty victory had turned to defeat.

Now Napoleon's enemies—and even some of his allies—joined to defeat him. In 1814 he was forced to abdicate and was exiled from France. Under Louis XVIII (Louis XVI's brother), France became a constitutional monarchy. In March, 1815, however, Napoleon decided he had enough support to seize power again. He left the Mediterranean island of Elba and returned to France; Louis XVIII fled. Napoleon was emperor of France once more, but only for 100 days.

What began in Russia in 1812 ended on the battlefield at Waterloo, not far from Brussels, Belgium, in 1815. In June a multi-national army, led by the English Duke of Wellington and the Prussian Field Marshal Gebhard von Blücher, defeated Napoleon for the last time. He was exiled once more, this time to St. Helena, a tiny island in the South Atlantic.

Two Revolutions—1830 and 1848

Louis XVIII was restored to the French throne. For 15 years he and his successor, Charles X, ruled France. Both acted more and more as if the revolution had never taken place. The vote was restricted, parliamentary power reduced, and the press strictly censored. The Church played an increasingly important role in controlling education. The early 19th century brought the Industrial Revolution to France, as it did to the other nations of Europe. More and more Frenchmen were drawn to the cities in search of jobs and a better life. At the same time, the middle class grew larger—and wealthier. These Frenchmen were resentful of the government's policies.

In July, 1830, the King dissolved the parliament, reduced the vote still further, and destroyed what little remained of a free press. Strikes and riots broke out in Paris, and Charles was forced to abdicate. This revolution gave France a revised constitution and brought Louis Philippe, the Duke of Orléans, to the throne.

At first, Louis Philippe seemed satisfied to rule as a constitutional king. Industrialization continued. Cities grew larger, especially in the textile centers of the north and the mining areas of the east. The government did almost nothing to improve conditions for the workers or to help the unemployed. There was dissatisfaction with foreign policy as well.

By 1848 liberals had joined discontented workers in a campaign to draw attention to their demands. Strikes were widespread. In February, demonstrations and riots in Paris led to clashes between royal troops and the rioters. A new revolution seemed underway. Louis Philippe abdicated and went into exile. France was a republic again. The provisional government of the Second Republic called for a constitutional convention and made attempts to help the workers. But a majority of conservatives were elected to the convention. In June the Paris workers revolted against their rule and were put down by the Army.

Napoleon III and the Second Empire

Elections were held under the new Constitution of 1848, and Louis Napoleon (a nephew of Napoleon I) was chosen president of the Second Republic. By 1851 he had decided to follow in his uncle's footsteps. Because the Constitution allowed him only one term, he arrested his opponents, dissolved the National Assembly, and called for a national vote to make France an empire once more. He was crowned Napoleon III in December, 1852.

Napoleon III's main aim was to make France the most powerful nation in Europe. He had Baron Georges Haussmann, a leading city planner and administrator, redesign much of Paris as a modern capital city. Napoleon III encouraged the expansion of industry and communications, especially railroads. After an agreement with the Egyptian Government, French engineers, led by Ferdinand de Lesseps, dug the Suez Canal, gaining a foothold for France in the Middle East.

Napoleon III's ambitions also involved military glory. In 1854 he led France into the Crimean War against Russia, which had been trying to win an outlet on the Mediterranean. Five years later he supported the Italians in their fight for liberation from Austrian control, and France annexed the Italian territories of Nice and Savoy. He tried to extend French influence to the New World by putting the Austrian archduke Maximilian in charge of a Mexican "empire." (The venture failed, however, and Maximilian was executed by a Mexican firing squad.)

The Franco-Prussian War. But France was in a period of economic decline, and Napoleon III's wars were costly. Opposition to his policies grew steadily. There was also a threat from outside. The north German kingdom of Prussia had grown powerful under the leadership of Chancellor Otto von Bismarck. In July, 1870, Bismarck created a situation in which France was forced to declare war. Within 3 months Napoleon's armies had been defeated, he had been captured, and Paris was under siege. Prussia's peace terms were harsh—France lost most of Alsace and Lorraine and had to pay 5,000,000,000 francs to Germany. The Second Empire had been destroyed.

The Third Republic

Upon learning of Napoleon III's defeat and capture, the citizens of Paris had revolted and proclaimed France a republic once again. After the peace treaty of 1871, much internal unrest continued. When the elected National Assembly decided to meet in Versailles, site of the royal palace, Parisian workers and liberals, fearing a return to monarchy, set up their own revolutionary government—the Commune. For more than 2 months they tried to win national support, but the Commune was finally crushed by Versailles' troops under Marshal Patrice de MacMahon.

The Third Republic quickly paid the war indemnity to Germany and put France on the road to economic recovery. Industrial and agricultural output increased. Shipping and trade expanded. France gained colonies in Africa, including Morocco and Tunisia, and in Indochina (now Laos, Cambodia, and Vietnam). By the late 1880's the Third Republic had weathered many storms. There had been dissent from disappointed royalists and from newly born socialist groups and labor unions, some of which drew inspiration from the history of the Paris Commune.

The Dreyfus Case. In 1894 a young Jewish army captain, Alfred Dreyfus, was accused of selling military secrets to Germany. He was court-martialed, convicted, and sent to Devils Island—the French prison colony off the coast of South America. His family attempted to prove his innocence and gained the support of men like novelist Emile Zola and journalist and political leader Georges Clemenceau. In 1906 Dreyfus was completely cleared.

The Dreyfus Case was more than an injustice against one man. It was a national upheaval, and it became a focus for many of the political and social questions of the day. The division between the conservative forces of the Church, Army, and monarchists and the liberals was intensified. As a result of the Dreyfus Case, by the early 20th century the Army's influence in government had been largely destroyed, and the monarchists were also no longer politically effective. In 1905 the Concordat with the Catholic Church was repealed, and Church and State were completely separated. But little was done to improve working conditions in France. There were constant strikes and protests. Liberals, led by Clemenceau, tried but failed to put through reforms, including old-age pensions, workmen's compensation, and an income-tax bill.

World War I. In 1907 France signed the Triple Entente with England and Russia, each pledging its support should the others be attacked. Italy and the Austro-Hungarian Dual Monarchy joined Germany, which had grown more powerful since 1870, in the Triple Alliance. By 1914 almost every nation in Europe had entered one alliance or another, and when war broke out in July, it involved all of Europe.

The French fought the German invaders bravely, using every resource at their command. Nevertheless they were pushed back, and the Germans drew closer and closer to Paris. At one critical moment even Paris taxicabs were rushing reinforcements and supplies to the defending troops. The French capital was saved. On the western front, a stalemate gradually developed. By 1915 France had lost almost 800,000 men, although neither side had gained much ground. As the war continued, the French had some military successes. But again, the cost was enormous. In 1916, during the defense of Verdun alone, there were some 500,000 casualties.

The United States entered the war in 1917. Before the end of 1918 a combined French, British, and American army was able to push the Germans out of France.

Between the Wars

In 1919, by the Treaty of Versailles, France regained Alsace and Lorraine, with their rich mineral resources. The German coalfields in the Saar Valley were ceded to France for 15 years. Germany was disarmed and had to pay billions in damages. But over 1,300,000 Frenchmen had died in the war, and France had been devastated. French agriculture had been ruined and its factories destroyed. Shipping and trade were at a standstill.

The work of rebuilding the economy was begun. Industry and agriculture were modernized, and prosperity began to return. At the beginning of the 1930s France had a thriving economy, and the franc was stable. But during 1931, the worldwide Depression hit France. Thousands were out of work, and there were renewed strikes and demonstrations. In this situation no single party could maintain control for long, and within 5 years there were 14 cabinets. In spite of intensive efforts to stabilize the country, the divisions within France grew deeper.

Perhaps most important, a re-armed Germany under the leadership of Adolf Hitler again presented a threat to peace in Europe. In September, 1939, when Hitler's armies marched into Poland, France and England came to the support of their ally. Soon all of Europe was at war once again.

World War II

The Maginot Line, which the French had built along the border with Germany, proved useless when the Germans chose to strike at France from the Low Countries. France fell in June, 1940. Marshal Pétain, a World War I hero, signed an armistice with Germany. Most of northern and central France, including Paris, was under German occupation. In southern, unoccupied France a new government was set up, based in the resort town of Vichy. Led by Pétain and Pierre Laval, the Vichy government worked with Nazi Germany.

But most of the French did not collaborate, and internal resistance movements sprang up. Their efforts ranged from work slowdowns and sabotage to the guerrilla tactics of the fighters known as the Maquis. There was resistance outside of France as well. In 1940, the French general Charles de Gaulle escaped to England, where he issued a call to continue the fight. He put himself at the head of the Free French movement, which worked with the Allies against Germany. Later de Gaulle was recognized as a leader of a French provisional government organized in liberated North Africa. (The Vichy forces in Tunisia, Morocco, and Algeria had surrendered almost immediately.) In retaliation, the German Army occupied all of France, and the country became part of Hitler's Festung Europa ("fortress Europe").

On D-Day—June 6, 1944—the Allied counteroffensive began. American and British forces landed on the beaches of Normandy and began fighting their way inland. Allied planes struck from the air, and the German defeat was underway. By late August, Paris was liberated. General de Gaulle led a triumphal march down the Champs-Elysées, and within a few months, all of France was free.

De Gaulle had become a worldwide symbol of French resistance, and for over a year after his return to France he was a virtual dictator by acclamation. In the fall of 1945 an elected constitutional convention

The old port of Honfleur, in Normandy, is near the D-Day invasion sites.

named him provisional premier-president of the new Fourth Republic. In January, 1946, however, de Gaulle resigned because he felt the constitution that had been drafted did not provide enough power for the president. Nine months later, in spite of de Gaulle's opposition, a new constitution was finally adopted. France returned to regular political life for the first time since 1940. But once again there were so many factions and so much party rivalry that the resulting coalition governments could not stay in power long.

Postwar France

Because of the desperate political situation, French recovery from the war was slow at first. Prices rose, the franc was unstable, and there was serious inflation. Strikes were the order of the day, and the Communist Party gained strength as discontent grew.

By 1949, however, the situation had improved. Under a plan designed by economist Jean Monnet, and with Marshall Plan aid from the United States, French industry was rebuilt and modernized. Coal and steel production in Lorraine increased, and gradually all French industrial production reached or surpassed its prewar strength. French agricultural output expanded too, as farming methods became more modern. The French merchant marine was soon carrying French exports all around the world once more. As the country became more prosperous, tourism again grew in importance.

After the war, many European leaders felt greater economic recovery and strength could come through co-operation and union. In 1948, for example, a customs union among Belgium, the Netherlands, and Luxembourg (Benelux) went into effect. In the 1950's the French statesman Robert Schuman took the lead in proposing that the countries of Western Europe pool basic resources. This led to the six-nation Coal and Steel Community. Soon thereafter came the European Economic Community, or Common Market. France both contributed greatly to and gained much economic strength from these European developments. Many French leaders believed that genuine European unity—political as well as economic—might eventually follow.

Although the French economy grew stronger, politics remained shaky. There was also trouble in the French colonies. Indochina had revolted at the end of World War II, and 9 years later the French Army still had not been able to regain control. In North Africa, too, France was faced with multiplying difficulties—especially in Algeria. A drive for independence began there in the 1950's, but the *colons* (French-Algerians, many of whom had never lived in France) and the Army were equally determined that Algeria remain French. Tunisia and Morocco were also demanding independence.

In 1954 Pierre Mendès-France, an economist and statesman, became premier, with a sizable majority in the National Assembly. Under his leadership France withdrew from Indochina. Economic progress continued. Premier Mendès-France also granted more self-government to Tunisia and introduced reforms in Morocco. In Europe, the Mendès-France government signed economic agreements with West Germany and continued French participation in the Council of Europe and NATO.

But the Algerian situation, which had become a full-scale revolution and civil war, could not be resolved. By 1958, the question had so divided France that effective government was at an end.

De Gaulle and the Fifth Republic. In May, 1958, faced with a *colon* and Army uprising in Algiers, the National Assembly called General de Gaulle to power. His condition for accepting leadership again was the adoption of a new constitution, with strengthened powers for the executive branch, as well as economic and social reforms. France had grown tired of unstable politics and cabinet crises. The constitution was accepted by approximately 80 percent of French voters.

De Gaulle's Fifth Republic began in June, 1958. By 1962 the Algerian conflict was settled, and Algeria became independent. The new Constitution had also created the French Community—an association of France and its former colonies.

De Gaulle was president of the Fifth Republic for 11 years. During this period he attempted to reshape France so it would develop according to his aims. He believed that France should be strong internally and that it should be the leader of Europe as well. Because of this, in 1966 he withdrew France from NATO military affairs, and he consistently blocked Britain's entry into the European Economic Community (EEC).

But eventually, dissatisfaction grew. In 1969, de Gaulle's proposals for further constitutional reform were rejected, and he resigned. Later presidents governed France along conservative lines until François Mitterrand, a Socialist, was elected in 1981. He nationalized some banks and industries, but was forced by conservative gains to moderate his policies. Mitterrand was reelected in 1988, and in 1991 made history by naming France's first woman prime minister, Edith Cresson. In 1993 legislative elections, a huge defeat for the Socialists resulted in a dramatic shift toward the right. Public dissatisfaction with the Socialists was echoed in the May 1995 presidential election, won by conservative Jacques Chirac. During the subsequent years, though, the conservatives fell out of favor with the public, and Chirac called for an early parliamentary election in 1997. The Socialists gained a narrow majority, and Lionel Jospin was appointed prime minister.

French Overseas Departments and Territories

France once controlled a vast empire. Today it retains only a few holdings. It has three Overseas Departments in North America. The islands of Saint Pierre and Miquelon off eastern Canada (discussed in a sidebar in Volume 5's NORTH AMERICA article) form one department. The other two are the islands of Guadeloupe and Martinique in the Caribbean Sea. (See the article CARIBBEAN SEA AND ISLANDS in Volume 5.) France's other Overseas Departments are French Guiana in South America (discussed in a sidebar in SOUTH AMERICA in Volume 6), and the island of Réunion in the Indian Ocean (an article on RÉUNION appears in Volume 1).

The French Overseas Territories are the South Pacific island groups of French Polynesia, New Caledonia, and Wallis and Futuna Islands (see the article OCEANIA in Volume 2). France administered the New Hebrides group jointly with the United Kingdom until it became the independent nation of Vanuatu in 1980 (see the article VANUATU in Volume 2).

Soon after the French Community was established in 1958, 12 of the African colonies became independent. For some years, economic, cultural, and defense ties were maintained among the member nations through the Community. But eventually, the African nations forged links directly among themselves and with France, and the Community ceased to exist. France's last African colony, the Afar-Issa Territory (now Djibouti), became independent in 1977. France's involvement with its former colonies has been much reduced in recent years.

The Future

In spite of changing governments, economic progress, and new and different ways of life, the essential nature of France remains unchanged. Not long ago, a prominent Frenchman said, "France is not only a land, a people, and a State, it is also a spirit." On many occasions, this *esprit* has brought France to the peak of European power. It also has helped France to rise from total defeat to new life. France is a nation that brings to the future of Europe and the world a heritage of intellectual and cultural leadership and a belief in the power of human intelligence.

JEAN JOUGHIN, The American University

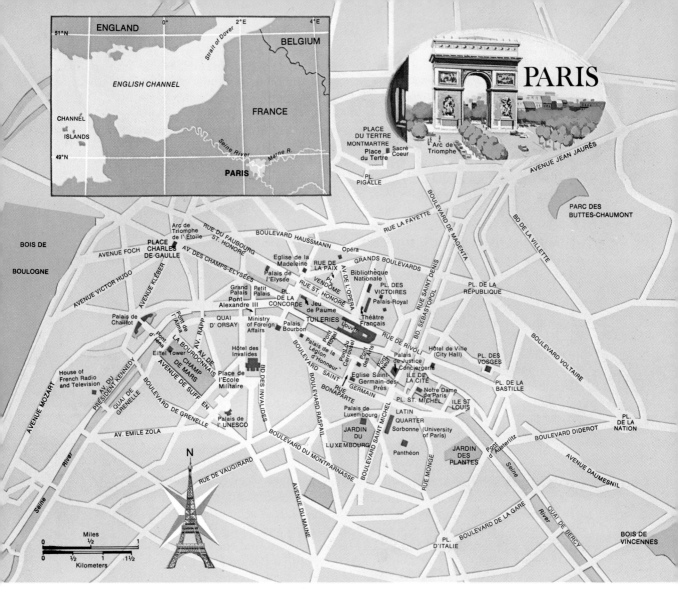

Paris

In 16th-century France, conflict between Huguenots (French Protestants) and Roman Catholics erupted into full-scale civil war. Prince Henry of Navarre, a Huguenot, was recognized as the heir to the French throne in 1589, but he had to fight to gain his kingdom. He had brilliant military successes—up to a point, for Paris refused to submit. Without Paris Henry knew he could never win the country, so in 1593 he took the only course left and gave up his Protestant faith. According to tradition, he said, "*Paris vaut bien une messe* [Paris is well worth a mass]." Within a year he was crowned King Henry IV of France.

Almost 350 years later, during World War II, a very different kind of European leader also recognized the great symbolic value of the French capital. Adolf Hitler had given orders to General Dietrich von Choltitz—his commander in German-occupied Paris—to mine many of the city's great buildings. If the Allies took Paris, the general was to light the fuses. As the Allies reached the suburbs, the time had come. But even after a personal call from Hitler in Berlin during which the Nazi leader demanded, "Is Paris burning?" the mines were not set off. Von Choltitz said later that he could not take on the responsibility of destroying a city that was such a vital part of the heritage, not only of Frenchmen, but of people everywhere.

PARIS AND ITS RIVER

What has often been called the most beautiful city in the world began about 2,000 years ago as Lutetia Parisiorum ("Lutetia of the Parisii"). Then it was a tiny community on an island in the Seine River in northwestern France. Its people, the Parisii, lived by fishing and trading. After Roman legions conquered Gaul in the 1st century B.C., the town began to expand, mainly onto the left bank of the Seine. Today Paris has more than 2 million inhabitants, and covers an area of some 41 sq. mi. (106 sq. km.) on either side of the Île de la Cité ("island of the city"), where it began.

Location on a river with access to the sea was always important to the growth of Paris. It was a trading center in its early days, and today various canals have made it a major inland port. Goods from many countries are loaded and unloaded at its docks. Barges from all over Western Europe pass under its bridges and can be seen tied up below the embankments.

The Seine is also one of the beauties of Paris, and in this role, too, it is central to the life of the city—so much so that it is easy to understand why one old song describes the river as "a lover whose beloved is Paris." Parisians and visitors alike enjoy quiet walks along its quays and embankments. Fishermen can still be seen at many locations along the Seine, though their catches are usually so small that they are thrown back. Another Seine attraction is the *bouquinistes'* stalls, found mainly along the Left Bank quays. These large stalls, filled with old books and prints, offer many happy hours of another kind of "fishing" to the stroller.

As the Seine curves through Paris, it divides the city into two sections. The Rive Droite, or Right Bank, lies north of the river, and the Rive Gauche, or Left Bank, lies to the south. A trip on the river in a *bateau mouche* (sight-seeing boat) under its *ponts* (bridges) and past many of the city's great buildings on either bank is an ideal—and restful —way for the visitor to get a feeling for the many cities that are Paris.

Île de la Cité and Île Saint-Louis. On the Île de la Cité stands the majestic Cathedral of Notre Dame, begun in the 12th century. On clear days, its soaring spires and arching buttresses cast their reflections in the rippling waters below. The sculptures on the portals of the cathedral are considered among the world's finest examples of Gothic art. The cathedral tower offers an excellent view of Paris, as well as a close-up look at the gargoyles. These grotesque stone monsters, whose fantastic horned and beaked heads are popular symbols of Paris on postcards and posters, were added to the cathedral during a 19th-century restoration.

Also on the Île de la Cité is Sainte-Chapelle, built for King Louis IX of France (Saint Louis). The 13th-century building—which actually houses two chapels—is known for its beautiful stained-glass windows,

The glowing stained-glass windows of Sainte-Chapelle—a building that is a masterpiece of Gothic architecture and one of the great beauties of Paris.

The Pont Neuf spans both arms of the Seine at the tip of the Île de la Cité.

depicting scenes from the Bible, and for its richly decorated interior. Its graceful, gilded pillars and arches form a lovely contrast to the red and blue walls and ceilings, embellished with gold fleurs-de-lis (the royal symbol of France).

Near Sainte-Chapelle is the massive Conciergerie, a building that witnessed a grim period in French history. A visit to its cells still summons up reminders of the French Revolution and of those who were imprisoned there before going to the guillotine.

Across from the Ile de la Cité is the Ile Saint-Louis. With its 17th-century mansions and quiet courtyards, it is a peaceful place in the middle of Paris, and a walk around the island is like a journey back in time.

The oldest bridge in Paris crosses the Seine near the western end of the Ile de la Cité. It is one of the many contradictions that make up Paris that the bridge is still called Pont Neuf ("new bridge"), though it was completed in 1604. Below the bridge, on the very tip of the Ile de la Cité, is the small Square du Vert Galant. Named for King Henry IV (who was called the evergreen gallant because of his lifelong interest in women), this tiny park with its sheltering trees is one of the most charming—and romantic—spots in Paris.

THE RIGHT BANK

Downstream, the next bridge across the Seine is the Pont des Arts, and on the right bank of the river are the vast buildings of the Louvre, one of the world's greatest art museums. Originally a royal palace, its halls and rooms contain countless masterpieces. The Louvre is grander than ever after a 15-year, $1.7 billion renovation completed in 1998, featuring a stunning glass pyramid designed by I.M. Pei. Among its treasures are the ancient Greek *Vénus de Milo* and *Winged Victory*; Leonardo da Vinci's *Mona Lisa*; and James McNeill Whistler's *Arrangement in Gray and Black* (better known as "Whistler's Mother").

The Louvre's impressionist and postimpressionist collections, once housed in the Jeu de Paume, former site of the royal tennis courts, are now impressively displayed in the new Musée D'Orsay, a glittering, renovated former railway station. Found there are the splendid paintings of Edouard Manet, Claude Monet, Paul Cézanne, and Paul Gauguin.

The Tuileries is a formal park, with bright flowerbeds and ancient shade trees, and it makes a lovely oasis amid the city's bustle. Parisians and visitors alike enjoy strolling there, often stopping for a drink or a snack. For children, the gardens offer pony rides, miniature carousels, and other activities. Toy boats can be rented; seen against Paris' blue skies, their white and scarlet sails echo the colors of the French flag.

A few steps from the Tuileries is the Place de la Concorde. This great square, with its fountains and statues representing eight French cities, is one of the most beautiful in the world. It also has some of the world's most notorious traffic jams, which even the Paris police have difficulty unsnarling. In 1793, during the French Revolution, the guillotine was set up in the square. Louis XVI and his queen, Marie Antoinette, were only two of its many victims.

The Place de la Concorde faces the broad, tree-lined and café-lined Avenue des Champs-Elysées, which stretches 1.25 mi. (2 km.) to the Place Charles de Gaulle, with the Arc de Triomphe at its center. This structure, the world's largest triumphal arch, was begun in 1806 as a memorial to Napoleonic victories. In its shadow an eternal light burns over the tomb of the French Unknown Soldier. Though there is an elevator, many visitors seem to prefer climbing the dark, 164-foot (50 meters) winding staircase to the roof. The view from the top of the arch is excellent, and it also explains the former name of the place, l'Étoile, because 12 wide avenues radiate from it like the points of a star. (Étoile means "star.")

Every Bastille Day (July 14) the tricolor is seen all along the Champs-Élysées, and a brilliant military parade is held there. Tanks bearing the names of great French generals and victories thunder down the avenue, followed by field artillery and *pompiers* (fire engines). The horsemen of the Garde Républicaine ride by, their spurs jingling and their golden helmets flashing in the sun.

The streets branching off the Champs-Élysées are lined by many of the elegant hotels, restaurants, and theaters for which Paris is known. Many of the houses of *haute couture* ("high fashion") that have made Paris a world fashion center are located there as well. In the 19th century, an Englishman named Charles Frederick Worth opened a dressmaking shop on the Rue de la Paix. When Empress Eugénie (wife of Napoleon III) began to patronize Worth, a Worth gown—and soon a Paris gown—became a symbol of style, elegance, and luxury. Fashion became an important Paris industry. Today, for many women a trip to Paris would be incomplete without a stop at the fashion houses of Dior, Chanel, Givenchy, St. Laurent, or any one of at least a dozen others.

Paris' most elegant street, however, is the Rue du Faubourg-St. Honoré, which starts near the Place Vendôme. Site of the Élysée Palace, home of French presidents, the street is best-known for its shopping. Both

The magnificent fountains in the Place de la Concorde are copies of those at St. Peter's Square in Rome.

Bastille Day. Jet smoke trails paint the tricolor across the Paris sky.

sides are lined with shops offering a dazzling array of fine goods to tempt the shopper and collector. From the graceful symmetry of the Place Vendôme, with its column built from cannons captured in the Napoleonic victory at the battle of Austerlitz (1805), it is only a short walk to the Madeleine. This massive church, designed like a Roman temple, was built as a "temple of glory" for Napoleon and his armies. To the east, down the Boulevard de la Madeleine, is another landmark, the Opéra. The ornate, 19th-century building has long been a magnet for music lovers from all over the world.

Nearby are the Grands Boulevards—a series of wide avenues that run roughly from the Place de la Concorde to the Place de la Bastille. The avenues include the Boulevard de la Madeleine, the Boulevard des Capucines, and the Boulevard des Italiens. These streets, too, are known for their cafés, restaurants, movie houses, theaters, and shops. Two of the largest department stores in Paris—the Galeries Lafayette and Au Printemps—are located on the Boulevard Haussmann. This avenue was named for Baron Georges Haussmann, who was appointed prefect of the Seine by Napoleon III in 1853. Under Haussmann's direction many of Paris' streets were widened to relieve traffic congestion, and new connecting avenues were laid out. The city was divided into 20 arrondissements for more efficient administration. Haussmann is also remembered for his modernization of the Paris sewers, and even today a trip through the *égouts* in a boat is one of the most curious ways a visitor can get to know Paris. A memorable scene in Victor Hugo's 19th-century novel *Les Misérables* involves a chase through their dank depths. The sewers also carry the city's telephone and telegraph cables as well as the complex network of the *pneumatiques*—tubes through which letters, in metal containers, are transmitted rapidly by compressed air.

South of the Grands Boulevards is another Paris attraction. At the Comédie-Française, the French national theater, the works of great classic

The Champs-Élysées, Paris's finest avenue, is lined with busy cafés, shops, hotels, and theaters.

playwrights are produced. The spot also has other associations, for Joan of Arc was wounded here in 1429, during the Hundred Years War.

At the eastern end of the Grands Boulevards, near the very old section of Paris called the Marais, is the Place de la Bastille. Nothing remains there of the ancient royal prison—symbol of the oppressive power of the French monarchy—that was attacked on July 14, 1789, signalling the beginning of the French Revolution. Only a column commemorating the 1830 and 1848 revolutions marks the spot today.

Also near the Grands Boulevards is the Forum des Halles, a modern leisure complex of glass and concrete, containing shops, cafés, restaurants, and movie houses. The Forum was opened in 1979. For eight centuries the site had been occupied by Les Halles, the central meat, fish, and produce market that the 19th-century author Emile Zola called *le ventre de Paris* ("the belly of Paris"). No longer able to handle the vast volume of goods, the ancient market was moved to the suburbs in 1969, and two years later its old iron pavilions, dating from the mid-19th century, were torn down.

Close by the new Forum, on Rue St. Martin, stands the ultra-modern Georges Pompidou National Center of Art and Culture, named after the second president of the Fifth Republic. When it opened in 1977, its architecture, with its visible plumbing and electrical pipes, transparent escalators and elevators, and prominent structural beams, was a shock to many conservative tastes. The building houses the National Museum of Modern Art, an industrial design center, a large public library, research facilities, and a children's workshop. Besides the attractions of its excellent collections and temporary exhibits, the Beaubourg Center, as it is generally known, has already become a focal point where street artists, musicians, and mimes ply their trades to throngs of *les vrai Parisiens* ("true Parisians") and tourists alike.

Les Halles' new location covers some 1,540 acres (623 hectares) at Rungis near Orly Airport, south of the city. Orly is among the world's busiest international airports. With its modern facilities, shops, restaurants, and hotels, it has been described as a self-sufficient city. North of Paris, at Roissy, is the new Charles de Gaulle Airport. Larger than Orly, it is in the same category in terms of air traffic. Closer to Paris is the city's domestic airport, Le Bourget.

THE LEFT BANK

For many visitors to Paris, the essence of the city is still found on the left bank of the Seine. Since the 13th century, when the Sorbonne (now part of the Universities of Paris) was founded there, the Left Bank has traditionally been the students' section of the city. The area was also called the Latin Quarter because Latin was the universal language of learning in the Middle Ages.

Much of the life of the Latin Quarter centers around the wide Boulevard Saint Michel, known affectionately as the Boul' Mich. Its many cafés are popular with students, who often meet there to discuss their work. Just off the Boul' Mich is the Palais du Luxembourg, built in the 17th century for Marie de Médicis, widow of Henry IV. The Jardin du Luxembourg (Luxembourg Garden), with its lake, terraces, and flowerbeds, is also a favorite spot for students.

Another focus of Left-Bank activity is the Boulevard Saint-Germain, which intersects the Boul' Mich. The boulevard takes its name from the oldest church in Paris, Saint-Germain-des-Prés, begun in the 10th century. The church contains the tombstones of several famous Frenchmen, including the 17th-century philosopher René Descartes. Near the church, there is a bust by Pablo Picasso dedicated to the 20th-century poet Guillaume Apollinaire.

At the cafés and brasseries in the area the visitor can have an espresso or *une fine* (one of France's excellent brandies) while he enjoys all the activity and bustle going on around him. The narrow streets of the Left Bank are also fun for the visitor, for they are a shopper's delight, abounding with antique shops, bookstores, and art galleries. Every year, too, there are more and more of the tiny boutiques that sell inexpensive young fashions that bear the unmistakable stamp of Paris.

One of the city's best-known sights is the Panthéon, atop the hill of Saint Genevieve. Begun during the reign of King Louis XV, the building was to be dedicated to Genevieve, the patron saint of Paris. However, after its completion in 1789, the revolutionary government decided to turn the building into a *panthéon,* from the ancient Greek word for "a temple of all the gods." Great Frenchmen—the "gods" of their time— were buried there, from the politician Mirabeau to the philosophers Voltaire and Jean Jacques Rousseau. In the 19th century, the authors Victor Hugo and Emile Zola, and the teacher Louis Braille, who developed a method by which the blind can read and write, were interred in the Panthéon.

Another Left-Bank landmark is the Hôtel des Invalides, founded by Louis XIV in the 17th century as a home for disabled soldiers. Today it houses one of the world's largest military museums. But the building is best-known as the final resting place of the last remains of Napoleon, brought back from the South Atlantic island of St. Helena and placed there in 1840. Many people still visit the tomb of the man who brought France both glory and disaster, and who played such a central role in the history of the world.

The huge complex also includes two churches, one with a chapel dedicated to Napoleon. On sunny days, the Invalides' gilded dome, with its tall spire piercing the sky, is one of the most striking sights in Paris. The best view is from the right bank of the Seine, across the broad Pont Alexandre III, built in 1900.

The Métro

No one can truly say he knows Paris without having traveled on the Métro (short for Métropolitain). The Paris subway system was opened in 1900, and today its total length is well over 100 miles (160 km.). The Métro is one of the most efficient subways in the world. The Métro stations are clean and brightly lit, and some of them offer even more. The Louvre stop, for example, has recently been modernized. Reproductions of paintings decorate its walls and copies of sculpture stand in niches along the platforms. Most important, however, every station has clear, easy-to-follow maps that make it simple—even for a foreigner—to reach any destination.

Montmartre

One favorite trip for Parisians and visitors alike is out to Sacré-Coeur—the Basilica of the Sacred Heart—high on the Butte de Montmartre (Montmartre hill) in northern Paris. At a centrally located Right-Bank station, such as the one at Concorde, the Métro rider buys a ticket for the Porte de la Chapelle line. (Like most Métro lines, it is named for its last stop, one of the ancient gates of Paris.) He gets off at the Abbesses stop, in Montmartre. Near the pleasant, tree-lined Place des Abbesses, a funicular climbs the hill to the lower terraces of Sacré-Coeur.

The white domes of this church have been a symbol of Paris since 1914. After the overwhelming French defeat in the Franco-Prussian War (1870–71), French Catholics started a national fund for a church of the Sacred Heart. The church was to be a symbol of French hope and a new beginning. Some 50 years—and 40,000,000 francs—later, the huge building was consecrated. Statues of Saint Louis (King Louis IX) and Joan of Arc stand on the upper terrace, above a steep flight of steps leading to the entrance of the Basilica. Sacré-Coeur's steeple contains the Savoyarde, a 19-ton bell that is one of the largest and deepest-sounding in the world.

But there is more to Montmartre than Sacré-Coeur. The community on the hill is one of the oldest and most picturesque sections of Paris, and since the mid-19th century, it has been the home of countless artists and painters. One of the best-known was Maurice Utrillo, whose charming paintings of Montmartre's ancient, winding streets, usually with the domes of Sacré-Coeur in the background, captured the atmosphere of the area for people everywhere. Perhaps because of all the artists who lived—and still live—in Montmartre, it is also known for its night life. The cafés around the Place du Tertre are crowded every evening, as are

The whole panorama of Paris can be seen from the terraces of Sacré-Coeur.

the nearby nightclubs and dance halls of the Place Pigalle. The Moulin de la Galette, formerly a windmill, is one of these.

The Two Bois

Visitors can also ride the Métro out to the two *bois* ("woods") of Paris—the Bois de Boulogne in the west and the Bois de Vincennes in the southeast. The Bois de Boulogne, with its ancient trees, was a favorite spot for walks *à la campagne* ("in the country") as long ago as the 17th century. By the mid-19th century, Paris had grown outward until it reached the edge of the Bois. In 1852, Napoleon III gave the forest to the city. Because Napoleon admired everything English, Baron Haussmann based his designs for the Bois on London's Hyde Park. Shady paths wind through the trees and around the Bois' two lakes, where rowboats can be rented. Paris families often spend Sundays in the Bois, enjoying a picnic they have brought along. There are also several outdoor restaurants in the Bois, and nothing could be more pleasant than a peaceful lunch outdoors, watching the ever-changing patterns of the sunlight through the leaves and finishing the last of the wine. The Bois de Boulogne also contains an amusement park, a zoo, and the two Paris racetracks, Longchamp and Auteuil.

Some 9 mi. (15 km.) across Paris to the southeast is the Bois de Vincennes, with its 14th-century castle. Among those who died in the castle dungeons was King Henry V of England, in 1422. The Bois de Vincennes is also the home of the Paris Zoo, where most of the animals live in large enclosures that resemble their natural environments.

The Suburbs of Paris

Surrounding the city on all sides are its many suburbs. In the northern suburbs, industrial equipment and chemicals are produced. Farther west, along the Seine, are the Citroën and Renault plants—the two largest automobile manufacturers in France. The huge Euro Disneyland complex, opened in 1992, is located in Marne-la-Vallée, about 20 mi. (32 km.) to the west of the city proper. Most French movies are made in the southern suburbs of Boulogne-Billancourt and Joinville-le-Pont. Paris is constantly expanding, and each year finds new housing developments— and often whole new towns—growing up farther and farther away from the city center.

CITY OF LIGHT

The great capital is the center of France in every way. It is the country's biggest city. All major French roads begin or end there. It is the center of the French railway network, and some 1 million travelers use its *gares,* or stations, daily. It has the largest airport and is the focus of one of the biggest industrial complexes in the country. It is also the seat of government, from which the country is run. In all these ways, Paris can be compared to a huge, powerful magnet.

But the most fitting description of Paris is still as *la ville lumière,* the City of Light, for the capital is also like a great lamp, whose rays reach far beyond the city's boundaries. The decisions made in Paris, and the ideas born there, affect all of France. The city is the intellectual center of France —and, by extension, of much of Europe. Most of the 18,500 books published in France annually come from Paris, and many of them are written there as well. The country's most important newspapers, such as *France-Soir, Le Figaro,* and *Le Monde,* and its leading magazines, such as *Paris Match* and *L'Express,* are published there. It is the home of the French radio and television industry.

Because it is a city of ideas, with an atmosphere of freedom of thought, many international organizations have made Paris their headquarters. One of these, UNESCO (United Nations Educational, Scientific, and Cultural Organization), has added something special to the city. Besides its unusual architecture (it is shaped like a three-pointed star), the UNESCO building has paintings by Picasso and Rufino Tamayo, a contemporary Mexican artist; sculptures by Henry Moore of England and mobiles by Alexander Calder of the United States; and outdoor murals done in enamel by the Spaniards Joan Miró and Josep Artigas.

Across the Seine, past the level green fields of the Champ de Mars, and past the Eiffel Tower, is the Palais de Chaillot. Today the palace houses several museums, and in the years after World War II, some of the first meetings of the United Nations were held there.

The Eiffel Tower in Paris, erected in 1889 from more than 12,000 wrought-iron parts, is 1,056 ft. tall.

The Eiffel Tower

The Eiffel Tower was designed by the French engineer Alexandre Gustave Eiffel for the Paris Universal Exhibition of 1889. Originally considered an ugly blot on the city's landscape, the tower was almost torn down several times, but it eventually became the city's best-loved landmark. On clear days the view from the top extends more than 42 mi. (67 km.) over the many cities that are Paris—the Paris of some 2.5 million tourists per year, with its hotels, fine restaurants, and museums; and the Paris of some 2 million Parisians, as rich and varied as life itself. Traditionally, just before sunset is the best time to visit the tower. Then, for the people who love it, the City of Light takes on a special glow. A 16th-century Parisian, the essayist Michel de Montaigne, proclaimed that he was a Frenchman only because of the great city, which he called "the glory of France and one of the greatest ornaments of the world."

Reviewed by RÉGINALD DE WARREN, Counselor
Embassy of France to the United States, Washington, D.C.

Monaco, a tiny principality on the Mediterranean, draws thousands of tourists to its famous beaches and casino.

MONACO

The Principality of Monaco is a tiny independent country surrounded on three sides by France and on the fourth by the Mediterranean Sea. It has a 3-mile (5-kilometer) coastline on the part of the Mediterranean that the French call the Côte d'Azur ("azure coast") because of its lovely blue skies and blue waters. Hemmed in between high rock formations and a sweeping bay, with houses perched on cliffs overlooking the small, beautiful harbor, the whole country looks like a huge amphitheater.

WAY OF LIFE

About four-fifths of the residents of Monaco, which is less than half the size of New York City's Central Park, are foreigners, mostly French and Italian. The waiting list for Monacan citizenship is quite long. Roman Catholicism is the official state religion, and education is compulsory between the ages of 6 and 16.

The capital, **Monaco-Ville,** is on a rocky promontory, more than 200 feet (60 meters) above sea level. There, in addition to the castle, is the world-famous Oceanographic Museum, founded by Prince Albert I, great-grandfather of the present prince. A fine scientist, Prince Albert

FACTS AND FIGURES

OFFICIAL NAME: Principality of Monaco.

NATIONALITY: Monacan(s) or Monegasque(s).

CAPITAL AND CHIEF CITY: Monaco-Ville.

LOCATION: Southeastern France. **Boundaries**—Mediterranean Sea, France.

AREA: 0.7 sq. mi. (1.9 sq. km.).

PHYSICAL FEATURES: Highest point—about 459 ft. (140 m.). **Lowest point**—sea level.

POPULATION: 31,892 (1997; annual growth 0.49%).

MAJOR LANGUAGES: French (official), English.

MAJOR RELIGION: Roman Catholicism.

GOVERNMENT: Constitutional monarchy. **Head of state**—prince. **Head of government**—minister of state. **Legislature**—unicameral National Council.

ECONOMY: Industries and products—tourism, chemicals, plastics, cosmetics, food processing, glassmaking.

MONETARY UNIT: 1 French franc = 100 centimes.

NATIONAL HOLIDAY: November 19 (National Day).

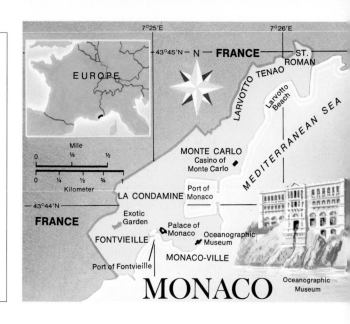

started Monaco on its way to becoming a center for modern oceanographic research. Albert also began the Exotic Gardens, which grow on the slopes of a rocky cliff. The gardens contain one of the world's finest collections of subtropical and semidesert flora.

This little country offers a great variety of sporting and cultural events. There is the Monaco Grand Prix, an annual event in which some of the world's greatest automobile racers speed through the hilly, winding city streets. The opera house, which is a part of the Grand Casino building, was the scene of the original presentations by the famed Ballets Russes de Monte Carlo of some of the masterpieces produced by the great choreographer Sergei Diaghilev. It was also the site of the first productions of a number of world-renowned operas.

Monaco is the site of an imaginative urban-renewal program. In 1964, the railroad that ran through Monaco was rerouted underground. The entire seafront area was rebuilt, and an area of 1,000,000 sq. ft. (93,000

The Monte Carlo Casino, off-limits to the native Monegasques, provides three percent of Monaco's revenue.

square meters) of land was reclaimed from the sea by filling in the shore-line with soil from nearby French hillsides and with rock from the 2-mile (3-kilometer) underground tunnel that was blasted out of a hillside to accommodate the railroad. A new highway was constructed, and new hotels, apartments, and restaurants were built. The program has continued with a larger reclaimed area beyond the rock. It will provide additional industrial sites and more land for high-rise luxury hotels. Monaco will thus be able to house more and more visitors who come to this miniature nation where, as Colette, the famous French novelist, said, the "frontiers are only flowers."

ECONOMY

The economic life of Monaco is based on the same ingenuity that has kept the country independent all these years. This is a state that has no national debt, no income taxes, and no inheritance taxes.

What is the basis for the fiscal magic? Profits from the tourists who flock here to enjoy the unfailingly delightful weather are most important. For most of the year the streets of Monaco are filled with foreigners, and the sparkling waters of the harbor are full of pleasure craft flying flags from all over the world. The government also profits from the sale of tobacco, a government monopoly, and from sales, customs, and business taxes.

A large amount of revenue comes from the sale of postage stamps. Ever since Monaco's first stamps were issued in 1860, collectors have prized the many artistic series illustrating the principality's famous landmarks and its major activities.

At the turn of the century the glittering Monte Carlo gambling casino brought in 75 percent of Monaco's revenue, but today it provides less than 4 percent. Despite the limited space and lack of raw materials, Monaco has a prosperous industrial community in the section called Fontvielle, near the western boundary. There, cosmetics, perfumes, elegant clothing, jewelry, fine art books, chocolates, and small precision instruments are produced. The bustling business section around the port is called La Condamine.

HISTORY AND GOVERNMENT

The coat of arms of the Grimaldi Family, showing two monks with raised swords, commemorates the capture of the fortress. In 1297, François ("the Malicious") Grimaldi, a member of a powerful family that had been exiled from Genoa, Italy, came to the gate of the town disguised as a monk and begged admittance. An armed band entered with him and conquered the town. Since then Monaco has belonged to the Grimaldis, except for a few brief periods; one of them was from 1793 until 1814, when Monaco was annexed to France.

Since the early 20th century, Monaco has been a constitutional monarchy. If the reigning prince should die without a male heir, the principality would be incorporated into France. For a while the people in Monaco worried that this might happen, but in 1956, the prince, Rainier III, married the famous American actress Grace Kelly. Three children were born: Princess Caroline, Prince Albert (heir apparent), and Princess Stephanie. In 1982, Princess Grace died in a tragic auto accident.

M.A. PALMARO and PAUL CHOISIT, Consulat General de Monaco, New York

Picturesque Esch-sur-Sûre, in Luxembourg's Ardennes region, dates from the Middle Ages.

LUXEMBOURG

To the tourist's first glance, the Grand Duchy of Luxembourg appears a fairy-tale kingdom. Beautiful towns and more than 120 medieval castles dot a romantic landscape of forested hills and rocky gorges. The capital, Luxembourg city, is an ancient fortress with great battlements and tunnels known as the Casemates. Yet the tiny country, about the size of Rhode Island, is very much of the modern world. One of the leading steel producers of Europe, Luxembourg has become a communications center and more recently a banking and insurance center.

THE LAND

Wedged between Belgium, France, and Germany, Luxembourg possesses two distinct geographic regions. In the north is the upland of the Ardennes; its most spectacular section is called Petite Suisse, meaning Little Switzerland. Mountainous and heavily wooded, with dramatic ravines and twisting rivers, it holds much game, including partridge and wild boar.

A smaller section in the south is the Bon Pays, or Good Land. Although not especially fertile, the land produces good crops of potatoes, oats, rye, wheat, corn, and roses. Some dairy products are exported. The southwest tip of the duchy contains a rich supply of iron ore and sufficient limestone (used in steel mills) to make the nation a steel-producing power.

Luxembourg city, the capital, is headquarters of the Grand Duchy's sizable steel industry.

The Our, Sûre, and Moselle rivers mark the long border with Germany on the east. Many other streams drain the Ardennes; the capital is located on the Alzette, which rises in France. For generations, Luxembourg has relied on its excellent railroad system for commercial shipping. Canalization of the Moselle in the 1960s connected the duchy to the waterways of the Rhine system and brought construction of a port at Mertert. The climate is mild, without great heat or severe cold, although the average winter temperature is below freezing. Rain falls often; in the Ardennes region, snow accumulates in the winter.

Vianden, a town near Germany, stands beneath one of many medieval castles found in Luxembourg.

LUXEMBOURG

THE PEOPLE

A Luxembourg saying proclaims: "We wish to remain what we are." The motto reflects the Luxembourgers' confidence in their way of life and desire for independence. Their spoken language of Luxembourgish (Letzeburgisch) has never been given satisfactory written form. German (with insertion of Luxembourgish words) is the chief language of the press and of the primary schools. French predominates in secondary schools, the civil service, and parliament. Many Luxembourgers are bilingual, and English is also widely spoken. There are post-secondary agricultural institutes and one university, but most students seeking higher education must go abroad to study.

Everywhere in the strongly Roman Catholic nation there is a sense of stability. The people like hiking, fishing, hunting, movies, and eating their famous good foods. These range from the white wines of the Moselle region to sausages, pâtés, wild game, and fresh trout.

A large majority of the population resides in the south, nearly 20 percent in the capital. The population growth rate is low. Demand for additional labor in times of peak steel production is met by numbers of guest workers, especially from Italy and Portugal.

THE ECONOMY

For all its greenery, Luxembourg is highly industrialized, with considerable prosperity and high per-capita income. Agriculture involves only 3.4 percent of the population and makes up roughly 3 percent of the gross domestic product (GDP).

The iron and steel industry is one of the most important sectors of Luxembourg's economy, accounting for some 30 percent of all manufacturing output in 1990. Chemical, rubber, and plastic products together provided 16 percent of this output.

The service sector of the economy employs close to 65 percent of the duchy's work force. The greatest growth has taken place in banking and insurance. Luxembourg's central location in Europe, multilingual staff, political stability, and laws protecting secrecy of accounts and records lure foreign banks and moneys to Luxembourg. The chief financial institution of the European Union (known until late 1993 as the European Community), the European Investment Bank, is located in the capital. International insurance companies are also clustered in the duchy.

Although the European Parliament meets in Strasbourg, France, its Secretariat is located in Luxembourg, as are the European Court of Justice, the Court of Auditors, and the offices of numerous European Union (EU) commissions. Powerful Radio Luxembourg sends popular music to most of Western Europe; a commercial station, it is the duchy's single largest taxpayer.

HISTORY AND GOVERNMENT

It was in A.D. 963 that Siegfried, Count of the Ardennes, acquired by barter the site of a Roman fortress overlooking the Alzette. Lucilinburhunc—or "little fort," as the Celts called it—grew as Siegfried's dynasty became established until it was the "Gibraltar of the North." In 1815, after centuries of both independence and domination by various states, Luxembourg was declared a grand duchy by the Great Powers. Portions of the duchy joined with the Belgians in their revolt against the Netherlands. The current borders were set by treaty in 1839.

A crisis over the possible sale of Luxembourg to France led the powers in 1867 to declare and guarantee the duchy's neutrality. After German invasions in 1914 and 1940, the duchy abandoned neutrality in 1949 and joined the North Atlantic Treaty Organization (NATO).

Luxembourg supports European integration. It shares a common currency and customs regime with Belgium as a result of the Belgian-Luxembourg Economic Union of 1921. It became part of the Belgian-Netherlands-Luxembourg (Benelux) Economic Union in 1948, and the European Economic Community (now the EU) in 1957. The duchy maintains only a small army.

The Grand Duchy of Luxembourg is a constitutional monarchy. The succession rules for the House of Nassau-Weilburg brought the separation of Luxembourg from the Dutch throne in 1890. Under the Constitution of 1868 and its amendments, the grand duke serves as head of state, while the parliamentary government is led by the prime minister. The ministerial Council of Government is responsible to the elected Chamber of Deputies. An advisory Council of State is appointed by the grand duke for life. The Christian Social and the Socialist parties have been dominant since World War II. The first has wide support, is Roman Catholic in orientation, and internationalist in outlook; the second draws support from blue-collar workers in the capital and south, and favors strong social legislation.

JONATHAN E. HELMREICH
Allegheny College

Bruges, now mainly noted for its lovely canals and bridges, was a leading commercial city in the Middle Ages.

BELGIUM

The greatest distance between two points in Belgium is just 175 miles (280 kilometers). Yet this small country, only slightly larger than the state of Maryland, hosts great cultural and economic diversity; and its history reflects much of the history of Western Europe.

The northern portion of the country, somewhat more than half, is known as Flanders. This is the home of the Flemings, who speak a variety of Dutch. The southern region is Wallonia, and its French-speaking people are called Walloons. Differences between these groups have grown ever sharper since Belgium gained independence from the United Netherlands in 1830. In recent years those differences have forced the government into a form of federalism. The country has three primary subdivisions: Flanders, with about 7 percent of the population; Wallonia, with a third of the population; and bilingual Brussels, the capital and home for about 10 percent of the citizens. The Flemings and Walloons each have their separate cultural communities, as does a small group of German-speaking Belgians in the east.

Despite, or perhaps because of, its own nationality differences, Belgium is a leader in international cooperation. The European Economic Community (Common Market), the North Atlantic Treaty Organization (NATO), the Belgian-Netherlands-Luxembourg Economic Union (Benelux), and other international agencies have offices in or near Brussels. So, too, do many international businesses and banks. Long famous for castles, refined art, music and ballet, and culinary delights, Belgium was also a leader in the 19th-century industrialization of the continent. Modern shipping communications, financial activities, and machinery and chemical production today augment the traditional income derived from textiles, specialized agriculture, tourism, glass manufacture, and the declining coal, iron, and steel industries. The mix of ancient culture, pleasant modern living, dynamic trade, international cooperation, and the challenge of accommodation of linguistic differences give Belgium political significance and cultural and economic excitement much greater than its size.

THE LAND

Belgium is a country of lowlands and low plateaus that rise gently from sea level along the North Sea coast to a high point at Botrange, located in the extreme east near the German border. Geographically, Belgium may be divided into three land areas. To the north there is a 42-mile (67-kilometer) coast on the North Sea. This area of wide beaches and dunes, where fashionable and popular seaside resorts are located, stretches south to a low plain of rich farmland drained by canals and protected by dikes. Polders, land long ago reclaimed from the salt marshes and protected by dikes, add close to 200 square miles (520 square kilometers) of fertile grazing areas. These blend with another low, sandy, marshy region to the east known as the Campine.

Central Belgium is the most populous area and the site of Brussels and other important cities. Higher than the coastal region, it has rolling fields and rich soil. The coal seams and iron ore deposits of the Borinage sector in its south nourished the early development of Belgium's steel industry; their exhaustion has brought severe unemployment.

South and east of the Meuse River is a higher plateau that reaches its greatest height at Botrange (2,283 feet; 696 meters) in the Ardennes. The woods and hills of the Ardennes, although providing lovely landscapes and good hiking and hunting, are not sufficient to block invasion. The lack of natural boundaries has greatly affected Belgium's history. Despite the elevation of the Ardennes, the altitude of the country as a whole is just over 525 feet (160 meters); the eastern third averages only 60 feet (18 meters) above sea level. No wonder that Belgium, like the Netherlands, is called a Low Country.

Belgium's Rivers

Rivers contributed to Belgium's early success as a trading center and to its continuing prosperity in the transshipment trade. The two largest, the Scheldt (or Schelde) and the Meuse, rise in France, flow through Belgium to the Netherlands, and empty into the North Sea. These rivers

FACTS AND FIGURES

OFFICIAL NAME: Kingdom of Belgium.

NATIONALITY: Belgian(s).

CAPITAL: Brussels.

LOCATION: Northwestern Europe. **Boundaries**—North Sea, Netherlands, Germany, Luxembourg, France.

AREA: 11,780 sq. mi. (30,510 sq. km.).

PHYSICAL FEATURES: Highest point—Signal de Botrange (2,277 ft.; 694 m.). **Lowest point**—sea level. **Chief rivers**—Scheldt, Meuse, Lys.

POPULATION: 10,203,683 (1997; annual growth 0.32%).

MAJOR LANGUAGES: Flemish (Dutch), French, German.

MAJOR RELIGIONS: Roman Catholicism, Protestantism.

GOVERNMENT: Constitutional hereditary monarchy. **Head of state**—king. **Head of government**—prime minister. **Legislature**—bicameral Parliament.

CHIEF CITIES: Brussels, Antwerp, Ghent, Liège.

ECONOMY: Chief minerals—coal, natural gas. **Chief agricultural products**—sugar beets, fresh vegetables. **Industries and products**—engineering and metal products, processed food and beverages, chemicals, basic metals, textiles. **Chief exports**—iron, steel, automobiles, petroleum products, diamonds. **Chief imports**—fuels, foodstuffs, chemicals, grains.

MONETARY UNIT: 1 Belgian franc = 100 centimes.

NATIONAL HOLIDAY: July 21 (National Day).

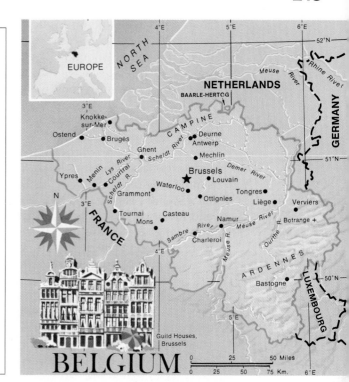

BELGIUM

have been linked by canals to the Rhine and other waterways. The great harbor of Antwerp, located well inland on the Scheldt, is an important port of entry to the continent for goods from Britain and has prompted that nation's solicitude for Belgian independence.

The North Sea affects Belgium's climate, as the proximity of the warm Gulf Stream keeps winter from being too harsh; snowfall, except in the Ardennes, is usually light. Winds from the sea keep summers cool and bring frequent clouds and showers. There may be flashes of bright sun each day, but rain falls some 150 to 200 days each year.

THE PEOPLE

The region we now call Belgium was probably first settled by tribes of Celts. Julius Caesar and later Romans conquered much of the area. They so established their influence in the southern portion of Belgium that, even though tribes from across the Rhine later conquered Gaul, the Latinized tongue of Wallonia was not replaced by the Germanic speech of the Frankish invaders.

The Flemings and the Walloons

The line of linguistic demarcation separating the Flemings and Walloons originally ran from near Boulogne in France to Cologne in Germany. Along the coast it has shifted north and now coincides with the French-Belgian border; inland, it has moved south. Traditional stereotypes picture the Fleming as unemotional and the Walloon as excitable. The Fleming has been historically more active in the life of the Roman Catholic Church; the Walloon attends Mass less regularly. Protestant and Jewish congregations in either region are not numerous. Flanders has a markedly higher birthrate than that of Wallonia. Historically,

Flemings have tended to prefer closer ties to Britain, while the Walloons have looked to France for support.

Many old distinctions between Fleming and Walloon, especially those concerning style of life, are increasingly less valid in modern Belgian society because they were based on economic status differences that are rapidly disappearing. In the years after the nation's founding, Walloons dominated government, commerce, and the professions. Dutch-speaking citizens were tried in courts conducted entirely in French, and Walloons considered Flemish a language spoken only by the working class. Flemings served primarily as laborers and developed a simple way of life. This included cooking based on stews, sausage, potatoes, and beans that is praised and practiced today for its nourishment and flavor. In 1898 the Dutch language won equality with French as the legal language of the country and its laws. Money and postage stamps were printed in Dutch and French.

Expansion of the right to vote gave Flemings a greater voice in politics in the period between the world wars. Better organized and angry over social and economic inequities, the Flemings pressed their demands. In 1921 the linguistic regions were officially separated. The government drew an imaginary line along the traditional language boundary from the western border near Menin to the eastern border east of Tongres. North of the line was decreed to be Dutch-speaking; south, French-speaking. The capital region of Brussels became a bilingual region, though at present it is more than 20 miles (32 kilometers) north of the linguistic border. The city center is still predominantly French, but the working class is Flemish (or increasingly consists of foreigners such as Turks and Indians), and many suburbs are Flemish speaking. The University of Ghent was changed to a Flemish-speaking institution. Laws of 1932 and 1935 decreed that government offices, courts, schools, and business were to be conducted only in the language of the area. A child in a state school must be taught in Dutch north of the line and in French south of the line. In Brussels, children study in either French or Dutch, according to whichever language is used in the home.

In the late 1960's, a bitter dispute centering around the University of Louvain caused the fall of the government. Louvain, the world's largest Catholic university, was founded in 1425. Situated just inside the Flemish border, it continued to teach in French but introduced a Dutch section. This did not satisfy the Flemings. Riots and strikes led to a parliamentary decision to divide the ancient university and to build a new French section just inside Walloon territory.

In 1980 the Belgian parliament passed a law establishing regional assemblies in Dutch-speaking Flanders and French-speaking Wallonia. These bodies control local matters such as culture, health, roads, and urban projects. Although intermarriage and national economic and defense concerns tie the linguistic groups together, their rivalry remains strong. It continues to cause the fall of government cabinets, most of which are carefully balanced coalitions among representatives of the two linguistic groups as well as among political parties. Such was the case in 1987, when the elected mayor of a commune in the Flemish zone that contained numerous French-speaking residents refused to conduct official business in Dutch, although familiar with the tongue. The issue became one of national proportion and brought the prime minister's resignation. The politician agreed in 1989 not to run again, permitting the issue to fade from prominence.

The Belgian Way of Life

The Belgians are hard workers, with little respect for idleness. They are politically aware, and illiteracy is almost unknown. In the many small cafés at which they gather with their friends after working hours, they will discuss politics and movies and read the particular newspaper that matches their political views. Circles of acquaintances may be large, but intimate friendships are limited, usually formed in childhood years and maintained throughout life. Belgians are very attached to their neighborhoods, homes, and well-tended vegetable gardens; rather than move, they prefer to commute some distance to work on their well-run network of railways and trolley cars.

The Belgians are especially fond of music and sports. Symphonies, piano and violin competitions, noon musicales, opera, choral ensembles, driving rock and jazz, and village brass bands are all part of the musical scene. Professional bicyclists and soccer teams are cheered. At the local level, there are organized clubs for bicyclists, motorcyclists, soccer, chess, and the like. A favorite lunchtime break is a game of *boules* (a form of lawn bowling). Festivals based on history, legend, and religion are widely enjoyed and involve many participants. Some, such as the procession of the Holy Blood in Bruges, the march of the Gilles at Binch, the Procession of Giants at Ath, *Ommegang* at Brussels, *Lumeçon* at Mons, and numerous carnivals before or at mid-Lent have become tourist attractions. In good weather, the Belgians love to walk and picnic in parks, such as the Soignes Forest outside Brussels, or camp in the Ardennes. During other parts of the year, they may seek vacation sun in Italy or Spain.

Belgians eat well; their cooking is world-famous. Fresh fish is available everywhere—mussels, shrimp, oysters, sole, turbot, trout, and eels. There are specialties, such as Flemish *waterzooï,* a rich soup made with vegetables and chicken; Ardennes ham; specially grown grapes, strawberries, and endive; eels in green garlic sauce; and an incredible array of sausages and pâtés. Traditional mainstays include beefsteak, mussels, and french fried potatoes, and *carbonnade flamande* (a beef stew cooked in beer). More beer per capita is consumed in Belgium than in any other country; more than 300 varieties are brewed. Desserts may include fruit tarts; delicate pancakes called *crepes,* filled with jelly; *cramique,* a raisin bread; *pain d'épices,* a type of gingerbread; or many other delightful pastries.

Cities

Within Europe, Belgium is second only to the Netherlands in population density. Many quiet towns dot the countryside. It is in the great cities of Belgium, however, that is found the mix of history, well-developed culture, and modern industrialization, technology, and commerce that identifies the country today.

In the heart of **Brussels** stands the Grand' Place, one of the great municipal squares of the world. Just blocks from its Gothic stone towers, skyscraper hotels soar and Common Market agencies and the Royal Library are housed in modern concrete architecture. To the west, neon

Imposing Gothic buildings dominate the Grand' Place, the center of Brussels' commercial district.

lights shine on lengthy streets of restaurants, department stores, and movie theaters. To the east stand art museums, holding the ancient treasures of Breughel and Van Eyck and the modern work of Ensor and Magritte; beyond lie the park and the stately royal palace. No visitor to Brussels should miss the Grand' Place, with its 15th-century city hall and old guild houses that were once the headquarters of the butchers, brewers, tailors, painters, and other artisans. Today these buildings, preserved in their original splendor, contain shops, restaurants, and municipal offices.

Brussels is such a busy city that it seems always under construction. Laborers from Turkey, Spain, Italy, India, and Algeria work alongside Belgian construction workers. The city is also filled with foreigners living in Brussels on assignment from their governments or their companies to work in the many European agencies and international businesses that have made Brussels their headquarters. Just outside Brussels is the seat of the North Atlantic Treaty Organization (NATO). At Casteau, near Mons, about 30 miles (50 kilometers) from Brussels, is the home of SHAPE (Supreme Headquarters Allied Powers Europe).

Antwerp, located 55 miles (90 kilometers) up the Scheldt River from the North Sea, has been a wealthy city for centuries because of its great port. It has a famous cathedral and wonderful museums, including the home the painter Peter Paul Rubens designed for himself. Antwerp is the center of the new industrial development in Flanders.

The third largest city of Belgium is **Ghent**. Long the heart of the Flemish textile trade, it is rich in art and historic treasures. So too is **Bruges**. In ancient times that city, busy with trade and textile manufacture, was larger than London. Today the people of Bruges live quietly along the city's peaceful canals. Nuns still dwell in the ancient abbeys, and chimes still sound from the many belfries. Visitors take motorboat rides along the canals, ducking their heads under some of the dozens of old bridges, and visit the many impressive, well-preserved buildings. There is the Hospital of St. John with its Memling gallery and dispensary active since the 12th century. There are the church of Notre Dame and the Gruuthuuse, a 15th-century merchant's palace that was used for women who had retreated from the world. To visit this museum city is to go far back in history.

Liège, in the east, an important modern industrial center, always has been the cultural focal point of French-speaking Belgium. Once again, modern industries may be found close by the ancient palace of the prince-bishops of Liège.

Many other cities of Belgium reveal this mixture of the modern with the ancient. Near Liège are the picturesque towns on the Meuse River and in the Ardennes forest. On the coast of Belgium are the seaside resorts of Knokke-sur-Mer and Ostend. Elsewhere are the cathedral town of Tournai, the university town of Louvain, and the old church center of

Antwerp, Belgium's largest city, is site of the Steen, a medieval castle that houses the National Museum.

Mechlin. Everywhere that one travels in Belgium, there are fine roads, a delightful place to lunch, an old chateau, monastery, abbey, or museum to visit, and modern industries nearby.

THE ECONOMY
Farms and Farming

Both at home and abroad, Belgium is known as an industrial nation, yet agriculture has always played an important part in the life of the country. By hard work, intensive cultivation, and use of scientific methods, the Belgians obtain high yields from their farms. Some foodstuffs, especially grains and citrus fruits, must nevertheless be imported.

Almost 50 percent of the land is under agriculture but is tilled by only about two percent of the total work force; nevertheless, the farms are among the smallest in Europe. Key products are livestock and dairy goods, poultry, sugar beets, and flax. Specialized farms and nurseries export Belgian endive (a salad delicacy) and shrubs and flowers such as begonias, azaleas, and orchids grown in the glass hothouses in the region between Brussels and Ghent. Belgian grapes, berries, and carrots, often grown in greenhouses, are found preserved or fresh in gourmet food shops in many countries.

Cattle graze beneath the memorial commemorating Napoleon's final defeat at Waterloo in 1815.

In Ghent, the ornate guildhalls that line the Lys River figured prominently in the city's history.

Trade and Manufacturing

Slightly more than a quarter of Belgium's working population is employed in industry. Many of these industries had their beginnings centuries ago. During the Middle Ages, Flanders, with its lace and tapestry makers and cloth weavers, was the textile center of Europe. Today's thriving textile industry is still centered in such old cities as Ghent, Tournai, and Courtrai, which produce cottons, linens, and synthetic fibers, and in Verviers, which manufactures woolens. Bruges, Brussels, and Malines (Mechlin) laces are famous. Liège still produces armaments and glassware, products for which it has been famous since the 16th century. Antwerp continues to be, as it has been for hundreds of years, a world center for diamond cutting and trade.

Coal was mined in Belgium in Roman times. Many of the early mines of the Sambre and Meuse valleys were depleted and have now closed. The steel mills located in regions about Liège and Charleroi, so important a few decades ago, must rely on imported ore and sometimes coal. This is expensive; the mills themselves are becoming outdated; and international competition is stiff. Some plants have been forced to close, creating unemployment and political unrest in Wallonia.

Meanwhile, newer coal mines and industries have been developed in Flanders. Since World War II, multinational chemical and electronic firms have established factories in Flanders. Their arrival was stimulated by growing demand for plastics and petrochemical products, nourished by the proximity of the sea terminals of Antwerp and Rotterdam and attracted by the legendary working capacity of the Flemish laborer. The rise of employment, property values, and prosperity in Flanders and the coincidental decline of Wallonia have given the Flemings more leverage in national economic and political issues.

Traditionally, Belgium has maintained an open, free-trade economy. It has imported materials such as cotton, electronic components, zinc, copper, and lead, processing them with skilled workmanship. After their value has been increased, the goods have in turn been exported as valuable products. Some 63 percent of Belgium's gross national product is exported annually.

Shipping

Belgium is also active in the transshipment industry. Lying at the heart of one of the world's most industrialized regions, Belgium is near the Ruhr region of Germany; Paris; and London. Its ports and well-developed canal, rail, and superhighway systems enable it to profit in the task of moving goods into and out of the European continent. Antwerp is the principal container-handling port of western Europe, and major

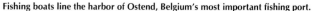

Fishing boats line the harbor of Ostend, Belgium's most important fishing port.

renovations have been made in the harbor at Zeebrugge to draw trade away from Rotterdam. All this commerce has stimulated the banking industry as well. More than a third of the population is employed in the services and transport sector of the economy. It is not surprising, then, that Belgium has been a leader in international agreements, such as the Benelux treaties and those establishing the European Economic Community (EEC, or Common Market), intended to reduce trade barriers. The EEC later became the European Union (EU).

Economic Problems

Income from all these undertakings, plus revenues from tourism, did not spare Belgium economic difficulties in the 1980s and 1990s. A key problem was the decline of the steel industry. Another was the high level of government-financed social services. Belgium was also hit hard by the Arab oil embargo in 1973 and the subsequent rise in oil prices.

Foreign borrowing grew as the country attempted to maintain its high standard of living. The national debt grew also, and in 1982 the government devalued the Belgian franc and provided subsidies to export industries to enhance the country's ability to sell goods abroad. The legal link between wages and inflation was severed to reduce the inflationary spiral of wages and prices.

Although steps to bolster the corporate sector and decrease imports intended for personal consumption affected living standards, the people demonstrated their acceptance of government austerity efforts in the elections of 1985. Further steps were then taken slowly to reduce the government deficit and unemployment. Two-thirds of Belgium's trade is within the European Union, and thus Belgium's ability to strengthen its economy is tied to the economic performance of its EU partners. To help solve this problem, Belgian trade leaders expanded relations with Eastern Europe, the Middle East, and China. Six huge trusts dominate the Belgian economy. The largest by far is the Société Générale, with vast holdings in Belgium and around the world. Efforts by an Italian financier to take over the firm in 1988, therefore, sent tremors into all sectors of the economy and government. In 1993, the recession in Germany, France, and the Netherlands was another factor in Belgium's economic woes. The Belgian economy nevertheless has made a slow but steady comeback, with 2.3 percent growth in 1994 and 1995, 2.25 percent in 1997, and about 2.8 percent in 1998. Unemployment and the national debt continue to be problems.

GOVERNMENT

The House of Representatives is the dominant body in the national legislature, and is directly elected by universal suffrage under a system of proportional representation. A portion of the Senate is elected by the regional councils, some by fellow senators, and the largest group by direct vote. The Belgian judiciary is modeled after the French system. The highest court, the Court of Cassation, is led by a chief justice appointed by the king. Courts do not examine the constitutionality of laws.

A special group consisting of senior statesmen, the Council of State, gives advisory opinions on legislation and in times of crisis. Each of the major political parties (Social Christian, Socialist, Liberal) has Flemish and Walloon wings, which sometimes act almost as independent parties.

The Palais des Nations in Brussels contains offices of the European Economic Community (Common Market).

There are more extreme nationalist Flemish and Walloon parties and growing ecology parties, plus a small Communist party and a few revolutionary cells of Communist Combattants. Movement toward further federalism in Belgium is blocked by an inability to reach agreement regarding the place of Brussels in a federated state.

HISTORY

Belgium's history is shaped by its valuable location and commerce coveted by aggressive neighboring states, by its limited military strength, and by internal linguistic and religious differences. After the decline of Roman rule, the territories of modern-day Belgium became part of Charlemagne's realm. In the feudal period following the disintegration of that empire, Belgium was split among many hereditary princes, bishops, and other local rulers. It was a period of prosperity, the flowering of the trade guilds, and the development of a wealthy, educated middle class. In the 15th century, a series of pacts, noble marriages, and wars brought Belgium under the control of the dukes of Burgundy. Belgium subsequently passed under the rule of Spain (1517–1715), Austria (1715–94), France (1794–1815), and the United Netherlands (1815–30).

King William I of the Netherlands treated the Belgians as second-class citizens, forcing them to assume responsibility for the large Dutch national debt and to pay unpopular taxes. He did not grant them equal representation by population in the national governing body. However, he did ensure freedom of religion, a policy opposed by Belgian Catholic conservatives who wished to keep Dutch Calvinism out of the country.

The king's actions forged an alliance of Belgium's Catholic and liberal factions that earlier had fought each other. On August 15, 1830, stimulated by news of revolt in Paris and by the performance in Brussels of an opera filled with appeals to liberty (Auber's *The Mute from Portici*), the people of Brussels looted the homes of the Netherlands ministers. The revolt spread and caused a meeting of representatives of the great powers in London. The French were sympathetic to the Belgians, while the British did not wish Antwerp to fall into the hands of France. In December 1830, the powers agreed on the separation of Belgium from the Netherlands. William I of the Netherlands objected and invaded Belgium. Despite opposition from the Netherlands, with the aid of French and British armies, Belgian independence was assured. In 1839 the European powers guaranteed Belgium's independence and perpetual neutrality.

Growth of the Nation

The Belgians chose as their king Prince Leopold of Saxe-Coburg-Gotha (reigned 1831–65), the uncle of Queen Victoria of England; he soon chose as his consort the daughter of French King Louis-Philippe. He negotiated well with the powers on behalf of Belgium and encouraged industrialization and development of trade. At the time, a republic was unacceptable to the great powers, still perturbed by the French Revolution of 1789, and to a majority of the populace. A constitutional monarchy was constructed that, while technically making the king the source of executive authority, gave most governmental control to the Council of Ministers. The council, headed by a prime minister, was responsible to the two parliamentary chambers: the Senate and the House of Representatives.

Leopold I and his son Leopold II (reigned 1865–1909) exerted considerable influence on the course of government. They also became deeply involved in colonial activities. Acting on his own as a private citizen, Leopold II founded in 1876 the International African Association, which in turn became the huge Congo Free State, ruled by Leopold. It was eventually taken over by Belgium as a colony in 1908. In subsequent decades the immensely rich province would become an important source of copper and uranium, as well as rubber. Of tremendous significance to the Belgian economy, its separation from Belgium in 1960 as the independent state of Zaïre (now the Democratic Republic of Congo) caused much political and economic stress in Belgium.

The Two World Wars

Despite its status as a neutral, Belgium was invaded by Germany in 1914. Under the leadership of King Albert (reigned 1909–34), the Belgian army fought throughout World War I, even though most of Belgium was occupied. Following the war, the Belgians abandoned neutrality, signed a military accord with France, and struggled to rebuild their economy. The linguistic controversy became more bitter. In 1936, King Leopold III (reigned 1934–51), in an effort to gain the support of both factions in strengthening the army to face the threat of Hitler's Germany, declared Belgium once again neutral. This course did not deter a German invasion on May 10, 1940.

After the surrender of the Belgian army, the king chose to remain in his country rather than follow his cabinet into exile in London during World War II. The German occupation of Belgium was particularly harsh. After the liberation of the country by the Allies in 1944, a controversy arose over whether Leopold should remain as king (he was accused of being pro-German), and he went into voluntary exile. A plebiscite held in 1950 favored his rule by a small majority, but continuing demonstrations, often led by Socialists, brought Leopold's abdication in 1951 in favor of his son, Baudouin I. In 1993, Baudouin's brother was crowned King Albert II when King Baudouin died childless.

Modern Belgium

The royal question divided the nation, but easier agreement was reached on other points. Women were granted the vote in 1948. The "school war," which since the 19th century had pitted the Catholic party first against the Liberals and then against the Socialists, was finally resolved 10 years later. Compromise settled the percentage of costs of church schools that would be paid by national taxes, upheld freedom of curriculum beyond a minimum prescribed by the Ministry of Education, and barred political propaganda from the classroom.

Continuing attempts to adjust the linguistic border provoked bitter parliamentary debate. As measures of reform, the constitution was amended in 1970 and 1980 to create a more centralized system of government. The country was divided into the three regions: Flanders, Wallonia, and Brussels. Flemish, Walloon, French-speaking, and German-speaking community assemblies and executives for regional and cultural affairs were created. In February 1993, Parliament voted to once again amend the constitution, creating a federal state of Belgium. Legislation to implement the reforms was enacted in July of that year.

International Cooperation

The experience of World War II convinced Belgian leaders of the importance of international cooperation. Belgium, linked in economic union with Luxembourg since 1921, joined with the Netherlands to form the Benelux Economic Union in 1948, with the goal of eliminating tariffs and economic barriers among these nations. In the 1950s, the Benelux countries joined in establishing the European Economic Community (now the European Union or EU). During the mid-1990s, Belgian officials debated a number of austerity measures to bring the nation's economy in line with EU requirements. Although a charter member of the North Atlantic Treaty Organization (NATO), Belgium decreased its support after the fall of Communism in Eastern Europe in the late 1980s and the breakup of the Soviet Union in the early 1990s.

JONATHAN E. HELMREICH, Allegheny College

Amsterdam, the Netherlands' capital and largest city, is called "Venice of the North" for its miles of canals.

NETHERLANDS

A famous story about the Netherlands is the tale of a boy who saved his country one stormy night by keeping his finger in a crack in a dike until help finally came. Like tulips and windmills and wooden shoes, the story is part of the mythology and charm of the Netherlands. And like most myths, it is based on reality but is not the whole picture. Today, the Netherlands is much more than a country of charming traditions. This small nation, with a high standard of living, has a modern, complex economy.

Few people outside its boundaries call the Netherlands by its formal name. Instead they speak of Holland, after its most populous and wealthy region, because it was Holland that led in the creation of the modern country. Inhabitants are rarely referred to as Hollanders or Netherlanders; almost always they are called the Dutch. Yet the Netherlands is an accurate name, for it means "the low lands," and this is the lowest country in the world, with more than two-fifths of its land below sea level. It is also the most densely populated, with more than 1,000 people per square mile (385 per square kilometer). A visitor, however, is struck by the way the Dutch manage to preserve a sense of space. Even where the towns are only a few miles apart, the land between is cultivated or used as parks.

Tourists continue to be charmed by the quaintness of the Old Holland of myth. Windmills with a distinctive shape dot the landscape, giving the country its most characteristic feature. Old buildings display their stepped gables. Farmers still wear wooden shoes with distinctive up-turned toes as they work the muddy soil. Canals cut their way through every city, where often buildings must be built on pilings sunk deep through the boggy land to the underlying hard ground. But this is not a country that lives off the tourist trade; it is a land of advanced industry and commerce as well as an agriculture whose efficiency is the envy of the world. If this were not so, the Dutch would not have achieved one of the highest standards of living in the world.

THE LAND

The Netherlands takes in almost the entire delta formed by three great rivers—the Lower Rhine, the Meuse, and the Scheldt—that flow together on its territory, dividing into numerous arms. The Rhine changes its name to the Waal as it leaves Germany and forms several tributaries before it empties into the North Sea. The Meuse is known in Dutch as the Maas and the Scheldt as the Schelde. These rivers link the Netherlands to its neighbors, Germany to the east and Belgium to the south. To the west and north the Netherlands borders on the North Sea. The Netherlands enjoys a moderate climate with abundant precipitation.

The unique landscape of the Netherlands is visible to visitors from abroad landing at Amsterdam Airport. As they look to the edges of the airfield, they will often see canal boats passing by on waterways considerably higher than the level of the airfield. Visitors will see, too, signs

The Eastern Scheldt Sea Barrier and other dams and dikes protect the low-lying reclaimed land from floods.

calling the airport "Schiphol," which means "Ship Hole" in Dutch. The two observations are linked: The land where the airport was constructed lies at the bottom of what was until the 19th century a very large lake. Like more than two-fifths of the country, this territory is reclaimed land below the level of the sea. The Dutch even have a special name for such land, "polder."

Pushing Back the Sea

In ancient times almost all the countryside west of the city of Utrecht was marshland, separated from the sea by a rim of dunes. People lived precariously on the dunes and on artificial mounds, called "terpen," built up from the bogs. They herded livestock, grew some grain, and fished. During times of high water, they drove their livestock up the terpen, and there both humans and animals stayed until the floodwaters receded.

In the 13th century, windmills came into use to pump the water out of land enclosed by dikes. At first, grain was grown on the new land, but it was discovered to be more productive as pastureland, and, ever since, dairy farming has been a major agricultural pursuit. Milk, butter, and cheese are produced for the constantly increasing population of the Low

Uniformed porters of the Cheese Carriers Guild add to the pageantry of the traditional cheese market days.

Countries and are exported to the outside world. In the 20th century the Dutch have employed the more powerful tools that became available—engines and pumps—to reclaim land from the sea. A 20-mile (32-kilometer)-long dike was built across the Zuider Zee from the tip of North Holland to Friesland, turning that sea into a fresh-water lake called the IJsselmeer (Ijssel Lake). Then, one by one, huge polders were constructed. The salt in the soil was leached by years of rain, and then modern farms were established and new cities built.

In February 1953, the dikes along the North Sea coast in Zeeland and southernmost Holland collapsed during a fierce winter storm, accompanied by high tides. The sea raced inland, killing about 1,800 people and destroying more than 70,000 homes. To prevent a recurrence of the disaster, the country embarked on a project called the Delta Works. All the outlets to the sea except the southernmost, the West Scheldt, and the northernmost, the Maas, would be controlled by dams with gates that could be closed in case of high water. The last dam was completed in 1987. In 1993, the Dutch began a radical plan to let in the sea. The constant need for drainage has led to immense land sinkage in some reclaimed areas. The Dutch hope to return about 600,000 acres to the sea.

Polders have given the Dutch landscape its distinctive look. The land is flat, divided into long, narrow strips by drainage ditches; there is little need for fences. The thousands of windmills that once drove the pumps are now chiefly ornamental, replaced by nearly invisible electrical pumps. The eastern part of the country is generally above sea level, with drainage canals less frequent. But everywhere canals are used for transport of goods. The landscape changes only in the extreme southeast, in Limburg province, where there is hill country above the valley of the Maas River.

Natural Resources. The natural resources below ground are limited. The coal mines in Limburg, with their veins largely depleted, have been closed. Today, the country's principal fuel is natural gas taken from an immense field in the northern province of Groningen. There are also large underground supplies of rock salt, which is used in the chemical industry. The supply of pure water for home consumption and industrial use is a persistent problem. The flat countryside does not permit the construction of large reservoirs, and the volume of rain water that can be retained in underground sand beds is limited. The principal source is water from the rivers, but removal of pollution is difficult and costly.

THE PEOPLE

A large majority of the Dutch are a Germanic people, and they have been clearly distinguished from Germans only since the 16th century. The name "Dutch," in fact, is the same word as the German's name for themselves, *Deutsch*. The country has long been open to immigrants seeking refuge from oppression or merely a better livelihood. These included many thousands from the Southern Netherlands (modern Belgium) in the 16th century, Jews from Portugal and Spain in the 16th and 17th centuries and from eastern Europe in the 19th century, and Germans from Westphalia and the Rhineland. The most recent are Turks and Moroccans who came as "guest workers" after World War II, and Indonesians and Surinamese from former Dutch colonies.

The Netherlandish Language

The language spoken by the Dutch is the same as the Flemish spoken in northern and western Belgium, with small differences in vocabulary and pronunciation; both the Dutch and Flemings call it *Nederlands,* "Netherlandish," because their common country was called the "Low Countries" until the 16th century. Modern Dutch speech throughout the country is based on the usage of Holland, although local dialects continue to be spoken, especially in the countryside. Dutch grammar is much like that of German, but simpler. Many words are taken from French and in recent times from English. Frisian, the native tongue in Friesland, in the north, is a distinct language, closer to English than Dutch; all Frisians also speak Dutch. Knowledge of foreign tongues is widespread; English is a second language for almost everyone, and German and French are widely spoken. Dutch schoolchildren start learning foreign languages at an early age. The sorry other side of this relationship is that Dutch is known by few foreigners, and few works of Dutch literature are translated into foreign languages.

The Dutch Way of Life

The Dutch spirit has tended to be realistic, sober, and concerned with ethical questions. Although the outward look of the Dutch pattern of life has lost virtually all of its obvious differences from those of its neighbors, Dutch society has retained important characteristics of its own. This is despite the ease with which the Dutch absorb other cultures.

A wide variety of groups that rose out of the turbulent religious and ideological conflicts of the 16th and 17th centuries have continued separate although parallel lives. Virtually all social activities were until recently conducted within associations based on religious or ideological identity: sports clubs, insurance companies, labor unions, agricultural communes, and political parties. These "pillars," as they are called, are weakening, but the ideal of the "melting pot" is far from universally accepted. The Dutch have on the whole stressed mutual tolerance of differences rather than making efforts to reduce or even eliminate them. Yet neighborliness, which may sometimes become prying interference, is emphasized over privacy.

This "pillar" system is maintained in the educational structure. All schools, public and private (which usually means church-affiliated), from kindergartens to universities, have equal right to financial support by the national government, which in turn closely supervises curriculum and administration. Elementary and secondary education have undergone considerable and frequent revision in recent years; and the universities, 12 in number, have been in turmoil due to government-imposed reforms. Among these are reorganization of programs and efforts to reduce expenditures, especially those limiting state aid to individual students and the number of years students may remain in school.

Most of the Dutch live in cities, which in the western part of the country have grown to the extent that today they merge into each other. Yet the Dutch retain a great love for life in the open—picnicking and playing in the parks, heathlands, and woodlands, which are carefully preserved. Modern homes, whether private houses or in apartment buildings, have large windows to let the sun pour in. The Dutch are famous for the cleanliness of their surroundings. Housewives for centuries have kept their homes—and the sidewalks in front of them—scrupulously clean, to the surprised admiration of visitors from less meticulous lands.

THE ECONOMY

The central fact in Dutch economic life is that the country cannot live in isolation but must draw its livelihood from intense participation in international commerce, both within Europe and outside. The Dutch for centuries have earned their living from agriculture, commerce, shipping, fishing, and industry. All continue to play a role, but the contribution of each to the nation's prosperity has changed immensely in the last century.

Dutch farmers have declined in number and now represent only a small percentage of the population. Their share in national income has also fallen, but the average income of individual farmers has risen. Dutch agriculture is one of the most efficient in the entire world; machinery and chemicals are employed intensively. Indeed, the large amounts of fertilizer put into the soils and the nearness of the fields to canals and rivers have caused severe water pollution, but the Dutch are addressing the problem with their customary efficiency.

Relatively little of the farm land is used for growing grains, which can be imported more cheaply. Dutch dairy farming, the most widespread agricultural activity, has become world famous; most of the milk produced is used for making cheese, of which the Gouda and Edam

Brilliant fields of flowers are cultivated in the Netherlands. Tulip bulbs are an especially important export.

varieties are best known. The Netherlands exports more cheese than any other country in the world. It is also the world's largest producer and exporter of flowers and bulbs, many of which are shipped by air freight across the oceans. The tulip fields near Haarlem attract huge crowds of tourists every spring to see field upon field of massed, exquisitely colored flowers. Less dramatic but hardly less valuable are the hothouses in the district called Westland, between Rotterdam and the sea, which grow fresh fruit and vegetables under glass the year round. These hothouse products are an important Dutch export.

For centuries the Dutch have also "tilled the sea" by fishing. More than 500 years ago they invented the pickling of fish at sea, so that in the days before refrigeration, their ships could venture far beyond the North Sea to the open ocean. Sole and herring are the principal varieties caught, although eels, caught in inland waterways, are a favorite delicacy. In recent years, when European commercial fishing has been controlled by decisions of the European Economic Community designed to preserve stocks from overfishing, the Dutch fishing industry has complained that it was given too small a quota.

Shipping and trade have long been the core of Dutch prosperity. Holland's location at the mouth of great rivers on the western shore of Europe put it at the crossroads of coastal trade between Southern and Northern Europe and riverborne trade to the continent's heartland. During the 17th century, Amsterdam was the storehouse of Europe, exchanging the grain and naval stores (pine products, especially tar) of the North for the wines, olive oil, and other luxury products of the South. After other countries, in particular England and France, began to trade directly with these lands and with their overseas possessions, Dutch trade with Germany increased in importance. A complex network of canal and river traffic moves goods to and from Dutch ports. Rotterdam is now the

Rotterdam is the world's largest port. The entire city was rebuilt after being gutted during World War II.

largest port in the world, although most of the goods it handles are transshipped. Its facilities for storing and refining petroleum are the biggest in Europe.

The most important shift has been toward manufacturing. Once a relatively unimportant economic activity serving the needs of commerce and shipping, it has risen since the late 19th century to become the leading producer of wealth in the country. The first large manufacturing industry was textiles in the late 18th and 19th centuries; but, faced with competition, especially from Asia, most textile factories have closed.

Steel mills were built at the beginning of the 20th century at the mouth of the North Sea Canal, meeting most of the country's need for steel. Most spectacular has been the rise of the electronics and electrical-appliances industry, with the Philips company based at Eindhoven one of the most powerful in the world. Other Dutch companies of worldwide importance include the Akzo chemical company, the Royal Dutch-Shell petroleum company, and the Royal Netherlands Airline company (KLM).

Dutch bankers and insurance and financial brokers have long been important factors in international finance. During and after the American Revolution, loans from Dutch bankers helped to keep the new republic afloat. The modern business of life and commercial insurance was in large part the creation of Dutch firms. The Dutch are also very active in overseas investment. Amsterdam traditionally has been a center for the diamond trade. Although it has lost a large part of the business to Israel, diamond cutting and trading remain an important industry in Holland.

Since World War II, the Dutch have taken the lead in economic-integration activities in Europe, including the formation of the Benelux customs union with Belgium and Luxembourg and the foundation of the European Economic Community (EEC, or Common Market). In the early 1990s, as the Common Market moved closer to economic and political union, the Dutch, like the other smaller members, were concerned about being treated fairly by the larger, more powerful member nations, and about maintaining their cultural identity in the new Europe.

CITIES

Amsterdam.   Founded in the 13th century on the Amstel River, the city got its original name, Amstelledamme, when the river was dammed. From its beginning, as wooden houses clustered in narrow streets, the city grew in size and importance to the point of having serious traffic problems. To ease these difficulties, a series of concentric canals were dug—the beginning of Amsterdam's modern network of canals. There are about 60 of them, crossed by more than 550 bridges, and they have made the city a composite of some 90 islands.

Among the city's highlights is the Rijksmuseum (National Museum), which is renowned for its extensive collection of paintings by great Dutch artists. The Stedelijk Museum contains an outstanding collection of modern paintings, including the works of Vincent van Gogh and the works of such 20th-century Dutch painters as Piet Mondrian, Kees van Dongen, and Karel Appel. Amsterdam's rich heritage from the past includes the Schreierstoren (weeper's tower), where 17th- and 18th-century travelers to the New World took leave of their relatives. It also is the site of the artist Rembrandt's house, which has been restored as a museum. Amsterdam is the home of the Concertgebouw, a leading symphony orchestra.

Amsterdam remains a world leader in the production of diamonds for jewelry and industrial purposes. The city's industrial complex ranks first in the nation. The port of Amsterdam, linked to international waters by the North Sea Canal, is one of the most modern in Europe. The city is the home base of KLM (Koninklijke Luchtvaart Maatschappij, or Royal Dutch Airlines) and the site of Schiphol International Airport, one of the largest duty-free airports in the world. All these combine to make Amsterdam a focus of international trade and travel.

Rotterdam and The Hague.   In a square in the center of Rotterdam, there stands a statue of a human figure with its arms raised despairingly and questioningly toward the sky. The statue represents the destruction of Rotterdam by German bombs in May 1940. Although the port was further damaged later in World War II, Rotterdam has not only managed to recover, but has far surpassed its former position. A huge extension called Europoort was added after the war, and today Rotterdam is the world's largest port. The city's location on an arm of the Rhine has earned it the name Gateway to Europe. Tugs and river barges take goods upstream to the countries of Europe, while others bring the products of European industry and agriculture downstream for export to the world. An exciting view of the port can be seen from the top-floor restaurant of the tall tower called Euromast, where one can also view the attractive modern buildings and museums of rebuilt Rotterdam. The city's subway —the first in the Netherlands—opened in 1968.

The Hague (known in Dutch as 's Gravenhage or Den Haag) is the third-largest city in the Netherlands. While Amsterdam is the capital, The Hague is the seat of government—where Parliament meets and where the country is run—and of foreign embassies. Various international peace conferences have been held in The Hague, and in 1921 the Permanent Court of Arbitration (International Court of Justice), or World

Court (associated first with the League of Nations and now with the United Nations) was established there. Three of the royal palaces are in The Hague and nearby Scheveningen.

GOVERNMENT
The Monarch

The Netherlands is a constitutional monarchy in structure and a democracy in practice. The head of state is a monarch (a queen for the last century) who succeeds according to the hereditary principle of primogeniture in the royal House of Orange-Nassau. Under the most recent constitutional revision, there is no preference for males over females. The monarch, who embodies the national sovereignty, is a symbol of national unity above political parties. The power of the state rests in the parliament, called by the historical name of States General, and the cabinet, composed of the premier and ministers who head government departments. Laws and decrees are issued in the name of the monarch, who in theory has all authority and is not answerable to parliament; but legislation must also be signed by a minister, who is responsible to it. Members of the cabinet do not serve in parliament; if they have seats in it, they must resign them. Even though the monarch theoretically has unlimited power, it would be unheard of for her to refuse to sign a duly approved piece of legislation. The sovereignty of the queen is therefore a useful constitutional fiction. In practice, the monarch uses her position above parties to facilitate the formation of a new cabinet after an election or when a cabinet resigns. With other members of the royal family, the queen performs a host of ceremonial functions and represents a unifying force in Dutch society.

The States General

The premier and ministers come before the houses of parliament to present bills for their approval and to explain and defend their political conduct. The States General is composed of two houses, the First Chamber, or senate, and the Second Chamber, or lower house. In the event of conflict with the senate over a bill, the approval of the Second Chamber is sufficient for the measure to become law. This arrangement reflects their respective electorates: The Second Chamber is elected directly by the people, the First Chamber by the Provincial States, which are the legislatures of the various provinces.

All adult citizens take part in parliamentary elections. In local elections, immigrants with established residence also have a vote. In elections for the Second Chamber there are no local constituencies but a nationwide system of proportional representation, which assures that the 150 seats in the chamber are distributed quite precisely according to the popular vote. Both major and most minor parties therefore have a voice in parliament. Because no party in modern times has been able to win a majority, cabinets are always coalitions. Although a few cabinets have been turned out of office between elections, there is a basic stability in personnel and policies. The three major parties, despite differences, all represent the center of the political spectrum. There is a wide variety of small and splinter parties, mostly on the right and left extremes; they usually do not sway the formation of cabinets but occasionally contribute new ideas for legislation.

How the Country Is Governed

The government of the Netherlands is unitary; that is, all power radiates from the center, and local governments derive all their powers from the national government. Although Amsterdam is called the capital (*hoofdstad*, "head city") in recognition of its size and preeminence, the seat of government is The Hague. There the States General meet in two ancient buildings together called the *Binnenhof* (Inner Court), which is also the popular name for the central government.

There are 12 provinces; all but one have the names of historic provinces, but their boundaries have been redrawn in modern times. The Provincial States, each headed by a royal commissioner, are allowed a considerable degree of self-government. The entire country is divided into local self-governing communities called *gemeenten* ("communes"), which vary in size from an entire city like Amsterdam to an assemblage of villages. They are headed by a mayor (*burgemeester*), named by the central government, and a board of aldermen, locally chosen. Provincial commissioners and mayors are not restricted to the party in power in the cabinet but are named upon the basis of the political complexion of their province or community.

Legal System. The legal system of the Netherlands is a mixture of Roman and the Napoleonic Code, which was instituted during the reign of King Louis of Holland (1806–10), as modified by almost two centuries of legislation. Judges hear minor cases singly and form tribunals for major cases. The rights of defendants are scrupulously observed. Prison sentences are relatively short. The constitution provides very broad civil rights.

HISTORY

The Netherlands as a separate nation and state dates back no further than the late 16th century. Until then it and Belgium were part of a loose unit called the Low Countries. In ancient times the area was peopled by Germanic and Celtic tribes called the Belgae, the Batavi, and the Frisians. In the 1st century B.C. they were conquered by the Romans under Julius Caesar, with the exception of those Frisians who lived on the farthest northwest coast. During the Middle Ages the northern Low Countries became part of the Holy Roman Empire (Germany), while some of the southerly provinces were under French rule. It was in these centuries that the province of Holland rose to importance for its shipping and fishing activities.

Between the late 14th and early 16th centuries all the Low Countries passed by inheritance and conquest under the rule of the French dukes of Burgundy. Their wealth enabled the duchy to establish its virtual independence from both the Holy Roman Empire and France. The chance for full separate existence was lost, however, when the dukes married first into the Habsburg family, whose members eventually ruled both the Holy Roman Empire and Spain. Charles V, who was born at Ghent in 1500, became Holy Roman emperor and king of Spain. When he abdicated in 1556, he divided his dominions between his brother, Ferdinand, who received the empire as his share, and his son Philip II, who received Spain and the Low Countries.

Philip's attempt to suppress Protestant heresies in the Low Countries and to rule them in the same absolutist way he governed in Spain led to riots in 1566 and a revolt in 1568, which were led by a great nobleman, William of Orange. After the rebels seized the little port of Brielle in Holland in 1572, they gained control of most of the northern Low Countries. William's most important supporters were the Calvinists, the most militant of the Protestant denominations. The rebellion spread to the southern provinces four years later but failed to maintain itself there. The northern provinces declared their independence of Philip II in 1581, becoming a new nation, the Dutch Republic.

The Dutch Republic

The republic, despite its tiny size, became one of the great powers of Europe in the 17th century. During most of the republic era, a member of the House of Orange led the country—but with the title of Stadholder rather than King. After 80 years, Spain acknowledged Dutch independence in the Peace of Westphalia (1648). The Dutch successfully defended their freedom in wars against both England and France, their former allies against Spain. Overseas they established colonies in the Americas and the East Indies. At home they created a haven for personal and religious freedom unmatched anywhere in Europe, although Calvinism remained the official church and increased its numbers to become almost a majority of the population. Dutch wealth expanded fabulously, providing the resources for a Golden Age. Dutch art, especially painting, reached the heights of achievement, with Rembrandt van Rijn only the most famous of dozens of great artists.

In the 18th century, the republic, exhausted by its immense military efforts, slipped well behind the rising power of England and France. It was, however, the first country to give full diplomatic recognition to the new United States of America in 1782.

The Evolution of the Monarchy

Between 1795 and 1813 the country was under French domination, first as the Batavian Republic (1795–1806), then as the Kingdom of Holland (1806–10) under Napoleon's brother Louis, and finally incorporated into the French Empire (1810–13). In this period political institutions were totally reorganized. The federal system of the republic was replaced by a unitary state, which was continued when French rule was thrown off in 1813, and a monarchy, still under the House of Orange, was instituted under King William I.

William shared his powers to a limited extent with a parliament (States General) but ruled with generally enlightened policies directed in particular to economic rehabilitation of a country badly hurt by a quarter century of war and occupation. He abdicated in 1840 after failing to prevent Belgium, which had been united with the northern Netherlands by the Congress of Vienna (1815), from winning its independence (1830–39). His son, William II, frightened by the revolutionary movements elsewhere in Europe in 1848, conceded full constitutional government as proposed by Johan Rudolf Thorbecke, who was the father of the modern Dutch system of government.

The Netherlands in the 20th Century

The next century brought full democracy to the Netherlands. The most difficult question was the school system, where dissident Protes-

An oil painting by Jacob van Ruisdael captures the essence of the 17th-century Dutch countryside.

tants and Roman Catholics sought state support for their private schools. This issue was not settled until a compromise, called the "Pacification," was worked out in 1917. By it, public financing of all schools was granted and universal suffrage was introduced. The Netherlands had effectively withdrawn from any major part in foreign affairs after Belgian independence, accepting a neutral status that was maintained until invasion by Nazi Germany in May 1940.

The cabinet, Queen Wilhelmina, and the rest of the royal family escaped to London, where a government in exile contributed to the Allied war effort. There was great suffering in the country, especially in the last winter of 1944–45, before liberation by Allied forces in 1945. Dutch Jews, who had lived in the country for centuries in safety, were hunted down by the Nazis and shipped to death camps; only about one in ten survived.

Peace brought freedom and the restoration of democratic, parliamentary government. Wilhelmina resumed her throne, and the first task was rebuilding the shattered economy. In 1948, Wilhelmina abdicated in favor of her daughter Juliana. For the next 15 years management, labor, and government collaborated. Strikes were avoided, and full use was made of American Marshall Plan aid. The policy of neutrality, which had not kept the country out of the war, was abandoned. The Netherlands enthusiastically joined the alliance of Western democratic states embodied in the North Atlantic Treaty Organization (NATO). It was unable, however, to retain its hold upon the Netherlands East Indies, which

Parliament buildings in The Hague. Although not the capital, The Hague is the seat of the Dutch government.

declared their independence as Indonesia; there was much bitterness against U.S. support for the Indonesian cause. The system of religious-ideological "pillars" was maintained and strengthened.

The 1960s brought significant changes. The discovery of natural gas provided new revenue, which was put to use in instituting a welfare system that included not only insurance for the aged, the disabled, and the unemployed, but also lavish support for education and culture. Within a quarter of a century, the public sector expanded to take in more than half of the gross national income. The strain upon Dutch industry, which depends upon exports, persuaded the coalition cabinet of Premier Ruud Lubbers to undertake a cutback of welfare expenditures in the 1980s and early 1990s. This policy was continued by Lubbers' successor, Willem Kok, who became premier after 1994 legislative elections. Kok was reelected in 1998, and his Labor Party increased its majority in the government.

The end of the Cold War and the dissolution of the Soviet Union in the early 1990s reduced domestic tensions over the nation's role in foreign policy. In the 1990s, Dutch industry prepared for the increased competition expected with the planned economic and political unification of the European Union (EU) nations. The Netherlands was particularly concerned about its place in the new Europe, since it was one of the smaller, less powerful countries. Nevertheless, in 1992 the Dutch cemented their commitment to the EU by signing and ratifying the Maastricht Treaty. The Netherlands also hosted a key EU summit meeting in Amsterdam in June 1998.

HERBERT H. ROWEN, Rutgers University

GERMANY: AN INTRODUCTION

The study of history—including that of a particular nation—is a prerequisite for an understanding of our own era. This is especially true of Germany, where the dramatic events of the past few years have helped to define the nature of the rapidly changing world around us. The dismantling of the Berlin Wall in 1989 captured both the symbolism and the substance of forces that altered, in the space of a few months, more than 40 years of history and ushered in the closing chapter of the period known as the Cold War.

Germans have always had a keen sense of history. For many years after World War II, entire generations of Germans— particularly in the West—felt subdued feelings of responsibility for the ravages of the war. The division of the country was a clear and inescapable reminder to citizens on both sides of the Iron Curtain of the tragic conflagration.

The German people balance these painful memories, however, with those of a grander time—for example, as when, centuries ago, the Holy Roman Empire of the German nation offered a framework for the peaceful coexistence of the peoples of Europe. Germans are also proud of their cultural heritage, their rich literature, their philosophers, their scientists, and especially their music.

From 1949 the Federal Republic of Germany (West Germany) built on the best traditions of German history and created a prosperous democracy that contributed much to the stability of Europe in the postwar era. A staunch supporter of the United States, West Germany became the chief proponent of a new European integration and the most forceful member of the European Community (EC).

Throughout the Cold War period, East Germany was a committed ally of the Soviet Union, and it was generally assumed that the regime would be among the last to give in to pressure for liberalization. While significantly below the standards for West Germany, the East Germans' standard of living was the highest in the Eastern bloc, and their military was one of the more reliable components of the Warsaw Pact.

The stability of the East German system, however, proved to be without foundation. Everything changed in 1989, when tens of thousands of East Germans migrated west through openings in the Iron Curtain provided by Hungary and Czechoslovakia. Since the West German Constitution recognized all Germans as citizens, the West German government provided resettlement assistance and social benefits to the escapees. There was jubilation in West Germany as families were reunited and East Germans tasted freedom for the first time.

Meanwhile, rapidly swelling demonstrations in dozens of East German cities brought down the Communist government. Erich Honecker, the party chief since 1971, resigned in October, and several weeks later the Berlin Wall was opened. The idea of a united Germany, which only months before had seemed completely out of reach, suddenly came close to reality. It took less than a year to work out the details, and on October 3, 1990, Germany became one country again.

By the time formal political unification was completed, however, the mood of many Germans was decidedly more somber than it had been during the dismantling of the Berlin Wall. It had become obvious that the integration of 16 million former East Germans into West Germany's economy and society would be no easy task.

The constitutional union of the two Germanys was relatively easy. The economic costs of the union, however, turned out to be astronomical. In 1989, Chancellor Kohl promised West Germans that no tax increases would be needed to pay for reunification, but he could not keep this promise. The actual costs, almost 200 million deutsche marks each year, were covered by the "solidarity tax" that West Germans were required to pay. Only in 1997 was this surcharge decreased, from 7.5 percent to 5 percent.

The unification proved to be a disappointment in other aspects as well. East Germans had lived within the Soviet bloc for 45 years, and were deeply influenced by Communist ideology and practice. They became citizens of a capitalist, democratic country overnight, and had no experience with a free marketplace or with open democratic debate. As late as 1995, about two-thirds of East Germans thought that "well-managed socialism" was preferable to a market economy.

In order to address the Communist legacy, the German government organized the files of the former East German secret police, known as Stasi, and made them available to the 6 million people about whom Stasi collected information. There were reports of broken friendships and shattered family relations when many discovered that they had been informed on by loved ones.

The government also put several former East Germans on trial. Some, including border guards who shot at people trying to cross the Berlin Wall, went to prison. Even Erich Honecker, the last East German leader, was on trial in 1992, but he was allowed to leave the country because of advanced cancer. He died in 1994.

Since 1990, Germany has had to deal with another consequence of the end of the Cold War: waves of refugees. As borders opened and fighting erupted in the countries of the former Yugoslavia and in other places, thousands of people started moving toward the wealthy Western world. Many of them have been crossing the German borders illegally. Until 1994, Germany accepted more than 800,000 immigrants annually, which made it resemble the America of the early 20th century. The newcomers were not always welcome, and anti-immigrant violence has been on the rise.

To add to the country's problems, by early 1998, there were about 4.4 million people unemployed; and the peaceful harmony between the labor unions, the heads of corporations, and the government had shown signs of cracks.

Yet despite all these difficulties, Germany continues to hold the distinction of being the economic giant of Europe. In contrast to previous decades, the country has begun to reassert its leadership role in European foreign policy, and its new pride has occasionally provoked unease among the country's European neighbors. Yet its postwar record clearly shows that the country has earned the right to take its place among the sovereign and democratic nations of the world. Despite all its current difficulties, it is a nation with a promising future.

High-rise buildings dwarf the medieval center of Frankfurt, a commercial hub in the central highlands.

GERMANY

For 45 years the dividing line between West and East in Europe ran through Germany. The line was real: an 858-mi. (1,381-km.) border strip of barricades, barbed wire, and mine fields. On one side of the border lay the Federal Republic of Germany, usually known as West Germany, a prosperous and democratic nation and a staunch member of the North Atlantic Treaty Organization (NATO). On the other side was the German Democratic Republic, known as East Germany. Throughout the decades of the Cold War, East Germany was a subservient, unflinching ally of the Soviet Union, and its government was a harsh Communist dictatorship.

The artificial division of Germany at the end of World War II separated families and divided people with the same culture and history. In 1989 and 1990, this division came to an end. First, in the fall of 1989, the barrier between the two countries was dismantled. Huge crowds cheered and danced in the streets as the Berlin Wall, separating East and West Berlin, was torn down. By mid-1990 the two countries had created a unified economy that used the same currency. The political union of the two countries followed on October 3, 1990. The speed with which this bloodless revolution occurred made it one of the most astounding events in recent European history.

The excitement of those days is almost forgotten, and in many ways Germany continues to be divided, even though the Berlin Wall is gone. Social scientists have even coined the phrase "underestimating the East German mentality." Viewed from the longer perspective, however, the turbulent 1990s have strengthened Germany, and the five new eastern states have changed beyond recognition—and for the better.

THE LAND

Germany lies in the heart of Europe—south of the Scandinavian countries, west of the Slavic ones, north and east of the Romance nations. It is a country that has varied greatly in size during the long existence of the German people.

Germany can be divided into three principal regions—the northern lowlands, the central highlands, and the southern alpine region, south of the Danube River. The northern region extends between the North and Baltic seas: the border is a zigzag line stretching from Cologne in the central west through Düsseldorf, Dortmund, Paderborn, Osnabrück, Hanover, and Magdeburg, to Wittenberg in the east. The geography consists of a mostly flat plain, dotted with marshes and lakes. Fertile soils lie near the coast and in the river valleys. Extensive parts of the region are sandy heathlands used for both sheep grazing and agriculture.

FACTS AND FIGURES

OFFICIAL NAME: Federal Republic of Germany.

NATIONALITY: German(s).

CAPITAL: Berlin.

LOCATION: Central Europe. **Boundaries**—Baltic Sea, Poland, Czech Republic, Austria, Switzerland, France, Luxembourg, Belgium, the Netherlands, North Sea, Denmark.

AREA: 137,803 sq. mi. (356,910 sq. km.).

PHYSICAL FEATURES: Highest point—Zugspitze (9,721 ft.; 2,963 m.). **Lowest point**—sea level. **Chief rivers**—Rhine, Elbe, Weser, Oder-Neisse, Danube, Main.

POPULATION: 84,068,216 (1997; annual growth –0.6%).

MAJOR LANGUAGE: German.

MAJOR RELIGIONS: Protestantism, Roman Catholicism.

GOVERNMENT: Federal republic. **Head of state**—president. **Head of government**—chancellor. **Legislature**—bicameral chamber.

CHIEF CITIES: Berlin, Bonn, Cologne, Dresden, Essen, Frankfurt, Hamburg, Leipzig, Munich.

ECONOMY: Chief minerals—iron, coal, lignite, potash, uranium, copper. **Chief agricultural products**—rye, wheat, barley, potatoes. **Industries and products**—iron and steel products, coal, cement, chemicals, machinery, shipbuilding, motor vehicles. **Chief exports**—machines, machine tools, chemicals, motor vehicles. **Chief imports**—manufactured products, fuels, agricultural products.

MONETARY UNIT: 1 deutsche mark = 100 pfennige.

NATIONAL HOLIDAY: October 3 (German Unity Day).

The dismantling of the Berlin Wall in 1989 set the stage for German reunification a year later. Only a few segments of the wall still stand.

The largest of these areas, lying between the cities of Hamburg and Hanover, is the Lüneburger Heide, a 55-mi. (89-km.) stretch of purple heather, golden gorse, and juniper trees.

Between the plain and the highlands lies a transitional belt known for the richness of its soil. It starts in the region around Cologne in the west and continues toward the east to the cities of Halle, Leipzig, and Dresden. From the early Middle Ages on, this area, which has long been one of the most densely populated regions of Europe, has been heavily traveled.

The central highlands offer a diversity of landscapes between the upper regions, with their rich stands of timber, and the lower slopes and valleys, where numerous crops are grown. The Harz Mountains, the best-known range in the highlands, straddle the line that for 40 years formed the border between the two parts of Germany. These mountains have peaks that exceed 3,000 ft. (914 m.) in altitude. In the western part of the

In southern Germany, picturesque villages lie nestled beneath snow-covered Alpine peaks.

country, the highlands form a series of plateaus into which the rivers, especially the Rhine, have cut steep gorges of great beauty. This area contains forests, fields, vineyards, and mountains. The town of Sankt Andreasberg in the Harz Mountains is famous for its singing canaries. To the east lies the Thuringian Forest, the site of many health spas. On the border with the Czech Republic are the Erzgebirge Mountains ("ore mountains"), which are named for the variety of minerals found there, including uranium ore.

No clear demarcation exists between the central highlands and the alpine areas of the extreme south. In the southwest is the Black Forest Range, named for the dark spruces and firs that line its slopes. These mountains, the home of the cuckoo clock and the background for many fairy tales, are a favorite vacation spot. The Danube River originates in these heights and flows eastward for about 400 mi. (644 km.) across southern Germany. (An article on the DANUBE RIVER appears elsewhere in this volume.)

The Bavarian Alps are an extension of a minor range of the Alps. On the border with Austria rises the highest peak in Germany, the Zugspitze (9,721 ft. or 2,963 m.). The snow-covered peaks and many lakes make the Bavarian Alps a favorite resort area.

Climate. A damp maritime climate prevails along the North Sea and Baltic coasts, but farther inland and toward the south, the pattern becomes more typically continental. The average January temperature is between 21° and 34° F. (−6° to 1° C.), depending on the location. In July the corresponding averages are 61° and 68° F. (16° to 20° C.). On the high plateaus, winter temperatures may be lower, and in parts of the Rhine Valley, the summers are sometimes a little warmer than the average.

Rain falls in all seasons, but generally more precipitation occurs in the summer. Precipitation is heaviest in the south, where most of it falls as snow, which attracts winter-sports enthusiasts. The northern lowlands and the central highlands receive more rain than snow.

Rivers, Canals, and Lakes. Germany has a number of navigable rivers and an extensive system of canals. The best-known river is the Rhine. Although it originates in Switzerland and empties into the North Sea in Dutch territory, the Rhine is generally thought of as a German river. This important waterway, together with its tributaries, carries more traffic than any other river system in Europe. (An article on the RHINE RIVER appears in this volume.)

The Weser, Elbe, and Oder rivers drain the northern plain. The Weser empties into the North Sea after flowing past Bremen and its port of Bremerhaven. The Elbe, which rises in the Czech Republic, flows northwest through the country, past Dresden and Magdeburg, to empty into the North Sea at Hamburg. Between 1949 and 1990, the lower reaches of the Elbe formed the border between the two Germanys. This river's chief tributaries are the Saale and the Havel. The Spree, which runs through Berlin, merges into the Havel.

The Oder also originates in the Czech Republic and, with its tributary the Neisse, forms most of Germany's eastern border with Poland.

A network of canals crisscrosses the country, connecting the various German rivers. The longest is the Mittelland Canal, which enables trav-

The Rhine flows past medieval Bacharach in its long gorge between Mainz and Koblenz.

elers to cross the whole length of northern Germany entirely by water. The Kiel Canal, farther north, connects the North Sea to the Baltic. More paying ships pass through the Kiel than through any other canal in the world. A connecting canal between the Main River and the Danube in the south provides a convenient link for ships traveling from the North Sea to the Black Sea.

In the south lies the Bodensee (Lake Constance), Germany's largest lake, and part of the course of the Rhine. Its surface is 208 sq. mi. (540 sq. km.), and it is more than 42 mi. (67 km.) long. The lake is shared by three countries: Germany in the north, Switzerland in the southwest, and Austria in the south. The deep Chiemsee in Bavaria is one of the most beautiful lakes in the country.

The northeastern part of the country contains a number of lakes, the largest of which is the Müritzsee, covering about 45 sq. mi. (117 sq. km.).

Natural Resources.   Germany's most important resource is coal. Bituminous coal is found in the Ruhr—a highly industrialized area that covers about 2,000 sq. mi. (5,180 sq. km.) in the western part of the country. The Ruhr is the center of the German iron and steel industries. Essen, Dortmund, and the Rhine port city of Duisburg owe much of their industrial power to the nearness of the seemingly inexhaustible supply of coal. Rich seams of coal are also found near the city of Aachen and in the Saarland.

Lignite, or brown coal, is mined chiefly in the central highlands. Before the unification of East and West Germany, lignite represented the backbone of East German heavy industry. This coal is of lower quality than bituminous coal, and its use has caused significant air and water pollution in the southern part of the former East Germany.

Although crude-oil deposits have been found in the Lüneburger Heide and around Schleswig-Holstein, as well as offshore in the North Sea, they are not sufficient for domestic needs. Some iron ore, lead, zinc, and copper are also mined. Potash salts are used as fertilizers: Germany is one of the world's largest suppliers of this substance. Germany also has considerable reserves of rock salt and kaolin, which is used in the famous Dresden china; kaolin is produced chiefly at nearby Meissen.

THE PEOPLE

The people known as Germans are really a mixture of three principal and several minor ethnic stocks. In the early years of the Christian era, tribes of Teutonic origin mingled with Celtic peoples in various parts of what is now known as Germany. In Roman times a Mediterranean strain was added to the Celtic-Teutonic stock. Further migrations brought in people of Baltic and Slavic origins, and repeated invasions through the centuries contributed still more variety to the mixture.

Roughly speaking, the western and southern regions are mostly Celtic and Mediterranean in composition, the central parts largely Celtic and Teutonic, and the eastern part Teutonic and Slavic. These generalizations, however, have become less true in recent times, and it is extremely difficult today to identify or separate the diverse elements that make up the German people.

The five new northeastern states—which until 1990 constituted East Germany—are much less densely populated than the western 10. Visitors

The North Sea island of Sylt attracts a great number of summer vacationers to its fine beaches.

often remark that the former East Germany looks in many ways like Germany before World War II. The Communist Germany was a country of small towns and hamlets: only 15 cities had populations of more than 100,000. In fact, the population declined over the years. Immediately after World War II, many people moved to the Western zones, prompting the construction of the wall through Berlin to stop the flow. Later years saw a low birthrate that was insufficient to sustain the population. East Germany imported foreign workers to supplement its labor force, mostly from Vietnam and other developing nations. After unification, many of these people were repatriated.

The former West Germany is one of the most densely populated regions in Europe. Over the years, the employment needs of the booming economy have attracted nearly 4 million foreign workers, many of them from Turkey and Southern Europe. Due to the wave of refugees in recent years, about 7.5 million foreigners lived in Germany in 1998. These immigration rates are comparable to those experienced by the United States in the early 20th century. As with other developed countries, however, Germany is becoming increasingly inhospitable, and by the late 1990s, the majority of applications for asylum were rejected.

A small Danish minority lives in the north. Dependents of U.S. military troops, foreign students enrolled at German universities, and businesspeople from other countries contribute to the cosmopolitan character of major German cities.

For several years after unification, Germany continued to host thousands of foreign armed forces. By late August 1994, however, all of the 370,000 former Soviet troops stationed in East Germany had left for their native countries. Germany contributed financially to their relocation. The combined U.S., British, and French forces still in Germany numbered about 150,000 in the late 1990s. By September 1994, all foreign troops had left Berlin.

Religion. Protestantism arose in Germany, and the dividing line between Catholic and Protestant Europe cuts through the country. Until unification, the West German population was almost equally divided between these two major denominations, but, with the addition of five new northeastern states, the balance has shifted in favor of Protestants. Bavaria has the highest percentage of Catholics.

Despite the official policy in postwar East Germany of creating a state without religion, churches remained an important aspect of life. Protestant churches played an increasingly significant political role by becoming centers for the nonofficial peace movement in the former East Germany in the 1980s; they were also the major organizers of the wave of demonstrations that swept the Communist regime in the fall of 1989.

Most Germans belong to Christian denominations. The Lutheran Church was founded in Germany in the 16th century.

Education. Because the Germans have traditionally placed a great emphasis on education, they have a well-developed educational system. School is compulsory from the age of 6 to the age of 18. For the first four years, all children attend a basic primary school. At this point, students take examinations that decide their future education. About 80 percent continue in primary school until they are 14 or 15. They may then attend school part-time, while they also work and learn a trade.

Students with greater ability take tests for the intermediate schools or the still more difficult secondary schools. Those students who go on to attend the six-year intermediate schools are usually trained for a business career. They must learn one foreign language, as well as mathematics, science, and business skills.

A student who passes the examination for secondary school, called *Gymnasium*, continues for nine more years. A Gymnasium stresses classical or modern languages or mathematics and science. At the age of 19, Gymnasium students must take another examination to qualify for the university. Talented young people who are already employed may qualify for higher education by taking evening courses.

Education in the former West Germany was noted for its excellent curriculum of foreign languages, particularly English. East German education was marked by all the ideological distortions of Communist regimes, but was quite good in sciences and in technical fields.

Germany's Young People. Many young people, particularly in the former West Germany, no longer fit into a truly national mold. Quite a few of them consider themselves Europeans rather than simply Germans. Having been exposed to European and world affairs through television

German vocational schools prepare students for employment, apprenticeships, or engineering colleges.

and other media, they are more questioning than their parents, and more open to liberal influences than was the prewar generation.

On the other hand, the influx of immigrants from the East in the past few years has led to a wave of racial violence, perpetrated in particular by young people belonging to neo-Nazi and skinhead groups. Many of these incidents took place in the former East Germany, most often in cities along the Polish-German border. There have been thousands of attacks on foreign workers and refugees, including firebombings of hostels for foreigners. More than 30 people were killed in these incidents during the 1990s.

Way of Life. The neo-Nazis and skinheads represent only a tiny extremist minority of the nation. Historically, Germans have been stereotyped as formal, punctual, hardworking, and officious, and while all these qualities exist to some extent, there is also a lighter side to the German character. In fact, Germans are quite similar to Americans: they take great enjoyment in socializing, partying, and all kinds of celebrations. The Bavarian Oktoberfest, which is held every September into October, is a well-known tourist attraction. But even in the staid former East Germany, the annual Shrovetide carnival was marked by dances in the streets, masked balls, and processions.

Since World War II, Germans have also become passionate tourists. Prior to unification, groups of West Germans, with their superb cameras, could be found in every country around the globe; their East German cousins, who were not permitted to travel anywhere but the Eastern bloc,

Tourists flock to Munich each October for the Oktoberfest, the city's annual beer festival.

were the most numerous tourists in countries such as Czechoslovakia, Hungary, and Bulgaria.

Food. Germans love to eat, and they take pride in their reputation as excellent chefs. Each section of the country has its specialty. In Bavaria, it is the delicious dumpling known as the *Knödel,* in all its infinite varieties. In Hamburg, every kind of fish and seafood is served including *Seezunge* ("sole"), prawns, and the popular eel soup. Westphalia has its dark-brown pumpernickel and its tender ham is a delicacy.

Germany is the land of the *Wurst* ("sausage"), and many different kinds are produced. Berliners are especially fond of the fat pork *Bockwurst. Leberwurst* ("liver sausage"), *Blutwurst* ("blood sausage"), *Knackwurst* (the name comes from the popping sound made by the first bite), and *Bratwurst* ("fried sausage") are but a few others. The frankfurter is the most famous German sausage, but though it is known by that name around the world, in Germany—and even in Frankfurt—it is called *ein Wiener Wurschen,* or "a Vienna sausage"! Among the best-known German contributions to international menus are *Sauerbraten*, a tasty pot roast in a sauce, and many varieties of *Kartoffelsalat* ("potato salad").

One of the most traditional of German meals is still the Christmas dinner. The meal takes days to prepare and includes Christmas fruit bread, or *Stollen,* and a wide variety of beautiful cookies. On this happiest of all German holidays, crisply roasted goose is served.

And of course, Germany is known for its beer, which Germans call "liquid bread." Brewing is a 1,000-year-old tradition, and some 6,000 varieties are produced today. Many of them are as popular in New York and Tokyo as they are in Germany.

Sports. Germans have always been sports-minded. Hiking and camping through the lovely countryside and mountain forests are ever popular. Excellent and inexpensive hostels and camping grounds are available. Skiing and winter sports attract people of all ages. Lovely seaside resorts such as Travemünde, on the Baltic Sea; the North Sea surf; or the pools in almost every town offer many opportunities for swimming. Sailing, handball, tennis, and riding are also popular.

Germany has a variety of spectator sports, which involve millions of people. When international soccer matches are played or other important sporting contests are held, fans crowd the stadiums or watch the events on television. Six-day bicycle races and automobile racing are particularly popular.

The former East Germany was a veritable sports machine, famous for its many Olympic successes: in the 1988 Summer Olympics, for instance, East Germans won 102 medals, second in number only to the former Soviet Union. These achievements now appear in a somewhat different light: since reunification a number of reports have indicated that the performance of many East German athletes was enhanced by illegal steroids. Furthermore, the connection of leading sports figures to the East German secret police has cast further shadows on the former East German athletic establishment.

In Germany, where the bicycle was first conceived, cycling remains a popular competitive sport.

Cultural Life. Germans are great readers and theatergoers. Books of all sorts sell extremely well. The works of post–World War II authors—such as Günter Grass, Uwe Johnson, Gisela Elsner, and Heinrich Böll (who won the 1972 Nobel Prize for Literature)—are especially popular. Wolf Biermann, Reiner Kunze, and Manfred Bieler began their writing careers in the former East Germany, but then moved to the West, finding enthusiastic audiences.

Opera, music, and dance are flourishing, and so are museums. More than 30 million people attend the theater every year. Most theaters are maintained by the federal, state, and city governments, but many private ones exist as well. Both classical and contemporary works draw large audiences. The controversial plays of Rolf Hochhuth have aroused much comment in Germany, as they have elsewhere.

Music is truly popular and—like the theater—heavily subsidized by state and city governments. New concert halls and opera houses have risen in many towns. Symphony concerts are among the high points of local musical life. From spring to fall, numerous music festivals are held. In many places, modern operas are performed. Electronic and other forms of avant-garde music are gaining popularity.

But music is not merely for professionals. Small groups of amateur musicians often assemble in private homes for chamber music. Choral societies abound and attract many thousands to their festivals.

East and West Germans. Throughout the postwar period of divided Germany, the peoples on the two sides of the Iron Curtain had a complex and often ambivalent relationship with each other. On the one hand were the bonds: the division of Germany cut through families, and virtually everyone had some relatives on the other side. One of the positive consequences of West German *Ostpolitik,* pursued after the early 1970s, was the increase in human contacts. Initially, only West Germans could visit their relatives in East Germany, but by the 1980s, even some East Germans were permitted to travel to the west to see their kin.

There were also grudges and arrogance. As West Germans became more affluent and cosmopolitan, they tended to look down on their East German compatriots, who in turn often envied all the luxuries and freedoms available in the west. West German television was watched in virtually all of East Germany, and its impact seriously contributed to the undermining of the Communist system: no other people in the Communist world were able to compare, on a daily basis, their own shabby surroundings and daily frustrations to the situation of their neighbors, who spoke the same language, had the same cultural and political heritage, but lived under a different system.

When the Berlin Wall opened and the rest of the wall was dismantled, West Germans welcomed their newly liberated neighbors with open arms and a great generosity. Since then, it has become obvious that unification alone will not make all Germans economically and socially equal. Many former East Germans now feel like second-class citizens (their wages are less than two-thirds of the wages in the west), while former West Germans complain that 40 years of Communism have greatly undermined the work ethic of "Easterners" or "Ossies," as they are derogatively called.

CULTURAL HERITAGE

A unified Germany is a relatively modern development. Before 1990, the German people had lived under one government for only 74 years, from 1871 to 1945; but throughout the centuries of their long history, they were held together by the bond of their culture and common language. These links made the Cold War division into two Germanys seem artificial and unnatural to Germans on both sides of the Iron Curtain.

Language and Literature

German is one of the Indo-European languages. From its origins thousands of years ago along the coasts of the Baltic and North seas, it gradually spread southward and westward as the Germanic tribes moved into new lands. One of the strongest influences on the developing language was Latin, and many German words still show clearly traceable Latin origins.

By the 9th century A.D. many different regional dialects had developed, but no single German language yet existed. Martin Luther's translation of the Bible in the 16th century and the use of movable type—an invention of the German Johann Gutenberg—helped create standard written German.

Modern German is an inflected language, with changing endings of verbs and nouns. It also has three genders— masculine, feminine, and neuter—plus other complicated grammatical rules. All of this makes German a difficult language to master, especially for those whose mother tongue is English, which is structurally simpler. Many common words in English and German, however, share the same roots.

Myths, sagas, and folklore, passed on by word of mouth during the wanderings of the early Germanic tribes, are part of the German literary heritage today. The earliest literature was written in Latin by the monks. Anonymous authors collected and recounted various old themes in the *Nibelungenlied* ("Song of the Nibelungs"), which tells of battle, bravery, treason, and revenge. It has become a national epic.

From the 17th century on, German writers produced many works of literature that, in the words of Johann Wolfgang von Goethe, "like all good things, belong to the whole world." Goethe, born in Frankfurt am Main in 1749, is considered to be Germany's greatest writer. From his lyric poetry, to his novel *The Sorrows of Young Werther,* to his masterpiece *Faust,* his ideas have continued to inspire people everywhere.

The 18th century was also the time of playwright-critic Gotthold Lessing, whose *Nathan the Wise* was a plea for religious tolerance. At this time, too, Friedrich Schiller helped to carry German literature to international attention. In such plays as *Die Räuber* ("The Robbers"), he showed his concern with the individual's place in society. Such 18th- and 19th-century German philosophers as Immanuel Kant and Friedrich Hegel have had great influence on moral thinking all over the world.

Children of all nationalities are familiar with the collection of fairy tales compiled by Jacob and Wilhelm Grimm in the early 1800s. In the 19th century, Heinrich Heine's verse included *Die Lorelei*, which told the story of the beautiful Rhine maiden whose singing lured sailors to their destruction.

Two 19th-century philosophers who had a tremendous impact on 20th-century thought were Friedrich Nietzsche and Karl Marx. Nietzsche's idea of a moral superman found an erroneous echo in Hitler's theory that every German was an *Übermensch* ("superman"). Marx's *Communist Manifesto,* written with Friedrich Engels, and his monumental *Das Kapital* became the foundations of Communism.

A major figure of 20th-century German literature was Nobel prize-winner Thomas Mann, the author of such enduring novels as *Buddenbrooks* and *The Magic Mountain*. In 1933 Mann left Germany and went into self-imposed exile in Switzerland and then the United States.

True intellectual life in Germany ceased under Hitler. On the evening of May 10, 1933, torchlight parades in Berlin and several other cities ended with the burning of thousands of books, many written by authors of international repute. Art, music, and literature all eventually came under Nazi control. Ultimately, Heine's prediction came true—"Where books are burned, people are burned in the end."

The Arts

All Germans share a rich heritage of the great contributions made by their countrymen to music, literature, and art. Early German art often expressed Christian themes in ivory carvings and illuminated manuscripts. The strong religious character of the art also found an outlet in the stark and emotional Gothic sculpture of the 13th and 14th centuries.

"The Street" (1913), an oil painting by Ernst Ludwig Kirchner (Museum of Modern Art, New York City).

In the years between 1500 and 1550, several artists were active who later became known for their outstanding use of color, line, and detail. Albrecht Dürer was a fine painter, but it was the masterly use of line and design in his drawings and etchings that made him a major artist. Matthias Grünewald used color superbly in his greatest achievement, the *Isenheim Altarpiece*, now in a museum in Colmar, France. Part of this magnificent masterwork portrays a realistic Crucifixion showing the Agony of Christ. Hans Holbein the Younger is noted for his superb portraits —among the best known is that of King Henry VIII of England. Lucas Cranach the Elder brought freshness and charm to his many mythological and court paintings, as well as to his portraits of the leaders of the Reformation.

In the 17th and 18th centuries, when rococo and baroque architecture flourished in Europe, many richly decorated churches and castles were erected. Some charming buildings of this period have been preserved or restored. The Pilgrimage Church of the Wies, near Steingaden in southern Bavaria, is one of the loveliest examples of German baroque architecture.

In the late 19th and early 20th centuries, all the arts adopted a modern and simpler style. In her lithographs and etchings, Käthe Kollwitz portrayed the emotions of working people. The German love of color was seen in the *Blaue Reiter* (Blue Rider) group, in which artists such as Franz Marc moved German expressionism toward abstract art. In the

Dresden's ornate Semper Opera, bombed in World War II, finally reopened in 1985.

same period, Ernst Barlach's sculptures in bronze and wood captured the suffering of the common man.

At the Bauhaus, an art school established in Weimar in 1919, new ideas for industry, architecture, and crafts were generated that influence industrial design to the present day. Architects such as Walter Gropius and Ludwig Mies van der Rohe were great innovators in their field.

Music.   The German people have always loved music. It is not surprising, then, that over the centuries, German composers have contributed a great deal of superb music—symphonies, concerti, chamber music, and opera—to the world. And churchmen, noblemen, and common people all contributed to early German music. From the Church came the musical reading of Latin texts, called Gregorian chants after the 6th-century Pope Gregory I, who was one of the first to collect them. The Minnesingers were knights and lyric poets of the 12th and 13th centuries who traveled from court to court singing their poems of love and nature. The Meistersingers, who believed that the art of music could be learned like a trade, flourished from the 14th to the early 17th century. The music of the Meistersingers and a great wealth of *Volkslieder,* or "folk songs," originated from the common people. With the Protestant Reformation, church music was introduced to people as hymns.

To call the roll of German composers is to read much of the repertory of orchestras around the world. In the early part of the 18th century, baroque music reached its height in the works of Johann Sebastian Bach. He composed the world's greatest organ music as well as incomparable cantatas, fugues, and concerti. A contemporary, George Frederick Handel, who composed much of his wide range of work in England, is perhaps best loved for his oratorio the *Messiah*.

Probably the greatest of all German composers was Ludwig van Beethoven, who began his immortal work at the end of the 18th century. His nine symphonies and five piano concerti are among the world's most moving music. Beethoven's chamber music and his opera, *Fidelio*, are also part of his great legacy.

In the 19th century, Robert Schumann composed melodious piano music and symphonies. He is also known for the warmth and charm of his *Lieder* ("songs"). Felix Mendelssohn finished his first mature work, the overture to *A Midsummer Night's Dream*, at the age of 17. Many of his later compositions, such as the *Italian Symphony*, are still worldwide favorites. Johannes Brahms produced beautifully clear, lyric symphonies, as well as chamber music and *Lieder*. Richard Wagner brought a new dimension to German opera with his theory of the *Gesamtkunstwerk* ("total work of art"). Wagner was interested in every aspect of the opera, from the subject to the set design. In such operas as *Die Meistersinger von Nürnberg* ("The Mastersingers of Nuremberg") and *Der Ring des Nibelungen* ("The Ring of the Nibelung"), he used old German themes as the stories. In the Bavarian town of Bayreuth, a *Festspielhaus* ("festival theater") was specially built in which Wagner could produce his operas. Today visitors from all over the world come to attend the Wagner festival held every summer in Bayreuth.

Another composer of the period, Richard Strauss, carried German music into the 20th century. Strauss also used old German folk themes. In one of his many tone poems, he used the music to describe the merry pranks of a popular folk hero, the rascal Till Eulenspiegel. Strauss' other compositions include the operas *Electra* and *Ariadne auf Naxos*.

In this century, composer Paul Hindemith created new harmonies. German conductors such as Bruno Walter and Otto Klemperer won acclaim everywhere. Today, composers such as Hans Werner Henze and Karlheinz Stockhausen have gained worldwide recognition.

THE ECONOMY

At the end of World War II, the German economy was almost completely ruined. The excessive demands of the Nazi war machine had drained the resources of the country, and air raids had devastated the cities and industries. In addition, the Allies dismantled many of the remaining industrial plants for reparations. The nation's economic life came to a halt. In rebuilding their economies, the two parts of postwar Germany took widely divergent paths, leading to very different results.

East Germany

Although the devastation of the war was about the same in the East and the West, important differences in the East slowed its recovery. The German Democratic Republic had none of the magnificent resources of West Germany's Ruhr district; it had few resources to work with except farmland, potash, and brown coal. It also suffered from massive dismantling of its industrial plants by the Soviet Union in reparation for the losses the U.S.S.R. had incurred at German hands during the war. There was no Marshall Plan to aid the economy, as there was in West Germany.

The country faced the future with crippled industries, insufficient agricultural output to feed its people, and nothing to trade for raw materials.

Nationalization of the economy on the Soviet model brought further problems. It resulted in a large-scale flight to the West of the skilled labor force that was the backbone of industrial production. Not until the erection of the Berlin Wall in 1961 was the mass emigration effectively halted. Most manufacturing and retailing was transferred to public ownership. Centralized planning and mismanagement reduced incentive and efficiency.

In comparison with other Communist states, however, East Germany was the most prosperous. It established international recognition for its optical equipment, but most of its other products were significantly inferior by Western standards. Automobiles (including the little Trabants, which were the butt of many jokes), drugs, household appliances, toys, and musical instruments were exported to Eastern Europe and some nations of Asia and Africa. East Germany also had an active chemical industry, producing plastics, petrochemicals, textiles, and fertilizers. East German industry was tied closely to the Soviet Union by a 2,500-mi. (4,023-km.)-long oil pipeline from deep in the Soviet heartland.

Pollution and other environmental problems plague many cities formerly in East Germany.

The farmlands in East Germany were historically parts of large estates rather than the small, owner-worked strips that were the rule in the West. When the Soviet Union occupied this area in 1945, at the end of World War II, a radical program of land redistribution was begun. The small farms established by this program, however, were not as productive as had been hoped. There was a great shortage of labor as people moved to the cities for work. The Soviet Union took the best of the draft animals and machinery. Fertilizers were scarce.

In 1952 an attempt was made to gather the small farms into cooperatives that shared land, or machinery, or, in the case of people without land, their hours of labor. As an inducement a certain amount of the

Shopping malls in Hamburg and other German cities have a distinctly American feel to them.

yield of the land or livestock could be held for private use. The program was unsuccessful until 1960, when the majority of farms were finally collectivized.

West Germany

Unlike East Germany, which was slow to recover, West Germany soon after the war experienced an economic comeback of such magnitude that it has been called a *Wirtschaftswunder,* an "economic miracle." Much of that miracle, however, was due to the help given West Germany under the European Recovery Program. From 1948 to 1952, the Marshall Plan—as the program was popularly called—poured no less than $3.5 billion into the country.

The money received was wisely used. Invested in modern machinery and complete retooling of industrial plants, it enabled West German industry to manufacture products efficiently and inexpensively enough to compete in the world market.

A combination of many factors brought prosperity beyond anything Germany had ever experienced. The Federal Republic had no military expenditures during the early postwar years. (After it became a member of the North Atlantic Treaty Organization—known as NATO—in 1955, Allied troops remained at their stations as West Germany developed its defense forces.) Moreover, in a country where 20 percent of the dwellings were completely destroyed or heavily damaged at the end of the war, the need for new housing was enormous. Capital from an increasingly healthy economy spurred the expansion of building. The hunger for all kinds of consumer goods provided an excellent market for industry. A strong demand for West German manufacturing products throughout the world in the postwar period also helped bring about the "economic miracle."

After the first impetus, a general expansion of world trade began. Because of German production and marketing skills, the country's export volume doubled, redoubled, and more than doubled again. West Germany's charter membership in the European Economic Community (EEC, or Common Market) in 1958 helped to increase the nation's prosperity. The elimination of all tariff barriers between the six Common Market nations in the heart of Europe greatly expanded the interchange of goods between them.

Before the Berlin Wall was built, the flow of skilled refugees from East Germany, as well as a stream of workers from other parts of Europe attracted by high wages, provided West Germany with a strong supply of labor. While East Germany suffered from the loss of its craftsmen, West Germany profited from their skills.

Industry

The heart of Germany's industrial might lies in the state of North Rhine-Westphalia, whose coal mines, steel plants, and huge industrial concerns employ about 3 million workers. The coal supply of the Ruhr keeps the blast furnaces and rolling mills turning out large quantities of steel for every use. As a result, Germany is one of the world's largest producers of steel.

The skyline of Düsseldorf, the capital of North Rhine-Westphalia, is graced by skyscrapers. This city, the home of many of Germany's metalworking plants, owes its growth to its location on the Rhine and its rail connections to the Ruhr.

Other sources of income for Germany include growing chemical and textile industries, particularly in the field of synthetics. Germans have enjoyed a reputation as fine craftsmen for hundreds of years. Their optical and precision instruments, fine cameras, and watches are sold everywhere. Electronic equipment, television sets, radios, and musical instruments are all part of the stream of German products. Imaginatively designed and intricately decorated toys have long charmed children all over the world.

Germany has experienced an uninterrupted rise in exports of heavy machinery, machine tools, electrical equipment, and chemical products. Another leading export is automobiles. From Volkswagen to Mercedes-Benz, German cars are popular all over the world.

The former East Germany went through an unprecedented industrial collapse just after unification. Of more than 3 million people employed in industry, about 2 million lost their jobs. Thanks to large investments from the West, however, the economy in the former East Germany is slowly improving, particularly in the state of Saxony.

Agriculture and Fishing

For many years, Germans have been moving away from the country and farming and into the cities and industry. Today, only about 6 percent of the population of the former West Germany is engaged in agriculture, forestry, or fishing. Most of the farms are small—about 22 acres (9 hectares) on the average—and are worked by their owners.

Germans are good farmers. Crop rotation, the proper use of fertilizers, and modern machinery have helped to increase productivity. The most important crops are wheat, barley, potatoes, and sugar beets. Dairy farming and the raising of livestock—cattle, pigs, sheep, horses, and chickens—are responsible for a large part of agricultural income. Despite the efforts of the government to protect and help the farmer, however, Germany must import at least 25 percent of its foodstuffs.

The growing of grapes and the accompanying industry of winemaking, although a small part of the national economy, are part of a heritage that dates back to Roman days.

A thriving fishing industry is centered around the North Sea ports. Bremerhaven is one of the busiest fishing ports of Europe. Many fishermen travel to faraway grounds in the North Atlantic or even in the Arctic Ocean in search of seafood. Herring makes up the bulk of the catch, but cod, sole, and flounder are also caught in some quantities.

The Welfare State

Although the cost of reunification has been much higher than projected, workers in the western part of the country continue to enjoy a better life than workers anywhere else. Their average workweek is only 37.5 hours, they have an annual vacation of six weeks, and they often retire at the age of 60. They have comprehensive health care and very generous pensions. When their children want to study at a college or university, they don't have to worry about huge tuition costs.

Germany is a very comfortable and efficient place to live. Intercity trains are equipped with on-board computers that show travelers how many minutes until the next stop. Public transportation is well developed, and many cities boast "pedestrians only" zones. Germany employs prudent environmental policies that discourage unnecessary waste.

As in most other developed countries, however, the population is growing older, and there are proportionately fewer young people to support the retired public. Many worry that the German social and economic system can no longer support such generous benefits.

Economic Crisis?

In the late 1990s, many Germans were feeling dissatisfied and fearing an economic crisis. The word "crisis" is obviously an exaggeration, but Germany seems to be at a crossroads—it has to make its economic and social system more flexible and innovative. Social security, so valued by older generations (Germans were seldom laid off and few companies went bankrupt), does not seem to concern younger Germans, who increasingly turn to Anglo-American models—more individual responsibility coupled with greater risks, yet greater chances for success. Germany is still very bureaucratic. In some states a new business needs the approval of almost 90 government offices before it can open. The regulations also affect services, which have always been Germany's weak point. For example, each state strictly enforces shopping hours, and stores are closed Saturday afternoons and on Sundays. In contrast to the United States, salespeople are often grumpy and disobliging.

The German model thus needs reworking, and German businesspeople are providing solutions. Many critics remain optimistic, hoping for a new burst of German energy, pragmatism, and competence.

German farmers run highly efficient, very productive operations. Most German farms are very small.

Tomorrow's Germany

The economy of the former East Germany has begun to improve, and in some ways it points toward the future: many entrepreneurs in the east are more flexible and innovative than their counterparts in the west. They dispense with complex bureaucratic rules and achieve higher productivity. Many old East German factories were in such poor condition that it was more economical to dismantle them and start building new facilities from scratch. For example, a new Opel automobile factory built near the town of Eisenach in 1992 is now one of the most efficient car plants in the world. Foreign firms investing in the region numbered 1,700 by the late 1990s.

An important factor in Germany's economic development will be its relationships with the countries to the east. Immediately after the fall of Communism, German politicians realized that financial aid to the countries of the former Soviet bloc would ultimately be beneficial to them as well. And so they provided more than half of the overall assistance to these nations. German investors can expect little profit in the near future, but once political conditions stabilize, the successor states of the Communist regimes will represent a huge new market at Germany's doorstep.

THE CITIES OF GERMANY

German cities are as distinctively varied as the German people—they can be firmly rooted in the past, thoroughly up-to-date, or both at the same time.

Sections of many cities were reduced to rubble at the end of World War II. In their determination to restore the old, medieval parts of cities, known as *Altstadt,* the Germans sometimes duplicated well-remembered streets down to the last cobblestone. This has caused many traffic jams, as cars from modern four-lane highways are funneled into narrow replicas of streets laid out centuries ago. Skyscrapers, housing developments, or modern factories can also be found alongside much older buildings, and crenellated castles sometimes hover over newly built supermarkets. Around the cities of Essen, Hamburg, and Munich, huge metropolises have sprung up. In the former East Germany, on the other hand, the growth of large cities at the cost of smaller towns and villages was slower than in West Germany.

Berlin, the largest German city and its capital since 1991, is treated in a separate article that follows this one. Other major cities include:

Hamburg.   Germany's second-largest city after Berlin, Hamburg is a busy, cosmopolitan port with a certain English influence. Shipyards, docks, and wharves line both shores of the Elbe River as it flows toward the North Sea.

One of the leading seaports in Europe, Hamburg has many faces. A skyscraper rises in the center of the new university complex. Hagenbecks Tierpark is at once a park and a zoo. In the Planten und Blumen botanical garden, the displays of flowers, the open-air theater, the children's playgrounds, and the restaurants on the lake make the area a pleasure park for young and old alike.

The Inner Alster and the Outer Alster, two lakes in the heart of the city, provide a delightful setting for the many office buildings and homes that rim their shores.

The leading seaport of Germany is Hamburg, near the mouth of the Elbe River.

Lübeck.   Northeast of Hamburg, on the Trave River near the Baltic, is the small city of Lübeck. Residents still take pride in their city's fame as "queen of the Hanseatic League"—the medieval association that controlled shipping as far away as Norway and the Netherlands. On the riverbank are the steeply gabled salt warehouses, reminders of the 14th and 15th centuries, when quantities of salt were used to preserve fish. The twin towers of the 15th-century Holstein Gate are often reproduced in marzipan—Lübeck's best-known product. This almond paste, which originated in the Middle East, is also shaped into fruits, vegetables, and many other forms and has gained worldwide popularity.

Potsdam.   Just southwest of Berlin is Potsdam, where the palace of Prussia's King Frederick II (Frederick the Great) is located. He was a lover of all things French, and he named his castle *Sans Souci* ("Carefree"). This 18th-century monarch invited many of Europe's intellectuals to visit and exchange ideas with him. In the palace are the rooms used by the French writer Voltaire when he was Frederick's guest. The building, with its lovely gardens, set in a picturesque spot, is now a popular museum.

At the Potsdam Conference in 1945, a few months after the end of World War II, the victorious Allies decided to divide Germany into four occupation zones.

Düsseldorf.   This port on the Rhine is the business center for the Ruhr industries. The city is the capital of the richest state in Germany, North Rhine–Westphalia. Its main street, the Königsallee, has many fine shops displaying goods from all over the world. Completely rebuilt after the war, Düsseldorf has modern buildings as well as many lovely parks. It also has several museums, including two art museums, an economic museum, and a Goethe collection.

Cologne.   The Rhine River city of Cologne is famous for its Gothic cathedral, begun in 1248 but not finished until 1880, and for its university, which is the second oldest in Germany, founded in 1388. In the 18th century, an Italian chemist named a new product for the city—*Kölnisch Wasser,* or "eau de Cologne."

Bonn.   In 1949, when the Federal Republic of Germany was formed, the quiet university city of Bonn was chosen as the capital. It sits on the Rhine River, about 15 mi. (24 km.) south of Cologne. Many new buildings, including the *Bundeshaus,* or parliament, were erected to house the government. During the 1990s, the government was transferred to Berlin.

It was in Bonn, in 1770, that composer Ludwig van Beethoven was born. His birthplace is preserved as a museum. In the concert hall that bears his name, a music festival is held every two years. It seems that all the inhabitants of Bonn are music lovers, for the concert halls are packed for every performance.

Aachen.   West of Cologne and Bonn, near the Belgian border, is the famous city of Aachen. A health resort since Roman times, it was the capital of the 9th-century Holy Roman Emperor Charlemagne, who built his palace there. The 14th-century town hall was erected on the ruins of that palace. Winding streets and ancient red-brick houses surround the cathedral, begun during the emperor's reign and containing his tomb.

Leipzig.   After East Berlin, Leipzig was the largest city in East Germany. About 90 mi. (145 km.) southwest of the capital, it has been an important trading center since the early Middle Ages. The Leipzig Fair, a showplace for merchants' goods, has been a tradition for more than 800 years. Today this international exhibit takes place twice a year. All kinds of machinery, from computers to tractors, and all kinds of consumer goods, from cosmetics to musical instruments, are on display. Leipzig is also a center of publishing.

The great composer Johann Sebastian Bach, who died in Leipzig in 1750, is buried in the Thomaskirche (Church of St. Thomas) in Leipzig. Bach, the greatest member of a famous musical family, was the director of music at the church. The choir of St. Thomas may often be heard singing his lovely music.

Dresden. Another important city located in the former East Germany is Dresden, which had been the capital of the medieval and Renaissance duchy of Saxony. During World War II, Dresden, 65 mi. (105 km.) southeast of Leipzig, was the most heavily bombed city of Germany. In February 1945, more than 700 British planes, followed by American aircraft, rained fire, destruction, and death on Dresden. Firestorms raged for almost two weeks. According to most accounts, about 135,000 people were killed, including many refugees, prisoners of war, and slave laborers from Eastern Europe. More than 70 historic buildings were completely destroyed, and hundreds of thousands of people were left homeless. One of the most vivid portrayals of this event is in Kurt Vonnegut's novel *Slaughterhouse Five* (1969), which was also made into a movie.

Many of Dresden's famous buildings were restored according to the detailed paintings of the Venetian painter Bernardo Bellotto Canaletto, who worked in Dresden in the 18th century. The most famous restoration is the Zwinger. This ornate building contains some of the best-known paintings in the world, including the *Sistine Madonna* by the Italian artist Raphael.

After World War II, Dresden became a busy industrial city. The delicate Dresden china that is its best-known product, however, is made in the town of Meissen, about 15 mi. (24 km.) away. There are important deposits of kaolin nearby that have been used since the 17th century for the manufacture of china. Meissen has a porcelain museum with a magnificent display of exquisite china.

Weimar. In the wooded hills some 55 mi. (89 km.) southwest of Leipzig is the peaceful town of Weimar. Germany's greatest literary figure, Johann Wolfgang von Goethe, lived and worked there for a good part of his life. He died in Weimar in 1832. In the Goethe Haus today, visitors can see the desk at which he wrote his masterpiece, *Faust*. Germans come here each year to pay tribute to and discuss the works of this great writer. It was in this town, after World War I, that the constitution for the short-lived Weimar Republic was written.

Frankfurt. On the Main River in central-west Germany is the old city of Frankfurt (the full name is Frankfurt am Main, to distinguish the city from Frankfurt an der Oder, near the German-Polish border). The meeting place of the electors of the Holy Roman emperors for centuries, Frankfurt today is a busy, modern city, with one of the largest airports in Europe. It has been an important banking center since the Middle Ages, and is also home to major machinery, leather, and chemical industries.

Its cathedral, begun in the 13th century, and the ancient Römer (the *Rathaus,* or city hall) are only two of the many restored buildings in Frankfurt's *Altstadt* ("old city"). The birthplace of Frankfurt's most famous son, Goethe, with the original furnishings, draws many visitors.

Rothenberg in southern Germany is known for its completely preserved medieval section.

Heidelberg. South of Frankfurt, nestled in the Neckar Valley, is the town of Heidelberg, with its 13th-century castle and its world-renowned university. The university, the oldest in Germany, was founded in 1386. Much has been written about student life in Heidelberg, with emphasis on the dueling. Members of the *Burschenschaften* (fraternities) proudly displayed facial scars as proof of valor. Dueling was forbidden by the Allies after World War II. But traditions die hard, and some dueling, though legally outlawed, may still be going on to this day.

Munich. Munich, the capital of the state of Bavaria, is the fastest-growing city in Germany. The charm and vigorous pace of this south German metropolis, the fine Ludwig-Maximilian University, and the high wages paid by its many factories have made it a magnet for thousands of newcomers every year.

This fascinating city has much to offer, and it no longer bears the scars of war. Almost every building was damaged by air raids in World

Heidelberg is noted as the site of Germany's oldest university.

War II. The Frauenkirche (Cathedral of Our Lady), whose copper-domed spires are the city's landmark, has been restored. The Alte Pinakothek, one of Europe's great museums, is in perfect condition. The National Theater and the charming Cuvilliés Theater have also been rebuilt.

Munich's outdoor pleasures include the Botanical and Zoological Gardens and the many fine walks in the Englischer Garten.

The joyous side of Munich's life starts with the pre-Lenten carnival, the Fasching, with parades, floats, and masked balls. In March and May, there are beer festivals, with extra-strong beer on tap. For hundreds of years, Munich has maintained a reputation for its fine beers. The many *Bierstuben, Biergarten, Bierhallen,* and *Bierkellern* (beer rooms, beer gardens, beer halls, and beer cellars) serve every variety.

But the greatest festivities take place during the Oktoberfest, a 16-day holiday that begins at the end of September. Huge tents, amusement parks, yodelers, bands, folk dancers, mountains of food, and rivers of beer are all features of this Bavarian festival.

Nuremberg. About 95 mi. (153 km.) north of Munich is the city of Nuremberg, home of the 16th-century artist Albrecht Dürer. Much of the medieval part of this town has been restored, including the Dürer Haus, the 14th-century Schöner Brunnen ("beautiful fountain"), and the lovely Gothic Frauenkirche (Church of Our Lady). Nuremberg has long been the center of the German toy industry. Each December the Christkindlmarkt (Christmas fair), featuring handmade tree ornaments and glittering Nuremberg tree-angels with gold-foil wings, is held there, as it has been for many years.

But Nuremberg's past has its dark side, too, particularly in the era preceding and during World War II. The city was the scene of the massive torchlight parades of the Nazi Party. The infamous Nuremberg Laws of 1935 deprived the Jews of their civil rights. And at the conclusion of the Nazi era, the war-crimes trials took place there.

HISTORY

It was only in 1871 that the first political unification of Germany was completed and a centralized government was formed. In this respect, Germany is one of the newer nations of Europe.

Although there was no Germany until the 19th century, the history of the German people goes far back in time. Germans were first mentioned in recorded history by the Romans, when they extended their conquests northward from Italy in the 1st century B.C.

In A.D. 9, Germanic tribes were victorious against the Roman legions in a battle in the Teutoburg Forest beyond the Rhine River. From then on, the Romans were content to remain behind their protective ramparts on the lower Rhine and upper Danube rivers. They founded cities and brought Roman civilization to the nearby tribes. Vestiges of their presence can still be seen in towns along the Rhine.

In the 4th century A.D., barbarian tribes from the north and the east began to attack the Romans. The Roman Empire started to collapse, and Germanic tribes from beyond the Rhine-Danube border poured into Western Europe. Some became Christians as they mingled with the Romans and adopted Roman customs. Smaller groups merged, and gradually some tribes, such as the Alemanni, the Saxons, and the Franks, became more powerful than others.

The Holy Roman Empire (First Reich)

The Frankish tribes carved out a kingdom in Gaul (present-day France) and on both sides of the Rhine. The greatest of the Frankish kings was Charlemagne, whom both the Germans and the French claim as their own. As he pushed eastward from the Rhine to the Elbe, Charlemagne brought Christianity to the warlike Saxons. In Rome, in A.D. 800, he was crowned by Pope Leo III and proclaimed "Emperor of the Romans." From his capital at Aachen, Charlemagne ruled the territories known as the First Reich.

With the death of Charlemagne, the empire began to fall apart. In 843 the Treaty of Verdun divided the empire among Charlemagne's three grandsons. One grandson took the German lands to the east, one took the western part (later France), and another took the center (later the Low Countries and parts of France and Italy).

Within the east Frankish kingdom, five great tribal duchies developed—Franconia, Swabia, Bavaria, Saxony, and Lorraine. Each was a power within the kingdom, and the dukes ruled their lands almost as if they were kings. Even within the duchies, lesser nobles—counts, bishops, and margraves—often fought for independence from the dukes who reigned over them.

In the 10th century, Otto, the duke of Saxony, grew strong enough to command unity. Because he repulsed the Hungarian invaders in A.D. 955, he was hailed as the savior of Christendom. Otto, too, was crowned in Rome as ruler of a revived Holy Roman Empire that was to last until the early 19th century. Succeeding emperors had to struggle to hold the empire together, gradually losing much of their power at home. And the German nobles grew increasingly more unwilling to give up power to an emperor.

The boundaries of the empire grew too narrow to contain the German people. From the 10th century onward, there was a steady migration eastward in search of new land. By the 13th century, Germans were firmly established in lands to the east that would later form the nucleus of the kingdom of Prussia. At the same time, there was a growth of trade, shipping, and industry. Some cities became strong enough to be free from the rule of princes or dukes. Other free cities, such as Bremen and Lübeck, banded together to protect their trade and shipping. This association was called the Hanseatic League, and it became the most powerful force in the North and Baltic seas.

Martin Luther, above in a painting by Lucas Cranach the Elder, was the founder of Protestantism.

The great unifying force in the divided country was the Roman Catholic Church. But in 1517 Martin Luther, a Roman Catholic priest, became the leader of a movement that would further divide the land. Martin Luther believed that forgiveness was a free gift from God, and not something to be purchased from the Church in a document known as an indulgence. His 95 theses on the subject of indulgences began the Protestant movement in Germany. Bitter religious strife ensued between Catholics and Protestants. Most of the south Germans and their rulers continued to worship as Roman Catholics. In the north, many of the princes and their followers accepted Protestant teachings and were anxious to have a Protestant king. Religious dissension touched off the Thirty Years' War, which involved many other countries, but was fought mainly on German soil. The Peace of Westphalia, which ended the war in 1648, paved the way for religious toleration. But Germany was a wasteland; its commerce was in ruins. One tiny Bavarian town, Oberammergau, still commemorates its deliverance from a terrible plague in 1633. Every 10 years the inhabitants enact Christ's last days on earth. Visitors come from all over the world to see the Oberammergau Passion Play, performed to fulfill a pledge made during the Thirty Years' War.

At the end of the war, there were more than 300 separate units of government. The Germanys, as they were often called, were actually a collection of petty principalities under the Holy Roman emperor.

The Rise of Prussia

With the return of peace in the 17th century, the various rulers tried to restore some prosperity. The most successful was Frederick William I of Brandenburg, who took over the duchy of Prussia. He devoted his reign to the task of building military might in his small state. His son took the title of Frederick II, king of Prussia, in 1740 and became known as Frederick the Great. Under the rule of the Hohenzollern dynasty (Hohenzollern was the family name of the Prussian kings), Prussia turned into a European power of consequence. To extend his control, Frederick the Great seized the province of Silesia in 1741, and in 1772 he joined with Austria and Russia in the first partition of Poland.

The Hohenzollern princes were schooled in stern discipline. All-important virtues were absolute obedience, hard work, and frugality, among others. As Prussia struggled to achieve power and success, it also glorified patriotism and militarism. These Prussian traditions exerted a profound influence on later German history, when Prussia became the center of German nationalism.

At the beginning of the 19th century, Napoleon I of France annexed much of Germany. He swept away scores of ancient mini-states in a series of reorganizations and reforms. Napoleon refused to recognize the title of Holy Roman emperor, and thus crushed forever the remains of the medieval empire.

Prussia, too, had been defeated by Napoleon. In a few years, however, it was Prussia that rallied the German states to rise against the French. In a "war of liberation," German armies pushed Napoleon back across the Rhine in October 1813.

The Rise of Modern Germany

The peace settlement reached at the Congress of Vienna in 1815 made Prussia even stronger by giving it the Rhineland, with the rich coal deposits of the Ruhr. At the same time, the congress further consolidated the country.

Democratic stirrings in the following generation led to the revolutions of 1848. In sections of Germany, as well as the rest of Europe, a struggle for political, economic, and social changes took place. The strong spirit of German nationalism found expression in a constitution drawn up in Frankfurt. The constitution called for a federal state of Germany, with a constitutional monarchy headed by the king of Prussia. The king of Prussia rejected the constitution, and even among the reformers, there was disagreement. Many Germans left their homeland for the United States when all revolt was crushed.

German unity under Prussian leadership was achieved a generation later by Otto von Bismarck. Bismarck, known as the Iron Chancellor, was a brilliant statesman and an advocate of autocratic Prussian power. He was ready to wage war to achieve German unification. In quick succession, he guided Prussia to military victories over Denmark (1864) and Austria (1866). In 1867 he organized the North German Confederation, which united German states north of the Main River.

In 1870 Bismarck maneuvered a situation that resulted in the Franco-Prussian War. A victorious Prussia pressed harsh terms on France and took most of the provinces of Alsace and Lorraine as well as huge reparations. During this period the south German states joined Bismarck's confederation. In 1871, at the palace of the kings of France in Versailles, William I of Prussia was declared the emperor of a Germany united as the Second Reich. The military character of the assemblage was symbolic of the part the army would play in the German Empire.

The German Empire and World War I

A united nation had now been created in the heart of Europe. Berlin was the capital of the new Germany, as it had been for Prussia. The new state was a constitutional monarchy, but Chancellor Bismarck kept an iron grip on the country. From 1871 to 1918, the people were officially called "German subjects" rather than citizens.

This was a time of great prosperity for the new nation. Germany became a leading industrial power. Arts and sciences flourished. Theaters, opera houses, and concert halls sprang up throughout the country. Universities were built, and because of their excellence, they attracted scholars from all over the world. Germany, seeking "a place in the sun," built up a colonial empire in Africa and in the Pacific.

It was also the time when some Germans, seeing their country hemmed in at the center of Europe, spoke of a fear of encirclement by its enemies. The young Emperor William II, who had ascended the throne in 1888, wanted to run the empire in his own way, and in 1890 he dismissed Bismarck.

The brief period of peace and prosperity that Germany enjoyed beginning with unification was consumed in the fires of World War I. In 1914, after Archduke Francis Ferdinand, the heir to the Austrian throne, was assassinated by a Serbian student, Austria made impossible demands on the Serbian Government. Germany backed Austria in these demands. In World War I, Germany and Austria faced Britain, France, and Russia. By the time the United States entered the war in 1917, the conflict had taken a terrible toll on the battlefield and was beginning to cause much suffering on the home front in Germany. In 1918 the military leadership sued for peace. The kaiser (emperor) was forced to abdicate.

The Weimar Republic

In 1919 a democratic republic was proclaimed. Because the national assembly met in Weimar to write a constitution, the new government became known as the Weimar Republic. The new state started under difficult handicaps as it tried to meet the terms of a severe peace treaty.

At the same palace in Versailles where the German Empire had been declared in 1871, a German delegation received the terms of peace. The Treaty of Versailles of 1919 returned Alsace and Lorraine to France and stripped Germany of its colonies. New boundaries were drawn for Germany that took away border areas that had large non-German populations. Germany was not allowed to own or manufacture tanks or military planes. The armed forces were to be held down to 100,000 troops. A huge amount of money was to be paid in reparations.

The Germans found it difficult to accept these terms, and even more difficult to make a recovery. Inflation destroyed the buying power of Germany's currency, the mark. At one point in the early 1920s, an American dollar could buy billions of paper marks. Life savings were wiped out, and people had to carry their salaries home in suitcases, only to find that the money could scarcely buy a loaf of bread.

But many Germans refused to acknowledge that Germany had been defeated on the battlefield. The Weimar Republic became identified with the loss of the war, the humiliation of the Versailles Treaty, and the hunger and inflation of the postwar years. By the late 1920s, however, a stabilized currency had halted the devastating inflation.

A worldwide depression, triggered by the U.S. stock market crash of 1929, shook Germany just when some stability had been achieved. Millions of Germans lost their jobs. By the winter of 1932, more than 6 million people were unemployed. Breadlines formed in all of the cities.

The economic crisis opened the door for Adolf Hitler. He was the leader of the Nazionalsozialistische Deutsche Arbeiterpartei (National Socialist German Workers Party). The Nazis, as they were generally called, promised a rebirth of German greatness. Despite the violence of their tactics, their appeals to national pride attracted thousands of people to their ranks.

Hitler was a passionate and hypnotic speaker. His promises to restore prosperity and to regain Germany's lost territories won him many followers. His vicious attacks on the Jews gained support from those who were happy to find a scapegoat for the country's woes.

The Third Reich

In January 1933, although the National Socialists had not obtained a majority in free elections, aging President Paul von Hindenburg was persuaded to appoint Adolf Hitler as chancellor of Germany. Hitler was given dictatorial powers by an act of the Reichstag and became *führer* ("leader") of the Third Reich. Hitler established a totalitarian and utterly ruthless dictatorship. He outlawed all other political parties, as well as the trade unions, and turned the press and radio into instruments of Nazi propaganda. Opponents of the regime were imprisoned and often murdered. The 600,000 German Jews were deprived of citizenship by the Nuremberg Laws of 1935, and those who could not emigrate faced unbelievable horrors.

But many Germans were eager to identify with Hitler and Nazism because the man and his movement seemed to be restoring Germany to its prewar glory. Youth camps and public-works projects helped to relieve unemployment. Rearmament, too, provided new jobs, as Hitler openly disregarded the Versailles Treaty ban on German arms.

In March 1936, Hitler ordered his soldiers into the demilitarized Rhineland. At this point, he probably could have been stopped. But France and Britain, unable to agree on what to do, looked the other way. In October of the same year, Benito Mussolini, the Italian dictator, and Hitler formed an alliance, often called the Rome-Berlin Axis. Later Japan joined Germany in the Anti-Comintern Pact, supposedly aimed against the spread of Communism. Italy became the third member in 1937.

Encouraged by the ease with which he had taken the Rhineland in 1936, Hitler went on to annex Austria in March 1938. Half a year later, at a conference in Munich, Britain and France agreed to Hitler's "last demand"—the Sudetenland. This was an area of Czechoslovakia that had a large German-speaking population. The Munich Pact, which became a symbol of appeasement (a policy of trying to pacify an aggressor), lasted only six months. In March 1939, Hitler broke his pledge and seized all of Czechoslovakia. It was the last of his bloodless conquests.

HOLOCAUST

Troops liberating the Nazi concentration camps at the close of World War II were shocked by the condition of the inmates.

World War II, the cataclysmic event of the 20th century that cost 45 million people their lives, is remembered in different ways by the countries involved in the war. In the former Soviet Union, for example, the period is commemorated as the Great Patriotic War, in which the gallant Red Army crushed the Nazi enemy. In Western Europe, countless books and movies celebrate the heroic feats of Resistance fighters. In the United States, World War II stories revolve around D-Day, the Battle of the Bulge, and the struggle in the Pacific.

For the Jewish people around the world, World War II is remembered as the

In August 1939, the leaders of Nazi Germany and of the Soviet Union astounded the world by signing a nonaggression pact. Secure in the knowledge that they would not have to wage a war on two fronts, Nazi troops advanced into Poland on September 1. Britain and France, honoring treaty commitments to Poland, declared war on Germany, and World War II began. The following year, in a *Blitzkrieg* ("lightning war"), Germany overran Denmark, Norway, the Low Countries, and France. The German *Luftwaffe* (air force) bombed Britain mercilessly, but the Royal Air Force saved it from invasion.

When Hitler turned on his Russian ally and invaded the Soviet Union in June 1941, he was the master of most of Europe. He had gained control of the Balkans, but the battle for Yugoslavia and Greece had delayed his timetable for entering and conquering the Soviet Union. This had disastrous consequences because Hitler's armies would now be confronted, not only by the Soviet Army, but by the brutal winter in the U.S.S.R.

On December 7, 1941, Japan attacked Pearl Harbor. The United States entered the war against the Axis. America's productive capacity, the fortitude of the Russians, the vastness of the Soviet front, and the wrath of the peoples under the Nazi heel were to spell doom for Hitler. The tide turned when the Russians held firm at the Battle of Stalingrad in 1942. Thereafter the Russians kept smashing westward toward Germany.

While the Nazi armies were engaged in battle, other Nazis killed and tortured countless men, women, and children in special camps set up in Germany and in conquered territories, particularly in Poland. Although the Jews were by far the worst sufferers, millions of other victims were confined under atrocious conditions. Extermination centers, prisoner-of-war camps, and concentration camps held people of almost every European nationality, as well as many Germans who had protested against the

Holocaust. This Greek word, which until the 1950s was translated and used literally to mean "burnt sacrifice," now generally refers to the systematic massacre of about 6 million Jews during the Nazi period. This dark chapter of Germany's history is also described as *genocide,* a term adopted by the United Nations to describe policies that deliberately result in the extermination of a large national or ethnic or religious group.

The "Final Solution," a code name for the total annihilation of European Jewry, was formalized by Nazi leaders in a protocol signed in 1942. The persecution of Jews, however, began immediately after the accession of Hitler to power in 1933, and it gained in intensity in 1935, with the passage of the Nuremberg Laws depriving German Jews of many basic freedoms. The first concentration camps were set up before the beginning of World War II, and after the war started, many more camps were established in the conquered territories, especially in Poland.

Some of the camps later became extermination centers, in which inmates—mostly Jews—were killed in specially designed gas chambers. In Auschwitz, 1.5 million people perished. Thousands of other Jews died in pogroms; one of the worst atrocities was the slaughtering of almost 34,000 Ukrainian Jews at the Babi Yar ravine near Kiev.

In recent years, some publicists have argued that the figure of 6 million is exaggerated, but these numbers were first given by Nazi leaders themselves, at the Nuremberg Trials, and later were confirmed in hundreds of studies.

regime or were suspected of anti-Nazi feelings. The iron grip of the German security forces (known by the feared initials "SS") made any protest difficult and dangerous. Yet resistance—even at the penalty of death—became widespread, tied up large German forces, and ultimately sabotaged the Nazi war machine.

As the Allies opened new theaters of war and counterattacked on all fronts, Germany's military triumphs were slowed. Battles in North Africa and Italy, and then the brilliantly executed Allied D-Day invasion of Normandy on June 6, 1944, began to push back the German armies. The Red Army advanced westward from battlefields deep within the Soviet Union. Allied air raids reduced many German cities to rubble.

A group of German conspirators tried to assassinate Hitler on July 20, 1944. Hitler escaped and crushed the uprising in a wave of blood and terror that took thousands of lives. But the end was drawing near. By March 1945, Allied troops had crossed the Rhine and were marching into Germany. As the Russian troops entered Berlin from the east, Adolf Hitler committed suicide. On May 7, 1945, the German high command surrendered unconditionally. The Nazi era—the Third Reich—lasted only 12 years instead of the 1,000 that Hitler had predicted.

Oddly, two of Hitler's major objectives, German unity and the end of Communism, have only recently become reality, decades after his death. The irony, of course, is that neither of these developments bears any resemblance to his plans, and they actually refute everything for which he stood. The unification of Germany and the collapse of the Communist regimes in Europe and in the Soviet Union are both evidence of the economic and moral strength of the forces that defeated Hitler. Liberal democracy and freedom of expression are the goals of today's movements.

In one major respect, Hitler's legacy is the exact opposite of his ambitions. The *Holocaust* (see the sidebar beginning on page 272), as his campaign to exterminate the European Jews is now called, culminated not only in the creation of the first Jewish state in 2,000 years, but also in the growing awareness of the role that the Jewish people have played in European civilization.

Germany's Rebirth—The Years After World War II

Armies of the United States, Britain, France, and the Soviet Union occupied Germany during the final phase of the war. For purposes of the occupation, Germany was divided into four zones: American, British, French, and Soviet. In the same fashion, Berlin was divided into four sectors.

At the Potsdam Conference in the summer of 1945, the United States, Britain, and the Soviet Union discussed denazification, demilitarization, and the reeducation of Germany. No peace treaty was drafted, but territorial adjustments were made. Part of East Prussia was given to the Soviet Union. Poland received all of Germany east of the Oder and Neisse rivers. A forced removal of Germans from Poland, Czechoslovakia, and Hungary resulted in a movement of about 10 million people, most of whom went to the Western zones.

East Germany

When the Soviet Union took over its zone in Germany, it set up a Communist system. Walter Ulbricht, who had been a German Communist leader and parliament member before Hitler came to power, became the head of the government. It was clear in 1946 that the Social Democrats would attract a larger following than the Communists, and therefore the two parties were merged. The resulting Socialist Unity Party (SED) was the ruling party in East Germany until 1989.

In June 1948, the Soviets tried to force the hand of the Western Allies by imposing a travel ban through East Germany to West Berlin—the so-called Berlin Blockade—which in fact denied the city most of its necessities. For nearly a year, all supplies to West Berlin were brought in by a smoothly organized airlift. It was after the failure of the blockade and the establishment of the Federal Republic of Germany in May 1949 that the Soviet Union proclaimed the German Democratic Republic.

Mostly because of economic hardships, there was a revolt of construction workers, industrial workers, and other East Berliners in June 1953. Russian tanks put down the revolt, and, after this event, the government introduced a number of measures to improve economic conditions. Despite these improvements, however, many skilled workers and professionals continued leaving for the West. To stop the flow, East Germany in 1961 built a wall separating East and West Berlin.

After Erich Honecker replaced Walter Ulbricht as head of the party in 1971, East and West Germany entered a period of rapprochement. In 1972 they signed a treaty allowing closer ties, which reduced incidents of hostility. Still, East Germany remained a staunch ally of the Soviet Union until 1989. Because it was widely believed that East Germany would resist the liberalization processes taking place in neighboring countries, the speed and remarkable lack of violence with which the regime collapsed astonished nearly every international observer.

Turkish children playing in a Berlin neighborhood reflect Germany's new multiethnic society.

West Germany

The United States, Britain, and France combined their zones, and in 1949 the Federal Republic of Germany was formed as a self-governing state.

Under Konrad Adenauer, elected federal chancellor in 1949, the Federal Republic of Germany (or West Germany) joined a number of important international organizations. It made valuable contributions to the Council of Europe, the North Atlantic Treaty Organization (NATO), and the European Economic Community (EEC). Through the EEC, or Common Market, West Germany became part of an economic bloc with France, the Netherlands, Belgium, Luxembourg, Italy, and, later, Britain, Spain, and Portugal.

Willy Brandt, the Social Democratic Party leader, became the federal chancellor in 1969. He advocated the "Eastern policy," which aimed at improving relations with the Communist countries. A West German-U.S.S.R. nonaggression pact in 1970, in which the Oder-Neisse line as the border of East Germany and Poland was accepted, was the first success of this policy. In 1971 the United States, the Soviet Union, France, and Britain reached an accord that eased access to West Berlin, and Willy Brandt was awarded the Nobel Peace Prize. In the next year, a treaty normalizing relations between the two Germanys was signed, and in 1973 both countries joined the United Nations. Brandt's successor, the Social Democrat Helmut Schmidt, continued to develop economic and political ties with Eastern Europe and the Soviet Union.

The East German flag was furled for the last time in October 1990, when Germany reunified.

United Again

The closing page of the postwar chapter of German history began in May 1989, when Hungary dismantled the barbed wire on its border with Austria. During the summer, some East Germans vacationing in Hungary took advantage of this opening to cross into Austria and then West Germany. Hundreds grew into tens of thousands, and later Czechoslovakia became a second transit point for a rising flood of East German citizens eager to leave. Street protests and demonstrations in many East German cities added pressure until the Communist Party ousted Council Chairman Erich Honecker, who had led the country for 18 years. In November the entire cabinet resigned, to be followed by most of the Politburo. Honecker and other former Communist leaders were arrested on corruption charges, and the government was forced to agree to hold multiparty elections.

The first free elections in East Germany were held in March 1990, resulting in an overwhelming mandate for reunification with West Germany. A coalition government was formed with a free parliament, and negotiations on the mechanism of reunification began almost immediately. The talks were held in consultation with France, Britain, the United States, and the Soviet Union, since these four countries still technically exercised authority as the occupying powers of World War II.

By mid-1990 reunification had already become a fact in many administrative areas. In July 1990, the two Germanys adopted one currency—the West German *Deutsche mark*—giving the East Germans access to Western goods and markets. On October 3, 1990, the two Germanys merged into one state, and the first all-German elections since 1937 took place in early December.

The chief architect of German unification was Christian Democrat Helmut Kohl—the German chancellor from 1983 to 1998—who was the longest-ruling German leader since Bismarck. Kohl belonged to the group of important post–World War II European politicians. For him, the German unification was a part of his overall vision of a unified Europe, which he had embraced at a very early age. Even before he reached the age of 20, shortly after World War II, he became convinced that the only way to prevent another war was to unite the continent. And the first step toward that unity was improved relations between France and Germany, the traditional European enemies. Kohl's goal of a united, democratic, and peaceful Germany at the heart of a united, democratic, and peaceful Europe remains key to the continent's future. Nevertheless, the more immediate problem of high unemployment led to Kohl's defeat by Gerhard Schroeder of the left-leaning Social Democratic Party in elections held in September 1998—the first time in the postwar period that Germans voted an incumbent chancellor out of office.

THE GOVERNMENT

Shortly before the two Germanys were unified, East Germany reestablished five historic states, which replaced the 15 counties into which the country had been divided since 1952. The new states were Mecklenburg–West Pomerania, Brandenburg, Saxony-Anhalt, Saxony, and Thuringia. Following unification, these states then gained the same status as the 10 states that had constituted West Germany under the Basic Law of 1949, which functions as a constitution. These 10 *Länder* ("states") are Schleswig-Holstein, Bremen, Hamburg, Lower Saxony, North Rhine–Westphalia, Hessen, Rhineland-Palatinate, Saarland, Baden-Württemberg, and Bavaria. The Basic Law stipulated that any part of pre–World War II Germany could be admitted as a new state, providing the mechanism for reunification. Unified Berlin became the 16th German state.

The highest authority in the republic is the bicameral federal parliament. The larger, and more powerful, of the two houses, the *Bundestag* (Federal Diet) has 622 members popularly elected for four-year terms. The other chamber is the *Bundesrat* (Federal Council), whose members have been elected by the state governments.

The head of state is the federal president, elected for a five-year term by a special assembly made up of the *Bundestag* and an equal number of delegates chosen by the state legislatures. The president, however, has no actual power—presidential functions are purely formal and ceremonial. Real executive power is wielded by the chancellor, or head of government, who is chosen by a majority of the *Bundestag*. The *Bundestag* can at any time, by a simple majority, vote a chancellor out of office. Each state (*Land*) has its own legislature and government.

Political Parties. The two major political parties are the Christian Democratic Union (CDU) and the Social Democratic Party (SPD). The Bavarian Christian Social Union (CSU) has been allied with the CDU since the late 1940s. A small Free Democratic Party (FDP) has alternately allied itself with CDU/CSU and with SPD. The environmentalist Green Party, which in 1983 gained representation in the *Bundestag*, won nearly 7 percent of the vote in the 1998 elections. The former dominant party in East Germany renamed itself the Party of Democratic Socialism.

PAUL FREEDMAN, *The Journal of Commerce*

The 1990 German reunification drew jubilant crowds to the historic Reichstag building in Berlin.

Berlin

Many of the pivotal moments in 20th-century European history took place in Berlin, a city that epitomizes the recent and current fate of Germany. For Germans, Berlin will always have a special place in history —not only because it was the first capital of unified Germany in 1871 and a flourishing dynamic metropolis in the 1920s, but also because it was the site of the famous Berlin airlift of 1948–49 and of the infamous Wall, a tragic division between two worlds, where more than 200 young people lost their lives trying to flee to freedom. Since 1989, Berlin has also become the symbol of a reunified Germany, and in 1998, it resumed its role as the capital of the country.

Berlin covers an area of 342 sq. mi. (886 sq. km.) and has a population of about 3.5 million, making it the fourth-most-populous city in Europe (after Moscow, London, and St. Petersburg). The River Spree connects the city with the Elbe and thus with Hamburg, an outlet to the North Sea.

From Fishing Village to Imperial Capital

Seven hundred years ago, Berlin was a small fishing village on the Spree. An early member of the Hanseatic League, the city gradually expanded into a busy marketplace. In the 15th century, when the Hohenzollern rulers of Brandenburg made it their capital, Berlin developed various industries, including breweries, for which it later became known.

The Thirty Years' War in the 17th century ravaged Berlin and left it impoverished and depopulated. But Frederick William and his successors, Frederick I and Frederick II (the Great), revived the city and made it the capital of the Prussian kingdom. During this period the famous avenue of Unter den Linden was laid out, and the city was further graced with numerous new buildings. By 1871, when it became the capital of the newly united German Empire, Berlin had become the country's intellectual capital as well, with a population of 800,000.

Berlin Between the Wars

In the following decades, the city grew into an industrial and commercial center. Spared damage in World War I, Berlin in the 1920s became known as one of the most glittering and stimulating capitals of the world. Writers, artists, musicians, and filmmakers found the new air of freedom and spirit of "anything goes" in the city inspiring. Playwright Bertolt Brecht and composer Kurt Weill collaborated in the writing of *Die Dreigroschenoper (The Threepenny Opera)*. Concerts led by Bruno Walter and Wilhelm Furtwängler and performances at the Municipal Opera were part of the city's musical wealth.

Modern styles of architecture also found their most enthusiastic supporters in Berlin. George Grosz's satirical drawings of postwar Europe appeared. The Berlin atmosphere, or *Berliner Luft*, called "champagne air" because of its dry clarity, was heady with fresh talent.

The successful 1972 movie musical *Cabaret*, with Liza Minnelli and Joel Grey, vividly captured the spirit of Berlin in the early 1930s. It was still a vibrant, free city then, but the clouds of Nazism were already gathering ominous strength.

When Adolf Hitler came to power, all intellectual life in Berlin was crushed. Many of the most talented artists were forced to leave or left on their own because they refused to work under the constraints of the tyrannical new regime.

Divided City

During World War II, the city was subjected to intense bombing. By late April 1945, Soviet troops had surrounded Berlin, inflicting additional damage with heavy artillery fire.

Berlin was captured by Soviet forces on May 2, 1945, two days after Adolf Hitler killed himself. The end of the war found the former metropolis of 4 million in ruins. Trees in parks were cut down for firewood, and hungry people planted vegetables in the cleared ground. In July the United States, the Soviet Union, France, and Great Britain took over the administration of the city, each one responsible for a particular sector. In 1948 the Western powers united their sectors into a single administrative unit, although the three military sectors—American, British, and French—formally remained. A few months later, the Soviet Union declared that the four-power administration of the city had ceased to exist. The Soviet Union tried to force the western part of the city into a union with the eastern part by imposing a blockade that denied West Berlin heat, light, and food. But from June of 1948 to May of 1949, a magnificently timed and managed airlift by American, British, and French planes brought food, fuel, and other necessities to the beleaguered city. The people of West Berlin stood up to the pressure, preferring cold and hunger to surrender.

East Berliners, meanwhile, continued to flee to West Berlin. To stop the flow of refugees from East Germany through the intersections and subway tunnels of Berlin, the East German government built a heavily fortified wall across the city in August 1961.

West Berlin. Because of Cold War tensions within the postwar four-power administration, West Berlin was in the peculiar situation of being a city-state without a country. Postwar West Berliners elected nonvoting representatives to sit in the West German *Bundestag,* but they had their own House of Representatives with about 200 elected members. The executive body of West Berlin was its Senate.

Young people found it difficult to live in West Berlin during the years when it was surrounded by a wall and other barriers and was isolated within a sometimes-hostile Communist country. The federal government offered a wide variety of incentives such as cost-of-living bonuses and freedom from military service in order to attract settlers. Despite the appeal of the city itself, many people chose to live elsewhere. Those who remained developed a distinctive way of life.

During the Cold War, West Berlin retained much of its charm. Postwar rebuilding plans provided for many *Grünanlagen,* or "green spaces." In addition, some of the buildings erected then are still notable. For example, Philharmonic Hall, ultramodern in design and acoustics, and the Deutsches Opern Haus contribute to the enjoyment of music. The broad-roofed, glass-walled National Gallery, designed by the great contemporary architect Ludwig Mies van der Rohe, is as beautiful as the art collection it contains. The Hansa Viertel ("Hansa Quarter") is a unique residential district designed and built by architects of international fame. A reminder of the war is the jagged ruin of the Kaiser Wilhelm Memorial Church, which is silhouetted alongside the glass and concrete of the new church and bell tower.

The Kurfürstendamm, or Ku-damm, is now one of Berlin's busiest streets, housing showrooms, offices, elegant shops, cafés, theaters, and nightclubs. Many engineering, textile, and food-processing companies have also set up their headquarters in what used to be West Berlin.

The Free University was founded in 1948 to replace the old University of Berlin that lay in the Soviet sector. Started partly by scholars who fled to the West, today the university is supported by both the city and federal governments.

Abundant parklands within the city were especially dear to West Berliners during the isolation of the Cold War. A favorite excursion was to the chain of lakes in the Wannsee area to the southwest. A day at Wannsee could remind citizens that, in the words of an old song, *Berlin bleibt doch Berlin*—"Berlin is still Berlin."

East Berlin. Unlike the citizens of West Berlin, East Berliners had no doubt about their postwar affiliation. The city was made the capital of the German Democratic Republic and fully incorporated into it.

Until the removal of the Berlin Wall in 1989, any foreigner wishing to go from West Berlin to East Berlin would have to pass through an entry point in the Wall nicknamed Checkpoint Charlie. A few blocks away one could see the 18th-century triumphal gateway—the Brandenburg Gate—

For 28 years, the heavily fortified Berlin Wall stood as a grim symbol of the ongoing Cold War.

whose reopening to free traffic in 1989 was one of the most emotional events of the period.

In contrast to West Berlin, East Berlin was a city that lacked a soul, a drab place of new, uninteresting buildings, constructed in the heavy Stalinist style. At night, there were few of the bright neon lights and little of the excitement, energy, and bustle that characterized West Berlin. The historic Unter den Linden boulevard, a former hallmark of Berlin, lost most of its sparkle.

Yet the city remained a cultural center. Two state-subsidized opera houses, the Deutsche Staatsoper (German State Opera) and the Komische Oper (Comic Opera), put on performances of exceptional quality. East Berlin's most famous theater company was the Berliner Ensemble, founded by Bertolt Brecht after he returned to East Germany from the United States in 1948. The best-known East Berlin museums were the Pergamon, with its fine collection of Greek sculpture, and the Egyptian Museum, with the 3,000-year-old bust of Egypt's Queen Nefertiti.

The German Metropolis Once Again

Since 1989, Berlin has experienced an injection of energy and dynamic change. Western investment and technical advice, along with access to new markets and ideas, have been transforming the former East Berlin and making it a vibrant addition to its twin.

The overall rebuilding of the city is on an overwhelming scale. The historic Potsdamer Platz is being enlarged, and when its reconstruction is completed, it will be the largest square in all of Europe. Close by is a new government area, comparable in size to the Washington Mall. Berlin is also attracting artists and musicians from all over the world and is thus becoming one of the greatest and liveliest European cities.

PAUL FREEDMAN, *The Journal of Commerce*

RHINE
RIVER

The snowy peak of Six Madun soars 10,000 ft. (3,000 m.) into the sky over southern Switzerland. From Lake Toma, more than halfway up the mountain, and from Paradies Glacier, two streams flow east through rocky gorges and ice fields to the green valleys below. Near the town of Reichenau, they unite to form the Rhine—the great river that, in its 820-mi. (1,320-km.) journey from the Alps to the North Sea, links not only the six countries touched by its waters, but, because of its economic importance, every country in Europe.

THE JOURNEY BEGINS

Past Reichenau, the Rhine turns northeast to form the borders between Switzerland and Liechtenstein and Switzerland and Austria. At Bregenz, Austria, the river enters the Lake of Constance. Surrounded by picturesque towns and villages, this lovely lake draws vacationers from all over the world. It also acts as a natural control for the Rhine. Because the lake is so large and deep, it slows the river's tumbling, rushing flow.

After it leaves the Lake of Constance, the Rhine soon gathers its strength again. Just below Schaffhausen, Switzerland, it plunges over a 65-ft. (20-m.) drop to form a spectacular waterfall that is sometimes called the European Niagara. The falls provide hydroelectricity for Swiss and German homes and industries nearby.

Basel, Switzerland, is the first major city on the Rhine. The river is responsible for Basel's industrial development and growth as a port, because the city is located where the Rhine first becomes navigable. From Basel, the river flows north to form the border between France and Germany. This section was once part of the boundary of the Roman Empire and has served as a battleground in every major European war.

Still flowing north, along a course that was artificially straightened and deepened in the 19th century, the river reaches Strasbourg, a crossroads of French commerce and industry. Canals reach out from its port to connect the Rhine with the larger French rivers. In a major industrial disaster in late 1986, some 30 tons of chemicals were washed into the river from a Basel-based company, killing about 500,000 fish and eels and so undoing a decade-old cleanup effort.

About 50 mi. (80 km.) downstream from Strasbourg, the Rhine enters Germany. It flows past large industrial cities such as Karlsruhe, Mannheim, and Ludwigshafen.

As the Rhine continues on its course, it flows past vineyards that date from Roman times. Today, the names of many riverside towns are known everywhere because of the excellent white wines they export.

THE LEGENDARY RIVER

Near Wiesbaden, on the east bank of the Rhine, there is a village called Winkel, which means "corner" in German. The river swings around the village to enter the most beautiful part of its course. Flowing west through a region called the Rheingau, the Rhine becomes the romantic river of legends that inspired hundreds of poets and composers. Golden vineyards cling to the steeply sloped riverbanks. Ruined castles, where once medieval robber barons exacted heavy tolls from those who used "their" river, perch on hilltops and on islands in midstream.

The river leaves the Rheingau at Rüdesheim and turns north again, toward Coblenz. Ships and barges take on special pilots to steer them through this dangerous part of the Rhine, with its whirlpools and narrows. The perils of this part of the river inspired the legend of the Lorelei. This lovely maiden sat atop a rock, singing so beautifully that she lured sailors to their doom. She was immortalized in a poem by the German poet Heinrich Heine. The golden treasure of the Nibelungs—a legendary family of Norse and German mythology and of Richard Wagner's Ring operas—is said to be buried at the foot of Lorelei's rock.

At Coblenz, where it meets its longest tributary, the Moselle River, the Rhine leaves the land of legends. Soon the river reaches Bonn, the birthplace of Ludwig van Beethoven, which also served as the capital of the Federal Republic of Germany. Farther downriver at Cologne, the towering twin spires of the city's great Gothic cathedral dominate the landscape.

Tourists take cruises on the Rhine between Mannheim and Bonn to view the medieval castles and quaint villages.

At Coblenz the Rhine shows its other face—an important highway of trade.

THE INDUSTRIAL RHINE ONCE AGAIN

After the broad, placid river passes Cologne, it enters the Ruhr region, with its coal mines and iron foundries, blast furnaces and steel mills. The heavy industries of the Ruhr depend on the Rhine as a highway for the delivery of raw materials and the exporting of finished products. The bustling cosmopolitan city of Düsseldorf and the great inland port of Duisburg (Western Europe's largest) are both symbols of the Ruhr's—and Germany's—economic recovery after World War II.

When the Rhine leaves the Ruhr, it begins to flow west, as if it already felt the pull of the sea. Almost everywhere on its course, the Rhine takes on the characteristics of the countries it flows through, and when it crosses the Netherlands border near Emmerich, it becomes a Dutch river. In this low, flat country—much of it below sea level or actually reclaimed from the sea—the Rhine branches out into a vast delta. The last arm of the river is a 16-mi. (26-km.) human-made passage called the Nieuwe Waterweg (New Waterway), which extends from Rotterdam to the North Sea. Through this canal, ships flying the flags of many nations bring their cargoes to Rotterdam's harbor. As ships and barges leave Rotterdam's docks to start the upstream journey, their bells are rung three times. Traditionally, this means "In God's name, a good voyage" on one of the world's most important commercial rivers—the Rhine.

Reviewed by INGEBORG GODENSCHWEGER, German Information Center, New York

Grindelwald, one of many Swiss "picture-book" towns.

SWITZERLAND

Since the 19th century, when tourism first became widespread, the Alps have been the most important part of the world's image of Switzerland. This picture of the country is usually completed by small wooden chalets clinging to sheer hillsides, meadows blanketed by brilliantly colorful wild flowers, and pastures dotted with contented cows and agile goats. Yodeling cowherds can still be encountered in the mountains, and the Swiss also continue to be famous as cheesemakers, chocolatemakers, and watchmakers.

To a great degree the Swiss themselves contributed to this image—most notably the author Johanna Spyri. Her novel *Heidi*, the tale of a little orphan who finds a happy life with her grandfather in the Swiss Alps, has been loved by children around the world since 1881. (Not long ago, Swissair, the national airline, used the words "Heidi wouldn't lie" in an advertising campaign!)

But Switzerland is more than mere quaintness surrounded by some of the highest and most beautiful peaks in Europe. It is one of the most advanced industrial nations in the world, and it also ranks among the world's oldest democracies.

THE LAND

This small, landlocked country is bounded on the west by France; on the north by Germany; on the east by Austria and tiny Liechtenstein; and on the south and southeast by Italy. Although Switzerland often seems to be all mountains, within its area of almost 16,000 square miles (41,000 square kilometers) it possesses a wide variety of geographical features. In the northwest the soft folds of the Jura Mountains, lined with lush green meadows, form part of the border with France. To the south and southeast the land soars upward to form Switzerland's landmark, the Alps—a majestic company of wild and lofty rocks, snowy peaks, deep gorges, and vast glaciers grouped around the Saint Gotthard and the Bernese Alps. The Swiss Alps reach their highest altitude at 15,203 feet (4,634 meters) in the Dufourspitze of the Monte Rosa group, near the border with Italy. Over 50 Swiss peaks rise higher than 12,000 feet (3,600 meters)—among them the piercing Matterhorn, the towering Finsteraar- horn, the treacherous Eiger, and the dazzling Jungfrau. (An article on the ALPS appears in this volume.)

Still farther south the Alps descend in steep shelves, finally sloping down to one of the most surprising facets of Switzerland—Ticino. Gone is the looming majesty of gleaming peaks. In Ticino, an almost Mediter- ranean breeze from Italy stirs the oleanders and the palms, and small stone houses painted in pastel tones offer a friendly welcome.

Between the Alps and the Jura lies the central plateau. About two thirds of the Swiss people make their homes in this peaceful region, with its gently rolling hills and pleasant valleys. It is a rich agricultural area, and it is also where most of Switzerland's cities are located.

Rivers and Lakes

The Alps form a vast watershed, and, not unjustly, Switzerland has been called Europe's mother of rivers. The meltwaters of mountain snows and glaciers drain into the sources of two of the continent's great rivers—the Rhine and the Rhone. Two other major rivers that start in the Alps are the Ticino, which joins the Po in Italy, and the Inn, which joins the Danube on the Austro-German border. After carving their way through the rocks of their birthplace, sometimes cascading downward as sparkling waterfalls, all of them flow peacefully toward the seacoasts of Europe, hundreds of miles away.

Another distinctive feature of the Swiss landscape is its approxi- mately 1,500 lakes, ranging from small, icy, crystal-clear ones high in the Alps to larger, more placid ones—Geneva, Lucerne, Zurich, Neuchâtel, Constance, Lugano, and Maggiore—at lower elevations, with cities and resorts on their shores.

Climate

Switzerland's climate is strongly influenced by its Alps. Though tem- peratures vary with altitude, in most parts of the country winters are cold and summers warm. In the higher mountains winter comes early, with the first snows often falling before the end of October. Most of the peaks above 9,000 feet (2,700 meters) are snow-covered all year round, and, while this contributes to much of the country's beauty, it also presents a grave danger—the avalanche. In the spring, alpine winds melt and loosen huge masses of snow. As the snow hurtles down the

SWITZERLAND

FACTS AND FIGURES

OFFICIAL NAME: Swiss Confederation.

NATIONALITY: Swiss.

CAPITAL: Bern.

LOCATION: Central Europe. **Boundaries**—Germany, Austria, Italy, France.

AREA: 15,942 sq. mi. (41,290 sq. km.).

PHYSICAL FEATURES: Highest point—Dufourspitze (15,204 ft.; 4,634 m.). **Lowest point**—shore of Lago Maggiore (636 ft.; 194 m.). **Chief rivers**—Rhine, Rhone, Ticino, Inn, Aar. **Major lakes**—Geneva, Zurich, Constance, Neuchâtel, Lucerne, Lugano, Maggiore.

POPULATION: 7,248,984 (1997; annual growth 0.57%).

MAJOR LANGUAGES: German, French, Italian, Romansch.

MAJOR RELIGIONS: Roman Catholicism, Protestantism.

GOVERNMENT: Federal republic. **Head of state and government**—president. **Legislature**—bicameral Federal Assembly.

CHIEF CITIES: Zurich, Basel, Geneva, Bern, Lausanne.

ECONOMY: Chief mineral—salt. **Chief agricultural products**—grains, fruits, vegetables, meat, eggs. **Industries and products**—machinery, chemicals, watches, textiles, precision instruments. **Chief exports**—machinery and equipment, clothing, precision instruments, metal products, textiles, foodstuffs. **Chief imports**—machinery and transportation equipment, agricultural products, chemicals, textiles, construction materials.

MONETARY UNIT: 1 Swiss franc = 100 centimes.

NATIONAL HOLIDAY: August 1 (Anniversary of the Founding of the Swiss Confederation).

mountainside it gains momentum and sometimes buries everything in its path—trees, animals, houses, and even whole villages.

But in some parts of Switzerland, the mountains also offer protection. The climate in the central plateau is moderate, without great extremes of temperature; and in Ticino, on the southern slopes of the Alps, summers are hot and winters mild.

ECONOMY

Legend has it that in the 17th century an Englishman traveling in Switzerland asked a blacksmith to repair his watch. The blacksmith studied the complicated mechanism, repaired it—and also made a copy, thus starting the Swiss watchmaking tradition. Fine watches soon became one of the country's best-known products. About 25 million watches and clocks are produced for export each year.

With almost no mineral resources of its own, except salt, Switzerland must import the raw materials for industry. But the Swiss have harnessed many of their rivers, using them as "white coal" to produce hydroelectric power for factories and mills. The Swiss metal and machine industry manufactures turbines, diesel engines, locomotives, precision tools, and scientific instruments, and accounts for almost half of total exports.

Switzerland's second-most-important industry is centered in Basel, where some of the world's largest chemical and drug companies have their headquarters. Besides medicines and vitamins, this industry produces plastics, inks, and dyes. While many of these are exported, the dyes are also used in turning out high-quality Swiss textiles. The old Swiss tradition of fine craftsmanship continues, too, in book production and printing.

Switzerland's banking system is the third most important in the world. The secrecy of individual bank accounts attracted rich depositors, but because this anonymity was sometimes abused, banking laws were amended in 1991 to eliminate most of the anonymous accounts as of September 1992.

Agriculture

Although Switzerland is one of the most highly industrialized nations in Europe, agriculture remains a vital part of its economy. Only about one-quarter of the country's area can be farmed, so Switzerland depends heavily on imported foods. On the most fertile land—most of it in the central plateau—wheat and other grains, potatoes, sugar beets, and a variety of vegetables are raised. In the central plateau, too, and in Ticino there are orchards where apples, pears, cherries, and apricots are grown. Known for their size and flavor, these fruits are used to make preserves and fiery brandies. Grapes were introduced by the Romans, and today several cantons produce fine wines.

But it is the pastures that are associated with the country's most important agricultural products. On the high—sometimes incredibly high—Alpine meadows, sheep, goats, and cows graze. Their rich milk is made into butter, cream, and cheese. Switzerland produces over 100,000 tons of cheese a year, mostly the Emmentaler generally thought of as Swiss cheese. But there are many others, including Gruyère, Sbrinz, Bagnes, and Appenzeller (named for the canton in which it is made). The cheeses are Swiss precision products, scrupulously tested for shape, color, flavor, butterfat and water content, and number and size of holes. The same care is used in the preparation of the chocolate and chocolate products that delight "sweet teeth" around the world.

Tourism

Beauty is the basic resource for another major Swiss industry—tourism. Switzerland has an incredible variety of attractions.

The internationally renowned resorts—such as Davos, Gstaad, Zermatt, Interlaken, and Saint Moritz (site of two Winter Olympics)—offer the sports lover the world's finest skiing, skating, and bobsledding. There are many smaller but equally popular spots, including Pontresina,

The resort town of Zermatt. In the background is the Matterhorn.

Crans, Arosa, and Chur. All of them are year-round resorts, and in summer there is mountain climbing for experienced or novice climbers and hikes into the foothills of the Alps. Hikers may be rewarded by a glimpse of the surefooted ibex (mountain goat) leaping from crag to crag, or they may come upon edelweiss or other alpine flowers. At countless lakes there is swimming, boating, fishing, and simply peaceful relaxation. Switzerland's huge number of hospitable resorts and inns (over 7,000) has led to its being called a nation of hotelkeepers.

An excellent railway system, good roads, bridges, cable cars, funiculars, and ski lifts serve the country. Long ago the mountains presented much more of an obstacle than they do today. Now, often in cooperation with neighboring countries, automobile and railroad tunnels have been built through even the highest passes, such as the Simplon, Saint Gotthard, and the Great Saint Bernard. The last is near the monastery that used to send out St. Bernard dogs (with kegs of brandy around their necks) to rescue lost travelers.

It is also possible to enter the country from France, Germany, Austria, and Italy on the passenger steamers that ply the lakes of Geneva, Constance, and Lugano.

THE PEOPLE

Unité par diversité ("unity through diversity") is the motto of the Swiss people. Switzerland is a country where loyalty to a hometown or canton is often as strong as—and more immediate than—national feeling. Swiss diversity is emphasized by its four languages. The largest number of people (about 65 percent, mostly in the northern and eastern cantons) speak German, and smaller groups speak French (mostly in the west) and Italian (in or near Ticino). A fourth national language is ancient Romansh, a Latin language. There are also many regional dialects and variations based on each of these.

Way of Life

Every child must attend school up to the age of 16, and there is no illiteracy. Over 100,000 young people, including foreign students, study at institutes of higher learning, which include seven universities.

Numerous Swiss have made their mark in literature, theater, music, arts, and science. Carl Spitteler and the German-born Hermann Hesse won Nobel prizes for literature; the best known contemporary author is probably the playwright Friedrich Dürrenmatt. Paul Klee was a famous painter and Le Corbusier a leading European architect. Naturalized citizen Albert Einstein developed his theory of relativity while working in Bern. Other important 20th-century personalities include psychiatrist Carl Jung, psychologist Jean Piaget, and theologian Karl Barth.

In many areas, skiing is a necessity rather than a sport. Other popular activities, according to the season, are skating, swimming, sailing, camping, and, of course, mountain climbing.

The Swiss is essentially a family man, whose home is his sanctuary. The care of the home, however, is mainly the woman's realm. Swiss homes are kept spotlessly clean, and at the entrance little squares of felt may be parked, on which family and visitors obediently skate across the immaculate mirrors of the floors.

It has been said that Switzerland has "food barriers" as clearly defined as its language lines. Much of German-speaking Switzerland has a marked preference for sausages and flour foods; in the French-speaking areas, steaks, *pommes frites,* and omelets are popular; and in Italian-speaking Ticino savory pasta dishes are served.

Nevertheless, there is a typical Swiss cuisine. It comes generally from areas where cheese was victorious over pork and beef, and its best-known dishes are *raclette* and Fondue. More than meals, they are ceremonies performed at the table.

For *raclette,* a 3-month-old loaf of Bagnes cheese is cut in half and brought close to an open fire to melt slowly. Then it is scraped onto a plate, spiced with pepper, and accompanied by pickled onions and sour gherkins for taste contrast. Small, boiled potatoes are usually served with *raclette,* and fresh plates of melted cheese replace empty ones.

Even more of a ritual surrounds Fondue, a bubbling mixture of grated Gruyère and Emmentaler cheeses, garlic, wine, and kirsch (clear, powerful cherry brandy). It is prepared in an earthenware pot over a small spirit stove on the table. Each guest, armed with a long fork, dips small chunks of bread into the fondue. He tries not to lose any bread in the pot, for if he does he must traditionally pay a forfeit—a bottle of wine, or a kiss for his hostess and the other women at the table.

Other Swiss specialities include delicious *rösti,* crusty cakes of crisply fried potatoes; and Grisons beef (or *Bündnerfleisch*), thin slices of meat dried in the open air, cooked by the sun.

Bears—the emblem of Bern, Switzerland's capital, and the source of its name.

CITIES

In many other countries, industrialization has meant a top-heavy growth of huge metropolises. Swiss cities, however, are relatively small. The five largest—Zurich, Basel, Geneva, Bern, and Lausanne—had fewer than one million inhabitants all together in 1992.

Bern

Bern, the federal capital of Switzerland, was founded in the 12th century on the Aar River, a tributary of the Rhine. In its course from south to north, the river ate a steep-sided U-shaped bed in the area's rocky soil, creating a small, high peninsula. It was only natural that a fortress was built in this dominating position, and equally natural that the fortress later grew into a thriving town.

Today Bern, although not large, is a busy, modern city, yet it still retains many reminders of the past. The sidewalks of its narrow streets, lined with heavy solid houses, are often covered by arcades. There are innumerable lovely fountains, graced by statues of historical or mythological figures. In the center of Bern stands its Gothic cathedral, which dates from the 15th century. Nearby is the city hall, which is also over 500 years old.

Bern's ancient university, founded in 1528, is one of the oldest in Switzerland, and there are also many professional schools and colleges. The Fine Arts Museum has a large collection of works by Swiss and foreign artists. It also houses the Klee Foundation, honoring the painter Paul Klee.

As the seat of government since 1848, Bern is the site of the Swiss Parliament, as well as of the Supreme Federal Tribunal and the National Library and State Archives.

The Limmat River flows through Zurich, the largest city and center of the banking industry in Switzerland.

But not all of Bern centers on Swiss official life. There are many beautiful parks and many spots offering dazzling views of the alpine peaks to the southwest. Bern's 16th-century Clock Tower puts on spectacular hourly performances with its mechanical clowns, puppets, roosters, and dancing bears. Bern's Bear Pit is another well-known attraction. Visitors spend hours watching and feeding the bears, whose favorite treat is bottled soda pop.

Zurich

Zurich is Switzerland's largest city. Located in the northern part of the country on Lake Zurich, by the 18th century Zurich was already an active international market, especially for silk. It has expanded this reputation by becoming the center of Swiss business and banking and a main attraction for tourists.

In addition to silk and other textiles, Zurich's industries include paper manufacturing, printing, and machine tool works. But no sooty factory chimneys soil the face of Zurich, which embraces the northern end of the Lake of Zurich. And business has not suffocated culture—the city's modern architecture has had full respect for the winding lanes, narrow houses, and ancient churches of the Old Town. The latest stock market quotations are posted side by side with announcements of Zurich's Theater Company or Art Museum.

The Federal Institute of Technology is located in Zurich, as well as one of the country's seven universities. Zurich's Pestalozzianum is named for Johann Heinrich Pestalozzi, the Swiss whose theories revolutionized the field of education in the 18th century.

Visitors can enjoy the elegant shops and cafés along the Bahnhofstrasse ("railroad station street"), Zurich's main street, and leisurely walks along the Limmat, watching the ducks and swans that paddle there. They can take a funicular up to the wooded Dolder Hills, where one of Europe's largest swimming pools provides artificial waves—the only waves in Switzerland. And, if they come in April, when winter releases its grip on the country, they can take part in Zurich's Sechseläuten ("six o'clock bells") festival. The cathedral bells signal the beginning of this ancient expression of joy. There is a colorful, costumed parade culminating in the burning of the Böog—a symbolic snowman stuffed with firecrackers.

Basel

Only 57 miles (92 kilometers) west of Zurich, on a sweeping bend of the Rhine, is Basel. Basel is Switzerland's second largest city. Its location on the river where three countries—Switzerland, Germany, and France—meet has long made Basel a crossroads of trade. The Rhine gives Switzerland its outlet to the sea, and on both banks of the river Basel has some of the most modern port facilities in the world. Many of the exports and imports so vital to the Swiss economy enter and leave the country at Basel's docks, including the products of the city's chemical, pharmaceutical, and dye works, textile mills, and breweries. Every spring Basel holds the Swiss Industries Fair—a trade show for manufactured goods from all over Europe.

Basel is also proud of being an intellectual town, with an excellent Art Museum and a famous university. In the 16th century, the Dutch philosopher Erasmus and the Flemish-Belgian anatomist Vesalius taught there. Some 200 years later, the university's professors included the Bernoullis, a Swiss family of scientists who made many important discoveries in mathematics and physics.

Today, though Basel is a thriving, modern city, in its beautiful patrician houses, fountains, and narrow streets it has also preserved the slow contemplative pace of the past.

Geneva

Geneva is located at the southern tip of Lake Geneva near the border with France. It is often considered Switzerland's most French city and its road signs, which all seem to point toward Paris, underline this idea. (Only on one road can one proceed into the rest of Switzerland, via Lausanne.) Many of Geneva's streets have a Parisian flavor, with hundreds of jewelry shops and stores selling other luxury goods.

But although Geneva seems French, it is actually even more international in character. Since the 19th century, when a Swiss businessman, Jean Henri Dunant, helped to found the International Red Cross there, the city has been the home of countless international organizations. Overlooking the lake is the Palace of Nations, built in the 1930's to house the League of Nations. Today, the vast, beautiful building is the European headquarters of the United Nations. Geneva is also the seat of the International Labor Organization, the European Commission for Nuclear Research, and almost 200 more international organizations. In addition, the city hosts many congresses and conferences.

A Genevan landmark is the 426-foot (130 m.) Jet d'Eau—one of the tallest fountains in the world. Among the other attractions of the well-planned city are many parks, an opera house, dozens of art galleries, and several museums. Geneva is the home, too, of one of the world's leading symphonies, the Orchestre de la Suisse Romande. The annual Bol d'Or (Gold Cup) yacht race is a popular sailing competition.

Geneva is European headquarters of the United Nations and a center for international diplomacy. Switzerland, however, because of its strict neutrality, does not belong to the U.N.

The university, which dates its founding to 1559, includes the International Interpreters School and a school of education named for Jean Jacques Rousseau, the 18th-century philosopher whose ideas helped set the stage for the French Revolution. Rousseau was a Genevan, but artists and thinkers from other countries also found the city a magnet—among them the French philosopher Voltaire, the English historian Edward Gibbon, and the English poets Lord Byron and Percy Bysshe Shelley.

Atop the highest hill in Geneva's Old Town is its cathedral, and near the university stands the towering Reformation Monument. Both recall Geneva in the 16th century, when men like John Calvin, Guillaume Farel, John Knox, and Théodore de Bèze made the city a center of European Protestantism. Under Calvin's strict rule, daily life in Geneva was austere. He would hardly recognize—and perhaps not approve of—the busy, cosmopolitan city it has become today.

Lausanne

Some 40 miles (64 km.) east of Geneva, also on the shores of the lake, is Lausanne. Its university and innumerable private schools and colleges have given Lausanne its reputation as an educator of Swiss and foreign youth. The presence of these students accounts for a gaiety and lightheartedness unknown to other Swiss towns. Lausanne's setting, too, endows it with a special, happy charm. Built on steep hills clustered high above the lake, it is a multilevel city. Among the hills, crowned by the cathedral, is La Cité, the center of old Lausanne; and bustling Place St. François, heart of the city's business district. Nearby, from the 2,100-foot (640-meter) Signal, there is a fine view of the city, the lake, and the mountains in the distance. Down below, among the flower-bordered promenades of Lausanne's Ouchy lakefront section, are luxury hotels, fine restaurants, and cafés. From there, visitors can take steamers to other lakeside towns.

A favorite excursion is to **Montreux,** long a popular resort. Near the town, on a rock in the lake, stands the ancient Castle of Chillon. In 1816 Lord Byron based his poem "The Prisoner of Chillon" on events that took place there during the Reformation. Another pleasant trip is to **Vevey,** a charming town between two mountains. Vevey is known for its lovely beaches, and for its wine festivals, held every 25 years. It is also famous as the place where milk chocolate was invented in 1878, and it is still the headquarters of Nestlé, one of the largest chocolate companies in the world.

Other Cities

Located almost in the center of the country, on the Vierwaldstätter-see (Lake of Lucerne, or Lake of the Four Forest Cantons) and the Reuss River, is **Lucerne.** It is a bustling modern town, yet there are still many signs of other times around every corner. The covered wooden bridge over the Reuss has painted panels depicting important events in the town's—and Switzerland's—history. Funiculars run up the city's hills, and about 15 miles (24 kilometers) away, Mount Pilatus boasts the steepest cog railway in the world. Lucerne has several excellent libraries and museums, and in August and September the city holds its music festival, featuring performances by leading orchestras and soloists from around the world.

Time dawdles in the Jura Mountains, some 30 miles (48 kilometers) west of Lucerne. At their feet lies the pearly mirror of the Lake of Neuchâtel, with the city of the same name on its western shore. **Neuchâtel** is a peaceful town, proud of its university and its active intellectual life. It is the site of the Swiss Laboratory for Watchmaking Research and of the Neuchâtel Observatory—both signs of the city's leadership in watchmaking. The people of Neuchâtel are renowned for their special esprit (spirit) and politeness.

Other major Swiss cities include Winterthur, near Zurich, with important metalworking industries; and Saint Gall, near the Lake of Constance in northeastern Switzerland, a textile center known especially for the fine lace produced there. The largest cities—Zurich, Basel, Geneva, Bern, and Lausanne—contain a third of the Swiss population.

HISTORY

The English humorist Sir Max Beerbohm wrote, "Switzerland has had but one hero, William Tell, and he is a myth." To this day, no one knows whether Switzerland's national hero really existed or not (though there are statues of him in almost every Swiss town). Nevertheless, he symbolizes the proud independence and love of liberty that characterize the Swiss people.

Roman and German Switzerland

The recorded history of Switzerland begins in the 1st century B.C., with Julius Caesar. On a plaque in Geneva today there is an excerpt from Book I of his *Commentaries.* He boasts of his victory over the Allobroges, who occupied the Geneva region; and over the Helvetii and Rhaeti, who lived in the area enclosed by the Rhine, the Alps, and the Jura.

Roman control of what is now Switzerland lasted some 300 years. Throughout most of this time, the Roman garrisons existed peacefully

One of Lucerne's main landmarks is the ancient wooden bridge on the Reuss.

side by side with the area's Celtic population. Fortifications were built in various places along the Rhine, which was considered the northern frontier. In the mid 3rd century, however, Alemanni, a German tribe, using military roads built by the Romans to defend their empire, overran the region. About two centuries later Burgundians from what is now France invaded from the west and took over the region of the Lake of Geneva. It is because of these two invasions that today's Swiss speak several languages.

In the early 6th century, the Franks struck from the east and overthrew the Alemanni, the Burgundians, and the Rhaeti—making Switzerland part of the Frankish kingdom. Under King Clovis, Christianity was introduced into the area. In 843, after some three centuries of unity under the Franks, the kingdom was divided among the grandsons of the great ruler Charlemagne.

Switzerland was reunited in 1032 under the Holy Roman Empire, which also included much of western and central Europe. However, unity within the empire offered no insurance against internal conflict, and Swiss peasants became involved in power struggles between landowners. By the end of the 13th century, the Austrian Habsburgs grew powerful in the area. One focus of trouble was central Switzerland, around the Lake of Lucerne.

Independent Switzerland

On August 1, 1291—partly according to history and partly to tradition—men from Uri, Schwyz, and Unterwalden met on the Rütli meadow above the Lake of Lucerne. They swore a solemn oath forming a perpetual alliance to support each other and to fight foreign invaders.

In this way they founded the Swiss Confederation, which has lasted until today.

William Tell. It was the circumstances of the Rütli pact that gave birth to the story of William Tell. According to the best-known version (made popular by the 18th-century German playwright Friedrich Schiller), Tell refused to bow in homage to a hat placed in the market square of the town of Altdorf. The hat belonged to Gessler, the Habsburg governor of Uri, Schwyz, and Unterwalden. Tell was brought before Gessler and condemned to shoot an apple off his son's head. An experienced marksman, he split the apple with the first of two arrows. With the second, he stated boldly, he would have shot Gessler if his son had been harmed. The furious governor ordered that Tell be cast into irons. However, Tell escaped shortly afterwards and ambushed and killed Gessler near Küssnacht. He then became one of the leaders of the fight for independence.

Gradually the confederation expanded. More and more towns and cantons (as the Swiss states are called) joined. But the alliance was threatened from the outside, especially by the Habsburgs, and war followed. Though they were often far outnumbered, in a series of battles—Morgarten, Näfels, Sempach, and Dornach—in the 14th and 15th centuries, the confederation defeated the Habsburgs. The Swiss dissolved their allegiance to the Holy Roman Empire. They also gained a reputation for military prowess, and their soldiers were soon in demand all over Europe. (The Swiss Guard that serves in the Vatican today dates from this period.)

But in 1515, in a battle against the French at Marignano (now Melegnano, Italy), the Swiss forces were crushed and thousands of lives were lost. The defeat helped lead the Swiss to adopt the policy of neutrality they still follow today.

The Reformation

The 16th century also taught Switzerland its religious lesson. In Zurich, Neuchâtel, and Geneva, men like Ulrich Zwingli, Guillaume Farel, and John Calvin preached for sweeping reforms of the Roman Catholic Church. As the Reformation spread, there was much conflict between Catholic and reformist cantons. After the battle of Kappel am Albis in 1531, where Zwingli was killed and the reformists defeated, came the wise—and typically Swiss—decision that each canton should choose the religion it pleased. (Legend has it that this kind of peaceful coexistence had already been put into practice on the battlefield. The two opposing armies, one short of bread, the other of milk, agreed to cook a milk soup together. The Catholics provided the milk while the Protestants contributed the bread, and the soup was cooked and eaten with unanimity from one pot.)

From 1648, when Switzerland's independence was confirmed, until the end of the 18th century, Switzerland enjoyed peace and prosperity. Yet however neutral they were, not even the Swiss could avoid Napoleon when he began to change the face of Europe. In 1798 he transformed the country into a centralized, French-style republic, which lasted about four years. In 1802, at bayonet point, he reasserted his control over Switzerland. At the Congress of Vienna (1815) after Napoleon's final defeat, Swiss neutrality was officially recognized.

Modern Switzerland

With the return of peace, the Swiss soon realized that they needed some central authority. In 1848, after a referendum, the 22 cantons that then comprised the confederation (a 23rd canton was added in 1978) accepted a new constitution transforming the confederation into a federal state modeled on the United States. Modern Switzerland, with its capital at Bern, was born. Its policy of neutrality succeeded. During the Franco-Prussian War, World War I, and World War II, Switzerland fortified its frontiers, aided refugees—and maintained neutrality.

Neutrality did not always mean freedom from involvement in wartime events, however. In the 1990s, the Swiss government was accused of selling arms to Nazi Germany during World War II, thus possibly prolonging the war. At the same time, family members of people killed during the Holocaust filed lawsuits against Swiss banks, charging that the banks were illegally keeping money, jewelry, and other assets deposited by Holocaust victims before and during the war. After much wrangling and litigation, and threatened by sanctions, several banks agreed in August 1998 to a $1.25 billion settlement. The Swiss government did not participate in the settlement.

As the union among European nations approached, Switzerland held fast to its independence. Voters turned down membership in the European Economic Area (EEA) free-trade zone in a referendum in 1992. However, in 1993, Switzerland was granted observer status in the new EEA. Public opposition to joining the European Union (EU) also remains quite strong. In 1995, for example, voters rejected a referendum on relaxing foreign-property-ownership regulations to conform with EU standards.

GOVERNMENT

Switzerland's seven-member Federal Council has executive power and also acts as the cabinet. Each minister serves as president for a one-year term. The two-chamber parliament—the Federal Assembly—includes the National Council, directly representing the people, and the Council of States, representing the cantons.

But the real foundation of Swiss democracy is the commune, or local government, in which every citizen takes an active interest. In 1971, a constitutional amendment was passed granting Swiss women the right to vote in federal elections, and in 1981, an amendment was passed providing equality under the law for women. In 1990, Swiss women finally won the right to vote in all cantons.

Two institutions—referendum and initiative—help the Swiss to influence their country's policies. A law adopted by the Federal Assembly goes into effect only if, during a 90-day period, no petition is made against it. But if at least 30,000 citizens petition for referendum, the people themselves decide whether to accept or reject the law. By initiative, on the other hand, the people—with at least 50,000 signatures—can propose a new law or request revision or rejection of an old one.

A referendum was held in 1989 on the question of whether to abolish Switzerland's armed forces, retaining only a militia for domestic emergencies. In a large turnout, voters soundly rejected the proposal. In 1994, voters defeated a referendum that would have allowed Switzerland to contribute up to 600 troops to United Nations peacekeeping forces.

DOROTHEA SPADA-BALLUFF, Editor in Chief, *Abitare* (International Edition)

Mountaineers have been challenged by the Alps for centuries.

ALPS

The majestic Alps are Europe's most important physical feature—a 680-mi.- (1,100-km.)-long chain of mountains with snowcapped peaks, narrow valleys, deep blue lakes, immense glaciers, cascading waterfalls, and icy streams. Nestled here and there in the Alps are romantic castles, lovely chalets, quaint old villages with flower-bedecked houses leaning over crooked streets, and some of the world's most popular resorts.

Covering an area of about 80,000 sq. mi. (210,000 sq. km.), the Alps extend in an arc from the Mediterranean coast between France and Italy, through Switzerland, Germany, and Austria, and then along the Adriatic coast of Slovenia, Croatia, and Yugoslavia to Albania. The high, sharp peaks of the Alps show that the mountains are young in geological time. Geologists believe that the Alps were still being formed 70 million years ago. The highest of all the Alps, and the tallest mountain in Western Europe, is Mont Blanc (15,781 ft.; 4,810 m.). Other skyscraping alpine peaks are the Dufourspitze in the Monte Rosa group, which reaches 15,203 ft. (4,634 m.), the Matterhorn (14,701 ft.; 4,481 m.), and the Jungfrau (13,653 ft.; 4,161 m.).

Although a great deal is known about the history of the Alps, no

The Matterhorn looms over a tiny alpine village.

one is quite sure how they got their name. Some authorities believe the source of the name is the Celtic *alp,* meaning "height." Others believe that the correct root is the Latin *albus,* meaning "white." Both words describe the snow-topped mountain chain that looks so formidable but has in fact been a home for men since prehistoric times and a route for travelers, traders, and armies for as long as human records have been kept.

Living in the Alps

It has never been easy to live in the Alps because the climate is not always gentle and there is a shortage of good farmland. Besides, there is often the threat of an avalanche hurtling down the slopes, sealing roads shut, and burying entire villages. We can guess that the people who chose to live in the mountains did so because the mountains provided a natural shelter from the wars and revolutions that regularly disturbed the life of men in the flat, less fortresslike parts of Europe. In time, the alpine people came to be known for their fierce love of liberty.

Many of the alpine people make their living as dairy farmers. During the short summer season, flocks are taken to the high pastures (also called alps) to fatten on the sweet grass. In winter, men and their cattle return to their homes and villages. It is the time when such old crafts as wood carving and weaving flourish.

Life is a little gentler on the southern slopes of the Alps, where the

Skiers cross a slope of Mont Blanc, Western Europe's highest peak.

climate is somewhat milder. The lower mountain slopes are covered with grapevines, and in the valleys corn is grown. There are even orange and lemon groves on the shores of Lake Garda in Italy.

On both sides of the Alps farming is now less important as a source of income than it used to be. The "white coal" of the rushing rivers is being harnessed to provide hydroelectricity for chemical manufacturing, textile production, and metal processing. However, the leading alpine industry today is tourism.

Traveling in the Alps

Until the middle of the 18th century the Alps did not attract tourists. The mountains were something to be crossed as easily as possible or to be looked at with awe from some safe, low level. In the old days the trip across the Alps was extremely difficult and uncomfortable. A horse-drawn carriage rumbling and bumping over the packed dirt road on the Mont Cenis pass, for example, had to be disassembled and carried over the steepest part of the route. The passengers were carried over that part of the road in chairs.

In spite of such hazards, the mountains eventually came to be thought of as a vital part of a young man's education. If the Grand Tour of Europe's leading cities taught him fine manners, then the mountains existed to inspire him with a taste for natural beauty. Later, poets and artists came to the Alps to capture in words and oils the beauty of alpenglow (the reddish light of sunrise and sunset on the mountains),

Farms nestle in the valleys near Switzerland's snowcapped Jungfrau.

the great glaciers like the 16-square-mile (41 sq. km.) Mer de Glace ("sea of ice") on the northern slope of Mont Blanc, and the distant, cloud-wrapped peaks.

Sometimes one of these visitors would express a wish to climb one of the distant peaks, but he was quickly discouraged by tales of fire-breathing dragons that lurked in the ice crevices, sudden death-dealing avalanches, and the treacherously changeable weather at the higher altitudes.

In 1760 a wealthy Genevan, Horace Bénédict de Saussure, tried to put an end to such talk by offering a reward to the first man to climb Mont Blanc. One year passed, then another and another. Men tried to scale the mountain and failed. It was not until 1786 that Michel Paccard and Jacques Balmat succeeded in making the climb. The news of their triumph electrified Europe. English children played a game called "The Ascent of Mont Blanc," which included all the possible pitfalls of the climb. Their fathers and uncles set off for the continent and a try at the Alps. One by one the mountains were climbed. On July 14, 1865,

This ice tunnel is inside the Rhone Glacier in south central Switzerland.

Gstaad, Switzerland, is one of the many ski resorts that abound in the Alps.

the last great challenge that remained—the stony spire of the Matterhorn—was conquered by Edward Whymper and his team of climbers.

Mountaineers still find a challenge in the Alps. Athletes also find the mountains ideal for sports such as skiing, ice skating, and bobsledding. The Winter Olympics have been held in the Alps nine times since the games were begun at Chamonix, France, in 1924. In the summer the mountains are perfect for hiking or for swimming and waterskiing on one of the deep lakes like Constance, Lucerne, or Geneva.

It is becoming easier every year to travel through and across the Alps. There are cableways and cog railways up many of the peaks and superb highways over many passes. The Simplon Pass has the world's longest railroad tunnel—12.3 miles (19.8 kilometers) long. The tunnel cut through Mont Blanc and the Arlberg tunnel in Austria are among the world's longest automobile tunnels. Switzerland is also planning to build two more railway tunnels that will run through the base of the Alps. The tunnels will be used by both freight and high-speed passenger trains. Germany, Austria, and Italy are considering drilling a railway tunnel under the Brenner Pass, and in France, there are plans for a tunnel through the Mont Cenis massif.

Although engineers constantly find new ways to make it easier to travel through and across the Alps, the beauty of the mountains remains unchanged. The mountain air is clear and exhilarating; the scenery is always superb and always peaceful.

Reviewed by SWISS ALPINE CLUB

The Lake of Lucerne, at the foot of Mount Pilatus, is one of the loveliest alpine lakes.

Prince's castle in Vaduz, Liechtenstein's capital.

LIECHTENSTEIN

Tucked into the valley of the Rhine, between Switzerland on the west and Austria on the east, is the tiny principality of Liechtenstein. With its snowy peaks, its meadows covered with wildflowers in summer, its rushing streams, and its crystal-clear lakes, Liechtenstein might almost be a miniature Switzerland. And yet this tiny country has its own history and its own character and customs.

THE LAND

The agricultural and industrial part of Liechtenstein lies to the west in the fertile Rhine Valley, where the river forms a natural boundary with Switzerland. Most of Liechtenstein's towns, including Vaduz, the capital and seat of government, also lie in this area. To the north are Schaan, a resort that is Liechtenstein's only stop on an international railroad line; Bendern; and Schellenberg. To the south are Triesen and Balzers, whose Gutenberg Castle has been overlooking the Rhine since the Middle Ages. All these villages seem like stage sets for operettas. Their small houses have flower-covered wooden balconies, and there are neatly kept orchards and gardens and picturesque inns that are often hundreds of years old.

The eastern part of Liechtenstein, which borders on Austria, is an area of mountain scenery and green pastures dotted with wooden chalets and small white chapels. There are also shady forests that abound with game. This part of the country is a botanist's paradise, too. In springtime the deep-blue shimmer of gentians—Liechtenstein's national flower—spreads over the higher slopes, and in summer, alpine roses paint the mountainsides a glowing red. Many kinds of wild orchids can be found in Liechtenstein. The landscape has inspired many of Liechtenstein's ancient legends, such as the story of the *Wildmannli* ("little wild men"), the shy dwarfs who leave their mountain caves at night to do chores for the sleeping villagers. There is also the tale of three heartless sisters transformed by an angry god into three craggy mountains. Located in the extreme southeast, near Switzerland and Austria, the "Three Sisters" include the Naafkopf, one of Liechtenstein's highest peaks.

HISTORY

Liechtenstein's true history also reads like a collection of legends. In 15 B.C. the area called Rhaetia, which included parts of present-day Switzerland and Germany as well as Liechtenstein, became part of the Roman Empire. In succeeding centuries the Rhaeti had to defend themselves against Germanic invaders and Huns. In A.D. 536, Rhaetia fell to the Franks, eventually becoming part of Charlemagne's kingdom and the Holy Roman Empire. In 1699 Johann Adam von Liechtenstein, an Austrian prince, bought the Barony of Schellenberg in the Rhine Valley and, in 1712, the county of Vaduz. In 1719 the area was consolidated by Holy Roman Emperor Charles VI, who declared it the Principality of Liechtenstein. It remained part of the Holy Roman Empire until 1806.

From 1806 to 1815 Liechtenstein was a member of the Confederation of the Rhine set up by Napoleon I. After Napoleon's final defeat in 1815, the principality became a free and independent state, which has never been conquered since. According to Liechtenstein tradition, there was an attempted invasion in 1939, when Germany sent a well-armed battalion to Liechtenstein. The invaders were met by Liechtenstein's 10-man police force and 9 Boy Scouts, mustered up at the last minute by a Vaduz priest. At this sight, and probably because they considered the country too insignificant, the Germans abandoned the idea of the invasion.

Liechtenstein is still ruled by the hereditary princes of the House of Liechtenstein. Prince Franz Joseph II died in 1989 after reigning for 51 years. His son, Prince Hans Adam, who took over executive authority in 1984, assumed his father's title.

THE PEOPLE

Liechtenstein has a population of about 30,000. They are hard-working and outgoing, with a welcome for friends and strangers alike. Until about 1945 most Liechtensteiners earned their livings as farmers. Though today Liechtenstein's major source of income is industry, some 8 percent of the people still follow the traditional way of life. They raise corn, wheat, and potatoes, and they tend their herds of Brown Swiss dairy cows, whose bells echo across the valleys as they graze the mountain pastures. On the lower slopes of the Rhine Valley, Liechtenstein's carefully tended vineyards have been producing excellent wine

FACTS AND FIGURES

OFFICIAL NAME: Principality of Liechtenstein.

NATIONALITY: Liechtensteiner(s).

CAPITAL: Vaduz.

LOCATION: Central Europe, Alps. **Boundaries**—Austria, Switzerland.

AREA: 62 sq. mi. (160 sq. km.).

PHYSICAL FEATURES: Highest point—Grauspitz (about 8,530 ft.; 2,600 m.). **Lowest point**—about 1,410 ft. (430 m.), in Rhine Valley. **Chief rivers**—Rhine, Samina.

POPULATION: 31,461 (1997; annual growth 1.09%).

MAJOR LANGUAGE: German.

MAJOR RELIGIONS: Roman Catholicism, Protestantism.

GOVERNMENT: Hereditary constitutional monarchy. **Head of state**—prince. **Head of government**—prime minister. **Legislature**—unicameral Landtag.

CHIEF CITIES: Vaduz, Schaan, Balzers, Triesen.

ECONOMY: Chief agricultural products—corn, potatoes, vegetables, wheat, grapes, livestock. **Industries and products**—electronics, metal manufacturing, textiles, ceramics, pharmaceuticals, food products, precision instruments, tourism. **Chief exports**—small specialty machinery, dental products, stamps, hardware, pottery. **Chief imports**—machinery, foodstuffs, metal goods, textiles, motor vehicles.

MONETARY UNIT: 1 Swiss franc = 100 centimes.

NATIONAL HOLIDAY: August 15 (Assumption Day).

grapes since Roman times. For the farmer or the factory worker in Liechtenstein, good conversation over a glass of Vaduzer (a rosé wine) is still a favorite pastime.

In the 1950s, hydroelectric plants were built in the Samina and Lavena valleys, harnessing the rivers' power for homes and industry. Today Liechtenstein's factories produce chemicals, machine parts, optical instruments, and computer components, as well as the more traditional textiles, sausage skins, and dentures. Liechtenstein's most famous product, however, is its stamps, which have been an important source of income since 1912. Collectors all over the world prize Liechtenstein's stamps for their vivid colors and beautiful designs. Tourism is increasing in importance, and every year more and more people from all over the world come to Liechtenstein to enjoy the beauty of its landscape and the warmth of its hospitality.

Vaduz, Liechtenstein's tiny, bustling capital, lies in a valley surrounded by towering mountains. The city was founded in the Middle Ages. It is especially noteworthy for the great art collection, owned by the royal family, which can be seen by natives and tourists alike.

GOVERNMENT

The Principality of Liechtenstein is a constitutional monarchy, whose government is based on the Constitution of 1921. The legislative body is the 25-seat Landtag, which is elected for four years. The head of government is the prime minister, who leads the five-member cabinet and is appointed by the reigning prince from among the members of the majority party in the Landtag. All legislation must be approved by the prince. In 1984, women were finally given the right to vote. Liechtenstein became a full member of the United Nations in September 1990.

A country church spire soars in an Austrian Alpine valley.

AUSTRIA

Where the Danube River leaves the hills and turns south into the Great Hungarian Plain, north meets south and east meets west in Europe. As a result, Austria's great role in history has been as a frontier post—the protector and defender of Western civilization against the invading tribes that time and again threatened to overrun the whole of Europe.

The Romans used the Danube as their line of defense against the wild tribes of the north. In the 8th century, Charlemagne, emperor of the Franks, a Germanic tribe, designated the region we now call Austria as the Ostmark—the "east march," or boundary. He made it his bulwark against threatened invasions by the Huns and Vandals from the east. In the 10th century, a German emperor made the region into a duchy, whose purpose was to protect his empire from invasion by the Magyars moving in from the southeast. This small frontier duchy was named Ostarichi—"east kingdom"—and it is from this word that Austria's modern German name, Österreich, comes.

Until Yugoslavia dissolved in a bloody civil war in the early 1990s, neutral Austria had served as a buffer land. Its borders touch on seven nations—Germany, Switzerland, Italy, Liechtenstein, the Czech Republic, Slovakia, and Hungary—as well as Slovenia, of the former Yugoslavia.

Vienna's Volksgarten ("people's garden") and Hofburg (Imperial Palace).

The three eastern nations were part of the vast empire ruled by Austria's Habsburg emperors from 1278 to 1918. At its greatest extent the empire stretched from the borders of Poland in the northeast to the Adriatic Sea in the south. The empire included all of Czechoslovakia and Hungary, as well as large parts of present-day Italy, Yugoslavia, Rumania, and Poland. Then, at the end of World War I, the empire was erased from the map of Europe. The much smaller Austrian republic took its place. But, like the lilting waltz music for which Austria is famous, the melody of the old empire lingers on.

THE AUSTRIAN PEOPLE

There is, of course, far more to the legacy of Austria's past than its glittering mementos of the emperors, or even the splendor of the art they inspired and supported. The Austrian Empire united under one flag some 50,000,000 people, speaking over a dozen different languages. A glance through the current Vienna telephone book is like a tour of the old empire, for it is filled with German, Czech, Hungarian, Polish, Slovenian, and Croatian names. The empire, in spite of the shortcomings that finally overwhelmed it, was a step on the road toward a united Europe.

Language and Religion

No matter where they came from, the people who have made their home in Austria are united by their language and their religion.

German, the official language of Austria, is spoken by about 98 percent of the population. Slovenes, Croatians, and Hungarians make up the small linguistic minorities, but German is their second language. Like the language of Germany, Austrian German evolved from Old German to the High German—*Hoch Deutsch*—that is spoken today. But if you learned German in school, you might be a little surprised to hear Austrian German spoken, for it incorporates words from French, Italian, Latin, and English in a seemingly carefree fashion. The gentle, witty, and melodic dialect of Vienna, almost another language in itself, perfectly reflects the character of the inhabitants of this worldly, fun-loving city.

About 90 percent of the Austrian people are Roman Catholics—another legacy of the Roman Catholic House of Habsburg. The only sizable Protestant communities are in Burgenland and Vorarlberg—the easternmost and westernmost federal provinces of Austria—where the Catholic Counter-Reformation did not succeed in suppressing the Protestants. In fact, it was not until the late 18th century that Protestants were granted toleration in Austria. And until the late 1930s the Roman Catholic Church in Austria exerted an important influence on politics. Since World War II the church has not been involved in government, although some Catholic lay organizations still take an active interest in public affairs. The number of Jews in Austria dropped from about 185,000 before the war to a little more than 11,000 when the war ended.

Education

Ever since Empress Maria Theresa ruled Austria, in the 18th century, elementary education has been compulsory. All children must attend school until they are 15 years old. Students planning to attend a university go to a preparatory school called a Gymnasium. At the end of Gymnasium a student takes a final examination called a *Matura,* which he or she must pass in order to be admitted to one of Austria's four universities. The oldest of the Austrian universities, Vienna, was founded in 1365. The other universities are at Salzburg, Innsbruck, and Graz. Besides the usual university studies, a student may attend one of the special academies devoted to music, art, applied arts, or acting. There are also technical, commercial, and industrial schools.

Food

The Austrians, who have made a fine art of cooking, love good food. They have, in the course of their history, taken what they liked best from the vast variety that the cuisine of the empire offered and created a unique style of cooking from that great and colorful selection.

Austria and especially Vienna are names to reckon with in international gourmet circles. A number of Austrian recipes, such as Wiener schnitzel (breaded veal cutlet), have become world-famous. When you are offered the same dish in Italy as *cotoletto milanese,* you should remember that Milan was once part of the empire.

Cakes, creams, and pastries are produced in infinite, mouth-watering variety in Austria. The larger cities are dotted with *Konditoreien*—"pastry shops"—which can only be entered when one throws all thoughts of dieting to the wind. The many coffee shops also serve all sorts of delicious pastries, from the simple crescent-shaped vanilla cookie called *Kipferl* or briochelike *Golatschen* to elaborate cream-filled cakes.

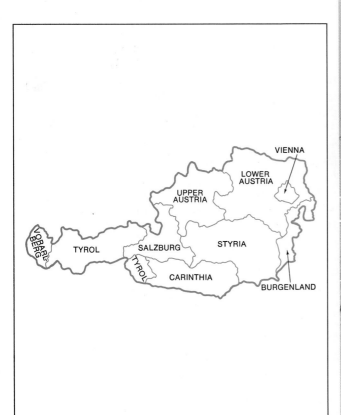

FACTS AND FIGURES

OFFICIAL NAME: Republic of Austria.

NATIONALITY: Austrian(s).

CAPITAL: Vienna.

LOCATION: Central Europe. **Boundaries**—Czech Republic, Slovakia, Hungary, Slovenia, Italy, Switzerland, Liechtenstein, Germany.

AREA: 32,375 sq. mi. (83,850 sq. km.).

PHYSICAL FEATURES: Highest point—Grossglockner (12,461 ft.; 3,798 m.). **Lowest point**—Neusiedler Lake (370 ft.; 113 m.). **Chief river**—Danube. **Major lake**—Neusiedler.

POPULATION: 8,054,078 (1997; annual growth 0.36%).

MAJOR LANGUAGE: German (official).

MAJOR RELIGIONS: Roman Catholicism, Protestantism.

GOVERNMENT: Federal republic. **Head of state**—president. **Head of government**—chancellor. **Legislature**—bicameral Federal Assembly.

CHIEF CITIES: Vienna, Graz, Linz, Salzburg, Innsbruck.

ECONOMY: Chief minerals—iron ore, petroleum, magnesite, coal. **Chief agricultural products**—grains, fruits, potatoes, sugar beets, cattle. **Industries and products**—food, iron and steel, machines, textiles, chemicals. **Chief exports**—iron and steel products, machinery and equipment, lumber, textiles. **Chief imports**—machinery and equipment, chemicals, textiles and clothing, petroleum.

MONETARY UNIT: 1 Austrian schilling = 100 groschen.

NATIONAL HOLIDAY: October 26 (National Day).

Perhaps the best-known of all Viennese cakes is Sacher torte. Sacher torte is named after a Viennese hotel and restaurant. Although it may seem to some to be no more than a delicious iced chocolate cake with a bit of apricot jam, the real recipe is a well-guarded secret, and lawsuits have been filed by the Sacher family for the misuse of the name and title.

Austrians often congregate in fashionable coffeehouses, where friends can socialize over a fresh cup of coffee and a favorite pastry. Vienna has been home to such cafés since coffee was introduced to Austria in the 17th century.

A highway across the Grossglockner, Austria's highest peak.

THE LAND

The land the tourist discovers is best described in one word—mountainous. Almost three fourths of Austria is covered by the Alps. It is only north and northeast of the Danube River that the land begins to roll more gently as it nears the Great Hungarian Plain, across which invaders from the east swarmed into Europe thousands of years ago. The Alps dominate all the rest of Austria, reaching their highest point in the Grossglockner ("great bell").

Climate. In the mountains the climate is marked by heavy snowfalls in winter and almost daily rain in summer. Northern Austria has a milder climate than the mountains, with rainy winters and cool, moist summers. Eastern Austria has a more typical continental climate, with hot, relatively dry summers and cold winters.

Austria's Nine Provinces

Austria's nine provinces—Vorarlberg, Tyrol, Salzburg, Upper Austria, Carinthia, Styria, Burgenland, Lower Austria, and the city of Vienna—are governed as a federal republic. Most governmental authority is in the hands of the federal government, which is parliamentary in form. At the head of the republic there is a president, but real power is represented by the office of the federal chancellor, who is appointed by the president and leads the government. However, welfare and local administration are directed by the provincial governments. Each of Austria's provinces is like a mini-nation, with its own unique attractions, customs, and traditions.

Vorarlberg, the westernmost of Austria's provinces, has an exquisite setting between the towering, snowcapped Silvretta Group of the Alps and the Lake of Constance. Bregenz, the provincial capital, rises from the edge of the lake and is known for its beautiful setting and its annual music festival. The best-known products of the province are embroidered goods.

Once part of the Roman province of Rhaetia, Vorarlberg was added to the Hapsburg crownlands in stages between the 14th and 16th centuries.

Tyrol, which is also in western Austria, has been called the Land in the Mountains because of its spectacular alpine setting. A mecca for tourists and sportsmen, the Tyrol is still crowded with visible reminders of times gone by. The capital city is Innsbruck ("bridge on the Inn"), which was settled in the 5th century B.C., grew during the Roman occupation, and reached its economic height as a trading center during the Middle Ages. In 1964 and 1976 Innsbruck was the site of the winter Olympics, and it is a popular year-round center for visitors from all over the world. In villages all over the Tyrol one can still find people proudly wearing their attractive national costumes, performing folk dances, or simply enjoying the music of a brass band or the tune of a yodeler. Of the province's many products salt, which is mined near Solbad Hall, is one of the most abundant.

Salzburg and its capital city, which is also called Salzburg ("salt city"), offer the typical variety of Austrian attractions—spectacular mountain scenery, the legacies of a long history, and every kind of cultural event. Located in west central Austria, the province was occupied by the Celts and then the Romans, and from the Middle Ages until the

A medieval fortress rises above the Salzach River at Salzburg.

Seefeld, near Innsbruck, is one of the many winter resorts in the Tyrol province.

18th century it was governed by archbishops. It became part of Austria only in the early 19th century. The city of Salzburg, which was the birthplace of Wolfgang Amadeus Mozart, has a Mozart Museum, a Mozarteum music academy, and the Salzburg Festival as memorials to its great 18th-century son. The province also boasts Europe's highest waterfall, near Krimml; Europe's largest ice grottoes; and spectacular salt mines.

Carinthia in southern Austria once included parts of Italy and the former Yugoslavia. With the signing of the World War I peace treaty in 1919, Carinthia's borders shrank, but the province still attracts visitors by the thousands to exquisite alpine lake resorts. The province's industries —metals, lumber, and farm products—play an important part in the Austrian economy. Here, as everywhere in Austria, the past lives on in the present. There is the Hochosterwitz—a fortress-castle with 14 towered gates—and the handsome Romanesque cathedral at Gurk. Carinthia also is the site of the excavated remains of the largest Celtic city that has been uncovered in Central Europe.

Styria, which is known as the most forested province in Austria, is noted for its location in the scenic, mineral-rich eastern Alps. Styria's Erzberg—"ore mountain"—contains the world's largest open-face iron mine. Here, as elsewhere in Austria, the landscape is dotted with hotels and inns, castles and spas. Graz, capital of Styria, is Austria's second largest city and a center of industry, transportation, and culture. Among its most notable landmarks are the Schlossberg, with its ancient clock tower, the Johanneum Museum, which has a great collection of medieval art, the opera house, the Gothic cathedral, and Eggenberg Castle, which houses the world's largest collection of medieval weapons and armor.

Upper Austria, in northern Austria, lies between the Bohemian Forest and the Dachstein peak at the point where the eastern Alps begin to slope gently downward into rolling hills. The region, which was made a duchy in the 12th century, is known for such resorts as Bad Ischl, which was once a favorite vacation spot for European royalty. Here Anton Bruckner and Franz Lehár composed some of their best-known works. The province's industries are clustered around the capital city of Linz, which is known to dessert-lovers as the birthplace of Linzer torte—a delicious lattice-topped cake that is made of nuts, spices, and fruit jam.

Burgenland forms a unique part of the Austrian landscape because the rolling foothills of the Alps flatten out into the plain that separates the Alps and eastern Europe. The large Neusiedler Lake, which lies partly in Austria and partly in Hungary, is in a wine-grape-growing region. Elsewhere in Burgenland nomadic tribes from the east left their mark, and ancient fortress-castles still stand as silent sentinels guarding the land against possible invaders. Today the gentle landscape is better-known for its contribution to Austrian agriculture. Thatch-roofed houses, high-booted, costumed Burgenlanders, gypsies, and storks nesting on chimney tops add their color and charm to the province that was the home of Joseph Haydn, the famous 18th-century composer.

Lower Austria, the largest of Austria's nine provinces, lies astride the Danube and surrounds Vienna. There are tiny typical riverside villages and great castles that once sheltered robber barons. The old monasteries of Klosterneuburg, Melk, Göttweig, and Maria Langegg are counted among the province's most fascinating attractions. Perhaps the most famous single landmark of the region is Dürnstein, in the beautiful Wachau region of the Danube. It was here in 1193 that Richard the Lion-Hearted was imprisoned on his return from the Third Crusade to the Holy Land. Blondel, Richard's troubadour and faithful servant, traveled up and down the land in search of his master, singing melancholy songs in the hope that he would be heard and answered. According to the old tale, Richard heard his minstrel from the prison window, and Blondel hastened to ransom his king, who was released and allowed to return to England.

VIENNA

Vienna, Austria's ninth province, is the nation's capital city and one of the great cities of Europe. As home to about a quarter of the entire Austrian population and as the center for a large part of Austria's industries, it is indisputably the heart of the nation. Located strategically at the edge of the foothills called the Vienna Woods and on the Danube, Vienna has played a major role in the country's history since it was first settled about 2,000 years ago by the Celts. When the Romans occupied what they called the *municipium* of Vindobona, they made it into the strongest military fortress on their eastern boundary. The 2nd century Roman Emperor and state philosopher Marcus Aurelius died in Vindobona.

From Roman times until quite recently the city grew up along the

These buildings were the first public housing in Europe.

banks of the Danube River. The river's course has been changed, and today it is the Danube Canal and not the Danube proper that runs through the city. The city, however, has changed very little since Emperor Franz Joseph I ordered the medieval walls removed in 1857. In place of the walls there runs a wide circular boulevard, which on one side is referred to simply as the Ringstrasse and on the other side, where it borders the Danube Canal, as the Kai. This makes Vienna an easy city to explore, for the fashionable Inner City is more or less identical with the old city. Along the tree-lined Ring are some of the handsomest buildings in Vienna—the Rathaus (City Hall), the Burgtheater, the university, and the city's two great museums—the museum of art and the museum of natural history. Nearby is the vast palace called the Hofburg, with its treasures. Farther along the Ring is the State Opera house.

In the very center of the Inner City stands the beautiful Gothic cathedral of Saint Stephen, whose slender spire dominates Vienna. The cathedral, like all the churches of Austria, has been added to in the course of the centuries. Like those of many other architectural monuments, many of its valuable ancient murals and structural elements have been replaced by whatever was modern at the time. Indeed, the elaborate 18th-century baroque style of architecture has almost everywhere obliterated the former facades and interiors, which gives the impression that the city was founded in the 18th century. Walking through the streets makes you realize, however, that for Vienna 18th-century baroque is not just a style of architecture. It is a style of life!

A visit to Vienna, the capital and chief city of both imperial and republican Austria, can be a nostalgic journey into the past. There is scarcely a corner of the ancient city that does not evoke a memory. A grapevine planted by Roman legionnaires is still growing in the heart of the city. Throughout Vienna there are handsome reminders of the centuries when the city was an imperial capital. The Habsburg winter palace, the Hofburg, which is now open to the public, contains the twin symbols of Austria's power—the imperial crown of Austria and the crown of the Holy Roman Empire. In the state dining room, the table is still lavishly set with the imperial gold service, just as if the emperor and his court were about to come in for dinner. The imperial jewels are on display in another part of the Hofburg. Elsewhere in the city—in museums, stately homes, and churches—the countless facets of the imperial life may be seen. They range from marble memorials to such curiosities as the car in which Archduke Franz Ferdinand was shot to death at Sarajevo in 1914, signaling the beginning of World War I.

Yet there has always been another Vienna too—a little removed from splendid victories and great festivities. It is the Vienna of the people —the merchants, the winegrowers, the clerks, and the apprentices. They have always lived in the shadow of great events. The wars, the plague, the sieges did not make them into a morose, melancholy lot, but rather the contrary. A happy-go-lucky people, full of humorous pranks, they always have made fun of their own misfortunes. Over a glass of wine they discuss politics to forget their everyday troubles. The untranslatable word *Gemütlichkeit* is uniquely fitted to the Austrians, who try to create an atmosphere of comfortable happiness in a place where living is never too fast, never too noisy, never too strenuous and, above all, never too serious.

The Arts

In this setting, which gave a sense of tranquillity even when swords were clanging all around, great music has been born. The irresistible charm of the city on the Danube, surrounded by wooded hills and vineyards, was a powerful inspiration to musicians from all over the world to settle there. First we must mention the greatest—Wolfgang Amadeus Mozart, Joseph Haydn, Ludwig van Beethoven, Franz Schubert, and Anton Bruckner. Then there are the lighthearted geniuses—the two Johann Strausses, Karl Michael Ziehrer, and Franz Lehár—and the moderns, of whom the best-known are Gustav Mahler and Anton von Webern. Grand opera and operetta provided music for everyone in a city where everyone was musical. And the memory of these great men survives in more than their music. Countless streets and lanes are named after them, as well as some airplanes of the Austrian Airlines. The Royal Academy of Music still attracts pupils from all over the world, and every young singer or musician knows that the concerts given in Vienna are a must in his career.

Once a year the great Vienna opera house opens its doors to society people from all over the world, when the famous opera ball takes place. It is the greatest fashion show of the year, and the bejewelled ladies and the gentlemen dressed in black and white, dancing the Grand Polonaise under the brilliant light of the chandeliers, bring back a memory of past glory.

The great city also attracted great minds—the annals of the Vienna medical school include the names of Albert Billroth, the great surgeon;

Ignaz Semmelweis, who discovered the cause of puerperal (childbirth) fever; and Sigmund Freud, the founder of psychoanalysis. The Royal Academy of Art drew people like Egon Schiele, Gustav Klimt, and Oskar Kokoschka; and the University of Vienna sent its professors to teach all over the world. And there were, too, the poets and writers. To them the Vienna Burgtheater was a great center of attraction. This theater is still among the best in the German-speaking countries. Franz Grillparzer, Gotthold Ephraim Lessing, Ferdinand Raimund, Johann Nestroy, and, later, Arnold Zweig are among the greatest names in German literature. Their works are part of the theater's repertoire.

Vienna has a number of fine theaters. The most famous is still the Burgtheater, which was founded during Maria Theresa's reign. It now stands opposite the City Hall on the Ring, and its beautifully elaborate loggia is sometimes opened on warm spring evenings to let theatergoers catch a breath of air. Unfortunately, the bombs of the last war destroyed most of the auditorium, but on October 16, 1955, the theater again opened in all its splendor to play its traditional repertoire of the great European classics.

However urgent it was after the war to rebuild Austria's industries, the Viennese knew that there were some things more worth rebuilding. These were the landmarks—Saint Stephen's Cathedral and the State Opera. The former—a part of the city for eight centuries—had been almost completely burned out in the last days of the war, and stood as a haunting empty shell reminding the people of past horrors. The latter, even more badly damaged, was a different symbol altogether—for it stood for Austria's name as a center of music and culture the whole world round. To rebuild it not only was the wish of every Austrian, but it was a signpost of the future—a solemn promise never to give up what generations of music lovers everywhere had admired and respected. And so, even before houses and industries were rebuilt, the Viennese rebuilt their cathedral and their opera house and made both even more beautiful than before.

ECONOMY

Austria cherishes its abundant natural resources with the same intelligent care that it has lavished on its cultural and historical landmarks. Unlike the stripped and barren mountain slopes of southern Europe, Austria's mountains are still well-forested. This is the result of centuries of careful management by mountain farmers, who have realized that the forests are more than a source of fuel and lumber. The forests also help to protect the high-perched farms from landslides, avalanches, and the slower damage of erosion.

Many swift-flowing, glacier-fed streams and rivers rise in the mountains, providing Austria with one of its most valuable resources—water for hydroelectricity, the "white coal" of Austria. Although Austria has not yet fully developed its hydroelectric resources, it is able to export electrical power to its neighbors, Germany and Italy. There are hydroelectric stations on the Inn, Enns, and Salzach rivers, all of which are tributaries of the Danube. The Danube, navigable for its entire length through Austria, is the country's most important river and vital link with the nations of eastern Europe.

In addition to its scenery, its power resources, and its forests, Austria

Farm workers bring in the hay harvest in the Salzach Valley.

has a wealth of minerals. It is one of the world's leading producers of high-grade graphite. The country is also well supplied with minerals used by modern industries. Coal is mined in Styria and Upper Austria. Oil production in fields near Vienna is sufficient for Austria's needs. Austria also produces considerable iron ore, with the most important mines located in the Erzberg region of Styria. Other important mineral resources are copper, lead, zinc, and antimony. Nuclear power was rejected in a 1978 referendum.

Less than one fifth of the land can be used for farming in this mountainous nation, but the Alpine slopes provide excellent pastureland. Most farms are small, and many are perched on steep hills and mountain slopes. Careful use of the land and hard work make Austria nearly self-sufficient in food production. Meat, milk, butter, and cheese are the most important food products.

Austria's industries manufacture a wide variety of products, including iron and steel products, chemicals, and consumer goods such as textiles. Ancient traditions of craftsmanship are still evident in such Austrian products as blown and cut glass, leather goods, pottery and ceramics, wrought iron, jewelry, lace, and petit point. Most of these goods are still made by men who have served three to four years as apprentices before being recognized as journeymen, and finally as master craftsmen.

Hallstatt in Upper Austria, the site of an Iron Age settlement.

HISTORY

The journey into Austria's past begins in the early Iron Age at Hallstatt in Upper Austria. Here careful excavation of ancient burial grounds has revealed the existence of a flourishing community that mined and traded salt. When the Celts moved into Austria about the 3rd century B.C., they took over the thriving salt trade in such towns as Hallstatt and Salzburg and extended their kingdom of Noricum until it included most of Upper Austria, Salzburg, West Styria, and Carinthia.

There is evidence that the Romans had penetrated the region we call Austria by about 100 B.C. By A.D. 10 they had established themselves as the sole rulers of the region they named Pannonia. The Romans were as interested in exploiting the trade of the area as they were in protecting their eastern frontier. The Danube River gave the Romans an east–west trade link. The most important north–south trade route was the so-called Amber Road, which extended from Jutland in Denmark in the north, across western Austria, south to Rome. Traders from the north carried whale tusks and amber (used for jewelry), which they traded for swords, pitchers, and, of course, salt.

For several hundred years the Romans were able to fight off the repeated attempts at invasions by barbarians from the north and east. During this period of relative peacefulness the Romans established the city of

Vindobona (Vienna), and brought their language and later the Christian religion to the region.

But from about A.D. 400 onward, the weakened Roman Empire could no longer successfully defend Pannonia. By the end of the 5th century the country lay open to attack by wave after wave of barbarian invaders—Huns, Slavs, Avars, and Magyars from the east; Teutons from the north; and Bajuvars from the west. It was not until the time of Charlemagne in the 8th century that the region knew stable government again. It lasted for only about a century.

In the year 976 Otto II, the Holy Roman Emperor, gave part of Austria to Leopold of Babenberg to rule as a duchy. The gift was perhaps a little less generous than it seems, for Otto II wanted to protect his eastern frontier from further invasions, and it became the Babenbergs' duty to keep the Magyars (Hungarians) at bay.

The Babenbergs set Austria on the road to steady growth in trade and prosperity. The eastern border of the duchy was never quiet, but it managed somehow to survive all attacks. After nearly 300 years of continuous rule, the last of the Babenbergs died in 1246 in a battle with the Magyars, their fiercest enemies. The Babenbergs had not only erected mighty fortresses to defend their duchy, but also built beautiful monasteries, such as the ones at Melk, Klosterneuburg, Heiligenkreuz, and Admont—splendid stone mementos of their deep religious faith. Christianity had come to the land in the 4th century when Emperor Constantine made it the state religion of Rome. Throughout the centuries that followed, the dukes, kings, and later the emperors of Austria took as their foremost duty the defense of Roman Catholicism against the heathens, the Muslims, and later the Protestant reformers.

Austria Under the Habsburgs

When the last duke of Babenberg died, Austria fell into the hands of King Ottokar II of Bohemia (now part of Czechoslovakia). The German Emperor, seeing the southeastern border of his territory threatened, quickly sent a relief army to Austria. The army, under the leadership of Rudolf of Habsburg, defeated Ottokar in 1278.

This event marked the beginning of Habsburg rule over Austria. It was to last for 640 years, until 1918. Under the Habsburgs, Austria became renowned as a center of music, art, and architecture. The Habsburgs developed another new and singular talent, which made their empire grow and grow until in the 16th century Emperor Charles V could say of his empire that the sun never set on it. This talent was based on a simple, strategic plan for marriages of the Habsburg children and grandchildren, which made duchies and kingdoms fall into Austria's lap like ripe apples.

The first Habsburg to put this strategy into practice was Frederick III, who ruled in the 15th century. He realized that this was a far better way to enlarge the empire than by bloody wars. The following verse should have been inscribed on his crest: *Bella gerant alii, Tu felix Austria nube* ("Let others wage war, You, happy Austria, marry"). Frederick's son Maximilian I added the Duchy of Burgundy (now part of France) and the Netherlands to the empire through his first marriage, to Maria of Burgundy. His grandson Philip made Spain and its colonies a Habsburg possession by marrying Juana of Castile and Aragon (Spain). Frederick

III's great-grandchildren married the heirs to the thrones of Bohemia and Hungary, unions that formed the core of the empire until 1918.

When Charles V came to the throne in the 16th century, Austria reached the height of its power. Charles inherited the Austrian lands and the right of succession to the thrones of Bohemia, Hungary, Burgundy, the Spanish Empire, the Netherlands, Sardinia, Sicily, and Naples. Charles V goes down in history as the great defender of Catholicism, and his strongest enemy, the one he never defeated, was Protestantism. Under Charles' direction, Martin Luther was excommunicated by the Diet of Worms in 1521.

The forces of Catholic Austria were pitted against the Protestants in the Thirty Years' War. During the long war Austria lost holdings in Germany and suffered a terrible loss of manpower. However, in 1620 at the battle of White Mountain, Austria re-asserted its control of Bohemia and Moravia (now part of Czechoslovakia). As its territory grew, the imperial bureaucracy became more strict. At one point the police even told each class of society what clothes to wear and what food to eat.

The Austrian Empire continued to be threatened from the outside. In 1683, 150 years after an unsuccessful attempt to take Vienna, the Turks were again at the city's gates. In a century of warfare the Turkish Army had overrun Asia Minor and the Balkan Peninsula, and the Turks were determined to take over the rest of Europe as well. A force of 300,000 Turks stood at the gates of Vienna to wipe Austria from the face of

Vienna's landmarks include the stately Burgtheater (foreground) and the Gothic-style St. Stephen's cathedral, whose majestic spire rises in the distance.

Schönbrunn, one of the magnificent Habsburg palaces, in Vienna.

the earth. Although the city seemed lost, it never gave up hope. For 2 months the Viennese starved and prayed. Deliverance came suddenly and unexpectedly when the armies of the Polish king, John III Sobieski, and Charles, Duke of Lorraine, swooped down from the wooded hills in a brilliantly timed surprise attack and destroyed the Turkish force. The leader of the Turks, Kara Mustafa, was beheaded by the sultan after what was left of the army fled wildly back across the Hungarian Plain.

All that the Turks left behind—the tents, the jewelry, and the arms— is preserved in Vienna's museums. The most coveted pieces of loot, however, were some sacks of coffee beans from which the Turks made a sweet black liquid that was an immediate success in Vienna. Soon coffee-houses sprang up all over the country. According to legend the delicious little cookies called vanilla *Kipferl* also date to the defeat of the Turks. Viennese housewives eager to celebrate their freedom from the Muslim threat shaped the dough like a crescent moon—the Turkish symbol.

When the Emperor Charles VI died in 1740, the male line of the Habsburgs came to an end, and with Maria Theresa, the first empress of Austria, another brilliant chapter of Austrian history began. Although most of her reign was a desperate fight to assert herself against such aggressive enemies as the Prussian emperor Frederick the Great, she managed not only to hold her own, but to make Austria, and above all Vienna, into the center of the European world. Indeed, she was a woman of extraordinary qualities, who somehow managed to look after the affairs of the state and to raise a large family with her husband, Franz Stefan of Lorraine. Her statue still stands majestically between Vienna's two great museums of art and natural history. The Empress, surrounded by her finest counselors, seems to look at the royal castle as if to say, "All this is mine." It was in Maria Theresa's time that the arts blossomed, when Mozart played to Her Imperial Majesty in Schönbrunn Palace, and the most significant baroque palaces and churches were built. Maria Theresa gave her imperial residence all the splendor of a great capital—a splendor that can still be felt today.

The Habsburg marriage policy, however, proved disastrous with Maria Theresa's daughter, Marie Antoinette, who married the French king Louis XVI and had to share with him the terrible death under the guillotine during the French Revolution. It was impossible in those days to liquidate any one ruling dynasty without in some way offending the House of Habsburg. And when Napoleon Bonaparte, a child of the French Revolution, tried to legalize his self-imposed imperial crown, he chose to marry the Habsburg princess Marie Louise. This, however, did not stop him from twice attacking and overrunning Austria. But at the end of this epoch, during which nearly the whole of Europe was laid waste, it was Austria that played the leading role in uniting Europe. In 1815, emperors, kings, princes, and dukes met at the Congress of Vienna to negotiate a peace. Their success can be measured by the fact that Europe's peace lasted for almost 100 years.

The statesmen of the 19th century were all agreed on one point: if Austria had not existed, one would have had to invent it. It was not like any other country. It did not consist of different nations, but of different peoples. It had a dozen different peoples—Austrians lived with Czechs and Slovaks, Poles with Italians, Croatians with Slovenes, Ukrainians with Bosnians and Germans—all united under one crown, the crown of the Habsburgs.

What is today an unfulfilled ambition, a unified European territory without customs or frontiers, was a reality in Hapsburg Austria. Thus, Austria was way ahead of its time. Yet it was, simultaneously, lagging far behind. In an empire of this size, appropriate reforms could perhaps have prevented the rise of a new and fearful age—the age of nationalism. Nationalism was the scourge of the 19th century, and Franz Joseph, the next-to-last Habsburg emperor, did not or would not understand that nationalism would finally destroy his empire. His reforms were too few and came too late. In 1867, for example, Hungary was granted almost equal status with Austria in the Austro-Hungarian Dual Monarchy. But this was only one small step when many great steps were needed.

The End of the Empire

When the heir to the Habsburg throne, Franz Ferdinand, was murdered in Sarajevo (Yugoslavia) in July 1914 by Gavrilo Princip, a Serbian nationalist, Franz Joseph saw only one way to save the honor of the Crown—war. When the Serbs refused to surrender the assassin, Austria's army marched toward Belgrade.

This not only was the death warrant of the monarchy, but also set off the chain reaction of war declarations that led to World War I. The whole of Europe took up arms, and even America came out of its isolation and joined England, France, and Russia to battle the Central Powers led by Austria and Germany. It was not until Germany and Austria were completely defeated in 1918 that an armistice was declared. The peace treaty left Austria with scarcely more than the little province that had long ago been given to the dukes of Babenberg. The crown lands were made into the independent republics of Czechoslovakia, Poland, Hungary, and Yugoslavia. Romania and Italy took shares of what was left of the empire. Of the approximately 50 million people who lived in the Austro-Hungarian Empire, only 6.5 million were left as Austrian citizens.

The last Habsburg, Charles, who was crowned in 1916 in Hungary, made a feeble attempt to draw Austria out of the war, only to find himself humiliated by Germany and misunderstood by the other allies. When Austria became a republic, he left the country.

The Austrian Republic

The Austrian Republic got off to a shaky start, since the nation's economy had suffered the double blow of war and the loss of imperial markets. Unemployment, hunger, and inflation plagued the small nation. By 1922, however, the country began to get back on its feet. A new constitution was passed, and a government took office that succeeded in stabilizing the economy and keeping peace within the country.

Unfortunately, just as Austria was regaining its stability in the late 1920s, the world experienced a severe economic depression. In Europe, this event was marked by a high rate of unemployment and the rapid growth of the fascist movements, especially in Italy and Germany. Little Austria was courted by Mussolini's Italian Fascist Government and infiltrated by Nazis from Hitler's Germany. The Austrian Nazi Party, which had been formed secretly and supplied with arms by the German Nazi Party, grew rapidly. In 1938 Hitler's troops annexed Austria.

In 1945, at the end of World War II, Austria was occupied by American, British, Soviet, and French forces. However, the four big powers, divided as they were on many other issues, soon agreed that Austria should not come under the influence of any one of them. Instead, a status of neutrality was agreed to for Austria, which it maintains today.

In 1955 all foreign troops left Austria, and since then Austria has been trying to pick up the threads of its old mission: to separate the combatants and to act as a mediator between north and south and east and west. In the 1970s it became the transfer point for Soviet Jews emigrating to Israel, as well as a haven for refugees from Communist states. In the 1980s thousands fleeing Poland found asylum in Austria.

The bitter legacy of the Nazi era was raised when former United Nations Secretary-General Kurt Waldheim was elected president in 1986. During his campaign, it was revealed that in World War II he was a staff officer with an army group that committed brutal reprisals against Yugoslav partisans and arranged mass deportations of Greek Jews to death camps. As a result, Austria was isolated diplomatically until 1992, when Waldheim was succeeded by Thomas Klestil. Klestil was reelected by a landslide in April 1998.

Government. Austria is a federal republic made up of nine provinces. The head of state is the president, who is elected for six years. The president appoints the chancellor, who serves as the head of government, usually from among the members of the majority party in the legislature. The legislature is composed of the Nationalrat (National Council), elected for four years directly by the people, and the Bundesrat (Federal Council), elected by the provincial legislatures.

HUGO PORTISCH, Chief Commentator, Austrian Television Corporation

DANUBE RIVER

DANUBE RIVER

Donau in Germany and Austria; *Dunaj* in Slovakia; *Duna* in Hungary; *Dunav* in Croatia, Yugoslavia, and Bulgaria; *Dunârea* in Romania; and *Dunai* in Russia and Ukraine—all are names for a river as varied and colorful as the countries on its banks—the Danube. Though it is often thought to be exclusively Austrian, or even Viennese, the Danube begins in Germany. It ends in the Black Sea, after wandering, winding, flowing, and sometimes hurtling 1,750 mi. (2,800 km.) through ten very different countries.

THE RIVER BEGINS

Near a castle in Donaueschingen, in Germany's Black Forest, there is a wishing well where tourists like to throw coins. This is the Donauquelle—"Danube spring"—and when its waters meet two local streams that rise in the Alps, the Danube is formed. The Danube flows gently northeast through this part of western Germany, gradually gaining in strength. By the time the river reaches Ulm, it is wide and deep enough for small boats to begin the trip downstream. Heavier craft must start at the ancient city of Regensburg, the northernmost point on the Danube. In the 2nd century A.D., Regensburg—called Castra Regina by the Romans—was a military camp and part of Rome's northern defense lines against invading barbarian tribes.

Even this early in its journey, the river is light brown, because it has already begun to pick up some of the silt that will eventually be deposited in the delta at the Black Sea.

At Passau the Danube enters Austria. Here the steamers of the Donaudampfschiffahrtsgesellschaft—"Danube steamship country"—start their trips downriver, passing Russian, Romanian, and Yugoslavian barges being towed upstream. This section of the river is full of contrasts, at once as new as tomorrow and as old as many yesterdays. The Romans called this part of the river Danubius, and they threw coins into its dangerous whirlpools to calm the river god. The Romans also started the vineyards here that are still the source of fragrant Austrian wines.

On this stretch of the river, there are four great hydroelectric dams, converting the river's energy into power for industries and homes. The dams—Kachlet, Jochenstein, Aschach, and Ybbs-Persenbeug—are symbols of everything new on the Danube. The river next flows through the Wachau region, with its many abbeys and castles, including Dürnstein, where Richard the Lion-Hearted was imprisoned on his way home from the Third Crusade.

FOUR CAPITALS ON THE DANUBE

Before reaching Vienna, the first of the four great cities on the Danube, the river flows past the Wiener Wald ("Vienna woods")—the inspiration for a waltz by the Austrian composer Johann Strauss, Jr. In spite of Strauss' most famous waltz, "The Beautiful Blue Danube," the river is truly blue only on the clearest days, when it reflects the sky.

Once the capital of the vast Austro-Hungarian Empire, Vienna today is still an important international city. It is also still a city of whipped cream, pastries, and beautiful music, as it was in the time of Mozart and Beethoven. Each year, from May to September, cruise ships take passengers downriver from Vienna to the Black Sea. And there are the much faster hydrofoils, appropriately called *Raketen* ("rockets") because they can make the trip to Budapest in less than five hours.

About 40 mi. (64 km.) east of Vienna lies Bratislava, the capital of the newly independent Slovakia. It is a 1,000-year-old city, which served as the capital of Hapsburg Hungary from 1526 to 1784 (at that time it was known by its German name, Pressburg). Bratislava is the gateway to the picturesque Carpathian Mountains.

The Danube, now running due south, divides Hungary's capital city, Budapest, into two parts—Buda, the old section, and Pest, the newer, more commercial section. From Budapest, the river continues south through the Great Hungarian Plain to Mohács, on the border with Yugoslavia. In 1526, about 28,000 Hungarians were slaughtered by 300,000 Turks at this place, giving the Ottoman Empire control of central and southern Hungary for almost 200 years.

The Danube at Ulm, Germany, where the river first becomes navigable for small craft.

Belgrade, Yugoslavia, is the fourth of the capitals on the Danube. Although it is a modern, Western-looking city, it still shows much of the influence of the East. The Kalemegdan, an old Turkish fortress on a bluff high over the Danube, is a reminder of the days when everything to the south and east could be controlled from here, and the Danube Valley rang with marching songs. According to an old saying, whoever was the master of Belgrade was the master of the entire Balkan Peninsula, and the city was destroyed over and over again as various armies fought to take it.

WITH THE DANUBE TO THE SEA

After it leaves Belgrade, the river suddenly becomes narrower and deeper. Only the best pilots can take ships safely through the treacherous currents and eddies of the Kazán Defile, whose name means ''boiling cauldron'' in Yugoslavia. Farther on, this same forbidding gorge is called the Iron Gate. No one knows when the name was first used, but the reason for it is clear—it seems as if the mountains will refuse to let the water through. Romania and Yugoslavia built a huge power dam here, and when the project was completed, in the early 1970s, a large lake was created in part of the gorge. Several villages were submerged and a monastery had to be moved to higher ground.

As if tired from its struggle with the Iron Gate, the Danube flows on placidly toward the Black Sea. Bucharest, Romania's capital, is only 40 mi. (64 km.) to the north, but the fishermen, shepherds, and buffalo who live along this part of the river make a 20th-century city seem many light-years away.

In Vienna, the Danube flows by the Donaupark Center, where many U.N. agencies are housed.

The Danube River, as it flows through Budapest, the capital of Hungary, on its course toward the Black Sea.

As the river slows down, so does the pace of life on its banks. Galaţi, Romania's main Danube port, is the last large city on the river as it approaches the delta. Near Tulcea, Romania, the Danube branches out into three main channels—the Kiliya, the Sulina, and the St. George—and hundreds of smaller ones. The Sulina channel has been deepened to allow ships access to the Black Sea, but many of the smaller channels are hardly wide enough to permit rowboats to pass through them.

The Danube Delta

The 1,000-sq.-mi. (2,600-sq.-km.) area between the Kiliya channel on the north and the St. George on the south is the vast Danube Delta, which is growing constantly as the river adds sediment. The delta is one of the largest bird sanctuaries in the world. There are ducks, geese, pelicans, and swans; herons, egrets, kingfishers, and cormorants; and hoopoes, spoonbills, ibis, and storks. Migratory birds from far and near spend the winter in the quiet delta region. The few people who live on the delta live from it, catching fish and gathering water chestnuts. Although parts of the delta were damaged by a reclamation scheme begun in the 1980s, these areas are now being restored by the Danube Delta Biosphere Reserve, created by the Romanian government in 1991.

So when the Danube finally reaches the sea, it has become many small streams instead of one great river. The waters that have been described by the gypsies as "the dustless road," which have formed a highway for trade and travelers and for countless armies as well, flow peacefully into the Black Sea.

Reviewed by THOMAS NOWOTNY
Austrian Information Service, New York

ILLUSTRATION CREDITS

The following list credits, according to page, the sources of illustrations used in Volume 3 of LANDS AND PEOPLES. The credits are listed illustration by illustration—top to bottom, left to right. Where necessary, the name of the photographer or artist has been listed with the source, the two separated by a dash. If two or more illustrations appear on the same page, their credits are separated by semicolons.

Cover photo, © Superstock, provides a rooftop view of Munich, the capital of Bavaria, in southern Germany.

Wraparound photo: © Chuck Savage/The Stock Market

DATE DU